THE EMPIRE
OF THE ST. LAWRENCE

THE EMPIRE
OF THE ST. LAWRENCE

By

DONALD CREIGHTON

TORONTO

THE MACMILLAN COMPANY OF CANADA LIMITED

PREFACE TO THE RE-ISSUE

THIS book was published originally in 1937 as *The Commercial Empire of the St. Lawrence, 1760–1850*. It appeared as a volume in a series called *The Relations of Canada and the United States*, which was sponsored by the Carnegie Endowment for International Peace, and directed by Dr. James T. Shotwell. The late Professor Harold A. Innis, Head of the Department of Political Economy and Dean of the School of Graduate Studies in the University of Toronto, was asked by Dr. Shotwell to act as editor for the volumes contributed by Canadians on the economic aspects of Canadian-American relations; and it was he who proposed that my book should be published in the series. I was, of course, only too glad to accept this invitation, since *The Commercial Empire of the St. Lawrence* was my first book and since, in those days, a work on Canadian history, by a Canadian, was published only with difficulty, and often, in part, at the author's expense. In the preface to the original edition I acknowledged my debt to Professor Innis and Dr. Shotwell; and I should like to repeat here my thanks for the encouragement and support which they gave me on that occasion.

In this new edition, called *The Empire of the St. Lawrence*, the original text has been reprinted without change. The book expounds and illustrates, through a narrative account, a certain thesis respecting Canada's historical development during a given period; and, in my opinion, such interpretative essays are injured, rather than benefited, by the revisions and additions which are sometimes made in more general histories, particularly text-books. I should perhaps be inclined to modify slightly, here and there, some of the views expressed in this book; but the idea of the St. Lawrence as the inspiration and basis of a transcontinental, east-west system, both commercial and political in character, is still central in my interpretation of Canadian history. Much of my later work has been based upon the idea; and I prefer, therefore, to leave this first, enthusiastic expression of it in its original form.

D. G. CREIGHTON

PREFACE

THIS book is a study in commerce and politics. It is an attempt to trace the relations between the commercial system of the St. Lawrence and the political development of Canada during almost a century of its history. The St. Lawrence river inspired and supported a trading system which was both transatlantic and transcontinental in extent, and political as well as economic in significance. Its needs could no more be satisfied within the sphere of commerce than its growth could be confined within the territorial limits of the Canadas; and it involved its supporters in the concerns of the British Empire, the affairs of the North American continent and the provincial politics of Canada itself. These political and economic interests, which were at once so wide-spread and so deep-rooted, were represented by the successive generations of Canadian merchants; and it is largely from the point of view of the commercial group that this study has been written. It was the merchants, above all others, who struggled to win the territorial empire of the St. Lawrence and to establish its institutional expression, the Canadian commercial state; and though their influence was undeniably less than the pressure which they persistently applied, they may be regarded as one of the most continuously important groups in Canadian history.

To stand, as the merchants did, at the junction of commerce and politics, is inevitably to lose sight of some portion of the wide fields which lie on either side. There can be no claim, nor is there any implication, that this study satisfies the traditional requirements of either a general economic or a general political history. The main purpose of this book is to set forth, as a related whole, the ambitions, programmes and struggles which had their central inspiration in the St. Lawrence river; and while the theme of the St. Lawrence is vitally important for Canada, and all-important for this book, it is not the only theme in Canadian history. There are historical problems of varying importance for which there can be little accommodation in this essay; and the limits of its design may dictate the cursory treatment of topics both economic and political without necessarily implying any judgment upon their

v

historical importance. *Empire of the St. Lawrence* is intended to serve
as an introduction to a theme of enduring significance in Canadian
development. It is not meant to provide a final and self-sufficient
interpretation of Canadian history.

It remains for me to thank those who, in various ways, have
helped me in the study of my subject or in the writing of this book.
The officials of the Public Archives at Ottawa, Mr. W. S. Wallace,
Librarian of the University of Toronto Library, and Dr. J. J.
Talman of the Provincial Archives of Ontario have all assisted me
in obtaining material. I am indebted to Professor A. R. M. Lower
of the University of Manitoba, who has kindly permitted me to
use some of his unpublished material on the Canadian timber
trade. From Mr. Charles Lindsey of Toronto, I have obtained
permission to consult the files of the *Colonial Advocate* and *The
Constitution*, which have been deposited in the University of
Toronto Library; and Professor R. A. MacKay of Dalhousie
University has generously put at my disposal a portion of his own
notes on William Lyon Mackenzie's newspapers. I am indebted
for much helpful criticism and many valuable suggestions to my
colleagues in the Department of History at Toronto: to Professor
Chester Martin, head of the department, Dr. G. W. Brown and
Mr. R. G. Riddell, each of whom has read sections of my manuscript; and to Professor G. P. de T. Glazebrook, who has read
nearly the whole of the study and who has helped me very greatly
with the maps. Dr. James T. Shotwell, the general editor of this
series, Professor J. Bartlet Brebner of Columbia University,
Professor N. J. Endicott of University College, Toronto, and
Professor G. S. Graham of Queen's University, have likewise
found time and patience to read my manuscript in whole or in
part; and the text has benefited greatly from the historical and
literary amendments which they have been kind enough to
suggest. Finally, I should particularly like to acknowledge the
great debt I owe to Professor H. A. Innis, head of the Department
of Political Economy in the University of Toronto, who has
aided me throughout with his interest and enthusiasm as well
as with his judgment and scholarship.

University of Toronto   D. G. C.
   October, 1937

CONTENTS

PART I

THE FIRST UNITY OF THE ST. LAWRENCE

PART II

TRANSITION IN THE REGION OF THE LOWER LAKES

PART III

THE STRUGGLE FOR THE SECOND COMMERCIAL EMPIRE

MAPS

vii

PART I

THE FIRST UNITY OF THE ST. LAWRENCE

THE EMPIRE
OF THE ST. LAWRENCE

CHAPTER I

THE ECONOMY OF THE NORTH

I

WHEN, in the course of a September day in 1759, the British made themselves the real masters of the rock of Quebec, an event of apparently unique importance occurred in the history of Canada. There followed rapidly the collapse of French power in North America and the transference of the sovereignty of Canada to Great Britain; and these acts in the history of the northern half of the continent may well appear decisive and definitive above all others. In fact, for France and England, the crisis of 1759 and 1760 was a climax of conclusive finality. But colonial America, as well as imperial Europe, had been deeply concerned in the long struggle in the new continent; and for colonial America the conquest of New France had another and a more uncertain meaning. For Europe the conquest was the conclusion of a drama; for America it was merely the curtain of an act. On the one hand, it meant the final retirement of France from the politics of northern North America; on the other, it meant the regrouping of Americans and the reorganization of American economies.

The conquest had a double significance, American and European, because the struggle in North America had not been one war, but two. It was a part of the history of both the old world and the new. In its more obvious and more imposing aspect, it was an extension of that war between France and England which filled the century from the Revolution of 1688 to the Peace of Paris in 1763. North America was merely one theatre in a world conflict, a struggle between imperial giants, which invaded the extremes of east and west; and this conflict appeared, in America, as in every other continent which it visited, to dominate the lives and to decide the destinies of lesser men. Its shocks and pauses both stimulated effort and imposed quiet on the seigniories of the St. Lawrence and the towns of New England. And when the war was won by the

1

capture of Montreal and concluded by the Peace of Paris, it might well have seemed that the struggle in North America was over for ever.

Yet concealed within this majestic imperial drama was a sub-plot, a conflict between the first Americans in America. And for them this secondary drama was the more prolonged and therefore the more important of the two. Two colonial societies, rooted in two different American landscapes, had come into existence on the continent; and while one was scattered sparingly along the giant system of the St. Lawrence and the lakes, the other, more compact and populous, had grown up on the Atlantic seaboard. These two societies differed from each other, and among the differences which distinguished them were some which had been imported from Europe. Fundamentally, the civilization of each society in North America is the civilization of Europe. An inward necessity, instinctive and compelling, had driven the immigrants to preserve the mysterious accumulations of their cultural heritage; and the price they were forced to pay for its preservation should not entirely obscure the extent of their success. Undoubtedly, these two societies, one almost exclusively French and the other predominantly English, were differentiated by race, language, laws and religion. The distinctions which had been inherited from the old world lived on in the new with an almost inextinguishable vitality; and undoubtedly they helped to foster and to prolong the rivalries between the first Americans.

But the society of the St. Lawrence and the society of the Atlantic seaboard were divided by something else, which was perhaps more fundamental and which was purely American. It was, in fact, the continent of North America itself. Immediately these migrants had to come to terms with the new continent. From it they had to wrest a living; and since they were Europeans and not Indians, a living meant not merely the food to sustain life but the amenities of West-European civilization which alone could make it tolerable. They had to find means to produce their own necessities and to pay for their imports from Europe. They had to live in and by the new world; and they were driven, by this double compulsion, to understand the possibilities of the new continent and to exploit its resources. They could escape neither the brutal dictates nor the irresistible seductions of North American geography; and in an undeveloped world the pressure of these prime phenomena was enormous and insistent. Each society, after long trial and recurrent error, had read the meaning of its own environment, accepted its ineluctable compulsions and prepared to monopolize its promises. And each, in the process of this prolonged and painful adjustment, had acquired an American character, a purpose and a destiny in America.

II

Chance flung the first English colonists on the edges of the Atlantic seaboard and opened the single great eastern waterway of the interior to the French. In the history of the different economies, of the cultural patterns which were to dominate North American life, these were acts of first importance. For each cultural group, the English and the French, fell heir to one of America's geographic provinces, and both these regions had their laws, their promises and their portentous meanings. Of the two, the Atlantic seaboard conformed more nearly to the geographic conditions of western Europe, which had been for centuries a forcing-house of nations. It was, for North America, a fairly small and compact area, sharply defined by obvious natural frontiers. From the coastline the land stretched westward to rise at last in the ridges of the Appalachians, which were unbroken from the St. Lawrence valley to the Floridas, save where the Hudson-Mohawk system gave access to the west. It was a boundary; but during colonial times it was not a barrier in the sense that it confined a restless and ambitious people determined upon its assault. Because they shaped the courses of the rivers, the mountains helped to focus the attention of the English-Americans upon that other boundary of the Atlantic seaboard, the ocean. Their faces were turned east rather than west; and during the greater part of the colonial period, the commercial energies of the population were concentrated in the numerous short rivers, in the bays and sounds and harbours which fretted the coastline, and sought their objectives eastward on the sea. For New England especially, whose economy was based upon its fisheries, the pull of the coastline and the submerged continental shelf beyond it, was enormous. The prohibitions, the invitations and the varieties of this seaboard empire directed, in a kindly fashion, the energies of an adaptive people. While the land configuration concentrated their pursuits, the climate and soil gave them variety. The area meant stolidity, gradual settlement, the inescapable necessity to produce and the possibility of diversified production. Seaward, it meant a commercial empire which would cease to be imperial because it would inevitably become oceanic.

The river up which Cartier ventured gave entrance to the totally different dominion of the north. It was a landscape marked off from the other geographic provinces of the new continent by the almost monotonously massive character of its design. A huge triangle of rocky upland lay bounded by a river and a string of giant lakes. It was a solemn country, with that ungainly splendour evoked by great, crude, sweeping lines and immense and clumsy masses. The marks of age and of terrific experience lay heavy upon it. It was an elemental portion of the earth, harshly shaped by the brutal catastrophes of geological history. The enormous flat bulk of the Precambrian formation was not only the core of the whole Canadian system, but it was also the ancient nucleus of the entire continent. It lay, old and sombre and ravaged, nearly two million square miles in extent. The ice masses, during the glacial period, had passed over and beyond it, and they had scarred and wrenched and altered the entire landscape in their advance and their retreat. Scouring the surface of the Shield itself, pouring boulder clay into the valleys to the south, the ice sheets had hollowed the beds of new lakes and had diverted the courses of ancient rivers. There was left a drainage system, grand in its extent and in the volume of its waters, but youthful, wilful and turbulent. The wrinkled senility of the Precambrian formation was touched by a curious appearance of youth. The countless meaningless lakes and lakelets, the intricately meandering rivers and spillways, the abrupt falls and treacherous rapids, which covered the face of the Shield, seemed to express the renewal of its primitive strength. To the south, below the Shield, the ice masses had throttled the waters into new lakes and had dammed the St. Lawrence into a long southern loop, leaving Niagara, the Long Sault and Lachine as evidence of the novelty of its course.

The Canadian Shield and the river system which seamed and which encircled it, were overwhelmingly the most important physical features of the area. They were the bone and the blood-tide of the northern economy. Rock and water complemented each other, fought each other's battles and forced each other's victories. The Shield itself, a huge lop-sided triangle, whose northern points were Labrador and the Arctic east of the Mackenzie, occupied over one-half of the land area which was to become the Dominion of Canada. For the French and for their successors it was unescapable and domineering. It hugged the north shore of the St. Lawrence as the river issued from the continent. Westward, in the centre of the lowlands of the St. Lawrence, the good lands began to peter out a hundred miles north of Lake Ontario in the scarred, blank rock, thin soil sheet and towering evergreens peculiar to the Shield. Relentlessly it followed the north shore of Lakes Huron and Superior and at last struck north and west for the Arctic Ocean. Its long, flat, undeviating plateau effected the complete severance of the St. Lawrence lowlands from the western plains. In the east it helped, with the northern spurs of the Appalachians, to cut off Acadia from Quebec. Settlement starved and shrivelled on the Shield; it offered a sullen inhospitality to those occupations which were traditional in western Europe and which had been transferred by the first immigrants to the Atlantic seaboard of North America. But from the beginning it exercised an imperious domination over the northerners, for though it was a harsh and an exacting country, it offered lavish prizes to the restless, the ambitious and the daring. It was an area of staples, creating simple trades and undiversified extractive industries; and its furs, its forests and its minerals were to attract three great assaulting waves of northerners. Fur was the first great staple of the north. And with the fur trade, the Precambrian formation began its long career in the Canadian economy as a primary, instead of as a subsidiary, economic region. It was upon these ancient rocks that the central emphasis of the Canadian system was placed at first, and the initial importance of the Shield is of deep significance in the history of the economy of the north.

To the south lay the lowlands of the St. Lawrence. Here the intense winters of the Precambrian formation were softened and

the hot, bright summers flamed more slowly out of long spring-
times and faded gradually into reluctant autumns. North of the
lakes, the lowlands stretched from Quebec city to Georgian Bay—a
narrow but slowly broadening band of fertility, crowded a little
oppressively by the sombre masses of the Shield. South and west,
beyond the river and the lakes, they lapsed easily into the central
lowlands of the continent and the basin of the Mississippi. In
the centre of this rich region lay that immense organization of
waters which issued from the continent by the river of Canada;
and this drainage system, driving seaward in a great, proud arc
from Lake Superior to the city of Quebec, was the fact of all facts
in the history of the northern half of the continent. It commanded
an imperial domain. Westward, its acquisitive fingers groped into
the territory of the plains. Aggressively it entrenched upon the
dominion of the Mississippi. It grasped the Shield, reached southward into the valley of the Hudson and at last rolled massively
seaward between sombre approaches which curved away southward
into the Maritimes and rose north-eastward past Quebec and
Labrador to Newfoundland.

It was the one great river which led from the eastern shore into
the heart of the continent. It possessed a geographical monopoly;
and it shouted its uniqueness to adventurers. The river meant
mobility and distance; it invited journeyings; it promised immense
expanses, unfolding, flowing away into remote and changing
horizons. The whole west, with all its riches, was the dominion of
the river. To the unfettered and ambitious, it offered a pathway
to the central mysteries of the continent. The river meant movement, transport, a ceaseless passage west and east, the long
procession of river-craft—canoes, *bateaux*, timber rafts and
steamboats—which followed each other into history. It seemed the
destined pathway of North American trade; and from the river
there rose, like an exhalation, the dream of western commercial
empire. The river was to be the basis of a great transportation
system by which the manufactures of the old world could be
exchanged for the staple products of the new. This was the faith
of successive generations of northerners. The dream of the commercial empire of the St. Lawrence runs like an obsession through
the whole of Canadian history; and men followed each other

through life, planning and toiling to achieve it. The river was not only a great actuality: it was the central truth of a religion. Men lived by it, at once consoled and inspired by its promises, its whispered suggestions, and its shouted commands; and it was a force in history, not merely because of its accomplishments, but because of its shining, ever-receding possibilities.

For something stood between the design and its fulfilment. There was, in the very geography of the region itself, a root defect, a fundamental weakness, which foreshadowed enormous difficulties, even though it did not pre-determine defeat. In the centre, by Lake Ontario and the lower reaches of the river, the drive of the great waterway was unquestioned and peremptory. But this power was not indefinitely transmissible, and the pull of a system stretching over two thousand miles was at long last relaxed and weakened. The outer defences of the St. Lawrence contradicted its inward solidity; its boundaries were not bold and definite, but a smudged faint tracery. Between the valley of the St. Lawrence on the one hand and the valleys of Hudson Bay, the Mississippi and the Hudson river on the other, the separating heights of land were low and facile; and over these perfunctory defences invasions might pass as easily as sorties.[1] The river's continuity was broken at Niagara: it stumbled and faltered at the Cascades, the Cedars and Lachine. As it drove east and north past Quebec and into its immense estuary, the river was caught, its influence narrowed and and focused by the uplands of the Shield to the north and the rolling highlands of the Appalachians below. There were breaks and obstacles; and over both its seaward approaches and its continental extremities the hold of the river closed and again relaxed, uncertainly and unconvincingly. Yet for all its inward contradictions and its outward weakness, the river was a unit, and its central entrance was dominated by the rock of Quebec and the island of Montreal.

III

Each of these two geographic provinces was a matrix in which a distinct American economy was crudely fashioned. The boundaries of these rival economies were coextensive with the limits of two conflicting political dominions and two antipathetic social groups.

It was certain that man, with his political capacities and economic resources, would modify the crude stamp of, the geographical matrix; and it was equally certain that the geographical matrix itself would alter slightly under the force of human ingenuity and effort. Yet, in the first simplicity of early settlement, the pressure of geography bore with continuous persistence upon an unprotected people; and a brutal necessity drove the first Americans to come to terms with the landscape they had inherited. To exist as men, to live as West Europeans, they must immediately read the meanings of their respective empires, capitalize their obvious resources, fulfil their manifest destinies. The riddle of all migratory peoples confronted them; they must tie together the cut threads of their material and spiritual history, they must weave a new pattern of existence out of the stuffs of their new homeland and of the old world of Europe. It was a gigantic task; and in their deep need and desperate hurry, they turned naturally to the most immediate and the most easily obtainable of their resources. What the continent flaunted, they took; they could not be made to seek what it seemingly withheld. Their economies grew naturally, organically out of the very earth of the new world. It was not the sage wisdom of European statesmen which determined their development, but the brute facts of North American life. And the character and development of these two economies were to affect decisively not only their separate relations with the old world, but their mutual relations in the new.

In the region of the Atlantic seaboard, which by the end of the first half-century of settlement the English had acquired for their own, there developed a richly diversified way of life. The area invited a varied agricultural production; it encouraged, on the sea, a complex, cunningly adjusted and truly oceanic trade. From the stubborn soil and stern north temperate climate of New England, the coastal plain broadened out into the more fertile amplitudes of the middle colonies and passed southward into the lush richness of a region warmed by hot skies and watered by innumerable rivers and creeks. The sub-tropical products, tobacco, rice and cotton, were added to the homely, traditional roots and fruits and cereals of western Europe. But everywhere production called for husbandry, settlement, the consistent effort of a population established on the land; and, as the hewn forests receded west-ward, the life of the ploughed countryside collected in little villages and became concentrated in towns. There was great vitality in this economy, but its development was conditioned by certain definite limitations. For the great majority of these migrants trade was inevitably oceanic and not continental. They were granted a hundred outlets to the sea; but they were denied the single great eastern entrance to the continent. What they wanted from the Indians, the inhabitants of the interior, was chiefly land, not goods; and beyond the established settlements there extended, not a vast spectacular commercial empire, but a narrow, laborious land frontier. The rivers broke and dwindled, the forests and the hills closed in upon this agricultural community; but eastward, in generous compensation, were the inviting expanses of the sea. It was a wide horizon, bounded by the old world of England, France, Spain and Portugal, and by the new world of Newfoundland, Africa and the Indies; and across these expanses the colonial merchants drew, not a few direct and simple trade lines, but an increasingly intricate network of commercial com-munications. Neither they nor the English could prevent it. The abstractions of the mercantile system could not link the colonies and the motherland commercially when the practical needs of Englishmen and Americans did not necessitate a close commer-cial relationship. The trade of the Atlantic seaboard was not to be carried on over commercial trunk-lines which crossed the ocean undeviatingly to converge upon England. The paths of American commerce radiated over the Atlantic and no mercantilist wisdom could focus them in London.

This commerce, which in part competed with the interests of Great Britain, expanded continuously during the colonial period. Newfoundland, England, southern Europe, Africa and the West Indies were all drawn into the widening circle of American trade. Back of this expansion was the commercial energy of Philadelphia and New England; and back of New England were the resources of the forest and the cod from the "silver mines of the Atlantic". In the north, that eastern pull to which the whole of the seaboard was subject, the pull of the coast and the submerged continental shelf, was irresistible; and the hoard which the fishermen of

Marblehead, Gloucester, Plymouth, Salem and Ipswich drew yearly from the banks and shoals and ledges stretching northward from Cape Cod, paid the way of the Americans around the ports of the Atlantic. The fishing industry enhanced the value and quickened the development of the subsidiary industries of the North Atlantic coast—lumbering, ship-building, distilling and the provision business.[2] Under the rapid and magically repeated transmutations of commerce, cod became molasses, molasses rum, and rum turned into furs and manufactures and gold and slaves. The strangely varied component parts of this system were deftly combined into a great integration. It had toughness, elasticity and expansive powers. American trade burst through the imperial system to become international. The slaves which the New Englanders bought on the Guinea coast and sold to the planter plutocrats of Jamaica and Barbadoes, fulfilled the beneficent dual function of consuming inferior New England fish and of producing molasses for active New England distilleries. At last this southern trade, geared to increasing speed and capable of greater volume, broke into the French West India islands of Martinique and Guadeloupe.[3]

On the continent, expansion paralleled and complemented expansion by the sea. Settlement, in search of closer bases for the ever-expanding fishery, felt its way instinctively and surely from New England up the coast to Acadia, which thus began to play its complicated role as an outpost of both the St. Lawrence and the north Atlantic seaboard.[4] Trade worked more deeply inland, for though Anglo-American commerce was chiefly eastern and oceanic, there had always been an outlet to the west. This was the Hudson river, a stream of deep significance in North American history, which alone of all the rivers of the coastal plain threw off the hold of the Appalachians and alone pierced the inner defences of the St. Lawrence. It became the pathway of both military and commercial aggression. The easy route by Lake Champlain and the Richelieu led into the political centre of the St. Lawrence system; the Hudson, the Mohawk and Lake Ontario gave entrance to the western commercial empire of the French. Rum, made by New England distilleries out of molasses paid for by New England fish, English manufactures, guns, powder, kettles and cheap cloth, enabled both Dutch and English merchants to compete effectively in an area which the French regarded as their own preserve.[5] In Albany, Schenectady, Oswego and the distant interior, was felt the final pressure of the first great synthesis of industry and commerce created on the Atlantic seaboard.

The economy of the north was in utter contrast with the industrial and commercial organization of the Atlantic seaboard. In the north, geography directed the activities of men with a blunt sternness; and it had largely helped to create a distinct and special American system. The lower St. Lawrence was for the French, as it is for the Canadians of today, the destined focus of any conceivable northern economy; and in response to an invitation which was at least half a command, settlement became inevitably concentrated on the strip of territory between Quebec and Montreal. Here were the lowlands of the St. Lawrence; but the restricted area drew men for other reasons than for its fertile land, and northern commerce was not to be built up upon a solid foundation of agricultural production. The river and the Shield, which seemed physically to overawe the valley with their force and mass, reduced the lowlands to a position of secondary economic importance. It was the final trunk-line of the western commercial system driving past Quebec and Montreal, which gave the rock and the river city their initial economic importance.

Agriculture struggled with an ineffectual persistence against the lures of the fur trade; and French officialdom, from Colbert on, tried to preserve settlement and farming from the too damaging encroachments of expansion and commerce.[6] But the first important Canadian market and the first source of Canadian staples for export lay, not in the lowlands, but in the west. Settlement, encouraged rather by the fitful favour of French policy than by the inner necessities of commercial Canada, huddled close to the lower reaches of the St. Lawrence or ventured timidly down the Richelieu. There it stuck. The seigniory of Beaupré became the eastern limit of continuous settlement and the manor of New Longueuil was to be its outpost on the west: beyond this, east and west, there were only tiny communities and around them the forest and scarred upland closed with appalling abruptness. Population, in a country where mere numbers were unneeded and unwanted, increased slowly; and at the conquest there were but a scant sixty-five thousand French Canadians while the English in the Thirteen Colonies numbered perhaps a million and a half. Unlike the Anglo-American farmers, the peasants of the St. Lawrence valley produced food-stuffs not for export but for subsistence; and right up to the conquest there were years when they could not subsist upon what they had produced.[7] The efforts of Talon and his successors to build up a diversified industrial system and to develop a trade in wheat and provisions were fated to be fruitless.

The trend of expansion from the St. Lawrence valley was towards the west; and the commercial empire of the north, in sharp contrast with that of the Atlantic seaboard, was inland and not oceanic. The St. Lawrence was incapable of playing an effective role in the task of building a vigorous union out of the maritime and continental colonies which had been established by the French. On the map, the number and the variety of these possessions were impressive. In the West Indies, the French held Guadeloupe, Martinique, St. Christopher and Tortuga—tropical islands which produced sugar and molasses. In the north, in that region bounded by Newfoundland, the Gulf of St. Lawrence and Acadia, where political dominion would be determined largely by mastery in the catch of fish, the French established little settlements in Gaspé and Acadia, at Isle St. Jean, Cape Breton and Placentia. These two groups of colonies—the sugar-producing and fish-producing settlements—together with the fur-producing colony of the St. Lawrence, made up the western dominion of the French. Puny and disconnected, they lay raggedly across the face of the new world; and the problem of uniting them in a robust integration despite the opposition of England and New England—of linking the St. Lawrence, the Maritimes and the West Indies together and with continental France—exhausted the strength and ingenuity of Frenchmen.

The New Englanders shouldered their way into the markets of the French West Indies. To the north, the French fishing settlements were overshadowed by Newfoundland which was growing with painful slowness as an outpost of the English fishery; and to the south, England's temporary ally, New England, flung the accumulating strength of its variously nourished economy into the fight for fishing grounds and markets. For over half the year, the connection between Canada and the French Atlantic colonies was broken by the ice barrier in the St. Lawrence; and the proximity of Acadia enabled New England to usurp the economic control of the maritime region. The French lost Acadia by the Treaty of Utrecht: and although within the restricted area of Gaspé, Isle St. Jean and Cape Breton they prolonged their resistance sufficiently to prove that the final fate of the fisheries region was uncertain, they failed either to make their maritime colonies self-sufficient or to link them effectively with the St. Lawrence and the islands to the south. France itself was incapable of exerting the inward pull which would draw these feeble and scattered American communities together. She could not compete effectively with England in the production of rough staple manufactures for colonial consumption; and, while she could take the furs and fish of America, she could not assist her north temperate colonies in supplying an adequate market for the produce of the French sugar islands. The lower St. Lawrence valley was the best possible centre of an integrated American economy of the French; but the St. Lawrence failed almost completely to emulate the example of New England and to offer independent co-operation to the motherland. The frozen river enforced the periodic isolation of Canada; and the colony was beset by the limitations and weaknesses of population, industry and commerce, which were inevitably inherent in a society based upon the river, the Shield and its furs. All this stunted the seaward expansion of the St. Lawrence;[8] and Cape Breton depended for its existence and the French West Indies for their prosperity upon the commercial strength of New England and not of New France.

The St. Lawrence lacked energy in those very spheres where the vitality of the seaboard was abundant and insistent. The lower valley of the river was not the source of the chief Canadian export; nor was it the base of a complex oceanic trade. Canadian expansion drove impulsively westward, along the rivers and into the interior. The energy and initiative which lay dormant in the lowlands grew exuberantly in the western wilderness of rock and water and forest. Radisson, La Salle, La Vérendrye and the other heroes of exploration stand out from the ruck of men who passed westward along the waterways and unremembered out of life because in them the common compulsion troubling a whole society became the intense, solitary excitement of genius. It was trade which drew them all; for the Shield and its outlying fringes gave up the first and simplest of the Canadian staple products, beaver fur. Furs, a product of the Shield, obtainable by the river system of transportation, weighted the already heavy emphasis of the Precambrian formation and the St. Lawrence. Furs impelled the northerners to win that western commercial empire which the river seemed to offer to the daring. The expansion of the French was the penetration, not the occupation, of the west; it meant travel not home-building, and commerce not agriculture. And the future Upper Canada, the first great granary of the north, which was scarcely touched by French settlement, was passed and distanced by French trade.

Thus the society which grew up in the northern geographic province instinctively created that form of endeavour which was to dominate Canadian life until the conquest and for nearly a century thereafter. This was the northern commercial system, of which furs were the first staple; and the fur-trading organization of the French was the elementary expression of the major architectural style of Canadian business life. It was a distinct North American system, peculiar to Canada, with the immensity and simplicity which were characteristic of the landscape itself. From the ports of France, the northern commercial organization plunged in a single trunk-line across the Atlantic and up the river to Quebec and Montreal; but beyond the river city it spread out in increasing amplitude and with infinite ramifications over the enormous bulk of the Precambrian formation and over the central lowlands of the continent. This western territory, where the goods of Europe were exchanged for the goods of America, was the inland commercial empire of the St. Lawrence. The colony, weak in agriculture, weak in industry and seaward commerce, was tied in utter bondage to France; but it revenged this subordination in the east by its extravagantly ambitious pretensions in the hinterland of North America. The whole landscape annexed to the river of Canada, the lands which spread out north and south and westward of the Great Lakes were claimed and largely exploited by the commercial state which was centralized at Quebec and Montreal.

It seemed, in the first assertive youth of the northern society, as if the St. Lawrence might take possession of inland North America, as if the western edges of the continent would be the only limits of this vast, facile, unsubstantial commercial empire. The young fur-trading colony concentrated with passionate intentness upon the fulfilment of its own peculiar destiny. La Salle and La Vérendrye pressed south and westward to assert the ultimate claims of the northern system; and a long struggle began with those competitors who controlled the Hudson river and Hudson Bay, the two routes which rivalled the St. Lawrence as highways to the interior. It became at once the greatest ambition and the chief task of Canadians to enlarge the extent of their commercial dominion, to centralize it upon the lower reaches of the St. Lawrence and to protect it from the encroachments of rivals from the south and from the north.

The pressure of this system was enormous. The colony grew curiously—ungainly, misshapen, almost distorted—stamped by tasks and ambitions which were, on the whole, too great for it. The western commercial organization, which lasted as the dominant economic form for two centuries of Canadian history, rooted certain tendencies deeply in the society of the St. Lawrence: there were virtues and weaknesses, loyalties and antipathies which became fixed and almost ineradicable. It was western commerce which helped largely to determine the part which Canada would act in the affairs of European empires and the role which it would play in the politics of North America. A colony which scarcely rose above the level of feudal industry and which failed completely to develop a diversified trade, required a mature European metropolis both as a market and as a source of manufactures and supplies.[9] Canada continued acquiescent and loyal within the French empire, for it was tied by every basic interest to the motherland. But while the northern commercial system inclined Canadian statesmen and merchants to passivity within the empire, it drove them to competition and conflict upon the North American continent. Their subserviency in the east was complemented by their aggressiveness in the west. Because they desired it as a commercial monopoly, the Canadians struggled to make the entire empire of the St. Lawrence a political unit. They sought to break the commercial competition of Hudson Bay and the Hudson river and to restrict the expansion of the Atlantic seaboard; for the bay and the river threatened to partition the western monopoly, and the march of settlement from the Atlantic seaboard involved the annihilation of the fur trade through the destruction of the hunting races. North and south of the St. Lawrence, Canada discovered its inevitable enemies; but in the centre of the continent, among the Indians, it found its natural allies. The primitive culture of the hunting Indians was essential to the fur-trading state;[10] and the fur-trading state would alone preserve the Indians from extinction. It was more than an alliance: it was a political union. It was even a strange amalgam of two widely different cultures. The commercial system threaded through the native culture of the continent in tiny, intricate ramifications, changing it, debasing it, but effectively prolonging its existence. The Indians, giving up to the new westerners the fruits of their experience, the cunning adjustments of their heritage, and something of their proud, passionate independence, helped, in their turn, to create that curious western world of half-tones, that blent society where Europe and America met and mingled.

It was western trade, moreover, which largely determined the style of Canadian politics. Transcontinentalism, the westward drive of corporations encouraged and followed by the super-corporation of the state, is the major theme in Canadian political life; and it was stated, in its first simplicity, by the fur trade. The trade enforced commitments and determined policies. The state was based upon it: it was anterior to the state. Until 1663 Canada was governed by a series of trading corporations; then it became a commercial and military state. Colonial government derived its strength from taxes paid directly or indirectly by the western trade; and that strength was expended in an effort to extend the dominion of the fur trade and to protect it from competition. From the first, the government was committed to the programme of western exploitation by the river system. The St. Lawrence was an expensive monopoly; and its imperious demands could be met—and even then inadequately—only by the corporate effort of the northern society. The immense capital expenditures of the nineteenth and twentieth centuries were anticipated with startling clarity in the expensive military policy, the fortified posts, the presents to the Indians, by which Frontenac and his successors endeavoured to realize the destiny of the north.[11] Inevitably, the instinct of both politicians and business men was towards unity and centralization, both for the management and the support of this monstrous western machine. Strong, centralized government was, of course, imported from old France; but its continuance in the new world was encouraged, rather than opposed, by the northern commercial system.[12] It is true that the distant western trader, whether he was the employee or the debtor of a Montreal merchant, shouldered his aggressive individuality through an inevitably relaxed restraint. But the laxity which obtained on the frontiers of the system was abandoned as the river in its last concentration drove north-eastward towards the sea. Here trade, its management and its final defences, were concentrated; and the twin cities, Quebec and Montreal, were the two symbols, military and commercial, of a single unified system.

IV

Two worlds lay over against each other in North America and their conflict was not only probable but certain. Between those who possessed and those who were denied the single great eastern entrance to the continent, the hostility of war could subside only into the competition of peace. With the whole pressure of its material and spiritual being, each society was impelled to maintain its separateness and to achieve its dominion. They contradicted each other, they crowded each other; and the wars and raids and surprises which fill the seventeenth and eighteenth centuries are but outward manifestations of a great, essential and slowly maturing conflict. When Dongan laboured to defy Montreal from Albany, when the British built Halifax to overawe Louisbourg, when Washington toiled westward against Fort Duquesne, they did not so much initiate clashes as reveal the points at which two ponderously moving systems would be forced into reverberating collision. Here were two geographic provinces occupied by culturally distinct peoples; here were two economies controlled by antagonistic national states. Of their essence, the St. Lawrence and the seaboard denied each other. Riverways against seaways, rock against farmland, trading posts against ports and towns and cities, *habitants* against farmers and fur traders against frontiersmen—they combined, geography and humanity, in one prime contradiction.

With the excuse and with the stimulation of the imperial wars, the conflict in North America developed on its own lines, created its own strategy and tactics and discovered its own battlefields. Along the arc which stretched from the Gulf of St. Lawrence to the Mississippi and wherever these two systems touched or threatened each other, the conflict flared or smouldered. The seaward extension of the St. Lawrence cut like a boulevard through the finest fishing grounds in the West European-American world; and the French, weak as they were in the region, were determined to keep the gulf, the islands and Acadia as the outposts of their inland, and as the citadels of their maritime, empire. From Newfoundland, which lay like "a great English ship moored near the Banks", the English fishery expanded competitively into the area. From the south, New England, with the strength of its fused industrial and commercial organization, developed its fishing interests and pushed its settlements into Acadia. A little westward of this, where the river flowed between the Appalachians and the Canadian Shield the St. Lawrence temporarily threw off the clutch of its competitors; and its inner strength was fittingly expressed in the lofty symbol of the fortress of Quebec. But almost immediately beyond this, the inroads of geography and humanity began again. The Hudson river, by its two extensions, Lake Champlain and the Richelieu on the one hand and the Mohawk on the other, pierced through the easy outward defences of the St. Lawrence into the quick of the whole system. New York, backed by the industrial and commercial power of the North Atlantic seaboard, developed this natural highway with a chain of outposts from Albany past Schenectady to Oswego; and as middlemen the Iroquois extended competition throughout the west.

In the central lowlands of the continent, La Salle and those who followed him had established a counterfeit dominion. There was deception in the very grandeur of the Great Lakes. The country which spread out around them in such easy undulations was not a single geographic province: and the lakes crowded a territory which was unexpectedly narrow for them. A short way below the northern system, a low and almost indistinguishable height of land separated the waters of the Mississippi from those of the St. Lawrence. On the north, the rivers of James and Hudson Bay—the Rupert, the Moose, the Albany and the Nelson—pressed dangerously close. Radisson and La Salle passed with easy confidence into territory which, even from a geographical point of view, was competitive; and time could only reveal more fully the enormous northern and southern pull of Hudson Bay and the Mississippi. The Hudson's Bay Company, backed by the great strength of commercial England, began to invade the north-western, fur-trading country of the French which centred at Lake Winnipeg. By the middle of the eighteenth century, land companies began the scramble for grants by the "western waters" of the Mississippi; and the first discontented pioneers from Virginia and Philadelphia began to mark out the trail that led by Cumberland Gap and the Wilderness Road to the Ohio.

At all these points, where the economy of the St. Lawrence clashed with the rival economies of North America, struggles necessarily arose. They were neither haphazard nor transitory, they were rooted in the continent; and they were to reveal an almost indestructible permanence in the future. The first inhabitants of North America did not create these prime contradictions: they discovered them. The vital quarrel in the new continent was not a mere extension of the political rivalries of Europe; it was not wholly a result of those cultural differences which had been imported from Europe by the first migrants. It was, in part, American, it was a product of North America. It was fought, not only by British and French regulars, but also by Americans—by explorers, seigneurs, fur traders and Indians, by fishermen, Boston apprentices, frontiersmen and Virginia planters. Never was this American conflict completely fused in the imperial war which overshadowed it: its beats and pulses could not be perfectly regulated by the timing of European wars and European diplomacy. To be sure, the naval and military strength of Europe helped to magnify these American disputes and European diplomacy marked the main stages in their evolution. But the tumult in the maritime region did not cease with the Peace of Utrecht and the conflict impending in the Ohio country was not prevented by the solemn affirmations of Aix-la-Chapelle. Irrepressibly, the struggle in North America developed in its own way, in response to its own inner urgencies; and, though Europe might enhance or weaken American forces, it could neither create nor destroy them.

The British conquest, therefore, while it made changes and portended others, did not alter certain fundamentals of Canadian life. The conquest did not end the rivalry between the economies of North America, for it could not. The French could be beaten in America; but the St. Lawrence could not surrender in Europe. The northern commercial system remained what it had been—a distinct and competitive American economy, strong enough, despite its undeniable weakness, to arouse jealousy and fear and to enforce a certain respect. The departure of one set of officials and the arrival of another could not change the main trend of its development. In a certain sense, the French were not really the builders of the northern commercial empire: they were its first owners, its first occupants. They read the meaning of the region, they evoked its spirit, and they first dreamed the dream which the river inspired in the minds of all who came to live upon its banks. What the French saw, what they did and what they failed to do formed an experience which had not merely a limited national significance: it was an astonishingly correct anticipation of the experience of successive generations of northerners. With the surrender of the transportation system of the St. Lawrence, there was passed on also to the victors the commercial philosophy based upon it. It was accepted without pause or question. The new northerners, who succeeded to the direction of the St. Lawrence after the conquest, diverged from the lines laid down by the French only in the attempt to repair their failures. They clung to the conquests of the French and they tried to recapture their concessions.

These facts were at first imperfectly understood. After the conquest of Canada, Great Britain held the whole of North America except the south-west sector—an empire which stretched unbrokenly from Labrador to Florida. The British imagined they could unify this empire and standardize its various parts. They tried, in 1763, to make Quebec a typical American colony in a unified continental dominion. But they were wrong: for Quebec was an unusual colony and it had no part or lot in the affairs of the Atlantic seaboard. It had its own organization and its own internal problems. It nursed a special ambition for the west of North America and it was bound by unusually strong ties to the metropolis in Europe. Thus the Peace of Paris and the subsequent efforts of the British to unify and standardize their American empire violated the logic of facts on the St. Lawrence as well as in other parts of the new continent. It is significant that the peace and the imperial reorganization were followed by twenty years of increasing tumult which culminated in the political division of the continent roughly upon the lines which the French had already established. The French and the British were both humbled in America; but through all the curious chances and reverses of the eighteenth century, the St. Lawrence managed to preserve its individuality and its separateness.

The conquest could not change Canada. In fact, in some ways, it strengthened the dominant impulse of Canadian life. It tied Canada to Great Britain, a commercial and maritime power far stronger than France; and it opened the St. Lawrence to the capital and enterprise of Britain and British America. To the defeated society of the north it brought fresh enthusiasm, a new strength and a different leadership. But this injection of new vigour, while it strengthened commercial Canada, necessarily raised the problem of assimilation. The conquest brought two groups of Americans, different even in terms of their Americanism, within the limits of a single colony; and it remained for the future to determine how long and how effectively they could co-operate in the struggle for the western trade. It was certain that the British Canadians would fight to realize the commercial empire of the St. Lawrence; but it was equally certain that they would be forced to fight in company with the Canadians of French descent.

CHAPTER II
THE MERCHANTS' POLITICAL PROGRAMME

I

THE enduring strength of the northern commercial system which had been developed by the French, was revealed in the very nature of the British occupation. There were two occupations of Canada at the conquest, the military and the commercial; and this commercial occupation shows as well as anything could possibly do, the real meaning which the St. Lawrence had for the West-Europeans and Americans of the eighteenth century. For them the conquest was the capture of a giant river system and the transference of commercial power. The first immigration of English-speaking civilians to Canada, which lasted from the invasion of the British armies in 1759 until the coming of the Loyalists a quarter-century later, was an immigration, not of farmers and frontiersmen, but of commercial brains and capital and energy. Over in London, they apparently expected that the new province of Quebec would attract agricultural settlers and develop into healthy normality. But Canada was not a typical American colony: it was different; and its distinction lay as much in the nature of its economy as in the race and religion of its population. To the men of eighteenth-century America, the St. Lawrence was not a farmland but a commercial system; and its natural appeal was altered, in the first place, only by the violent political disturbances of the American Revolution. The first British Canadians were merchants drawn northward by the promises of the river; and they came with the single, simple objective of making money by trade.

The immigration began with what was in the eighteenth century a normal commercial adventure. There were no commissariat services for the armies of those days, and British merchants followed the red-coats around the world to profit by their necessities. As sutlers, a group of merchants entered Quebec with Murray himself. Many of them were the representatives of English exporting and army contracting firms.[1] But there were also merchants from the Thirteen Colonies, like Alexander Henry, who came with the relieving forces in the following spring; and when Amherst published the needs of Canada and invited the merchants of Massachusetts, New Hampshire and New York to meet them, there was a further influx from the south in the autumn of 1760.[2] The army and the civilian population which had endured a two years' blockade, constituted the first market on the shores of the St. Lawrence after the conquest. But almost at once the northern economy began to select its future servants from the ruck of these first casual traders. In Quebec and Montreal, the enormous implications of the conquest rushed over some of these nomad merchants; and their sensitiveness, their sudden comprehension, are vivid still in the pages of Henry's journal. "Proposing", he wrote, "to avail myself of the new market, which was thus thrown open to British adventure, I hastened to Albany, where my commercial connections were, and where I procured a quantity of goods, with which I set out, intending to carry them to Montreal."[3] The northern commercial system began to recruit its new management, and the process of selection continued without interruption for the next two decades. Immigration continued. It was insignificant in numbers, but mere numbers were of small importance. It was not seriously considered by officialdom; but the advent of James McGill, Simon McTavish, the Lymburners and the Frobisher brothers was of as much importance as the arrival of the bureaucrats and soldiers whose comings and goings we are so concerned to record. Gradually, during the first quarter-century of British rule, and by a slow process of arrivals and departures, there was built up a new commercial personnel, devoted to the river and dedicated to the realization of its promises.

This commercial group acquired and maintained an enormous influence in Canadian affairs. It was the most self-conscious, purposeful and assertive of all the Canadian social classes. But its outward appearance was not particularly unusual or impressive. The English-speaking population in the province of Quebec during the first two decades after the Peace of Paris was numerically very small. The great majority of the merchants were Protestants; and in 1764 there were, according to Governor Murray, two hundred Protestant householders in the towns of Quebec and

Montreal.[4] In 1765, according to a more detailed list which dealt only with the district of Montreal, there were ninety-nine male Protestants in the town of Montreal itself and thirty-seven in all the rest of the district.[5] But of these a considerable proportion, the artisans, small tradesmen and innkeepers, whose lives lay outside the range of large-scale commercial activity, possessed no great objectives and played no important economic and political role. In the list of 1765, there were only about fifty Montreal Protestants who were designated as merchants; and it is probably true that during the first two decades of British rule the numbers of that ambitious and energetic group which can properly be called the commercial class of Quebec and Montreal, should be estimated in scores rather than in hundreds.

At first, their origins and early experiences varied considerably. It was not until the old century drew towards its close that the Scottish clan and family systems monopolized the North West Company and the innumerable connections of George Phyn, the unwitting patriarch of Canadian business,[6] began to dominate the commercial life of Montreal. The first British-Canadian merchants came from a score of different towns and villages scattered haphazardly over the old world and the new. There were a few foreigners, Wentzel, Ermatinger and Wadden and the Jews, Solomons and Levy. John Askin and William Holmes were natives of Ireland. Allsopp, Oakes, Gregory, Lees, Molson, the Frobisher brothers and many others were English. From Scotland came George McBeath, Simon McTavish, Richard Dobie, the McGills, Finlays, Grants, Lymburners and Mackenzies. A certain number of merchants were natives of the Thirteen Colonies and among these were Price, Heywood, Alexander Henry, the German-American Pangman and the illiterate, indomitable Pond. Another group, which included some of the real captains of the new northern system, was composed of British merchants who had had a longer or shorter American experience before coming to Canada.

In contrast with the innkeepers and small tradesmen, who were often discharged soldiers, the merchants were civilians, almost to a man. Born, the great majority of them, of lower middle-class parents and brought up in an atmosphere of shrewd, hard, intelligently directed endeavour, they shared in that tough competence

which was so characteristic a feature of the eighteenth-century
middle class and which was to make it the great political force of
the next century. The great majority of them were Protestants.
But with few exceptions, they were neither enthusiasts nor fanatics
and they displayed little of the sternness of Presbyterian Scotland
or the intolerance of Puritan New England. There was a growing
element of sedate and sober respectability among the group.
They gave some of their time and money to the Protestant
churches; and in 1791 a few of the principal Montreal houses and
the "Gentlemen of the Northwest" put up some three thousand
pounds to build the Scottish church in St. Gabriel Street, which,
like McGill University, was founded upon fur packs.[7]

It was, from the first, an urban group. A few of the traders
settled in very small places like Detroit and Three Rivers, but the
great majority made their permanent residence in Quebec or
Montreal. Although it is impossible to determine exactly, it is
probable that the commercial population of Canada was divided
not unequally between these two towns in the first decades of
British rule. Quebec attracted more merchants at the beginning
and it possessed for a generation a considerable advantage as the
sole ocean port of entry for the colony. But after the middle
sixties, when the fur trade began to pick up, the merchants in
Montreal increased in numbers; and the river city began its slow
rise to metropolitan stature, for the future of Canadian commerce
lay inevitably in the west. At the conquest both towns were small,
with probably no more than five thousand inhabitants each, and
despite the natural grandeur of their situations, a little gloomy,
ugly and congested. At Quebec, the church, the government and
the quality monopolized the salubrious upper town and the
business part of the population crowded together on the flats by
the river, in stone houses which packed the sides of narrow, twisting
streets, where the debris of the siege remained and dirt accumulated. Montreal, which had entirely escaped cannonading, was
more spacious and more regular. St. Paul and Notre Dame Streets,
the two main thoroughfares which stretched for nearly a mile
parallel to the river, were crossed at intervals by shorter streets.
This "rectangular parallelogram," as Peter Kalm somewhat
pompously called it, was surrounded by fortifications which grew

rapidly dilapidated; and beyond these and the few straggling houses of the suburbs, were green meadows, woods and wheat fields.[8]

In Montreal business men settled as close as possible to the harbour and especially about the old market-place. Most of the houses of the French régime were made of wood; but after the conquest, the merchants began to build in stone, for fires were very frequent. Windows were shuttered in sheet-iron, roofs were shingled with tin-plates, and except from a distance, where one could watch the glitter of the sun upon the roofs, the town had a somewhat grim and forbidding appearance.[9] It seemed, as did Quebec also, like a French provincial town, small, a little dull and unprogressive. But although Quebec was a sedate town which took itself a little seriously as the capital of the colony, there was a certain air of sprightliness about both places. The merchants assembled regularly of an evening at the coffee houses: there were lodges and clubs; and in the early eighties, Mr. Franks opened the Montreal Vauxhall, where the citizens dined and danced and promenaded.[10] Simon McTavish, who had money and knew both New York and London, described a winter in Montreal, a little extravagantly, as a round of dissipation. And the Montrealers assured the casual visitor that in winter the town presented the appearance of a large and happy family engaged in a perpetual carnival.

Between this little commercial community and the normal middle-class societies of West Europe and America, there were both similarities and differences. In Quebec and Montreal, as in Bristol, Le Havre and Boston, there was that rather close atmosphere of shrewd sobriety, of hard endeavour and narrow concentration. In the stone buildings which were at once homes and counting-houses, men lived in the same prosperous comfortable respectability as did their brother merchants in Europe and worked the same long hours in the familiar dank and musty counting-house twilight. Society was simple and unpretentious; but its robust vitality was more than slightly subdued by the fashionable refinement of the century. There was an air of polite gentility about the two towns. The merchants gave sedate dinner parties, they were sedulous in paying calls. At Montreal, they walked with their ladies in the Champ de Mars, or took tea and danced at Mr. Franks's Vauxhall;

and at Quebec, on summer evenings, they climbed to the upper town and listened correctly while the regimental bands played in the parade grounds.[11] In some ways it was a rather airless little world, peopled by a normal middle-class society, fundamentally healthy, prosperous, polite and complacent.

Below, however, and not very far below in Montreal, there was hidden something unusual, reckless and primitive. For if the commercial society of Canada was linked with the civilization of Europe, it was linked also with the savagery of North America. These British Canadians were some of the last merchant adventurers of the western world. The type had been the first great creation of the capitalist revolution in the West; but while it grew tamed in the centre of civilization, it acquired a fresh vitality in the outposts of empire and nowhere more so than in the valley of the St. Lawrence. Of the vast half-continent which these merchants must hold and work to prosper, settlement scarcely occupied a foothold; and beyond the last small outposts of the seigniories, the wilderness of rock and lake and forest closed in with menacing abruptness. They had to map their own empire, govern their own people, act as their own ambassadors to the savages of the west. In the strange, unreal and debased culture of the hinterland they escaped at once and completely from accustomed restraint. A sense of the treachery and violence of men and nature in the new world was in their blood; and their lives were governed by the incalculable chances of success and calamitous failure and sudden death. Their commerce was an adventure; and something of its tenseness, its exaggeration and its adaptability entered into the more normal concerns of their lives. They were good cosmopolitans, for they had seen two worlds in utter contrast meet and mingle. They watched life imperturbably with eager interest and an amused and cheerful cynicism. They lived hard and drank deeply; and there was an almost florid magnificence in the great formal meetings at Grand Portage and the famous dinners of the Beaver Club. It was a society which honoured physical endurance, courage and pride of life as much as it respected commercial shrewdness and organizing ability. The members of the Beaver Club were its aristocrats, and to the Beaver Club, whose motto was "Fortitude in Danger", only the real westerners were admitted.

II

It is impossible to understand the political objectives of the commercial class without an understanding of its business system. The first British Canadians were merchants before they were Britons, Protestants, or political theorists. Their political struggles were at times dignified by philosophizing or debased by racial strife; but it is doubtful if they were ever, at bottom, struggles of national loyalties, or political principles or racial passions. The merchants became a political power because they controlled and represented a commercial system of enormous potentialities; and it was the commercial system which, in turn, dictated their main political demands.

This system was still distinguished from others on the continent by the peculiarities which had developed during the French régime. Land, for example, had never been commercially exploited on a large scale; and after the conquest, the new governors noted with uncomprehending disapproval that the merchants were in no hurry to become landed proprietors. They gradually acquired town property and in 1788 they owned the greater number of the thirty seigniories which were claimed to be in the possession of the "old subjects".[12] But there was little money in it then or for decades later; and the land company, which was a characteristic expression of American expansion, did not make its appearance in Canada until the new century was well advanced. The merchants made their money in other ways, which had, most of them, been long established by the French. A few Quebec traders tried to interest the French Canadians in the making of potash, and small quantities of what was to be an important staple in the future, were exported to Great Britain. Lumber, hoops and staves, in slowly growing quantities, were shipped to England, the West Indies and southern Europe. George Allsopp, John Welles, Robert Lester, the Grants, the Bondfields and other merchants of Quebec were interested in the trade in wheat and flour and biscuit; and, in good years, there was often an excited scramble for grain in the "Nouvelle Beauce" south of the St. Lawrence. In Quebec also lived those merchants who were concerned in the fishery of the gulf. Bayne, Brymer, Allsopp, Lymburner and others[13] fought a long fight against

Governor Palliser of Newfoundland and the London mercantilists to save the old Labrador seal fishery for Quebec; and the export of cod and seal oil increased, particularly after 1774, when the Quebec Act transferred the northern maritime region back to the St. Lawrence.

But these were small trades—trades which, so far as Canada was concerned, were either of the past or of the future. And it is significant that Quebec, not Montreal, concerned itself with most of them. Quebec looked forward to the long decline of its commercial importance; and it possessed neither the immense purpose nor the undivided concentration of Montreal. The river city was the city of western commerce—the grand style of Canadian commercial endeavour; and the fur trade was its first expression. Eagerly the new northerners took over the direction of this business, acquired its old technique and pushed forward towards its old objectives. In the summer of 1761 Alexander Henry was on his way to Michilimackinac. According to his account, the traders Goddard, Solomons, Bostwick and Treacey were in the west in the very early sixties, and there were others without doubt. It was, in those days, a trade for heroes. The Indians looked upon the British newcomers with resentment, irritability and malevolence. The sullen, mounting tension which filled the whole west cracked in 1763 and there came the explosive fury of Pontiac's rising. From the window of a house in Michilimackinac, Henry helplessly watched the slaughter of his fellow subjects; and the Indians brought the "green scalps" of British-Canadian traders to the Hudson's Bay Company's post at Severn House. For two years the west was closed for trade, until the merchants in Montreal fretted with impatience; but at last, at the beginning of 1765, Murray began to issue licences once more. John Askin, George McBeath, James Finlay, Benjamin Frobisher, James McGill and Forrest Oakes were some of the British traders who first reached the west after the ban had been lifted. From the trading centres of Niagara, Detroit and Michilimackinac the "new" and "old" Canadian subjects competed for the south-west fur trade with the merchants of Pennsylvania and New York and with the French from the Mississippi; and of the sixty canoes which in 1767 went to La Baye, or by La Baye into the Mississippi country, the great majority were dispatched by traders from Montreal.[14] But the Canadians established contact with the north-west as well, where lay the great future of the trade; and in 1768–1769 James Finlay wintered on the Saskatchewan.

Thus, by motives simple, profound and compelling, the first British-Canadian merchants were committed to the success of the St. Lawrence. They took over the direction of the northern commercial system; and with it, as its inevitable accompaniments, they assumed the policies and methods, the rivalries and alliances, of the past. The business organization by which the manufactures of Europe were exchanged for the furs of the Indians across incredible distances of ocean, river, forest and plain, continued to involve the old commitments and the old extravagant demands. The Canadian system was at once transatlantic and transcontinental. The Canadian merchants were forced to enter the politics of the province of Quebec, of the British empire and of the American continent; and their programmes in provincial, imperial and continental affairs were but different aspects of the same policy, pursued fundamentally for commercial ends. The conquest had not changed these commercial ends and it had scarcely altered these political objectives. Great Britain had been substituted for France as Canada's imperial master; but the change had strengthened rather than weakened the necessary dependence of Canada upon a European metropolitan power. The northern economy, organized with rigid simplicity for the production of a single luxury staple, was bound to London by the single, simple trade route which stretched undeviatingly across the Atlantic from Quebec to the English Channel. A number of the Canadian merchants had originally been agents for English firms of army contractors. They kept up these commercial connections or formed new ones; and both they and the traders who had come from the Atlantic colonies were dependent for almost their whole supply of trade goods upon the English exporting firms. These firms granted the extensive credits by which alone the western trade could be carried on; and the whole production of the major Canadian staple industry was invariably consigned for England. The British-Canadian merchants were soon to become distinguished for their obstinate loyalty to the empire and for their old-fashioned devotion to the mercantile system.

The humbleness of their attitude to Europe was, however, balanced by their aggressiveness in North America, in largely the same way as it had been during the French régime. The fur trade continued as a race against commercial rivals, against the progress of settlement and the exhaustion of the beaver fields; it assumed vast areas for exploitation and dictated a grandiose policy of territorial conquest. The new northerners, like the old, tried to hold the whole area annexed to the St. Lawrence, the Great Lakes and the upper Mississippi. They asserted the individuality of the Canadian economy; they insisted upon its essentially separate, aloof and competitive character. And, in so doing, they discovered their destined enemies and allies precisely where the French had left them. It made no difference that there were brother Scots on Hudson Bay and brother colonists in New York and Pennsylvania. So long as it continued independent, the economy of the St. Lawrence was in a state of war with the Atlantic seaboard and with Hudson Bay; and the new northerners took up the old quarrels of their commercial dominion against the old rivals from the north and from the south. It made no difference that Pontiac and his Indians had slaughtered the British conquerors upon their first arrival in the west. The pressure of the northern economy obliterated these transitory political loyalties and hatreds. Reverence for the defeated French could not keep the Indians apart from the fur-trading state any more than ties of blood and tradition could bring the Americans and the British Canadians together.

Rapidly the Indians took up their old position as devoted and even fanatical citizens of the fur-trading empire which was centralized at Montreal. Official Indian policy, personified in Sir William Johnson and a long line of followers and subordinates, became sympathetic and generous, in the best French tradition; but it is a mistake to assume that the quickly established and long-continued fidelity of the Indians to the northern state was alone or even primarily the achievement of a few officials made wise and cautious by the lessons of the Pontiac conspiracy. The commercial system of the St. Lawrence linked the Indians with the northern commercial state: the merchants and the Indians were the eastern and western partners of the fur trade. Indian culture, though altered and debased, could alone survive in a fur-trading colony; and the fur trade could alone continue within Indian society with its sparse population and roving, hunting traits. Merchants and Indians alike opposed the advance of settlement from the Atlantic seaboard, for settlement meant both the ruin of the fur trade and the downfall of the hunting races. The political, the territorial claims of merchants and Indians coincided with almost absolute exactitude, for their economic interests were so inseparably allied. It was the fur trade which made the Indians the potent allies and the troublesome poor relations of the Canadian state. They were the western subjects of that state; and like any other group of subjects, they would demand protection and services in return for their loyalty and support.

The nature and the requirements of the northern commercial system forced the British-Canadian merchants into provincial politics, as well as into the politics of the British Empire and of the American continent. They were products of a society in which commercial capitalism and middle-class ideals had triumphed over an absolute monarchy and a feudal ethic more than a century before; and they were convinced that the strength and the success of the northern economy in America were dependent ultimately upon the extent of their own political power at Quebec. In their view the St. Lawrence was a commercial state. Its policies must be fashioned by merchants for the achievement of commercial ends. The laws, the customs, the political institutions of the St. Lawrence must be organized to combine with the river itself for the defeat of commercial rivals and for the capture of a geographic empire. The merchants were middle-class reformers who eventually became revolutionaries; but in this period their attack was directed only at the apex and not at the base of the social and political system of Quebec. Their quarrel, in the first few decades of British rule, was not against the great mass of the French Canadians; it was against the British governors, the British military, the British and French bureaucracy and the French-Canadian *noblesse*. The merchants accepted the bulk of French-Canadian institutions and customs because they were the superstructure of which the fur trade was the base.

The fur trade was a unifying force; it was, in fact, the first and the last great continental enterprise in which British and French Canadians ever intimately participated. Young Alexander Henry, sitting in the firelit room of the seigniory on a winter's night in 1761, and drinking in avidly the accumulated wisdom of the French fur trader Leduc,[15] is a symbol of the close relationship of the two races which was based so solidly on economic needs. Control and direction were indeed surrendered to the British. But the Cadots, the Chaboillez and the Blondeaus remained as teaching partners to pass on the rich heritage of French experience; and the system for trade in the interior down to the last homely and seemingly irrelevant detail was French—or French and Indian. The Pierres and the Antoines still kept their old, their key positions as canoemen, interpreters and guides. It was they who drove or carried the *canots du maître* and the *canots du nord* through the incredible difficulties of the river systems, who guided the trade into the recesses of the continent and who made the last vital connection of speech between the men of Europe and America. The trade was bilingual, but French was the dominant language of the west. The songs, the stories, the tragedies and legends which gave the trade at once its simple humanity and its mysterious distinction, were all French, or Indian in French disguise.[16] Scots clerks and traders waited patiently at the little church of St. Anne's while the Canadians paid their last duties to the patron saint of the western trade. Where the French river slipped at last into Georgian Bay, they listened curiously, while the canoemen appealed softly for the favour of the wind; and at the height of land between Lakes Superior and Winnipeg, they took the oaths and submitted to the baptism which made of them at last real *hommes du nord*.[17]

Despite the fact that the *voyageurs* were almost serfs who were expected to labour for long hours at incredibly difficult tasks, disputes between the *bourgeois* and their men were very rare.[18] The fur traders were not merely employers and employed: they formed an order, a brotherhood, a society in which of necessity the whole native hunting population of the west were citizens. And this unique society, this strange violent way of life had been permeated by all the wisdom and folly of a simple people. Its laws, its polite usages, its traditions, its philosophies, even that curious blend of Indian and French-peasant superstition which one may call its religion, had ripened and matured. It was the French Canadians who had created the system and who had humanized it. Ultimately it rested upon the shoulders of the *voyageurs*, the short, thickset, black-haired descendants of the northern French peasantry; and it was shot through with their heroism, inventiveness, imagination and inconsequence.

This close co-operation of the two races in the main trade of the northern economy was reflected in the social relationships of the period. The merchants did not despise the French language: they learnt and used it. From the first the French Canadians were admitted to the Beaver Club.[19] In Quebec and Montreal, the daughters of French *bourgeois* and landowners, the Mariannes, Genevièves and Angéliques married Scottish and English traders with a frequency which might surprise the modern inhabitants of the province of Quebec;[20] and it is not without significance that the three men who were perhaps the greatest of the first generation of British-Canadian merchants, Simon McTavish, Joseph Frobisher and James McGill, all married French-Canadian women. Allsopp, Lymburner, McTavish, Pangman and many others bought seigniories, tacitly accepting a land system alien to their own; and, as late as 1784, the British commercial minority made no specific demand for the establishment of the English system of freehold tenure. In the eighteenth century there was no frontal attack by the British on the social, judicial and political institutions of the St. Lawrence; and there is little evidence of any serious hostility between the two groups. "By all I can find", wrote Maseres soon after his arrival in the colony in 1766, "the English and French agree together tolerably well and speak well of each other: but there are great animosities between the English themselves one with another."[21]

III

This was true. The northern commercial system, which depended upon the co-operation of the two races, helped to reconcile the French and British to one another. But it forced the British merchants to do battle with their own kinsmen, both within and without the colony. As we have seen, the merchants had two main objects in America: the defence of the dominion of the St. Lawrence in the continent; and the capture of political power at Quebec. In the period from the conquest until the Quebec Act of 1774, it was chiefly the imperial authorities in England and the governing bureaucracy in Quebec which prevented the realization of these objectives. The imperial planners over in London tried to curb the commercial system of the St. Lawrence in the interests of imperial integration and harmony. The old-fashioned bureaucracy of Quebec attempted to preserve and strengthen the authoritarian, military and feudal elements in the colony of the St. Lawrence, in the alleged interest of the French Canadians. These two policies, which together denied the past and stunted the future of the northern economy, the merchants set themselves to overthrow. The controversies really began in 1763, for both grew directly or indirectly out of the famous royal proclamation of that year.

The proclamation of 1763 was the imperfect introduction of an imperfect imperial plan, which, like the problem it was designed to solve, was continental in its scope. As everybody knows, the grand scheme was preserved arbitrarily, spasmodically and inefficiently; but it was at bottom an attempt to bring strength, cohesion and order out of the contradictions and chaos of a vast maritime and continental empire, recently swollen by conquest. Each colony, however curious and unusual its character, was to conform at least roughly to an approved and standard pattern; and all colonies, however incompatible their interests and however complicated their extra-imperial relations, were to accommodate themselves to the just demands of their neighbours and the great necessities of the empire as a whole. Of this somewhat belated and clumsy movement for the organization and strengthening of empire, the proclamation of 1763 was the inauspicious prelude. With a few important exceptions, it concerned only the new colonies of

Quebec, East and West Florida, and Grenada; but it showed the same virtues and vices as the more comprehensive legislation of the later sixties. It was a plan whose irritation arose not so much from its narrow unfairness as from the very breadth of its complacent and righteous impartiality. It was not that it contradicted justice but that it denied life.

The proclamation of 1763 was the repudiation of Canada's character and history as a distinct American economy, continental, commercial and competitive. For Canada was to be sternly limited in the interests of imperial harmony; and it was to be recreated in the interests of imperial standardization. A great inland commercial empire, its life rigidly simplified and organized to combine with geography for the prosecution of a single staple trade, was to become a normal colony, limited in territory, devoted to agriculture, modestly typical and completely undistinguished. Its boundaries were narrowly contracted by the proclamation. The stunted little colony which the British named Quebec was but a contemptible fragment of what they had conquered as New France. Labrador and the islands of the gulf had already been divided between Newfoundland and Nova Scotia; and the proclamation confirmed the partition. The western hinterland, where lay the colony's one great market, was wrenched away from the province of Quebec to form a western Indian reserve, in which British officials could pursue in uninterrupted seclusion the solution of the Indian problem. Canada was to abandon its pretensions and to learn humility. When Egremont, the secretary of state, argued that the western Indian reserve ought to be placed under the jurisdiction of one of the colonies and that Quebec was logically destined for the task, the board of trade judiciously replied that the annexation of the reserve to Canada was especially objectionable inasmuch as it would give the Canadians an unfair advantage in the fur trade and their governor an overweening importance in the politics of the continent.[22] Somewhat ostentatiously, the British tried to turn the faces of Canadians away from the exciting grandeurs of the St. Lawrence. The new boundary, while it was meaningless from the point of view of geography and commerce which the French had emphasized, possessed a certain justification from the point of view of settlement, which they had neglected. Settlement was no longer to be neglected. "Canada", wrote the board of trade, was a place "where Planting, perpetual Settlement and Cultivation ought to be encouraged . . . ."[23] Governor Murray was instructed to survey the unoccupied parts of his province on the basis of English land tenure and to encourage the advent of aspiring agricultural frontiersmen, in order that Quebec might both relieve congestion on the Atlantic seaboard and develop into healthy normality itself.

All this, however, was not the whole of the proclamation of 1763. The document also contained the famous promise of an assembly and the "Benefit of the Laws of our Realm of England" for all the newly created colonies, including Quebec. English law, in its entirety, was much more than the merchants were to demand for years to come; but the assembly, in their view, was absolutely necessary as the only way in which their political control of the colony could be realized. They both revered and hated the proclamation of 1763. So far as the continent was concerned, it seemed the doom of their commercial ambitions; so far as the province was concerned, it appeared the hope of their political supremacy. And resentment emerged dominant out of the confusion of their emotions as it became increasingly obvious that only the objectionable provisions of the proclamation were to be enforced. The new boundaries were drawn, the Indian reserve set up and a series of obnoxious regulations and restrictions of their trade established. But there was no assembly.

To a very considerable extent, this was the work of the first British governors in Quebec and of the governing clique which surrounded them. James Murray, Guy Carleton and Frederick Haldimand, the three soldiers who in succession ruled the province for a quarter-century after the conquest, belonged, despite certain obvious differences, to a single type and carried out a singularly consistent policy. They were all born into professional and land-owning families and they grew up remote from that new world of commerce and middle-class ideals which arose in England on the ruins of the old monarchy and the old tory party. Murray was of Lowland Scots extraction; Carleton came of an Anglo-Irish family established in County Tyrone; and Haldimand was a French Swiss, born in a little town in the canton of Neuchatel. Their experience, almost purely military in character, was profound but narrow. Murray and Carleton entered the British army at the tender age at which it was customary in the eighteenth century for the aspiring sons of the gentry to begin their military careers; and Haldimand became a member of the national profession of Switzerland and hawked his military talents around Europe for decades with little concern for the colour of the flag so long as the colour of the money was satisfactory. By birth, training and experience, the three men became identified with an eighteenth-century type, from which even their marked personal characteristics could not dissociate them. Murray was impetuous and erratic, with a warm heart and a hot head. Carleton's manner was more formal and his temper more inclined to vindictiveness; and he possessed—what Murray completely lacked—the capacity to work out logical and coherent schemes upon the basis of given premises. Haldimand, who combined a practical instinct with an old-fashioned courtesy and a love of routine, had neither the emotional directness of Murray nor the calculating intellectuality of Carleton. But these minor variations of tone and emphasis could not alter the rigidly woven pattern of character and mentality which all three men possessed in common. They were members of the English governing class, trained in its most regimented department, the army; and they cherished the convictions characteristic of their profession and their order with bland assurance or with irritable pugnacity.[24]

Their role in Canada, which was essentially counter-revolutionary in spirit, was determined for them; it was dictated by their character, their experience, and by the structure of society and politics on the St. Lawrence. Instinct with the desire for order, obedience and subordination, they looked upon the civilian population as a troop of inexperienced children, either dutiful and well-mannered or disobedient and naughty. They saw themselves, somewhat naïvely, as parents whose indulgence must be corrected by discipline and as magistrates whose severity must be tempered by kindness. They liked Quebec; they began to feel rather agreeably paternal about its people. In Quebec there was much that soothed their professional consequence and satisfied their military and aristocratic convictions. They dwelt fondly upon these features of Canadian life; in their minds and their dispatches they assumed larger proportions than they did in actuality. There was a great military tradition in the colony which Murray relished; "the Canadians", he reported enthusiastically, "are to a man soldiers." The province had a strategic importance which impressed the soldier Carleton. If Quebec were linked with New York by an adequate chain of fortifications, it would help to preserve British power on the continent against the attacks of the French or the discontented colonists; and a garrison might be found to defend British interests among the sober and old-fashioned inhabitants of the St. Lawrence. There were, in the society of Quebec, the decayed remnants of a feudal hierarchy, which Carleton sympathetically exaggerated. The old government, it appeared, had taught obedience and subordination; and the Canadian people were obviously simple, docile and politically unambitious. The place had charm. Of all the American colonies, it was the most un-American; astonishingly, in the midst of the American forest, it appeared to preserve the old certainties and the old simplicities. All this was very soothing and highly acceptable to the first British governors. They wished to preserve this static little society; they resented intruders. And they became pro-French and anti-commercial.

They did not, of course, dislike trade in itself; and when trade involved some political consideration such as the protection of Canadian subjects or the extension of Canadian influence and frontiers, both Murray and Carleton were ready to take the side of the merchants. But for the commercial party as a political and social force they had nothing but a gentlemanly aversion and a professional contempt. To Murray, in his outbursts of choleric rage, the merchants were "ignorant, licentious, factious men"; and, in his occasional lapses into patronizing urbanity, they became "poor mercantile devils". Both Murray and Carleton maintained a contemptuous raillery at the expense of the birth and social position of their opponents. Haldimand, who had much of the charm and the inappropriateness of a medieval ruin, was appalled at the possible social consequences of the jury system in Canada. There were foreign troops serving His Majesty in America; and he shook his head solemnly over the dreadful prospect of a German baron being tried by a jury of Canadian

shopkeepers.[25] Carleton, who possibly had less scruple and more
political capacity than the other two, organized this odd assortment
of military yearnings, aversions and prejudices into a political
and social philosophy which became law as the Quebec Act. But
Murray, for all his erratic inconsistencies, prepared the way for
the revival of the decadent French system, and Haldimand tried
to preserve it with an old man's myopic stubbornness.

The governors believed that they fought the battle of justice and
humanity for the French Canadians. There can be no question of
the sincerity of these convictions; but, at the same time, there can
be little doubt that the governors, in yielding to the promptings
of their humanitarian instincts, were moved to preserve a political
and social system which secured the prolongation of their own
power and satisfied the prejudices of their class and profession.
The conflict which followed in Quebec was not a conflict between
altruism and self-interest, or between right and wrong. It was a
struggle between an old force and a new—a struggle for power.
On the one hand were the British governors, the Francophil
bureaucracy and the French-Canadian landowners, attempting to
preserve the paternalistic, military and semi-feudal colony of the
St. Lawrence. On the other hand was the middle-class commercial
group. In the commercial group was concentrated a great proportion of economic power—the wealth, the energy and ability of the
colony. Yet the merchants were jealously shut out from political
control. Here was the origin of their anger and the genesis of
political strife. Race, language and religion had, in this period,
practically nothing to do with it. It was a re-enactment, upon
a distant and insignificant stage, of the classic West-European
struggle—the struggle between insurgent commercial capitalism
and a decadent and desperately resisting feudal and absolutist
state.

IV

The merchants, then, had two policies which in their minds were
simply the two aspects, continental and provincial, of a single
commercial programme. They desired to recover the economic
unity of the St. Lawrence which had been broken by the proclamation of 1763. They hoped to make Canada a truly commercial state

by breaking the power of the bureaucracy and gaining the political influence which the proclamation had promised them. They became active first in provincial politics. Their first quarrel was with Governor Murray.

The military régime, which came to an end only in August, 1764, had lasted nearly a year after the proclamation of 1763. For the merchants it had meant billeting, military courts and such irritating absurdities as the garrison order which required everyone abroad after ten o'clock at night to carry a lantern. The régime probably helped to reconcile the French Canadians to the conquest, for the military governors found it easy to employ French-Canadian methods and institutions which were, of course, compatible with absolutist rule for the simple reason that they had developed under it. But the French Canadians, who had endured the whole crisis of the conquest with a resignation which bordered upon apathy, were not the politically active part of the population. The merchants were. To them it was a grievance that the military régime had lasted so long; it was also a grievance that James Murray lasted on after it. No commission as civil governor could make him anything but a soldier; and as time went on it became obvious that the civil government over which he presided bore an increasingly irritating resemblance to the military régime which it had supposedly replaced. He called no assembly. He could not find it in his heart to deliver the French Canadians into the hands of a few score merchants by establishing an assembly on the basis of the old religious tests; so he delivered the control of the whole colony into his own hands and those of a group of his political appointees. The Francophil bureaucracy, destined to a long and vigorous existence, was established in the council and the courts. The new council proceeded to pass ordinances which the merchants, not without some element of justice, denounced as "Vexatious, Oppressive, unconstitutional". Their bitterness mounted with uninterrupted rapidity; and in the autumn of 1764, since the establishment of civil government, they were not without means of protest and reprisal. They sat on juries and they had been appointed justices of the peace. At Quebec the first grand jury censured the government with solemn self-importance. In Montreal, the new magistrates, headed by the merchant Thomas

Walker, began to exalt civilians and humble the military with a natural, if somewhat excessive, zeal. A party of army hoodlums, irritated at this profane perversion of established social values, took the blunt, honest course of soldiers and gentlemen. They invaded Walker's house, fell upon him, beat him thoroughly and amputated a part of his ear.

The merchants now took action. They had a definite objective, the recall of Murray. The methods by which they organized their opposition and the arguments with which they justified it are of some interest, for they were employed again and again in the future. They petitioned the king against the governor.[26] Petitions and memorials long remained the formal device of the commercial lobby at London and Quebec. Like a good many of Murray's and Carleton's dispatches, these petitions were party documents which often degenerated into full-blooded propaganda. They were discussed and debated in taverns and coffee-houses, drafted by small *ad hoc* committees and left for a few days to collect signatures. The collective action of the Canadian merchants, based as it was upon a unity of economic interests and a natural social solidarity, was usually so spontaneous and easy as to make a permanent organization unnecessary. But sometimes, as in the case of the Quebec and Montreal committees which fought against the Quebec Act and corresponded with the American revolutionaries, a small executive body exercised temporary authority.

More important and more difficult was the relationship with London. Of all the social groups in Great Britain, the merchants were the most persistent in support of the policy of conciliation with America during the troubled decade from 1765 to 1775. The Canadian traders, like those of the Atlantic seaboard, found political support in England through their commercial connections; but, so far as numbers went, the British merchants trading to Canada were only a small fraction of the North American group as a whole. The merchants trading to the Atlantic colonies could, on occasion, muster nearly twelve hundred signatures in London alone.[27] But only fifty-six London merchants signed the memorial of April 18, 1765, which dealt with the Walker outrage;[28] and twenty-five individual traders and firms supported the Quebec petition for the dismissal of the governor.[29] The personnel of the group of Canadian merchants altered considerably in this period, for it was not until the formation of the North West Company that a few London firms got control of the greater part of the Canadian trade. The merchants met regularly at the New York Coffee House. The group was small, but it was active and fairly well organized, and as early as 1765 an executive committee had been created. Brook Watson, Robert Hunter, Henry Guinand, Isidore Lynch, Robert Grant and John Strettel were some of the most assiduous in promoting Canadian affairs in the period before the Quebec Act. Every mail which left Canada carried a sheaf of letters for the English merchants, which they not infrequently employed in their representations to the government. Every season at least a few Canadian merchants travelled over to London to discuss business and politics with their correspondents, as Bayne and Mackenzie did in the autumn of 1764. But in the recurrent crises of their affairs, the Canadians often required a special representative in England who would devote himself particularly to uniting the various commercial groups interested in Canada and to concerting Canadian policy. To meet this necessity, there appeared the agent, who in the future was to be sometimes a Canadian and more frequently an Englishman nominated by either the Canadian or British merchants. On this occasion, Bayne and Mackenzie, who were commissioned by the Quebec and Montreal merchants to begin the attack against Murray in England, came to terms with the first Canadian agent in April, 1765.[30] He was Fowler Walker, a lawyer of Lincoln's Inn, and the merchants offered him £200 for one year of his services.

The merchants employed every argument and every insinuation which their baffled fury could suggest. But they were not alone in their prejudices and their vehemence. The first British governors in Canada were not remarkable for their good manners, their good temper, their scrupulosity, or the generosity with which they treated political opponents; and the merchants gave back pretty much what they got. They were not lawyers, but indignant business men, intent upon winning a political victory; and the chief arguments upon which they grounded their case were chosen unconsciously for their direct appeal to the world of eighteenth-century England. England and its empire rested on the twin dogmas of parliamentarism and mercantilism. The Canadian merchants, who felt perfectly at home within this world, had merely to invoke the spirit and quote the texts of imperial philosophies long since grown respectable. When they denounced Murray's ordinances as "Vexatious, Oppressive, unconstitutional", when they demanded the "Blessings of British Liberty" and requested a governor "acquainted with other maxims of Government than Military only", they appealed to that religion of individualism, parliamentarism and *laissez-faire* which had conquered in England in the seventeenth century. "They made speeches", wrote Maseres later, "and wretched ones, about the liberty of the Subject and the prerogative of the crown, the petition of rights, the bill of rights and magna charta. . . ."[31]

In addition, for the benefit of a commercially minded England, they repeated with tiresome iteration all the old commonplaces of seventeenth-century mercantilism. Canada, as they and their London correspondents were at pains to point out, was a valuable colony. It conformed perfectly to the requirements of mercantilism. It supplied the staples, furs, fish and oil; it consumed and did not compete with British manufactures; and it provided an outlet for British shipping. It was unnecessary for them to prove the obvious truth that this trade, which in their view alone made the colony an object worthy of imperial attention, was almost entirely in the hands of British merchants in Canada and England. The Canadians asserted that they would never have engaged in the trade and the British affirmed that they would never have granted the long-term credits necessary for its prosecution, if it had not been for the promise of liberal institutions on the banks of the St. Lawrence. Both Canadians and British joined in insisting that unless Canada's affairs were governed by civilians in the commercial interests, its trade and consequently its prosperity would remain undeveloped.

The campaign against Murray succeeded. The governor was a vulnerable man. His own character and policy, the inefficiency of his servants, the rancours of his military associates and the rowdyism of the army had made the colony a chaos. In the autumn of 1765 Murray was recalled. Subsequently, when the privy council held a formal investigation into the conduct of the governor, the case against him collapsed. The merchants did not press their charges; and, even if they had done so, the probable acquittal of Murray would not have meant very much. Murray, like Strafford, was not a criminal. He was simply a choleric, arrogant, impetuous man who was cordially hated by a politically ambitious minority in much the same way as Strafford was. The formal investigation, like impeachment, was a clumsy, legal means of exploring the rights of a complicated political struggle. The merchants, having secured Murray's removal, were complacently uninterested in further proceedings. They had wanted the governor's recall, not his head. And since he did not return, they congratulated themselves upon a victory which, as the next few years were to show, was in reality completely delusive.

V

Immediately after they had won this unreal success in the province, the merchants became involved in a controversy in continental politics. Like the quarrel with Murray, it grew out of the provisions of the proclamation of 1763. The Pontiac conspiracy at last petered out. The west was officially declared open for trade; and the system for the control of the Indians and the regulation of commerce within the new western reserve established by the proclamation was set up, though not entirely as it had originally been planned. No civil government was provided for the reserve and General Gage, as commander-in-chief in North America, had final authority over the region. Acting on advices from him, Murray published at the beginning of 1765 the first of the new conditions which the Canadian fur traders were forced to meet.[32] They had to take out licences; they were required to give security of double the value of the goods they carried into the interior that they would obey the regulations to be established there; and they were allowed to trade only at the fortified posts. Sir William Johnson, who became superintendent for Indian affairs in the northern district, imposed, in addition, a series of more stringent regulations[33] which he mistakenly believed would maintain peace, distribute trade equitably and satisfy the Indians. Trade was confined strictly to the posts; traders must not trade *en route* or seek the Indians in their villages. They were not allowed to grant them credit, and they had to accept the list of prices fixed by the Indian commissaries at the posts.

When Captain John Howard attempted, not very impartially, to enforce these regulations at Michilimackinac, there was an immediate protest; and the Canadian traders set themselves to break the new system in its entirety. In the autumn of 1766 they petitioned several times against Johnson's rules.[34] In London, Fowler Walker sent memorials on the subject to the board of trade;[35] and he and the Canada merchants co-operated[36] in drawing up the case against the regulations for presentation to government officials. The new scheme cramped the matured technique of the northern trade and violated the spirit of *laissez-faire* and freedom which had been its distinguishing characteristic in the hinterland. The confinement of the trade to the posts was absurd, the Canadians argued, and especially ludicrous in the case of Michilimackinac. Trade had been pushed hundreds of miles beyond Michilimackinac among Indians to whom the very name of the post was unknown. The Indians could not and would not come to Michilimackinac; and even if by a miracle they could be induced to undertake the journey, they would lose every second year of their hunting because of the distance. The post was barren, ruinously expensive for the traders and totally incapable of supporting large groups of natives. Wintering among the Indians, credit to the Indians and all the other free and easy practices of the French régime must continue. If they did not, the trade and the Indian empire founded on it would be lost to the French of the Mississippi. The blame would justly fall not on Canada, but on Pennsylvania and New York. The whole system of control, the Canadian merchants argued, was a vile plot on the part of these weaker fur-trading colonies to steal the fairly-won superiority of Quebec.

With these arguments the merchants protested against the new system of regulation; and Carleton gave them vigorous official support. Thus the St. Lawrence struggled for itself; but in addition, more general economic and political factors in the continent gave the northern colony powerful if indirect assistance. By creating the Indian reserve, the British had left the Mississippi in isolation; and in isolation, the Mississippi of those days was economically

and politically weak. Without settlements it could have only a
commercial meaning and that meaning, for the British, could best
be read at Quebec. If the resources of the region were not tapped
and its strength maintained by the natural system of the French,
the British would be forced to create an artificial and expensive
establishment in the west. This—and the planners had admitted
the necessity—implied imperial taxation. But the whole scheme of
imperial taxation was breaking against the resistance of the
Thirteen Colonies. The strength of the Atlantic seaboard, as well
as the weakness of the Mississippi, advanced the interests of the
Canadians. Worried by the continually mounting expense and
harassed by other American problems, the home government
decided in 1768 to scrap a part of its ambitious western scheme.
The control of western trade was handed over to the colonies
chiefly interested in it.[37] The imperialization of all Indian affairs
was at an end. And the Canadian merchants had won the first
round.

The old competition instantly revived. Those colonies which
were intent upon winning the inland commerce of the continent
renewed the rivalries which the British planners had been unable
to control. The pull of the St. Lawrence became heavier and more
imperative, in part because of its own inner strength and in part
because of the temporary weakness of the Atlantic seaboard. The
decision to retain Canada instead of the sugar-producing Guadeloupe, the Sugar Act and the tightening of the navigation system
injured the North Atlantic colonies, which had based their competition in the west on cheap English manufactures and New
England rum. With the recklessness of desperation, they heaped
upon the restrictions of the British the restrictions of their own
non-importation agreements. Their hold on the marginal areas of
their economy weakened and relaxed. Montreal with English
credits and English manufactures at its back, began aggressively
to expand its trade; while down in Albany and Schenectady the
American traders began to realize the strength of the northern
route and the perilous insecurity of their own. In 1770, Phyn and
Ellice accepted the inevitable and for the first time shipped a cargo
of British merchandise to Quebec.[38] Peter Pond, after an apprenticeship in fur trading around the Detroit district, launched his first

cargo from Montreal in 1773 and two years later abandoned the Mississippi basin to push into the far north-west.[39] The Quebec Act and the renewal of non-intercourse with Great Britain by the continental association of the Thirteen Colonies, drove other traders northward. Simon McTavish, who became one of the organizing geniuses of the North West Company, moved up to Montreal. "I am confident", it was affirmed in a letter from Phyn and Ellice dated February 9, 1776, "that upwards of £30,000 value in skins was shipped from Montreal last fall by traders who (for the most part) used to send their property to this place [Albany]."[40] In that sterner competition which revived after 1768, Montreal was winning; and one of the best indications of its success is the advent of these traders whose early experience had been gained in the southern route.

But commercial success alone was not enough. The merchants wished to complete their commercial monopoly in the west by full political control of the region—to break up the narrow boundaries imposed on Canada by the proclamation of 1763. So strong was the tradition of western empire and so appealing were its political implications that Carleton and his council joined with the merchants in their attempt to upset British plans and to triumph over American competition.[41] They pointed to the west, which was full of turmoil; its weakness and confusion would continue as long as its isolation. When they had handed over the control of the fur trade to the different interested colonies, the British had illogically maintained the Indian reserve and the control of the superintendents over the Indians. The Indian superintendents had no ordinary civil jurisdiction within their vast domains; and the governors of New York and Quebec could not extend their juris-diction beyond the boundaries of their respective provinces. The co-operative control of the fur trade by the different interested provinces would, therefore, be only a partial solution of the problem. But while New York, which was commercially weaker, was inclined towards co-operative regulation, Quebec, which was competitively stronger, was intent with the whole force of its being upon monopoly control. In 1769, a committee of the Quebec council, appointed to consider the English and Canadian petitions on the trade, reported that an effective regulation was impossible by colonies so at variance with each other in a country over which they had no real control. "And here", they concluded, "we think we do not speak the Language of persons improperly devoted to our own Province, when we say that this has much better pretensions to give the Law upon this head to those Countries, than any other Government upon the Continent."

In 1770, when the assembly of New York passed a bill appointing commissioners to confer with commissioners of the other colonies for the regulation of the trade, Quebec found a good excuse for non-attendance in the unsuitability of the time appointed.[42] In 1771 the northern colony finally accepted the invitation of the pertinacious New Yorkers to a conference on the fur trade in December; but both its councillors and its merchants agreed in disapproving of the whole scheme which New York was certain to propound to the congress. The New York plan provided for the imposition of duties on trade goods in order to pay for the superintendence of the commerce. But the Quebec councillors explained that the northern colony was legally incompetent to impose taxes and the Quebec merchants, true to their principles of *laissez-faire*, asserted that the trade was incapable of bearing them.[43] This natural antipathy of the merchants and the officials on the St. Lawrence was reinforced by the disapprobation of London, for Hillsborough made quite clear his dislike of colonial congresses.[44] It was significant that Canada and the home government agreed upon the matter of colonial conferences and that they both disagreed with the Atlantic seaboard. The fur trade bound Quebec to London and isolated it in North America. The Canadian merchants had won the second round. There could be no co-operative control of the fur trade without the co-operation of Quebec and the blessing of the home government. Thus both the imperial plan and the colonial plan for regulation of the trade in the west broke down, for history and geography were against them; and the Quebec Act solved the problem, as the Canadians had always hoped it would be solved, by transferring the political control of the Ohio country to the St. Lawrence. The boundary clause was, of course, only one feature of the Quebec Act; and back of the Quebec Act as a whole there have been discovered a number of different purposes—purposes military as well as political in character and continental

as well as provincial in scope. But the unfortunate experience of
the British in the north-west provided at least a strong negative
argument for a radical change of policy; and the facts of geography,
the western commercial supremacy of Canada and the existence of
Canadian settlements like Detroit, which had developed to serve
the fur trade, all favoured the return of the territory which had
been torn from Quebec in 1763.

Carleton, though at first he was apparently opposed to the
westward extension of Canada's boundaries, had given the
merchants his support in their campaign against Sir William
Johnson's restrictive system of control. In the east, where the
strength of the northern economy and the ambitions of its commercial directors were persistent, if attenuated, he also gave
assistance. The eastern outposts of the St. Lawrence—Labrador,
Anticosti, the Magdalen Islands and Cape Breton—had been
transferred to the governments of Newfoundland and Nova Scotia.
Much in the manner of Sir William Johnson in the west, Sir Hugh
Palliser, the governor of Newfoundland, attempted to enforce an
arbitrary system of regulation over his enlarged maritime empire,
which included Labrador and the north shore of the gulf. He tried
to establish a "free" British cod-fishery on the strict mercantile
principles of the industry in Newfoundland. This, in effect, meant
the ruin of the "sedentary" seal fishery in the district. The British
merchants in the city of Quebec who had taken up the old seal-
fishery of the French, protested violently, much as the Montreal
merchants had protested, against a régime which violated long-
established property rights and imperilled a mature Canadian
industry. Daniel Bayne and William Brymer struggled for years to
recover damages for their losses under the Palliser administration.[45]
The clamours of the Canadians and the violence of the American
fishermen in the gulf helped to undermine Palliser's ambitious
scheme, and the British decided upon a further re-allocation of
territory. The Quebec Act restored Labrador to Canada. In 1774
the northern economy recovered its old territorial grandeur on
the continent.

VI

Both in Quebec and Montreal the merchants were indebted to Carleton. They were naturally disposed to like him. Carleton came out to the colony with a strong prejudice against Murray and his creatures; and even if he had sincerely abominated the whole of the ex-governor's Canadian policy, his early attitude to the Murray party could hardly have been more suspicious and truculent than it was. The merchants grew complacent over the sound views of their governor and the excellent returns of their trade. The agitation for an assembly was almost but not quite abandoned. Down in the Thirteen Colonies the colonial merchants renewed their agitation after the passing of the Townshend duties and resorted again to their old protest of non-importation. But the Canadians remained unruffled and quiescent. They did not share the indignation of the seaboard merchants nor did they adopt their methods of reprisal.

The calm became a little portentous. For Carleton was ceasing to be the antagonist of Murray and was becoming the governor of Quebec. The little party prejudices with which he had come to Canada disappeared rapidly before the reassertion of his more profound convictions. He did not really change his views; he discovered the only real views which a man of his particular character could possibly hold of his particular problem. His political ideal, for the "command" he held, was the soldier-aristocrat's ideal of order, obedience and "subordination from highest to lowest"; and inevitably he came to see what a soldier-aristocrat wished to see in Quebec society—an insignificant group of transient merchants, an influential landed gentry, and an overwhelming majority of simple, untutored, biddable peasants. Perhaps because of a more set aristocratic prejudice than Murray possessed or because of a theorizing tendency which Murray completely lacked, Carleton inflated Murray's simple soldier's philosophy with a lot of highly dubious feudalism. In Carleton, the soldier-aristocrat's view of conquered Quebec became complete, systematic —and more than slightly ridiculous. With a confident dogmatism which harked back to the logic of a feudal lawyer and dismissed the facts of Canadian life, Carleton insisted that the seigneurs were the real political and social leaders of Quebec. Upon the Canadian aristocracy and the Canadian church Carleton proposed to base his system; and these views, which were to irritate the *habitants* only less than the merchants, he poured out in a series of explosive dispatches to the home government.

The merchants, of course, remained happily in ignorance of these vehement effusions. When at last, in the Quebec Act, Carleton's feudal Arcadia was revealed in all its primitive simplicity, they were violently angry. But some of its features were discernible with more or less clarity in the late sixties and early seventies and these they welcomed enthusiastically. In the west both imperial and colonial control had broken down; and when the committee of the Quebec council reported in 1769 that the annexation of the territory to Canada was the only solution of the problem, the merchants could hardly fail to applaud. As early as 1771, in anticipation of the Quebec Act, the home government issued instructions that in future grants of lands should be made *en fief et seigneurie*, according to the old French custom.[46] As we have seen, the merchants, during this period, had not the smallest objection to feudal tenure; and after the instruction became known, there was even a little scramble for new seigniories. There were other reasons for a certain smug self-satisfaction in the Canadian commercial group. The American merchants were in difficulties but their own trade was booming. With the help of sympathetic juries they had completely frustrated the attempt of the local government to collect the old French customs duties. The imperial authorities appeared to be in no hurry to impose a new tariff by statute; and the Quebec council was legally incompetent to impose any taxes at all.

In Quebec, the agitation for an assembly was renewed in the winter of 1767 and renewed again a year later by the Irish innkeeper John McCord and by George Suckling, the late attorney-general;[47] but nothing positive was done. The London merchants trading to Canada were far more active than the Canadians. In 1768, the Canada committee, with headquarters at the New York Coffee House in London, sent Hillsborough two petitions for a Canadian assembly.[48] From the first the merchants had been quite ready to give Roman Catholics the vote; and now the

Londoners proposed that a number of them should be admitted into both the council and the assembly. This recommendation coincided with the still-prevailing official view. Shelburne and Hillsborough continued to believe in the wisdom of an assembly: and as late as July, 1769, the board of trade presented a detailed project for a Canadian representative body in which Roman Catholic land-owners would sit side by side with Protestant members from the towns. From Fowler Walker the merchants probably learnt of the official plan—at least in its broad outlines; which no doubt accounts for their comparative political inactivity during this period. They remained comfortably certain of an assembly and they expected it in the very near future.

In 1770 they received their first abrupt shock. It had, indeed, nothing to do with the assembly: it was an ordinance, passed on February 1, 1770, which concerned the courts of the province. But it was a distinctly disturbing measure, cloudy and ominous, and it may very well have created a vague general feeling of fore-boding. It took from the justices of the peace their civil jurisdiction and transferred it to the judges of the courts of common pleas: it reorganized these courts and changed their procedure. Both the Canadian merchants and the London merchants[49] interested in the Canadian trade protested. They had a number of practical criticisms to make of the ordinance, for they claimed that in various ways it hurt their trade; but, in addition, they made a broad political criticism of real importance. The justices of the peace may not have been very well qualified, but the magistracy was the one part of the provincial administration over which the commercial middle class had the slightest control. The loss of their civil jurisdiction meant the loss of all authority in the determination of suits concerning their business. This crucially important power was handed over to the four judges of the common pleas, a group of men no more technically qualified than the merchants to exercise jurisdiction, for not a single one of them had been trained to the law, and a group which included some of the most obstinately reactionary members of the French party. The merchants spoke their minds frankly. "The Scope and Tendency of this Ordinance", they argued, "is apparently to invest the Officers of the Crown with such a degree of Power and discretionary Authority, as would

enable a few in public Employments among Us to become the sole
Arbiters of the whole Property of the Province, and introduce
such a State of Slavery and Dependence among Us as has ever been
deemed dangerous to, and inconsistent with, the freedom of a
Trading Body."[50]

The idea of an assembly may have been given up by the imperial
authorities as early as 1771; but if this was so, the merchants
almost certainly knew nothing about it, for if they had known
they would have recommenced their agitation. They were not badly
served for information and assistance in London during these years.
The attorney-general Maseres had returned to England in the
autumn of 1769 with no particular affection for Carleton. Although
his opinions, particularly upon the capital point of the assembly,
did not always coincide with those of the merchants, he became
their adviser and assistant in somewhat the same way as Fowler
Walker had been in the 1760's; and Canadian merchants in
London must frequently have dropped in to chat with him over
Canadian affairs, as Thomas Walker and Zachary Macaulay did
in the winter of 1773. It was in July of that same year that Maseres
learnt definitely, from no less a person than Lord North, that an
assembly was not contemplated in the approaching legislation for
Canada,[51] and probably he passed on this shattering piece of news
to the merchants. That autumn, at all events, they began to act.
On October 30, over forty merchants met in Quebec, at Miles
Prentice's tavern in the upper town. In December, the merchants
of both Quebec and Montreal petitioned Lieutenant-Governor
Cramahé for an assembly; and when that seasoned military
bureaucrat, in a correct and wooden reply, referred them to higher
authorities, they petitioned the king. They enlisted the support
of Maseres.[52] They wrote over to their London correspondents
urging co-operation with the late attorney-general; and John
Patterson, a Quebec merchant in London, was instructed to
"facilitate intercourse" between Maseres and the London people.[53]
At the end of May the petition of the London merchants against
the Quebec Bill was presented in parliament; and Maseres drew up
a supporting memorial, in which the case of the British merchants
trading to Canada was argued with considerable force and address.

It was all very efficient and well-organized and it achieved precisely nothing. Lord North's parliamentary machine rolled over these Canadian protests as unhesitatingly, as solidly, as uncomprehendingly as it did over the many commercial appeals of that uneasy year. The Quebec Act became law. It achieved what might have seemed impossible: for though it was diametrically opposed in almost every particular to the proclamation of 1763 it produced far greater irritation. The proclamation of 1763 had promised an assembly, but it had cut off the west from Canada: the Quebec Act restored the west, but it denied an assembly. And the gratitude of the merchants for the territorial enlargement of Canada was lost in their anger at the perpetuation of the anti-commercial oligarchy at Quebec.

CHAPTER III
CANADA AND THE AMERICAN REVOLUTION

I

THE Quebec Act and the American Revolution shaped the policy of the commercial class in Canada for the next decade. John Brown, the agent of the Boston committee of correspondence, met the merchants of Montreal on April 3, 1775; and on May 1 of the same year, the Quebec Act went into effect. The new constitution and the revolution, which entered Canada together, were in some important respects complementary in their results. The feudal and bureaucratic régime, legalized by the letter of the Quebec Act, was sanctified by the necessities of the war and the spirit of national defence. The merchants, their demands for reform answered with unending reiteration by the patriotic parrot-cry that the times were unsuitable for innovation, found it almost impossible to break Carleton's and Haldimand's illegally reactionary application of a reactionary constitution. Though they could not win their way to power in Quebec, the merchants could at least continue their efforts to defend the St. Lawrence as a competitive and independent economy in North America; and during the period of the American Revolution, there was as much need for this defence as there had ever been before. In the Quebec Act the British made public the abandonment of the scheme for the imperial control of the west; but, no sooner had they done so, than the Americans, irritated by this acknowledgment of the separateness and importance of the St. Lawrence, attempted to impose a second continental system of their own. They failed. The independence of the Thirteen Colonies was not the only conclusion of the revolution. Great Britain could not keep the whole of North America as a political unit dependent upon herself; but the Thirteen Colonies were equally incapable of making the whole of North America a political unit independent of Great Britain. The colonies gained their freedom from Europe; but the St. Lawrence kept its independence in America.

When, in the first spring days of 1775, John Brown talked with the merchants of Montreal, there was every reason to expect that they would accept his proposals with a savagely joyful alacrity. As Simon McTavish reported, they looked upon the Quebec Act "with horror". They stood aghast at the parliamentary enactment of what they had always considered the professional prejudices of their governors. They crowded into taverns and private houses at Montreal and Quebec for long and angry meetings; they appointed new corresponding committees, and in the autumn of 1774 petitioned king, lords and commons. But the protests of 1774 against the Quebec Act were just as ineffective as the appeals of 1773 for an assembly. The merchants wavered in the accustomed manner between rage and self-pity. They were, as George Allsopp said later, "wounded"; they agreed mournfully that they had been "treated like step-children".[1] And at the same time, they detested and denounced Carleton as "the first contriver & great promoter of this Evil".[2] The growing indignation of the past fifteen years reached a climax. And the impact of American propaganda and the advent of American liberators coincided nicely with it. Who would not have expected, what Carleton and the bureaucrats evidently feared, that the merchants would play their historic middle-class role, join with a peasantry oppressed by tithes and *corvées* and throw the province into the American Revolution?

As a group they could not and did not do it. There were individuals, of course, who went over to the American side and the group as a whole was resentful, moody and apathetic. But when the American solution was presented to them, they could not accept it eagerly and whole-heartedly. Their local protest could not be fused in a continental opposition and their dislike of the régime in Quebec could not grow into a desire for freedom from London. The character of the St. Lawrence system had formed and hardened. The economy of the north was moving, slowly, gropingly, but purposefully onwards towards its own separate fulfilment; and, in the main, it dictated the attitude of the merchants in this crisis. Union with the Americans would at once submerge the identity of Quebec in a general American federation and cut the vitally necessary economic relations with England; and these consequences were inimical to every interest of the northern commercial state. It was true, of course, that the continental association, by which the insurgent Americans had stopped all commercial intercourse with Great Britain, was an offensive measure which would not likely outlast the struggle that had given it birth; and, although Americans talked grandiloquently about the prospects of world trade, it was a certainty, foreseen by many on both sides of the Atlantic, that the commercial relations between Great Britain and her colonies would be resumed, even though their political relations were profoundly altered. But the Canadian merchants were reluctant to accept even for a moment the embargo which the Americans had adopted as a war-time measure. To break temporarily with a metropolis upon which they were vitally dependent, for the sake of colonies with which they were in constant competition, was completely unacceptable to the traders of the St. Lawrence. They had no desire to endanger their own commercial system, even for an interval. They wished to dominate in Quebec; but they were unwilling to cut the connection with London or to abandon their competition in North America.

The conduct of the Canadian traders from the conquest onward anticipated their attitude to American propaganda and the American invasion of 1775. The controversies in the Thirteen Colonies and in the province of Quebec pursued different courses through calms and crises of their own. The Stamp Act, which roused both the American merchants and the American populace, produced discussions and arguments in Canada which formed a mere feeble, irrelevant anticlimax to the stern struggle with Murray. The *Quebec Gazette* humbly suspended publication on the day the Stamp Act went into force. In the summer of 1766, when the paper was once more being issued, a man named Cawthorne, who was apparently a brief resident in the province, undertook to attack the Stamp Act in the pages of the *Gazette*. But another and irate correspondent denounced him as a man who wrote "without the sanction or approbation of any number of the merchants of Quebec".[3] The Canadian traders delivered no petitions against the Stamp Act at either Quebec or London. In the autumn of 1766, when Sir Guy Carleton arrived in Canada, a majority of the merchants—seventy including French Canadians—proposed to include in their address of welcome to the new governor a prideful reference to their loyal acceptance of the Stamp Act.[4] This address "occasioned great disputes and very high words in the coffee house where it was left to be signed"; and a disgruntled minority of forty-six, including French Canadians, ventured with great daring to pen a second address in which this reference was pointedly omitted.[5] After this little argument over the problems of imperial relations, which contrasted so oddly with the ferment on the Atlantic seaboard, the merchants settled down to business. In the late sixties and early seventies, political agitation in Quebec declined while it was renewed with greater intensity to the south. In 1773 and 1774, when the Canadians recommenced their political campaign, it was not in sympathetic response to the movement in the Thirteen Colonies but in direct reaction to the policy of the Quebec Act. The petitions which the mercantile minority sent to London in 1773 and 1774 were severely local in their subject matter; and until the Americans determined to spread propaganda in Quebec, there are few evidences of sympathetic communication between the two groups of colonists. It is true that Quebec sent a thousand bushels of wheat and Montreal a bill of exchange to the distressed patriots in Boston, in the autumn of 1774;[6] but we have very little means of knowing how far these gifts were the result of really collective action of the merchants in either case. Jonas Clark Minot, who dispatched the present of wheat, was a native of Massachusetts, and not of sufficient political importance in Quebec to be included in either of the two committees of 1773 and 1774.

The link between Canada and the Thirteen Colonies was, to a large extent, a personal connection, maintained by a few American colonists in Quebec. It was strengthened at this time merely by a common sensation of embitterment, for the two societies had no real community of interests. In Canada this sullen resentment was almost entirely the effect of the Quebec Act. It was the new constitution which gave the Canadian merchants a momentary interest in the miseries and the new religions of the people to the south. If Carleton, as he wás instructed to do, had relieved the archaic angularity of the Quebec Act by the modern ornamentations of habeas corpus, juries, and English commercial law, it is probable that the number of American sympathizers would have been still more insignificant than it actually was. Five years later George Allsopp argued awkwardly but not unconvincingly "that if Governor Carleton . . . in the spring of 1775, had immediately convened the Legislative Council, and that they had as expeditiously passed such Laws as are held out in the said Additional Instructions . . . at a time when the minds of His Majesty's British Subjects were disquieted and it may be said the affections of many of them alienated . . . it is very probable, nay almost certain, that very few of the ill effects that have since been unhappily felt, would have resulted in this province, from the attempts of the rebellious colonies against it".[7]

II

It was in this state of disillusionment, resentment and despair that John Brown found the Canadian merchants. He presented the American proposals. Their objective was, of course, not the conquest of Canada, but the liberation of insurgent Canadian democracy. As their addresses, manifestoes, and congressional instructions clearly show, they hoped to persuade Canada to copy the accepted revolutionary procedure of the Atlantic seaboard—to elect a provincial convention, to accede to the union and to dispatch delegates to the continental congress. No doubt Brown presented this full programme; and Thomas Walker, who identified his province with himself and imagined both to be the victims of sadistic persecution, sponsored and supported him. But, when the merchants were faced with these concrete proposals, their anger seeped away with disappointing rapidity. In all probability they were profuse in polite expressions of sympathy; but they remained obstinately phlegmatic about direct action. Once more, as a hundred times before in the conflicts of the past, the necessities of the commercial state of Canada clashed with the demands of the Atlantic seaboard. To send delegates to the continental congress would involve Canada's acceptance of the non-importation agreements; and to cut the simple and essential tie with London would ruin the merchants and destroy their commercial state. In a lame and embarrassed letter the Montreal committee explained the difficulties to the Massachusetts committee of public safety.[8] But John Brown was more blunt. "There is no prospect of Canada sending Delegates to the Continental Congress", he wrote flatly to the committee of correspondence in Boston.[9] The St. Lawrence, the Shield and the commercial system based upon them separated the northern economy from the Atlantic seaboard; and neither a common embitterment nor a common ideology could really bridge the gap.

This was the real crisis. But, though the merchants had refused the American terms, they remained just as sullen and irritable as before. There was a mild revolutionary flurry on the day the Quebec Act went into force. In Montreal, some one decorated the bust of George III in the Place d'Armes with a chaplet of potatoes and an impolite inscription. One of the French-Canadian bureaucrats, Picottée de Bellestre, rumbled aloud concerning the atrocity of the deed and young David Salisbury Franks punched his eye for him. James Price travelled southwards as the "informal representative" of the Canadian merchants at Philadelphia; but he was not, of course, an official delegate to the congress and the extent of his powers and the numbers who supported him in the venture are alike unknown. Letters passed to and fro across the border. There was much assiduous hunting of traitors on the part of the government; and Hertel de Rouville, another member of the "aristocracy" who had an itch to become a bureaucrat, made himself painfully conspicuous as a detective.[10] The sense of deep injury remained among the merchants and with it a confused, angry desire for retaliation.

But, though the Americans had left a way open, they could not take it. As a group they could not begin the revolution in Canada nor could they commit themselves whole-heartedly to the American cause. The year 1775 did not witness the fraternization of two societies; it witnessed the invasion of the northern economy by the competing economy of the south. There was little that was novel about the invasion; it moved on what were, for America, venerably traditional lines. It was a renewal, on the part of the Americans, of that old struggle between the St. Lawrence and the seaboard which before 1763 had been magnified by the ambitions of Great Britain and France. The ghosts of Frontenac and La Salle had been conjured up by British statesmen and Montreal merchants. The Quebec Act affirmed the old aloofness of the northern economy and shouted its old defiance to the continent. Down in the Thirteen

Colonies, puritanical democrats spoke angrily of Canada's popery and despotism. New Englanders coveted its fisheries and New Yorkers resented the extension of its western boundaries. But out of the confusion of these different emotions emerged dominant the old fear of Canada as a base for armed attack. For what reason had the British protected and segregated this strange, alien, northern world of commerce and militarism, of red men and white, of popery and paganism, if it were not to strike from it, as the French had struck, and by the same old routes, against the rebellious colonies? It was these old jealousies and fears and not the novel religion of revolution which inspired the movement against Canada. In May, ten days after the Quebec Act went into operation, Ethan Allen, Benedict Arnold and the "Green Mountain Boys" took Ticonderoga and Crown Point. In November, a larger American army (for congress had sanctioned the invasion of Canada) captured St. Johns; and a few days later it began to close around the practically defenceless Montreal.

During all these proceedings, the merchants played a role which was partly equivocal and certainly unheroic. Carleton and the bureaucrats, who had considered the merchants politically unimportant before the passing of the Quebec Act, adopted the convenient but highly illogical belief that they were responsible for the disaffection in the colony. The French Canadians, those brave fellows who, according to the governors, were instinct with the warlike valour of their ancestors, showed pugnacity mainly in their refusal to follow their "natural leaders", the *noblesse*. Lieutenant-Governor Cramahé, an old soldier like Carleton, told the merchant Macaulay in great heat "that it was our damn'd committees that had thrown the province into its present state, and prevented the Canadians from taking arms".[11] This was a transparent excuse, for, as a Quebec correspondent remarked to Maseres, "they must make somebody or other bear the blame of their *faithful Canadians*, as they used to call them".[12] It was also an exaggeration. The merchants did not set any very shining example of loyalty to government; but, on the other hand, they did not leap forward to clasp the knees of their American liberators. When Allen first entered St. Johns in May, he was met only by a single Montreal merchant, Bindon, who had galloped south with the prosaic purpose of watching over a consignment of provisions valued at £200.[13] In September, when the threat to Montreal became serious, the merchants formed a militia company to defend the Market Gate. Some thirty of them took part in the absurd little battle of September 25, when Ethan Allen was captured; and at least one merchant, Alexander Paterson, lost his life.[14] Even after Carleton had abandoned Montreal, some of the merchants tried strenuously to bargain with the American general Montgomery for the surrender of the practically defenceless town.

But there were pro-Americans at Montreal; and at Quebec, on Carleton's invitation, a number of disaffected merchants, John McCord, Zachary Macaulay, Edward Antill and the Bondfields, marched out of the town just before the siege began. We have no right to say that all the merchants who viewed the Americans with sympathy, openly declared their profession of faith; but since the Americans at first swept all before them and since for a long time they held almost the whole of the settled part of the province, it is reasonable to argue that the active mercantile sympathizers were bold enough to declare themselves. The number of those who did so is quite small; and Carleton's list of twenty-nine persons,[15] while probably incomplete, contains all the important and some insignificant traitors. These men, Walker, Welles, Price, Heywood, Antill, the Livingstons and the Bondfields, are distinguished from the bulk of the Canadian merchants in several important ways. The large majority of them were natives of the Thirteen Colonies. A considerable number were professional men, army contractors or wholesale dealers in provisions; and with the possible exception of Thomas Walker, there was not a single important fur-trading name in the whole group. In other words, it was the men whose business activities were least attuned to the distinctive commercial system of the north, who went over to the enemy.

On the other hand, a great many of the more energetic, the more notable, the more thoroughly Canadian of the merchants had nothing to do with the whole affair. Isaac Todd, the fur trader, dropped out from the Montreal committee early in April, 1775. Thomas and Joseph Frobisher, Alexander Henry, Peter Pond (both Americans), Paterson, Holmes, and Blondeau were hundreds of miles away in the prairie country. Simon McTavish passed through the invasion with his usual cheerful detachment and reached Michilimackinac in May of 1776 to tell its gaping inhabitants a satirical tale about "the great matters transacted since last Summer in Canada".[16] It was, indeed, with a curiously uniform celerity that the fur traders either disappeared into the forest or faded into political obscurity during the difficult years of '75 and '76. Those who were most completely committed to the really Canadian commercial system which was based upon the fur trade could not assist an American invasion for the same reasons that they could not initiate a revolution themselves.

As early as John Brown's visit, one of these reasons was clearly evident: others appeared during the course of the invasion and the occupation. When the Americans closed in around the town, the citizens of supposedly "radical" Montreal presumed to offer terms[17] for the capitulation. Among these terms, which were signed by fur traders like Finlay and McGill as well as by rebels like John Blake, were included the unsympathetic demands that the town's inhabitants should not be forced to lodge American troops and that they should "not be compelled, on any pretence whatever, to take up arms against the Mother Country. . . ". But the third article was even more illuminating, for it affirmed once more, in the face of the enemy, the deepest necessities of the commercial system of the St. Lawrence. "That trade", so ran the third article, "in general, as well within the province as in the upper countries, and parts beyond the seas, shall be carried on as freely as heretofore, and passports shall be granted for that purpose." Here, in the very presence of their victorious liberators, the committee of the citizens of Montreal made no request for self-government and made no suggestion of union with the Thirteen Colonies. The merchants stuck to their commercial system and their trade.

It was precisely these deepest necessities of the northern commercial state which the Americans could not grant. They could not accept the merchants of Canada frankly and unconditionally. For back of the merchants as individuals was their collective commercial system; and their commercial system depended upon the close connection with London and unrestricted trade with the Indians in the far west. But the Americans were fighting the

British and they distrusted and feared the western Indians and the western garrisons. General Lee ordered Wooster, who was commanding at Montreal, to "suffer the Merch[an]ts of Montreal to send none of their woolen Cloths out of the Town";[18] and this stoppage of free trade in the west completed both the dislocation of the merchants' commercial system and the process of their disillusionment. Their commercial distress, and very significantly their commercial distress alone, moved them to address congress. In the only petition which was ever sent by any group in Canada to the so-called "continental congress" at Philadelphia, the fur traders, with one of the Frobisher brothers at their head, petitioned for the reopening of the western trade.[19] Their action was not without its irony. Congress had expected Canadian delegates and hoped for Canadian entrance into the union; but all it ever received from the northern commercial state was a polite request to take its heel off northern commerce. When the American commissioners, Chase, Carroll and Franklin, came up to Canada, they reopened the trade and began to issue passes in the spring of 1776. But it was then too late.

The fact is that neither the merchants nor their liberators could grant each other's demands or live up to each other's expectations. The Americans would have welcomed the town meetings and nocturnal cabals of which Carleton so much disapproved. The merchants met on February 5, 1776, to debate their petition against the restrictions of their western trade;[20] but no provincial convention and no committees of correspondence arose from even the free soil of Montreal. The traders stood apart in an aloofness which could be modified only by embarrassed politeness and often hardened into positive hostility. As early as December, 1775, Montgomery was writing to the generalissimo Schuyler at Albany that "we are not to expect a union with Canada, till we have a force in the country sufficient to ensure it against any attempts that may be made for its recovery".[21] In Montreal and the country-side the Americans, who had intended to masquerade as open-handed liberators, were forced to maintain their real role of suspicious tyrants. Wooster, who was in command at Montreal during the greater part of the American occupation, reported that the merchants were not disposed to assist him if they could avoid it.[22] "With respect to the better sort of people, both *French* and *English*," wrote the traitor Moses Hazen, "seven-eighths are Tories, who would wish to see our throats cut, and perhaps would readily assist in doing it."[23]

Of this estrangement which had existed from the beginning and which became merely more evident with time, there exists a further and a better proof in the matter of finance. Beneath all the distresses of the invaders was an enfeebling poverty which paralysed their own efforts and antagonized their potential supporters. Money was the one thing which lay in the power of the merchants alone to contribute; but they refused to make loans, to discount bills or to accept paper. James Price, who loaned some twenty thousand pounds, was an exception and was very significantly regarded by the Americans as almost their sole resource.[24] Although he touted assiduously for the Americans among his brother merchants, he admitted himself that he did not find any of the Montreal traders willing to lend.[25] The financial stringency had its comic as well as its serious results. The three wise men from Philadelphia, Chase, the wealthy Carroll and the complacent Franklin, arrived at St. Johns to discover that their reception had been somewhat imperfectly rehearsed. The courier which they dispatched in royal style to Montreal to warn the waiting city of their arrival, was stopped at the ferry on the St. Lawrence for the sufficient reason that he had plenty of paper money but no hard cash. Not a carriage would have moved from Montreal to bring back "the first civilized American" and the wealthiest citizen of the Thirteen Colonies, if a single Montreal sympathizer had not pityingly agreed to foot the bill. "It is impossible", wrote the commissioners to congress on their arrival in Montreal, "to give you an idea of the lowness of the Continental credit here. . . ."[26] They pledged the public, and their own private credit in vain; and Charles Carroll's sterling bills of exchange were hawked fruitlessly around the town for days.

As spring broke in 1776, the British fleet moved up the St. Lawrence, the American army drifted chaotically west and south, and the American commissioners decided it was time to go. There was a slight scurry in Montreal among those who had committed themselves too deeply for pardon, and Price, Heywood and Bindon

were busy with preparations for departure. But the bulk of the
merchants watched the Americans and their few sympathizers
press southward without regret or perturbation. The northern
fur-trading colony, with the military and naval power of Great
Britain at its back, had maintained its old independence in the
continent. The Americans, as time was to show, could beat the
British on the Atlantic seaboard; but they could not hold the
towns on the lower St. Lawrence, nor could they capture the
western hinterland of the fur-trading state. The Indian administration, the fortified posts and the friendship of the tribes were
the three political expressions of western commercialism which
naturally fell under the control of the northern fur-trading state.
The Americans set themselves in vain to break this formidable
combination. They were weak politically in the west for they were
weak commercially. It is true that on the outskirts of the northern
economy they won some military successes. In 1779 George Rogers
Clark captured the post at Vincennes and its commander,
Lieutenant-Governor Hamilton. But, on the whole, the Americans
made little impression on the west. They could effect the temporary
possession of a fort, they could and did prolong the unsettlement
of the region. But they could not make it really theirs, for they
could not break the commercial and military supremacy of the
northerners on the Great Lakes.

III

During this period of struggle—and in part because of it—there
occurred profound changes in the economy of the north. It was
one of the great periods in Canadian business, expansive in its
conquests, rich in its developments; and of these the most spectacular and the most dynamic in its results was the shift of trade
to the north-west. It was not, of course, that the south-west trade
declined disastrously in this period. During the eighties the areas
commanded by Detroit and Michilimackinac contributed the bulk
of the Canadian furs; and it was probably not until 1794 that the
fur production of the north-west territory equalled that of Michilimackinac and Detroit.[27] But, although from 1775 on Montreal
maintained a commercial monopoly over the whole west, there

were good reasons why the more enterprising traders should be drawn towards the northerly parts of the fur-trading state. The southern areas, though still productive, were not as rich as they had been in the very best furs. The failure of the Albany route and the migration of traders northward increased the Canadian trading population and stiffened competition. All along the frontier from Niagara to the Mississippi country, the war was bad for trade, either because of the actual turmoil it created or because of the tension and excitement it aroused. And British officers, officiously eager to prevent any communication between the rebels and possible northern sympathizers, placed all sorts of restrictions upon Canadian trade around the Great Lakes.

The push to the north-west began. Old François, the veteran Canadian pedlar, who may have been in the district a few years earlier, was certainly on the Saskatchewan in the summer of 1768,[28] and James Finlay wintered there in the winter of 1768–1769. There were enormous difficulties. The weather and the hostility of the Indians frustrated the traders in 1769, and the Frobisher brothers who in that year made their first effort to reach the north-west, were robbed and turned back by the natives. But the Canadians were indefatigable. They gained the assistance of an important Indian chief, Wappenassew, and with his help Thomas Corry successfully wintered at Cedar Lake in 1771–1772.[29] Others followed him, while every year the Hudson's Bay Company's men grew more apprehensive for their trade; and in 1773, the Frobisher brothers, Joseph and Thomas, made their effective entrance into the region. This was an event of real importance in the history of the Canadian trade, for Joseph Frobisher, who became one of the great builders of the northern commercial system, possessed immense daring and a bold, imaginative grasp of the trading situation in the north-west. It was the Frobishers who emphasized the northern drive of Canadian commerce. In 1774, the two brothers pushed north to the Churchill river in the hope of reaching the Athabaska Indians and stealing their trade from the Hudson's Bay Company; and in the spring of 1775 several of this adventurous party crept back to the Saskatchewan, beaten by the appalling privations of their journey.[30] Every year competition was increasing on the river. The Hudson's Bay Company founded an inland post, Cumberland House, on the Saskatchewan, but the roving Canadians spread around it in every direction to intercept the trade. In October, 1775, Matthew Cocking, master at Cumberland House, noted the report that twenty-three canoe-loads of Canadian traders were expected to winter in the Saskatchewan country;[31] and in the years 1774–1776, Paterson, Holmes, Pangman, Peter Pond, Alexander Henry and the Frobishers—some of the greatest names in the trade—were all actively trading in the region. The Canadians competed, not only with the people from the bay, but with each other as well. The necessity of union became quickly apparent and expansion continued without interruption. In 1776, the two Frobishers and Alexander Henry were on the Churchill, trading with the Athabaska Indians.[32] In the spring of 1777 Thomas Frobisher revisited the region, and finally in 1778–1779, Peter Pond wintered in the Athabaska country itself.

These were the great deeds in this period of Canadian history; and the men who performed them deserve to be remembered, for they were winning a new empire in the west, while the soldiers and officials who despised them were losing the old empire of the Atlantic seaboard. The vanguard of British-Canadian enterprise in the prairies was made up of men whose deeds survive only in the most barren of records and whose personalities are lost in a shadowy and heroic legend of ambition, cunning, bravery and violence. The Frobisher brothers and Peter Pond, who carried the trade north-westward across the iron expanse of snow to the Athabaska country, must stand for this half-forgotten company of battered, indomitable men. The Frobishers were Yorkshire people who combined the will to organize and the urge for commercial expansion with an amazing resourcefulness and endurance in the field. Though Thomas and Benjamin died early, Joe Frobisher lived on to unite in partnership with Simon McTavish, to dominate the North West Company and to build Beaver Hall, one of the first fur-trading mansions in Montreal. Pond grew up in poverty and obscurity in the town of Milford, Connecticut. Uncouth, illiterate, violent, born for the new west, he was carried away to a lifetime of adventure in the wake of the fifes and drums and banners which paraded through Milford streets in the first days of the Seven Years' War. His years of service in the army were followed by a long fur-trading experience around Detroit and in the upper Mississippi country. Then he abandoned a trading territory, which only the most intrepid could consider exhausted, for the new north-west; and after all these things were past and done with, he came back to the old poverty in the old New England town, leaving behind him his curious map, his fragmentary and misspelt journal and the sinister notoriety of unsolved murder on the prairie. In these men were personified the two strains, British and American, which united to form the leadership of the northern commercial state. All the rewards and dangers of the new north-west and all the qualities by which they were captured and over-come, were revealed in these careers. This disreputable group of untaught and assertive men possessed the necessary, the essential qualities—ambition, courage and endurance; and they founded the tradition of the "ancient northwest spirit" which was toasted reverently at Montreal, in countless dinner parties, for half a century onward.

The capture of the north-west was the greatest conquest of Canadian business at this time; and the new acquisition, together with the revolutionary war of which it was partly a result, began to have profound effects upon the northern economy. Every year the Canadian commercial system grew more nearly continental in extent; and the commercial class, like the makers of confederation a century later, stood face to face with the problems of continental organization. It would be idle to pretend that the difficulties of the eighteenth and nineteenth centuries were the same. But the central problem of Canadian history is the problem of building a continental dominion on the basis of the St. Lawrence and the Canadian Shield and this was faced in the first place by the Cana-dian merchants in the eighteenth century. The North West Company and the Dominion of Canada emerged for reasons which are, at bottom, very similar; and the Nor' Westers grappled with all the basic Canadian difficulties, with the problems of continental organization, of regions, of transportation and of freight rates.

The canoe route on the Ottawa could only be improved with difficulty; but it was possible to increase the shipping on the Great Lakes, both for the transportation of furs eastward and for the carriage of bulky supplies—flour, corn and pork—westward from

the agricultural centres about Detroit and Niagara to Michilimackinac. Already there were a few commercial vessels on the
Great Lakes: a sloop was built at Detroit for the traders in 1769
and a second in 1770.[33] It is probable that a period of fairly active
ship-building would have begun in the seventies; for, as we have
seen, several Albany merchants, accustomed to transportation by
boat on the Great Lakes, moved up to Montreal at the opening
of the revolution. But in 1777, as a war measure, Carleton prohibited the navigation of private vessels. The commerce of the
lakes, merchants' goods and government stores, jammed together
in the small tonnage of the provincial marine, grew greater and
more demanding. The strain upon the weaker sections of the long
route from Montreal to Michilimackinac increased, became
intolerable. Merchants complained indignantly and replied to
the officials with bitter recriminations.[34] But government, as well
as the commercial group, was concerned over the difficulties of
transportation and it was government, in 1779, that first began to
attack the problem of the St. Lawrence.

It was an insignificant beginning. It did not even imply the
slightest realization of the enormous task which was to press with
ever-increasing weight upon generation after generation of the
northern people. The task of the river became the greatest task
of Canadians; just as the river itself was the greatest actuality and
the greatest hope of their collective life. So much depended on the
river; and the river was so fatally defective. It was like a great,
healthy, powerful organism spoilt by an incongruous weakness.
For miles, as the flat boats travelled down it, the river moved with
the slow, comfortable ease of perfect adjustment. It knew its
landscape; it was certain of its future. It idled along, unhurried,
controlled, manœuvring its vast bulk with a practised dexterity,
working with a deliberate, ponderous intentness towards its goal.
Then, and with sinister and inexplicable rapidity, its whole
character was transformed. Out of the solid, almost unruffled mass
of water there shot up a great curved blur of spray. Its recoil
was terrific; it drove backward against the current. It was a sudden,
shocking reminder of the immense strength and speed of the
moving stream. For a few moments, beyond this, the river
recovered. The abrupt spurt of white fell back, died rapidly away

into the smooth level of solid water. But beyond again, with a kind
of stubbornly persistent wilfulness, a great broad bank of spray
flung itself into the air. From this there was no real recovery.
There followed a brief, troubled passage of excitement and expectation, in which the traces of disorder did not entirely die away, and
then the whole river seemed to disintegrate in fury. It curved
away, roaring and foaming; and the entangled, matted spray grew
thicker and thicker until the river, as it neared the horizon, became
a dense, unbroken band of white. It moved and disturbed the
spectator; it caused a kind of intent and fearful wonder in the
listener who heard it from a distance. And on windless summer
nights it could be heard from far away, roaring strangely and
massively through the darkness. These crucial weaknesses of the
river were first attacked in 1779. Between that date and 1783
there were completed a canal at Coteau du Lac, just below Lake
St. Francis, and a second series of little canals and mere "cuttings"
at the Cedars and the Cascades.[35] Scarcely more than ditches
dignified by a few locks and capable of carrying flat-bottomed
bateaux only, the canals were nevertheless heartily accepted by
the merchants who agreed to pay the heavy tolls imposed.

As it drove westward across the continent towards its completion, as it acquired the complex cares and commitments of its full
maturity, the northern economy evolved that organization by
which alone its oppressive burdens could be borne. The dead
weight of a trading organization, built with increasingly elaborate
complexity to cross a continent, was beyond the strength of the
individual trader; and co-operation and centralization arose out of
the deepest necessities of the northern state. The Revolutionary
War, which caused the failure of the Albany route, increased the
centralizing tendencies of the St. Lawrence; and the new international boundary of 1783, which cut across the transportation
system of the Nor' Westers, helped to drive them together in the
face of common danger. The Canadian economy responded
sensitively, as it was to do in the future, to the pressure from the
south; but, in the main, the North West Company emerged as the
only solution of an enormous continental task. It was the prototype
of the great Canadian business organizations; it was the first of
that long line of co-partnerships, companies and public enterprises

which began with continental objectives or developed them in course of time. But the North West Company came in the first flush of northern maturity and because it was an organization dependent ultimately upon individual heroism and endurance, it had more of the flexibility and the assertive freedom of youth. These intensely individualistic traders were taught to combine only with great difficulty, and after failures, quarrels and violence. The company was never chartered, never incorporated. It continued as it had begun, a loose co-partnership with engagements which periodically expired and were renewed; and, in the end, its loosely organized affairs degenerated into inextricable confusion.

From the early seventies onward, the movement toward unification was rapid. It was the shift to the Saskatchewan and the Athabaska country that forced the pace. Almost from the beginning the tendency was evident, for Thomas Corry, who was active in the far west in 1771–1772, was supported by an organization which included the Blondeau brothers, George McBeath, Isaac Todd and John Askin.[36] As the years went by, as the competition on the river became rapidly more severe, the traders in the interior were driven to co-operate, from the certain knowledge that if they remained alone they would ruin the trade. A series of "pools", or loose co-operative associations followed.[37] These "pools" were imperfect: for the first few years they were of very brief duration and they ended in renewed competition and disputes. But their persistent reappearance from 1774 on is evidence of the strength of the forces which were making for unification in the interior. Partnership was the only means by which the traders could give the necessary support to Pond and Wadden in their extended expeditions northward and it was the only method by which fatal competition in the far hinterland could be avoided. The development and, indeed, the very existence of the trade, depended on union; and after 1778, the "pools" in the interior became more general and more long-lived. In 1779 co-operation, which had been born of trading necessities in the far west, was extended east to Montreal; and the merchants formed the first sixteen-share agreement[38] which was the direct forerunner of the North West Company. But it was a tentative and somewhat clumsy arrangement, possibly too inclusive and democratic for the more domineering traders; and in the next few years it was drastically revised. The number of interests in the trade was reduced, by withdrawal, elimination and death; and the Frobisher brothers and Simon McTavish completed their brusque rise to commanding importance. The peace and the new boundary line which cut across the Canadian trade route to the west, hastened the new organization; and the North West Company, born of the Revolutionary War and of the shift to the north-west which accompanied it, emerged definitely in the year 1783. Joseph and Benjamin Frobisher were the first directors; and of the sixteen shares in the concern, the Frobishers, with Simon McTavish, probably owned or controlled ten in all.[39]

IV

In commerce, the period was one of expansion and new creations. But between commerce and government there existed a contrast which soon became preposterous and intolerable; for, while trade expanded, administration, both in its institutions and its spirit, became gradually more rigid, harsh and unyielding. The Quebec Act, which was a revival of the old feudal and absolutist structure of New France, coincided with the renewal of the old armed conflict between the northern colony and the Atlantic seaboard. The war seemed to justify the maintenance of the act unchanged; and a reactionary constitution became even more reactionary than its framers in England intended. For though the Quebec Act was designed to satisfy the supposed leaders of the French-Canadian majority in Quebec, it was not intended that the act should be applied, without modification, to the prejudice of the minority of British-Canadian merchants. Carleton's new instructions contained a number of moderate glosses upon the medieval austerity of the new constitution. The legislature, which was supposed to interpret the law of the act in the spirit of the instructions, was advised, in particular, to follow the British model of habeas corpus and "to consider well" whether English laws might not be established in whole or in part for all personal actions grounded upon debts, promises, contracts or agreements, whether of a mercantile or other nature.[40] Unfortunately, while the medieval elements of the new constitution were established by law, its modernities were merely suggested to a council composed of soldiers, bureaucrats and landowners, instinctively opposed to merchants and to middle-class reform.

The result was certain. Carleton violated some of his instructions and interpreted others in the spirit of his intense convictions; and the perversion of the constitution was continued by the stolidly conservative Haldimand to the end of the war. Carleton created the "Privy Council"—a body warranted only by a badly worded clause in the instructions—and in this small, selected group was vested the real political power in the colony. In January of 1777, the legislative council met at last for its first effective session. The French-Canadian councillors had already shown themselves singularly indisposed to repay the munificence of the British ministers in England by a little generosity to the British merchants in Canada. Carleton failed to communicate the clauses of his instructions which advised reform in favour of the merchants, though by another clause of the same instructions he was ordered to do so; and through Captain Cramahé, his fellow-officer and his lieutenant-governor, he intimated that he was entirely opposed to juries in civil suits. The council did not even consider habeas corpus. It voted down optional juries and English law in commercial suits; and it thus left the laws of New France completely unaltered for the whole civil business of the Canadian courts.

This was a decision disastrous for the merchants. "The Laws and Customs of Canada", said George Allsopp, ". . . form the most imperfect System in the World for a Commercial people."[41] Canadian commercial law was a kind of medieval curiosity: it was inadequate and antiquated. Both England and France, like other nations of Western civilization, had a common basis in the law merchant of Europe for their own separate systems of commercial law. The *code marchand* of France had been organized by Colbert. English commercial law, a perfectly clear and definite body of commercial customs, was taking its final place in the common-law system of the country, at the end of the eighteenth century, under the direction of Lord Mansfield. Either of these two systems would probably have satisfied the Canadian merchants; but both, for one reason or another, were denied them. The *code marchand* had not been regularly introduced into New France before the conquest; and the decision of the council ruled out English commercial law. The merchants were thus left without a clear right to the law merchant of Europe in either of these two national derivatives. The Custom of Paris, which was the law of New France, and the few local customs which had developed before the conquest were alone legally available and they were inadequate. In these circumstances, in the absence of any adequate and clearly valid body of law, an immense responsibility and an immense power was placed in the hands of the common pleas judges who had neither the learning nor the impartiality to deserve them. The chief justice was not a member of their bench. They were judges both of fact and law. And since there was no provision for appeal from their decisions to the court of king's bench, these half dozen bureaucrats were the final and irresponsible arbiters of all the difficulties and disputes of an ambitious commercial class.[42]

There were other commercial grievances. The Quebec bureaucracy, fortified in its natural tendencies by the war, repeatedly violated the sacred middle-class doctrine of *laissez-faire*. Carleton had prohibited the use of private commercial vessels on the lakes. Haldimand continued this prohibition and the system of licences, and he watched the merchants with a jealously suspicious eye as they went about their business. Their unusual activity perplexed his honest, sluggish mind. He was blind to the great development of trade on the Saskatchewan and in the Athabaska country; and like the other soldiers who had governed Canada, he naturally associated insubordination and treachery with tradesmen. He enforced the rules, "Conscious of the Rectitude & Purity of my Conduct in these Respects . . ." and replied to criticisms in a tone of injured virtue.[43] The merchants, compelled to use vessels whose first business was naturally the service of government and the transport of government stores, complained of delays, damage to their goods, high freight rates and the partialities displayed by government officials to certain of their members.[44] They protested also, on another occasion, when Haldimand revived hoary government regulations, characteristic, as an English legal adviser put it, of the "dark ages of Edward 6th & Philip & Mary".[45] There was an apparent shortage of grain, possibly real, possibly fictitious, with consequent high prices. Haldimand continued the previous prohibition against the export of food-stuffs; he issued a formidable proclamation against "forestallers, regrators and engrossers"; and in 1780 he tried in vain to persuade the council to pass legislation which would compel the sale of grain and flour at fixed prices. The governor turned instinctively to authoritarian trade methods which, though perfectly legal, had become archaic after more than a century of disuse.

He inherited and preserved the soldier's and gentleman's philosophy of society and government at Quebec. He liked his bureaucratic friends. New ideas produced in him a kind of dull unease; and he perfected a neat little formula by constant repetition, "the present is not the time for innovations". He maintained Carleton's "Privy Council" and he still withheld from the legislature the articles of his instructions concerning legislation which he was supposed to communicate. By two special additional instructions of March, 1779, he was ordered to abandon both these courses. The stern old soldier, who had learnt instant obedience in the hard school of the army and who lamented the uncertain loyalty of the Canadian merchants, found it inconvenient to obey these instructions of his superiors for a mere matter of two years, until he was compelled to do so by renewed and categorical orders. He then dropped the original instructions unsympathetically, with a kind of dull thud, in a Francophil council opposed to all reform.

The "opposition" from 1777 to 1783 had two eminently modest and respectable ambitions: it wished, first, to force the governors to obey their instructions; and secondly, to persuade the council to follow the reasonable advice of the authorities at home. Specifically, the opposition desired optional juries at least in civil suits, English commercial law and habeas corpus. The rank and file of the merchants in the colony played no active part in these controversies; they were fought out by a small group in the council among whom were Hugh Finlay, the postmaster, the merchant George Allsopp who had been a partner of John Welles, and William Grant, the deputy receiver-general who was connected in various ways with the business community of the province. Chief Justice Livius had headed the opposition in the session of 1778. But Carleton had rewarded his temerity with abrupt dismissal; and during the Haldimand régime, George Allsopp stood out easily from his colleagues as the chief protagonist of reform. He was a blunt, unrestrained controversialist who kept worrying away at the cause of reform with a kind of dogged persistence. The height of his offensive was in the legislative session of 1780 when he presented a long protest, containing a verbose, somewhat clumsy, but on the whole extremely able, critique of the administration in Quebec.[46] He failed then to persuade the council to introduce reform; and in 1782, after Haldimand had at last communicated the instructions which advised amelioration of the laws, he failed again. His only reward was political death. The councillors were supposed to have freedom of debate; but Haldimand, like all dictatorial bureaucrats before and since, believed that in the exercise of the right "decency ought at all times to be observed". Obviously, Allsopp had been "indecent"; and Haldimand moved with a kind of cautious, lethargic deliberation to effect his execution. In the autumn of 1780, in a letter to Germain,[47] he raked together all the incidents, circumstances, and mere suspicions which could possibly blacken the loyalty and good citizenship of his obstinate councillor. But the home authorities, who may have remained unimpressed by the catalogue of heinous errors, did not act upon the governor's broad hint. In the end Haldimand, like Carleton, did his own dirty work, and in January, 1783, he suspended Allsopp from his seat on the council. The Francophil bureaucracy had, as George Allsopp, said, achieved "the compleatest Despotism". It bestirred itself from its satisfied immobility only to strike down its opponents with brief violence; and the middle-class rule desired by the merchants was further away than ever.

V

In 1783, when the merchants were irritably preoccupied with these problems of politics and trade, there fell upon them the greatest blow in their entire history as a political force. This was the Treaty of 1783, by which the independence of the United States was granted and its boundaries defined. There are some catastrophes in the life of an individual or a nation which are so great they cannot possibly be duplicated; and, in the end, the Treaty of 1783 destroyed for ever the natural development of the

Canadian commercial state. The significance of this tragedy, in all its full and shattering completeness, was appreciated by the commercial class alone. At that time, the merchants were the only Canadians in the modern sense of the term; they alone thought in terms of a distinct and continental northern state. They looked upon the treaty with amazement and indignation; they believed in all sincerity that it was the result of the ignorance, negligence and spineless complaisance of the British negotiators. And this tale of the ancient and irremediable wrong of 1783 was handed down and repeated by the Canadian commercial class for a full generation beyond the signing of the treaty.[48]

There was, in fact, much to justify their indignation and to support their interpretation of the facts. The Treaty of 1783 is the ideal example, in Canadian history, of how a weak state can suffer alike from the ambitions of its competitors and the complaisant generosity of its supposed friends. Lord Shelburne cherished the delusion that it was possible to make the Americans grateful and friendly by generous concessions. Benjamin Franklin insisted that his fundamental objective was reconciliation, which he described feelingly as "a sweet word". According to Franklin's plan,[49] the main contribution of the United States to this pious object was to be their earnest desire for its achievement. Otherwise, reconciliation was to be promoted almost entirely by large concessions on the part of the British, among which Franklin modestly placed the cession of the whole of Canada. Oswald, the British agent at Paris, who, as a diplomatist, deserves chiefly to be remembered for his advanced age and his friendship with Adam Smith, was acutely sensible of Franklin's wisdom and might possibly have handed Canada over, if it had been in his power to do so. But back of Oswald were Lord Shelburne and the cabinet, and it seems evident that they never contemplated the surrender of the whole of Quebec. Lord Shelburne, however, "apparently knew less about Canada than about any other portion of the British Empire";[50] and he considered with equanimity the most grotesquely meaningless boundary lines. In the end, the line which the British accepted in the provisional articles of peace, was apparently as much the result of chance as of any deep appreciation of the vital issues involved.

West of the point at which the forty-fifth parallel of latitude struck the St. Lawrence river, the new international boundary followed the line of the Great Lakes and the rivers by which they were connected. It passed through Lake Superior north of Isle Royale; it struck north-westward from Lake Superior to Rainy Lake; and from Rainy Lake it followed the water communication to the Lake of the Woods. Beyond the most north-western point of the Lake of the Woods, it was intended to run due west until it struck the Mississippi river. This was, of course, an impossible juncture, for the Mississippi petered out before it could intersect a line drawn west from the Lake of the Woods. But this was the one serious inconsistency in the midst of a succession of unambiguous and shattering facts. By the treaty, Canada lost for ever that vast territory between the Ohio and the Mississippi rivers, which it had explored, which it had exploited, and which had been returned to it as late as 1774. Niagara, Detroit, Michilimackinac and Grand Portage—the forts, settlements, depots and trading-posts which had developed to serve the Canadian fur trade—were all surrendered to an enemy which had been incapable of effecting the capture of a single one of them. The very rivers and carrying-places, including the water communication between Lake Superior and the Manitoba basin, which the Canadians alone had discovered and utilized, were divided in joint ownership between the two countries or became the exclusive property of the United States.

It was characteristic of the whole nature of the negotiations that the Canadian merchants, who by their own efforts were making Canada a continental economy and who alone could speak for it, were never consulted in the matter at all. It was not until the provisional articles of the peace were made public that they learnt the full dreadful truth. At the end of January, 1783, the London forwarders who had to speak—and speak rapidly—for the whole of the Canadian trade protested as vigorously as they could to Shelburne.[51] In February, they met the aged but youthfully impressionable Oswald in person and renewed their angry complaints.[52] They told the officials bluntly that by the new boundary, Canada would lose the greater part of its major staple trade to the United States. All the fortified trading posts, the best carrying-places and the majority of the Indian tribes, had been presented with punctilious comprehensiveness to the new federation. The free navigation of the Mississippi, promised by article 8 of the provisional terms, was, the merchants claimed, a concession of no value to the trade, since the river was not navigable to the new boundary. They may have felt a kind of gloomy satisfaction in pointing out these obstinate geographical details to the omniscient politicians. But Oswald, according to his own account, answered them with great persuasiveness and eloquence; and he claimed that, in the end, they were completely satisfied.

It was a purely commercial satisfaction which he presumed to offer them. Ironically enough, though the Treaty of 1783 destroyed the old commercial empire of the St. Lawrence, it was itself the imperfect issue of commercial ideas. "You will already", wrote Shelburne to a friend in 1783, "have recognized in the treaties of peace, the great principle of free trade, which inspires them from beginning to end."[53] Both Shelburne and Oswald, a little consciously "modern" in their economic ideas, were critical or scornful of mercantilism. Lord Shelburne hoped that British trade with America, free and unencumbered with duties, would prosper; and like a number of politicians in England, he seems to have been impressed by the enormous possibilities of the St. Lawrence as a water boulevard to the trade of the developing west.[54] When, therefore, the American commissioners, particularly Jay, argued that Great Britain's real interest in the hinterland was commerce and proposed free access to the interior and free navigation of its rivers, Oswald and his principal could hardly fail to be sympathetic. In the first tentative articles of peace, signed in October of 1782, the principles of free trade and free navigation assumed even more grandiose proportions. The two nations granted the reciprocal freedom of their rivers, harbours, lakes, ports and places, for trade; and both agreed to treat each other's merchants as their own nationals and to impose the same duties upon them. Obviously this revolutionary clause implied the reform of the navigation laws in the interests of the Americans; and a little later the cabinet decided not to attempt this at the moment. At the instance of the British, the commercial article, with the exception of the part referring to the free navigation of the Mississippi, was deleted from the treaty; and the whole question of trade was left over for a separate commercial treaty to be negotiated later on.

Oswald met the merchants with all this in his mind. He poured it out in a burst of enthusiastic, persuasive confidence. He told them of the generous commercial proposals of the Americans, of the original commercial clause and of the reasons for its deletion. He insisted that the treaty, even as it stood, contained no unfair restriction of Canadian trade. "There is nothing in the Treaty", he argued, "to hinder an Englishman passing & transporting Goods over all or any part of America."[55] British traders, he said, might freely make use of the carrying-places; and the Americans, if they decided to take over the fortified posts, would not grudge their protection to the Canadians. He cheerily admitted that competition from New York and Philadelphia would revive after the peace; but he insisted that the Americans had no wish for monopoly and no power to effect it. His reason for this confident assertion deserves honourable mention as an early British howler in Canadian geography. "The Indians", he asserted, "could go to either Side at their pleasure with as little difficulty, as one may go out of Middlesex into Essex."[56]

The merchants seized upon the one valuable point in this long harangue. They were eager for certainty and they told Lord Shelburne that Oswald had assured them "that it was the real intention and spirit of the Treaty that a free participation of all the Lakes, Rivers and Carrying-Places would be enjoyed by the British Subjects of Canada on the same terms and conditions as by those of the American States. . . ".[57] These concessions, they urged the minister, should be specifically guaranteed in the coming commercial treaty, if such was impossible in the articles of peace. Their demand was the first indication that the Canadian merchants, who had been commercial and political monopolists, were about to become ardent free-traders. The new boundary, cutting across their old commercial empire, drove them to support a new internationalism in western commerce; and free trade became one of the fundamental principles in the revised commercial philosophy by which Montreal hoped to defeat the boundary of 1783. The Canadians intended, however, that the new and fashionable doctrine should have only a very limited application, so far as their trade was concerned. In their view, it was to be applied only in the west of North America, where they needed it. In the east it would have ruined them. The old and the new theories of commerce were, in the future, to be combined by the Canadian merchants in their attempt to force the produce of western North America down the St. Lawrence; and to them the navigation laws were just as necessary on the Atlantic ocean as was free trade in the west.

Historians, including Canadian historians, have praised Jay and Shelburne, berated the mercantilists and lamented the deletion of the generous commercial clause from the Treaty of 1783. These opinions, derived instinctively from nineteenth-century English liberalism, are valid certainly from the standpoint of the two contracting powers. The free navigation and the relatively free trade between Great Britain and the United States, desired by Jay and Shelburne in 1783, would no doubt have benefited these two countries; but they would probably have completed the ruin of the Canadian commercial state. Canada depended upon the navigation laws for a full generation after the Treaty of 1783; and Canadian merchants, in London, Quebec and Montreal, remained convinced mercantilists up to the very moment when Great Britain herself destroyed the mercantile system. It was the business of the Canadians to increase the competitive strength of the northern economy; and they came rapidly to realize how immensely the navigation laws could enhance the inward pull of the St. Lawrence route. The benefits and preferences of the mercantile system could be extended to the British subjects in Canada; and its prohibitions enforced against their American rivals. If Great Britain continued to act upon the hoary principles of mercantilism, it would open the doors of empire to the staple products of North America so long as they were brought down the St. Lawrence; and it would close the doors upon the same products if they were shipped by American citizens from the American Atlantic ports.

PART II

TRANSITION IN THE REGION OF THE LOWER LAKES

CHAPTER IV
FIRST CONSEQUENCES OF 1783

I

THE year 1783 was probably the most important year in the entire history of the northern commercial state. Canada then was a sparsely populated and undeveloped country; but the mere simplicity of the society in which the crucial changes of that year occurred should not be allowed to diminish their fundamental importance. Canada was changed both outwardly and in essence. For the year 1783 meant three things: peace, the advent of the Loyalists and the establishment of an international boundary where none had existed before—a boundary devoid of geographical and historical meaning which cut through the commercial empire of the St. Lawrence. Each of these changes, though the establishment of peace was unimportant in comparison with the other two, was heavy with meaning for Canada. The northern economy, though despoiled and partitioned, had at least kept its independence in North America. It had emerged at length from the long period of wars, of rumours and aftermaths of wars, which had lasted from the conquest; and peace lifted the dread of the last decades and weakened the instinctive reliance upon military forms. The bureaucracy at Quebec lost its most unanswerable justification. The civilian middle class recovered its assurance and resumed its old political activity.

The year 1783, however, meant much more than this. It began an economic and social revolution in the region of the Great Lakes which lasted for nearly four decades after the peace. The new international boundary partitioned the northern commercial state; the coming of the Loyalists initiated a radical change in its character. Both these changes were of great importance. But the full consequences of the migration were less immediately apparent than the results of the new boundary; and though in the next forty years the merchants had to revise their commercial machine as much in response to the settlement of the lower lakes as in answer to the new political division of the continent, it was the boundary

87

which first took most of their attention. They could not passively accept a line which divided the first unity of the St. Lawrence at the very moment when it had attained the height of its magnificence. They tried, in the meantime, by advocating a policy of free trade for Canada, to make the frontier a commercial nullity; but always they hoped that in the end it would cease to be a political fact.

This hope lasted until the conclusion of the War of 1812. And it was strengthened by active and irrepressible forces in the far west which maintained a stubborn vitality even into the new century. For a while the northern commercial state proved stronger than the diplomatists who had divided it between Canada and the United States. For the commercial state, like the Dominion of Canada which followed it, was not an artificial creation. It was a human achievement created in response to certain basic invitations and challenges of the new continent; and the assertive strength of these prime geographic and economic phenomena is nowhere better illustrated than in the early history of the frontier between Canada and the United States. The boundary of 1783 was natural inasmuch as it admitted the independence of the northern economy; it was artificial inasmuch as it denied the northern economy its full inheritance. And against the unreality of the new division Montreal and the west rose in a united protest. A primitive, weak, but natural economy made a prolonged and unavailing effort to throw off a political division imposed upon it by two vastly stronger states; and the tumult and uncertainty which filled the region of the lower lakes and the Ohio for thirty years after the peace are, at bottom, the result of this unequal contest between the spirit and the law. The merchants struggled to preserve their empire south of the lakes and the Indians fought to defend their hunting grounds. For a while the British, assailed by these equally clamorous appeals, helped the northern commercial state to keep its southwest territories in defiance of the Treaty of 1783. But with the Grenville-Jay Treaty this political support was withdrawn; and it was certain, after the War of 1812, that it had been withdrawn for ever. By 1821 this first main theme in the revolution in the valley of the St. Lawrence had reached its final conclusion; and Canada, having lost definitively in politics, was flung back upon a secondary and purely commercial policy. As a political unity, the empire of the St. Lawrence was gone for ever; it was possible to maintain it only as an economic whole.

The coming of the Loyalists was the second great factor in the revolution in the region of the lower lakes. The Loyalists brought settlement, agriculture and production for export into the heart of the primitive fur-trading state. Even alone, they constituted a disruptive force; but they were, of course, only one contingent of that vast army of people that closed in around the lower lakes, that settled Vermont and northern New York and founded the new states of Ohio, Indiana and Illinois. Over all this vast area, which Montreal regarded without distinction as its empire, the trees fell and the Indians retreated before the slow, inexorable onward movement of the frontiersmen. The emphasis of the northern economy was shifted from the Precambrian Shield to the lowlands. The St. Lawrence and the lakes gradually superseded the Ottawa as the main channel of western commerce; and the new staples, timber, wheat and potash, replaced the old staple, fur. With every year that passed, the frail fabric of the old society became more tattered and transparent; and the Canadian economic revolution, which opened with the advent of the Loyalists, closed appropriately in 1821 with the collapse of the great fur-trading organization which was centralized at Montreal. An agricultural society, more energetic, productive and demanding, climbed painfully out of the wreckage of the Indian culture of the west. It offered an opportunity and it posed a problem. If Montreal was to cater to this new market, if it was to bring the new staples down the St. Lawrence as it had brought the old, it must completely overhaul the rudimentary business organization which had served the fur trade. Banks, roads, canals, harbours and ship channels were needed for the development of the new northern economy; and the first step in its progress must be the liquidation of the semi-feudal system of the French.

Such were the main themes in the economic revolution and such was, in general, its challenge to the commercial class. The whole process of change took nearly forty years to reach its conclusion and its implications were only gradually revealed. The merchants entered a long and difficult period of readjustment and

reorganization which was far from complete when the economic
revolution itself had run its course. As before, they had to do
battle on three fronts. They had to devise a commercial policy
to meet the new boundary even while they still hoped that it would
be politically erased. They had to find and keep markets for the
new staples in England and the empire. And they had to reorganize
a fur-trading business system which every year became more
hopelessly inadequate to meet the new demands. It was this last
necessity which eventually completed the divorce between the
merchants and the old society of the St. Lawrence and helped to
set in motion a political struggle of increasing gravity. Frontier
agriculture and the commercial system based upon it could not be
reconciled with feudalism as the fur trade had been; and the
merchants, who were determined upon a fundamental reconstruction of their system, were baulked both by the political division of
the province, which was effected in 1791, and by the dogged
resistance of the French Canadians. A political revolution grew
slowly out of the economic revolution which had preceded it. By
1821 the tensions and maladjustments, arising inevitably out of the
clash between the new economy and the old and unsuitable
political and social forms, were growing towards their climax.

II

As we have seen, the Canadian merchants, in the winter of
1783, made desperate efforts to effect a revision of the proposed
treaty. They foretold the ruin of the Canadian fur trade; they
prophesied a rising of the betrayed and angry Indians; and they
urged that even if the proposed boundary were allowed to stand,
the fortified posts should not be surrendered for a few years until
the traders had had time to wind up their affairs and withdraw
their property from the American side. From Oswald they received
slight comfort; but for a time they were able to hope that the
incredible, negligent generosity of the Shelburne administration
would be corrected at the hands of others. The astonishing Fox-
North coalition came into its brief tenure of power and David
Hartley replaced Oswald at Paris. If the merchants had the
slightest inkling of the conduct of the renewed negotiations, they

must have been decidedly pleased, for a number of the additions
and changes which Hartley was pressing, were directly inspired by
their original protests.[1] In particular, Hartley urged the free
reciprocal use by the nationals of both countries, of the navigable
waters and carrying-places along the boundary, the establishment
of free trade in the region and the retention of the posts by Great
Britain for three years. But, though the Americans were prepared
to be accommodating about some of these proposals, the British,
in the end, abruptly abandoned their new position and offered
the original provisional articles, practically unaltered, for the
Americans to sign. The obnoxious document of the autumn of 1782
became the definitive treaty of peace.

On the capital point of the new boundary, the merchants were
temporarily silenced. They evidently expected that after the usual,
and very useful, diplomatic delays which accompanied such
solemn transactions, the fortified trading-posts at Niagara,
Detroit, Michilimackinac and elsewhere would be duly handed over
to the Americans. For this event they made a few—but, on the
whole, surprisingly few—preparations. The North West Company
was particularly concerned, for though its territory on the Saskatchewan and in the Athabaska country was happily beyond the
clutch of the Americans, the communication westward from Grand
Portage lay definitely south of the new boundary. In June of 1784
Edward Umfreville and Venance St. Germain were sent off to
discover a new all-British route from Lake Superior to Lake
Winnipeg. The North West Company, which went briskly into
the business of propaganda almost as soon as it came into existence,
played up this great national service for Haldimand's benefit and
promised in addition to explore the whole north-west to the ocean
between 55 and 65 latitudes.[2] In return for this, the company
begged the exclusive right to the new passage for a period of seven
years and urged that a new fortified post should be constructed on
Canadian territory above Sault Ste. Marie at Point aux Pins.[3]
Down at Niagara, the government began to build a road on the
Canadian side of the river, and in 1789 a group of traders organized
a transport service over the new portage. Beyond this the merchants
did little. Apparently they made not the slightest effort to wind up
their business south of the lakes. Much depended on the unpredic-

table actions of the Americans once they were put in possession of the posts and, in any case, the Canadian merchants felt fairly comfortably secure in their own trading strength. "For my own part," wrote James McGill, "I am clearly of opinion that it must be a very long time before they can even venture on the smallest part of our trade."[4]

In the meantime the delay which might naturally be expected to precede an important cession of territory had unaccountably lengthened. By article 7 of the treaty the posts were to be surrendered "with all convenient speed"; but during the years 1783 and 1784, three American deputations—two from the federal authorities and one from the state of New York—came up to Canada to make arrangements for the transfer of the posts and each returned without even a preliminary discussion. In August, 1783—which was, to be sure, before the signing of the definitive treaty—three *bateaux* from Schenectady, owned by Americans and loaded with rum for the Indian trade, appeared at Niagara. This immediate attempt of the Americans to capitalize the benefits of the new boundary and to revive the almost defunct competitive trading route from Albany, raised a great protest from the Canadian monopolists at Niagara. The boats were turned back; and Haldimand not only approved of what had been done but also gave orders, a little later, that any other Americans who came in future to treat or trade with the Indians should be turned back as well.[5] In the summer of 1784 he countermanded the proposed fort at Point aux Pins.[6] The Nor' Westers made no effort to shift from Grand Portage to the newly discovered Canadian route. The southerners continued to trade undisturbed by competition from Albany. The posts were retained; and the western monopoly of Montreal continued to flourish under the protection of the old political control.

The mystery of Britain's surrender of this vast western territory is only equalled by the mystery of Britain's reluctance to hand over what she had legally signed away. Obviously two general explanations can be suggested for the retention of the posts. The British may have kept the posts because they actually feared their loss; and they may have kept them because they wished to bargain further for their surrender. The retention may have been dictated by policy or it may have been devised in simple retaliation. When, in the future, the Americans protested against this British violation of the treaty, they were answered in terms unvarying and eventually stereotyped, that the posts would be returned when the Americans had done justice to the Loyalists and had made proper provision for the recovery of British pre-revolutionary debts. The posts were thus, officially, kept in retaliation and offered as a *quid pro quo;* but it is obvious that this official reply, while partly an explanation, was also partly an excuse. The west, as the British ought to have known before signing the treaty and as they had good cause to know thereafter, had other values beside its exchange value. It had vast potentialities, both for profit and for mischief; and these were revealed in a long series of petitions, representations and dispatches which flowed in upon the government from the moment when the merchants first addressed it in the winter of 1783.

This protest of the west was essentially the united protest of a fur-trading economy; but it was voiced, as it had to be, by two very different sets of people, by the Indians and by the merchants who traded with them. While at least a few of the traders shrewdly suspected that they could outsell the Americans, boundary or no boundary, for some time to come, they naturally presented the gloomiest possible picture of their commercial plight to government; and in estimates which were made shortly after the Treaty of 1783, they calculated that the cession of the posts would endanger from one-half to two-thirds of their trade.[7] Down at Niagara, Sandusky and Detroit, the Indians showed an angry resentment to the perturbed Indian superintendents.[8] Joseph Brant and John the Mohawk, deputed by the confederacy of the Six Nations, came all the way to Quebec to interview the embarrassed Haldimand on the subject of the treaty. It was their unconcealed and stubborn conviction that the British had betrayed them. The greater number of the tribes in the region of the lower lakes had declared for Great Britain during the Revolutionary War; and yet the British with careless injustice had handed over the territory of their allies, apparently without gratitude for their services or consideration for their rights. There lay evident to all a real danger in the indignation of the tribes. A generation which remembered the slaughter of Pontiac's rising, had good reason to fear that the Indians might begin a fierce resistance to the American occupation of their lands and in the end wreak impartial vengeance on both their ancient enemies and their ungrateful friends. It was this fear of an Indian rising which chiefly troubled Governor Haldimand; and it was his chief argument for the indefinite retention of the posts. He was, of course—and particularly in such an important matter as this—merely an agent of the administration in Great Britain. Until he received Lord Sydney's letter of April 8, 1784, he temporized with the Americans, not because he had formulated a definite policy of delay but because he had received no definite orders from England. He was scarcely in a position to initiate policy himself; but, as the man on the spot, his advice must have been a powerful factor in its initiation by others. While the merchants and their sympathizers urged the commercial value of the posts, he emphasized their political importance in relation to the Indians. Thus it can be argued that the British violated the treaty either to preserve the fur trade or to prevent a terrible Indian rising in the west.[9]

The difference between these two lines of argument is apparent only and at bottom unreal. The problem of the Indians cannot be separated from the problem of the fur trade: the protest of one social group cannot be weighed against the protest of the other. Indian society was not a separate and self-sufficient organism; it was vitally dependent upon the fur trade. And the fur trade, in its turn, could only exist in the primitive hunting community of the Indians. The political connection, partly fashioned by the British themselves in New York and partly inherited from the French in Canada, was based upon this economic and social connection which was, in the main, the product of the fur trade. The maintenance of the posts in the interior and the concern of the administration at Quebec for the Indians were not dictated by unique sympathy and humanity; the adherence of the Indians to Quebec was not the result of an inexplicable political preference. It was the great fur-trading economy of the St. Lawrence which linked the administration at Quebec with the Indians in the interior, for it was the basis of Quebec's western imperialism. It was essentially a single, primitive economy which lay at the bottom of this complex of political and economic interests. To defend the rights of either white or red men in the west was ultimately to defend the integrity of the commercial empire of the St. Lawrence; and one of the best proofs of this fundamental, if unacknowledged, unity of aim, shared by politicians, merchants and Indians alike, is the remarkable similarity of their arguments. Haldimand, for example, was not the only person, nor indeed the first, to put the case of the Indians before the British government. It was the merchants, back in the winter of 1783, who spoke of the Indian's conviction of their betrayal and who prophesied a bloody Indian rising.[10]

III

In the meantime, while the fate of the western posts was still distressingly uncertain, the merchants had recommenced their political activity in the province of Quebec. They rushed into the conflict with a vigour which was equally the result of increased confidence and mounting exasperation. In Quebec, the war-time business boom collapsed with sickening suddenness. For the past few years, John Cochrane, the local agent of the exchange contractors for the British treasury, had been selling his bills of exchange to the Canadian merchants on an extravagant credit basis; and when the war came to an end, the merchants, through their dealings with Cochrane, owed the government a very large sum.[11] Haldimand, acting under peremptory orders from the home authorities, was determined to recover the outstanding balances; and the merchants, so they said, were unable to pay. Cochrane, who occupied, of course, a position of great strategic importance, refused to "lend his name" to suits against his debtors in the way the government desired; and, in this dilemma, Haldimand decided to sue Cochrane himself, at the same time attaching the effects of his debtors under a usage of the *code marchand* known as the *saisie arrêt*. Adam Lymburner, George Allsopp, the Frobishers and most of the principal merchants in the colony were involved; and in the court of common pleas, they had to stand before a bench dominated by their most unyielding political opponent Adam Mabane,[12] who had already given his advice to government in favour of the suits. Despite the protests and appeals of the defence against the tactics of the prosecution and the partiality of the judges, the Cochrane suits were decided in favour of the crown. They involved almost the whole commercial community in litigation, financial stringency and failure, and they completed the merchants' indignant disgust for the chaos of Canadian laws and the partiality of Canadian judges.[13] In the first few years after the peace of 1783, their dutiful respect for authority in general was at a low ebb; and, on the other hand, the peace and the arrival of the Loyalists had given them a more lusty confidence in their cause.

If, however, the mood of the merchants had subtly changed, their old political objectives remained unaltered for a brief time to come. The great migration that was to people the area of the lower lakes was big with menace for the old economy of the north and the old society rooted in it. But the feudalism of French Canada was not yet an osseous growth in the living tissue of a young, new, vital social body. The old organism still lived in the superb maturity that preceded the slow hardening of atrophy; and the merchants were still unquestioningly willing to accept the bulk of French-Canadian institutions because they were the superstructure of which the fur trade was the base. They gave little provocation to the main body of the French Canadians. In the petition of November, 1784, they specifically requested that the ancient land law of the country be continued;[14] and they were able to exploit their still amicable relationship with the other race so effectively that hundreds of French Canadians signed this same petition. In this period, as in the past, the quarrel of the merchants was still with the bureaucracy, the judges and the *noblesse*. "It is here remark'd", wrote Finlay, "that there's two opposite interests in the Province. . . ." On the one hand were the "Placemen and Canadian Noblesse, whose sway would be affected, power annihilated, if any change should be made in the present form of Government"; on the other hand were "the mercantile body, some of the Noblesse, and the better sort of Bourgeois, new as well as old subjects".[15]

Moreover, the great energizing motive behind the merchants' political activity in this period—as in the past and in the future— was the desire to protect and enlarge their commercial interests.

They felt that government was not merely authoritarian in form, but was also anti-commercial in spirit. "General Haldimand", wrote Finlay, "has been uniformly averse from permitting any Regulation to take place tending to the improvement and extension of our Commerce, which, as a Soldier, he will never see in a proper point of view. . . ."[16] The military bureaucracy was inimical to business both because of the regulations it imposed and the assistance it withheld; and the merchants desired an assembly to control government in the interest of the northern commercial state. "I look on Representation and Freedom in Government", said Grant in council, "as absolutely necessary Springs to give Vigour and Motion to the new Commercial Machine. The Power of exciting to Industry should be greatly lodged in the hands of such persons as are most likely to make mercantile Objects their principal Occupation and Study."[17]

In the meantime, while the bigger battle for the commercial control of government was still undecided, the merchants set themselves to win the maximum of *laissez-faire* in trade. The system of passes for western commerce still lingered on from the days of the old western reserve, and the confinement of trade goods to the provincial marine survived the conclusion of the Revolutionary War. The retention of the posts probably led to the continuance of these war-time measures. But the mere existence of the general peace and the evident reluctance of the Americans to take by force what was legally theirs, made the whole system slightly ridiculous. "How the safety of the Province is to be endangered by permitting decked craft to ply on the upper Lakes", wrote Finlay, "is past my comprehension."[18] The Detroit traders complained that their merchandise was held up at Carleton Island and the Niagara portage;[19] and the Nor' Westers were unable to bring up sufficient supplies from Detroit to Michilimackinac and Grand Portage to meet the needs of their expanding business.[20] Inevitably the merchants had to meet the certainty of increased interest charges due to a slower turnover as well as the very real risk of the loss, depreciation or theft of their property. In 1785 some relief was granted; but the mere right to use their own canoes and *bateaux* on Lake Ontario was completely unsatisfying to a middle class impatient of every government restraint. "All the Company wishes for", wrote Benjamin Frobisher on behalf of the Nor' Westers, "is on any terms to be left to the management of their own business." And when this "reasonable request" was still refused, the traders became truculent and obstructive. In the end they flatly refused to come to an agreement for their unpaid and mounting transport charges[21] and in 1786 the government was thinking of instituting another set of suits against them.

During the war, the opposition had contented itself with pressing for such changes in the system of the Quebec Act as had been suggested in the royal instructions. Now the merchants resumed the old campaign for an assembly, modestly calling the attention of authority to the patriotic sense of duty which had restrained them from presenting petitions and memorials to an embarrassed government in time of war. The towns of Quebec and Montreal were alive with political controversy in the first few years after the peace. As early as September, 1783, the merchants presented the first of the new petitions for an assembly;[22] and in November, 1784, they concocted a second, and slightly revised, edition of the same appeal.[23] The English-speaking subjects in the province mustered in hundreds to sign the two memorials; and a great number of French Canadians, either through commercial cajolery or through a real interest in the commercial programme, were persuaded to sign the second petition of November, 1784. The Quebec and Montreal committees drew up a plan for an elected house. Even in the frigid and forbidding atmosphere of the council, the party of reform developed more hardihood and acquired a few more votes. At the very moment when the councillors were deliberating an address of gratitude to His Majesty for the great benefits of the Quebec Act, William Grant had the indelicacy and the presumption to propose a rival petition to the king for an assembly.[24] For the moment Grant occupied the place of leadership, left vacant by the dismissal of Allsopp and soon to be pre-empted by the new chief justice, William Smith. He was a seigneur, a man of wide business connections in the colony and he occupied the post of deputy receiver-general. "Mr Wm Grant", wrote an unfriendly political observer, "is a man of first rate abilities. . . . He has a readiness in discovering men's character & a talent of profiting by their foibles when he has any purpose to serve. . . ."

He is "a complete master of every sort of simulation or dissimulation & possesses a shameless composure of temper and countenance that cannot be moved by reproach or abuse. He is besides this a plausible and good orator; quick with his pen; and when requisite of indefatigable application."[25]

The petitions were presented and transmitted to England; and over in the capital, at the New York Coffee House, the big firms Phyn & Ellice and Dyer, Allan & Company, as well as traders like John Brickwood, John Strettel and Robert Hunter, met to support the petitions from Canada with their own representations to government.[26] From these memorials and from the debates and protests in council, the commercial case for an assembly can be easily understood. The merchants wanted power, partly as an end in itself—for their generation was fully converted to the religion of parliamentarism—but mainly as a means to other ends which were largely material in character. As Grant said in council, it seemed to them intolerable that a mere half dozen men in a thinly attended session of the legislature, could, according to the terms of the Quebec Act, make fundamental changes in the laws of the colony. They obviously hoped that an assembly would help to make Quebec safe for commercial prosperity. They definitely intended to use the instrument of taxation for the encouragement of industry and commerce. Naturally it was the deputy receiver-general who elaborated this argument most fully; but the whole mercantile class was very early aware of the enormous importance of public finance in a country like Canada and they wished to control taxation, credit and tariffs for their own purposes in the development of the northern commercial state. They argued also that popular government would help to content the new settlers and would attract further settlement. The fact that the Loyalists had declined to co-operate in their petition did not unsettle their faith at all. They and their sympathizers realized that the political division of the continent and the settlement of its central portion by a great army of migrants meant a slow social convulsion in the domain of the lower lakes which would inevitably uproot the foundations of the old system of government.

But the British government still delayed; and while the delay lasted the attempt to revise the Quebec Act piecemeal was continued in the province. The Cochrane suits had both deepened the depression and intensified the merchants' hatred for the odd assortment of English, French and French-Canadian laws which the judges said was the civil law of the country. The spectacle of judges, who were also councillors, deciding government suits against government's political opponents was all the more annoying since large sums of money were involved. Evidently the legal system was not merely a restriction upon commerce; it was also a political weapon in the hands of the bureaucracy. The petitions and the memorials of both Canadians and Londoners were full of open and scarcely veiled allusions to the confusion in the laws and the scandals in the courts of justice. A growing number in the council considered a certain measure of reform to be imperatively necessary. Even Haldimand, in a kind of dim, confused, unhappy fashion, perceived that the good old order was no longer sacrosanct in its entirety; and he proposed an ordinance for the introduction of habeas corpus which was carried in the session of 1784. Lieutenant-Governor Hamilton succeeded him as administrator of the province. He was the first civilian with a middle-class philosophy to interrupt the dynasty of soldier-aristocrats which had governed Canada since the conquest; and during his tenure of power, which was as brief as it was encouraging, the party of reform made a determined attack upon the legal system.

When, in the session of 1785, the ordinance for the administration of justice in the civil courts came up for renewal, the committee in charge of the new bill introduced various drastically novel clauses, which provided, among other things, for English law in all commercial cases, for optional juries in civil suits at the instance of either party, and for the extension of English laws of evidence to all cases tried by jury. The voting was excitingly close. By a stroke of ill fortune, Grant was absent in England; but Finlay, the deputy postmaster-general, and the little group of British and French liberals, fought strenuously for the controversial clauses against Mabane and the French party. "It is necessary for this as a Commercial province," wrote Finlay, referring to the article which introduced English commercial law, "Our prosperity depending on the extent of our Credit in England, It ought to be the first care of this Council to render the recovery of British Property in this

Country easy, and according to the Commercial Laws of England."[27] But despite the arguments and the long written protests which set forth the commercial case, the French party conquered in the main. Juries were ordered established in civil suits; but otherwise the old legal system continued, multiplying commercial grievances and gradually intensifying commercial discontent.

IV

While men fought out these issues round the Quebec council board, the first transformation in the economy of the St. Lawrence had already begun. The great deeds by which simple farmers originally possessed the cultivable land of North America—deeds which were repeated regularly as the frontier travelled westward until they became accepted commonplaces—have now ended with the exhaustion of the new land itself; and in another generation the last actors in this plain and unpretending drama will be dead. We stand at the full term of the immense process which the Loyalists initiated; and, looking back over their work and that of their successors, we can more fully appreciate the revolution which their mere presence started in the old Canadian economy. They began, from nothing, the task of building up the immense industrial civilization of the Great Lakes. They were the last persons to see—what had been the normal landscape of the Indians and the fur traders—the untouched forest, stretching down to the very water's edge, teeming with life yet to their eyes empty and terrifying, without tracks or lights or homes. In those first summers of settlement, in the hard, clear northern sunlight, the land lay drowsy with the intoxication of its own rich, full-blooded vitality, proud of the almost tropically swift and splendid maturity of its leaves and fruits and grasses, untouched, unconscious of its destiny, waiting for nothing but the flaming autumnal death of its vegetation. It had stood for ages, serene, indifferent and impregnable, before a society which was powerless to effect its alteration. For a century and more beyond the arrival of white men on the continent, the fur trade had prolonged its security. But to the Loyalists the destruction of the forest was the first condition of their success. The clearings made with pain and difficulty on the

edges of the water presaged the slow annihilation of the old world
of the lakes, the wreckage of the forests, the disappearance of the
animals, the degradation of the Indians and the westward flight
of the fur trade. At once the settlers began to plant the homely,
traditional roots and fruits and cereals of western Europe. Their
mere effort to survive and to progress established ever more firmly
the prosaic foundations of western civilization, homes and families,
farms and barns and villages. Even their successes, sufferings and
diversions—the first corn sown where the blackened stumps still
stood in rows, the child buried in the little clearing beyond the
valley, the dances under the yellow light of a few lamps—are
touched with a more normal, homely simplicity than the region
of the lakes had ever known before. The settlers pronounced
doom upon the forest and its people; and the ephemeral culture
of the Indians and the fur traders began its slow retreat from life
into recollection and from recollection into history.

The Loyalists were, however, merely the northern contingent
of that great army of people that was pushing into Vermont,
north-western New York and the Ohio country. Over all the region
of the lower lakes, which Montreal considered its dominion, the
transmutation had begun; and it would create new commercial
opportunities in generous recompense for those it would inevitably
destroy. The immense portent of the change for Canada was
realized almost from the moment of the peace. It was understood
by business men, by many officials in England and Canada, by
Lieutenant-Governor Hamilton[28] with his eager interest in the
commercial prospects of the country and by Carleton who had
altered in so much beside his title when he returned to Canada
as Lord Dorchester. It was the aim of all those who thus imagina-
tively foresaw the distant but eventual results of settlement, to
capitalize this new market for the northern commercial state;
to bring the new staples down the St. Lawrence and to pay for
them, as they had paid for furs in the past, by the manufactures
of Great Britain. The job of the merchants was to build up a new
unity of the St. Lawrence, while the protecting limits of the old
unity remained precariously intact. This meant a re-orientation
of their views and a reorganization of their commercial machine.

It led to the utterance of certain new, striking and almost presumptuous demands.

If the merchants were to realize to the full the success that haunted their imaginations, they must, as soon as possible, achieve three preliminary essentials. In the first place, the boundary between Canada and the United States must be commercially obliterated by free trade for all the unmanufactured products of the Americans. Secondly, the whole export of Quebec and Montreal, whether it came originally from south or north of the new boundary, must be accepted as Canadian in imperial markets and admitted to all the advantages which Canada had at the moment or might acquire in the future under the old mercantile system. Finally, in every other part of the empire but the Canadian border, the United States must be considered what it had elected to become by revolution—a foreign country, outside the charmed circle of the imperial commercial system and subject to as many of the old trade restrictions against foreigners as could be economically maintained in its despite. The Revolutionary War and the peace, which had helped to inspire these new demands, helped also to frustrate their easy accomplishment. The fact is that the emergence of the United States as an independent nation produced an immense dislocation in British imperial trade in the North American world. The trade relations between Great Britain and her Atlantic possessions on the one hand and the United States on the other were too vital to be severed unthinkingly by the mechanical enforcement of the letter of the old commercial law. In England, the mercantilists and the free traders commenced a controversy over the revision of the navigation laws in favour of the Americans. Canada's position was slightly dubious. Canada wanted a little something from both parties. It wanted free trade in the interior of North America; but it also wanted mercantilism on the Atlantic ocean, where mercantilism would work Canada's profit and hurt both British subjects in the West Indies and the citizens of the United States.

It was the backwoods state of Vermont which first brought up, in concrete form, the great general problem of trade relations between Canada and the United States.[29] Both economically and politically, Vermont's position was peculiar at this time. The St. Lawrence, *via* Lake Champlain and the Richelieu river, was the only channel by which its produce could be easily marketed in the eighteenth century; and for the first few years after the peace the state was at odds with the American Confederation which for some time it refused to join. The political quarrel with the United States and the economic dependence on Canada combined to produce impressive results. The Allen brothers, Governor Chittenden and the other separatists in the state of Vermont were anxious for commercial treaties with Canada, Great Britain and the West Indies, which, they broadly hinted, might be the first steps in Vermont's re-entrance into the British Empire. On the other side of the boundary, the merchants and their sympathizers regarded the material progress and the politics of Vermont with complacency and eager anticipation. In their memorial of February 8, 1786, the London merchants requested the opening of trade with Vermont. The traders of Quebec, Three Rivers and Montreal made precisely the same request when the legislative committee on commerce and police invited their opinions toward the close of the same year.[30] "The rapid settlement of that country is incredible," wrote Finlay exuberantly concerning Vermont, "they say there's 70,000 souls already fixed there. . . . Their situation makes them dependent on us for their necessary supplies of European Manufactures and West India commodities. The whole of the surplus produce of their lands round Lake Champlain & Lake George must pass down the River St Lawrence in British ships, or remain on hand and perish."[31]

At the start, however, the decisions of the authorities in England apparently blocked all possibility of the change. Tentatively, in some confusion and with occasional contradictions, the British were feeling their way towards a new commercial policy. They were willing, temporarily at least, to suspend the navigation acts to permit a certain necessary measure of trade between Great Britain and the West Indies, and the United States; but, in the first few years after the peace, they seem to have thought rather of the protection of Canada's agriculture and industry than of the promotion of its commerce. By an order-in-council of April 8, 1785, the British administration explicitly forbade all trade by

sea between Canada and the United States. This, in itself, did
not particularly perturb the Canadian merchants, for it was inland
trade which interested them. But on March 24, 1786, another
imperial order-in-council prohibited "the importation of all goods
and commodities of the growth and manufacture of the United
States into any of the ports of the Province of Quebec".[32] Faced
by this apparently categorical prohibition, Canada embarked upon
an ingenious study in interpretation, in which governor, councillors
and merchants all participated. Committee in council decided
that Vermont was not really a part of the United States at all.[33]
Dorchester came to the comforting conclusion that "any ports"
meant "any sea ports".[34] In April, 1787, the council passed the
first ordinance and Dorchester issued the first orders to the customs
which opened inland trade with the United States. Audacity in this
case succeeded. The board of trade, which was struggling heroically
with the complicated problems of the new era, reviewed the whole
matter and in July, 1787, advised that the Canadian legislature be
permitted to regulate inland trade with the United States as it
willed. By an ordinance in the following year, the legislative
council opened Canada to the free importation, by way of Lake
Champlain and the Richelieu, of American timber, lumber, naval
stores, cereals, dairy products, cattle, poultry and fresh fish.[35]

Thus, within five years of the peace, the commercial class
had attained its first objective—the unimpeded entry of American
natural products into Canada. But the American goods which
entered freely under this new dispensation, were still subject in
theory to alien duties in the imperial markets; and it was the
second object of Canada to remove this discrimination. If, by its
mere passage down the St. Lawrence, American produce could
acquire Canadian status and enter into all the imperial preferences
which Canada enjoyed, American shippers would be induced, by
still another powerful attraction, to make use of the northern
route. In February, 1790, a committee of the legislative council
requested that alien goods from Quebec be admitted into imperial
markets as Canadian; and Dorchester followed this up by a
persuasive letter written in July of the same year.[36] The educational
process, by which the Canadians endeavoured to convince the
British of the great role which the St. Lawrence might play in

the still surviving mercantile system, finally converted the board of trade. The board became an enthusiastic advocate of the scheme;[37] and by an imperial statute, passed in 1790, American produce brought down the St. Lawrence was admitted to all the duties and preferences accorded to Canadian goods in Great Britain.[38]

There remained the third object—the object of securing for Canada protected markets in England and its Atlantic possessions from which the United States would be excluded by the strict application of mercantile principles. Canada aspired to take the place which New England and the middle colonies had occupied in the old commercial system, and to supply the British fishing settlements and the British West Indies with their grain, flour, provisions and lumber. Over in England, Lord Sheffield, William Knox, Carleton, the ship-owners and all those whose interests were bound up in the old mercantile system, pleaded that Canada and the maritime provinces should be given their chance. But the economic necessities of the West Indies were too apparent. Their commercial ties with the United States, which were highly developed and efficiently organized, could not in justice be cut abruptly; and in the end the British fell back upon the inconclusive and somewhat contradictory policy of permitting a measure of trade in British ships between the West Indies and the United States as a temporary expedient until Canada, Nova Scotia, New Brunswick and Prince Edward Island would be capable of undertaking full supply. In fact, therefore, the Canadians were left to compete with the Americans, and they competed badly.[39] In part and for a time, their failure was due to the Quebec Revenue Act, which discouraged the direct importation of rum from the British West Indies to Quebec. But the old disabilities of the St. Lawrence, which had been so conspicuous during the French régime, were a greater and more permanent disadvantage; and, in the main, it was Canada's industrial weakness and its commercial ineffectiveness on the Atlantic ocean which caused its ill success.

The Canadians could not overcome the solid advantages of proximity, uninterrupted navigation and expert knowledge which the Americans possessed in the West Indies trade. Canada had no winter ports. Distance and isolation made it difficult for her to gauge the West Indies market; and the still recurrent failures of Canadian agriculture sufficed to paralyse the whole trade. In 1788, when the crop failed, the merchants and millers in the Canadian flour and biscuit trade admitted that they had nothing for exportation;[40] and in 1789 came the hungry year, when the province was unable to feed itself. The trade with the fishing settlements and the West Indies continued on an almost infinitesimal scale. It was in the home market of Great Britain, rather than in the markets of its American dependencies, that Canada was to secure its most favourable preferential treatment and to obtain its greatest commercial success. In the years which immediately followed the American Revolution these triumphs and failures were alike hidden in the future; but already the Canadian merchants had made some major conquests in commercial policy; and the St. Lawrence had begun to act that curiously versatile role which it continued to play with enthusiasm and conviction for the next sixty years. It linked and reconciled the apparently irreconcilable principles of mercantilism and free trade. It was the water boulevard which connected the rising industrialism of Great Britain with that agricultural economy which both Canadians and Americans were building up in the region of the Great Lakes.

These initial defeats were, however, clear evidence of the puniness of the new economy. The rise of agriculture paralleled the decline of the fur trade; but the movement toward equilibrium was extremely slow. The agricultural interest was as yet far from balancing the fur-trade interest which it would eventually outweigh. Montreal was the city of western commerce; and though Montreal was titillated by the new prospects, the serious business of its life was still unquestionably the fur trade. From the middle eighties the trade was carried forward in a career of uninterrupted and booming expansion, of which the main features were the conquest of new territory, the development of company organization and the tightening of capitalistic control from Montreal. As trade advanced into the interior, as its organization became more complex, and as transportation costs soared upwards, capital came to play an increasingly commanding role. In the south-west trade, it is true, the tendency was not very pronounced. The Michilimackinac Company of 1785 was a failure. Although the

Montreal firm of Forsyth, Richardson & Company came to control the lion's share of the forwarding business, individuals and small firms continued to trade in the southern areas. It was not until the new century, when John Jacob Astor's competition became acutely dangerous, that company organization was firmly established in the south-west and a few big firms dominated the trade. In the north-west it was very different. Here, though in the hinterland the energy of the single trader was essential and his individualism insistent and obstreperous, everything combined to force the trade into the form of the big company and to throw the company into the hands of the firms in Montreal. From 1785 on, the North West Company, though it was in intention a monopoly, had to do stern battle with the rival organization of Gregory, McLeod & Company, a competitively weaker firm which nevertheless possessed considerable trading strength in the persons of Peter Pangman, John Ross and Alexander Mackenzie. But the unrelenting and savage rivalry between the two organizations which culminated in the murder of John Ross in the winter of 1786–1787, proved once again, convincingly, the impossibility of ordinary business competition in the north-western trade. The two firms drew together in repentance, exhaustion and fear of reprisal; and in the summer of 1787, Gregory and his partners entered into a unified and enlarged concern. In the meantime, Benjamin Frobisher had died. Joseph Frobisher remained as the single surviving director of the North West Company as organized in 1783; and to him, in a letter written in April, 1787, Simon McTavish proposed the business partnership which became probably the most commanding concern in the whole Canadian trade.[41]

The two men stood out from the mass of their followers as complementary personalities who summed up the various qualities of an entire business generation. Both of them had that hard, enduring vitality, that easy, amused acceptance of life, that large capacity for pure, sensual enjoyment which were so characteristic of the brotherhood of the old west. In trade, their qualities were complementary. It was Frobisher who first began the exploitation of the Athabaska district; and it was McTavish who outlined in detail the whole scheme whereby the two traders became the directing and controlling force in the North West Company. Both were all-round men in a sense impossible in the twentieth century; but, though it is dangerous to generalize from the evidence, it is possible that Frobisher represented the older, less specialized type of merchant adventurer, while McTavish, who was apparently never west of Grand Portage, personified money power and financial intellectualism. In November, 1787, the firm of McTavish, Frobisher & Company came into being. In the new North West Company agreement of 1790, which was to come into operation two years later, it achieved the supremacy which was due to its strength. It owned or controlled half of the twenty shares in the new organization; and it was to do all the business of the North West Company at Montreal.[42] From 1787 onward, under the direction of unified capitalist control, the north-western business organization was overhauled and improved, while on the frontier expansion continued, in the explorations of Alexander Mackenzie and the enlargement of the Athabaska district.

Thus the fur trade continued to prosper; and its defence still remained one of the chief political tasks of Montreal. The British retention of the posts and the competitive strength of the northern economy kept for the Canadians the virtual monopoly south of the lakes which they had won during the Revolutionary War. The new American settlers, though their arrival helped to reduce fur-trading profits around Niagara and Detroit, could no more wrest the fur trade from the Canadians than could the traders of Albany and Schenectady. Settlement could not endanger Montreal's commercial supremacy; but it could and did threaten the hunting-grounds of Montreal's Indian allies. It was this threat which precipitated the crisis in the west. Despite repeated attempts to settle a new boundary between hunting-grounds and settlements, the disputes of the Americans and the Indians became chronic and rancorous. The United States did not dare to seize the western posts, but it was quite willing to chastise the Indians; and in 1790 and 1791 it sent military expeditions against them. The Indians stood at bay. They were the last defenders in the field of the old political unity of the St. Lawrence; and the merchants, realizing that Indians' resistance had brought up, in an acute form, the whole unsolved problem of the west, recommenced, with redoubled energy, their propaganda in favour of the retention of the posts.

They presented both the political and the economic sides of the problem. "The commercial and political interests", they wrote in one of their memorials, "are so blended and interwoven as to leave almost no discrimination."[43] They put forward all their old commercial arguments loaded with fresh statistical material. In 1790, they calculated that of the total annual production of the trade, about one-half, valued at £100,000, came from the American side; and they estimated gloomily that if the posts were surrendered, three-tenths of the trade alone would certainly remain to Great Britain, one-fifth would be dependent upon "contingent circumstances" and the remainder would be inevitably lost.[44] They believed that the Indians had rights and the British obligations in the west which could not be lightly abandoned. It was, in their opinion, Great Britain's duty to help the Indians, if possible by diplomacy, to secure a lasting peace between the Americans and themselves; and the only solid basis of a lasting peace was a new boundary which would give the Indians the protection which the boundary of 1783 had failed to provide.[45] The merchants were not thinking of trade alone. They were thinking of territory; they were thinking in terms of the political unity of the St. Lawrence. They were capitalists who became political imperialists by the easiest and most natural of transitions.

The joint protest of the Indians and the fur traders was a single desperate appeal for the defence of an economy and society based upon it. After the Treaty of 1783, it had helped to move the British to retain the fortified posts. Now, as the appeal grew more wildly importunate, they formulated a more definite policy to support and justify their retention of the posts. While the Indians successfully fought the Americans and while the merchants redoubled their propaganda, the British began to believe that they could mediate between the Indians and their enemies and force the establishment, on the American side of the border, of a neutral Indian reserve.[46] This, which was the policy pursued for the next few years, was in effect the last effort of British diplomacy to preserve the old political unity of the St. Lawrence.

V

In the last years of the existence of the old province of Quebec, when Carleton had returned as Lord Dorchester to govern the country and when the American William Smith had become its chief justice, the reform movement of the merchants in provincial politics became perceptibly more radical. In part this growing impatience and thoroughness was due to a realization that authority was no longer opposed to all change. Faced by the new and radically different Canada which had issued from the American Revolution, Dorchester never recovered the old assertive self-confidence of Carleton; and the vigorous reactionary who had imposed his own policy in 1774 was now prepared to accept the guidance of a liberal colonial lawyer. William Smith was a Loyalist who came from an able professional family in New York and who had risen to be chief justice of his native province. Unlike the baffled Dorchester, he was full of ideas for the reorganization of what remained of Britain's empire in America; and his views, which were British-American in colour, were likely to come in conflict with the usages of the Canadian French. Authority was now prepared—and was, indeed, expected—to plan reform; but, at the same time, the mere presence of the altered Carleton and his liberal mentor, Smith, does not entirely account for the more revolutionary character of the merchants' methods and objectives. Reform had been delayed so long. Delay had allowed the old weaknesses of the political and legal system to become aggravated, and it had permitted new defects to grow. With every year that passed since 1783, the inadequacy of the institutional structure of the St. Lawrence became more glaringly evident to the commercial class. A new economy and a new society, growing in strength, in purpose and in promise, were encased in the tight, hard, inert shell of custom which frustrated their development. Feudalism and the new frontier agriculture were in implacable opposition; and the merchants, who grasped eagerly at the fresh opportunities of the new era, were led gradually by their commercial interests into a frontal attack upon the very bases of French Canada which before 1783 they had been quite ready to accept.

In 1787, the merchants precipitated a new political crisis. The ordinance regulating the courts of civil justice had come up again in the council for its biennial renewal; and Chief Justice Smith introduced into the draft of a new bill a few amendments in favour of the merchants and the Loyalists. This gentle thrust at the conservatives was answered with an immediate, blunt, uncompromising counterstroke. Paul Roc St. Ours, one of the more intransigent of the French-Canadian members in council, introduced at the next session a rival bill, which not only omitted all Smith's reforms, but which also dropped the major concessions which had been granted to the merchants in the past. On two occasions, by a majority of one, the council voted to give St. Ours's bill the previous consideration which was not its by rights. On March 26, Smith and his followers presented a protest, in which, among other considerations, the complaints of the merchants and the commercial interests of the country were advanced against St. Ours's bill.[47] But the merchants, faced by the impending calamity of the passage of this reactionary measure, determined upon more forceful action. They secured the right to be heard in council against the threatening bill. They engaged Isaac Ogden and James Monk, the attorney-general, who secured Dorchester's permission to act on this occasion, to present their case for them. And, on April 14, Monk delivered in council a terrific denunciation of the whole system of Canadian justice.

Results followed swiftly. The governor ordered an investigation into the courts of justice over which the chief justice presided. The indefatigable Monk continued to act for the merchants and they crowded into the court of investigation to lay their complaints against the Francophil and reactionary judges of the common pleas. In the autumn, when the investigation was nearing its conclusion, they decided to send Adam Lymburner, a Quebec merchant, to England, to support their complaints against the judges, their demand for English commercial law and their previous petitions for an assembly.[48] Lymburner, who was the first Canadian empowered by the merchants to act on their behalf abroad, appeared in the house of commons in May of the following year, when the affairs of Quebec were up for debate, and told the old story of the chaos in the Canadian courts.[49] But Chief Justice Smith, though he had collected vast quantities of evidence, produced no findings; and after a year and a half of delay, the secretary of state came to the unexpected decision that the best interim reform would be, not the correction of the judges, but the dismissal of the attorney-general, James Monk. The indignant merchants took up the cudgels for their advocate. Already, however, they were beginning to believe that to the British, as to themselves, the problem of justice in Canada was bound up with the larger problem of the political organization of the colony; and as 1788 drew towards its close, they suspected that imperial legislation for Canada was definitely on its way. In the autumn of that year, armed with powers signed by both French and English in Quebec and Montreal, Adam Lymburner departed again for London, to put and keep the whole mercantile case before the British government.[50]

In the meantime, while the British pondered the problem of Quebec and Lymburner continued his almost futile propaganda, there were more signs of commercial radicalism in the province. Faced by the growing and vocal opposition of the seigneurs, the merchants, in the time-honoured fashion of their class, set out to prove how complete was the identification of their own interests with those of the colony. In a long petition, weighted with somewhat questionable statistics, they tried to prove how numerous and "respectable" was their own following, how great was the value of their landed and commercial property and how unimportant and unscrupulous were their opponents.[51] "Government . . . ", wrote John Richardson, "ought to acknowledge commerce as its basis, & the accomodation of the Merchant as one principal means of promoting the national prosperity."[52] In 1788, the council, which in many ways was definitely more favourable to the merchants since Dorchester's return, at length permitted the navigation of private vessels on the lakes. But the merchants, still unsatisfied, wanted to abolish the whole system of regulation and control. "The first principle of Commerce", they asserted with complete assurance, "is, that it be free and unfettered. . . ."[53] Finally a council committee, presided over by Grant, reported with an almost lyrical defence of unlimited free trade; and in 1791 the system of passes for trade in the interior was swept away entirely by ordinance.

But while these old requests were granted the merchants were cautiously making new demands. One of these was of vital importance, for it had to do with land. Despite all the work which has

been done on westward expansion in North America, it is doubtful
if the intimate connection between commerce and the frontier has as
yet received sufficient attention. It was natural that the Loyalists
should demand land on English freehold tenure; but it was equally
natural that the merchants should make the same request. Since
1783, land had suddenly become of immense importance to the
commercial class. The Loyalists were slowly taking the place of the
Indians as the advance guard of the commercialism of Montreal.
The merchants were soon to become the promoters, money-lenders
and carriers of the new agricultural society. In another decade
they were deep in land speculation and early in the nineteenth
century they were helping to form land companies in Upper and
Lower Canada. This new demand for free land under a popular
tenure brought them up with a crash against the inert feudalism
of New France. As early as January, 1787, the Quebec merchants
were demanding freehold tenure for the Loyalists in the interest of
population and the extension of trade; but there was soon general
agreement on this aspect of the matter and the far larger question
of the liquidation of the feudal régime arose. "Nothing remains
of the old feudal System", wrote Lymburner to the secretary of
state, "that can render it advantageous to the government or
beneficial to the people."[54] Letters passed between the provincial
authorities and the home government on the subject; and in
October, 1790, Chief Justice Smith was able to convince his
colleagues in council that soccage tenure was "essential to the
growth, strength, defence and safety of the province".[55] But
there was opposition. The council hesitated to legislate, with the
fateful result that when the Constitutional Act was passed and the
province divided, the great problem of decadent Canadian
feudalism remained unsolved.

By 1791 the long-delayed reform of the Canadian political
system had reached its final form in what we know as the Constitutional Act. In a document, which was neatly divided into fifty
clauses, Grenville, the new secretary of state, achieved the difficult
task of creating new problems for the merchants, without really
solving any of their old difficulties. Representative institutions,
which the merchants had fought for so long, were indeed granted.
But there were to be two assemblies, not one; for the prospective
division of Quebec was mentioned in the act and a little later a

proclamation created the two provinces of Upper and Lower Canada. Freehold tenure was established in Upper Canada; grants in freehold were permitted in Lower Canada if desired; but there was no provision whatever for the commutation of the existing seigniorial system. There was no reform of the laws. In effect, the statute was practically what its preamble asserted it to be, an alteration in the government clauses of the Quebec Act.

Over in London, Lymburner fought the measure as best he could, by remonstrances to the secretary of state, and by detailed criticism at the bar of the house of commons. Because the bill failed to establish habeas corpus, English commercial law and juries in civil suits, he attacked it for the same reasons that the merchants had always attacked the Quebec Act. But, if anything, he paid less attention to these old disabilities than he did to the unexpected and calamitous division of the province. Like the boundary of 1783, and for much the same reasons, the establishment of the two provinces appeared to the merchants to be an unqualified disaster. The Canadian committee wrote to Lymburner that, if the division were maintained, all the advantages of the new constitution would be lost.[56] When, in March, 1791, he was heard at the bar of the house of commons, Lymburner argued that the provinces were geographically and economically linked together, that the country was incapable of supporting two governments and that—since the only ocean ports were in Lower Canada—the two provinces would be involved in endless disputes over finance and fiscal policy.[57]

To the merchants who personified the needs of the Canadian commercial state, the division of the province was the second greatest blunder made by the British government in the first eighty years of British rule. 1791 was the complement of 1783. The empire of the St. Lawrence was partitioned by the Treaty of Paris and repartitioned by the Constitutional Act. And together these two great political decisions destroyed the economic unity of the north. The creation of the two provinces divided that ambitious and active party which was devoted to the success of the river system. The new boundary isolated Montreal in the midst of a hostile French-Canadian population. It nullified the vigour and initiative of Upper Canada by the lethargy of the lower province. And because of it Canada was left a quarter-century behind in the race for the trade of the new west.

CHAPTER V

THE RISE OF THE NEW STAPLE TRADES

I

THE decade which followed the Constitutional Act of 1791 and the establishment of representative government in the Canadas formed an important stage in the great transition through which the commercial state was passing. The decline of the fur-trading society in the region of the Great Lakes was now accompanied by the solid settlement of the fat, rich, forest-covered land. The rise of the new industries and the new staple trades was coincident with the beginnings of parliamentary government. This uninterrupted onrush of change demanded constant effort and adjustment; it inspired the enterprising and perturbed the conservative; and it brought forward new men and discredited old reputations.

The governors who presided over the two provinces in the first years of their existence were affected, like everybody else, by the spirit of the transition; and their very reponses, which were either whole-hearted or timorous, reveal the nature of the challenge which they were forced to meet. Dorchester, the soldier aristocrat who had been so sublimely sure of himself in the days of the Quebec Act, was now uncomfortable and uninspired in the midst of the problems of the new régime. It was Colonel John Graves Simcoe, the first lieutenant-governor of Upper Canada, who found in the new frontier society of the lakes a stimulus sufficient to arouse all his ingenuous enthusiasm and tremendous energy. Simcoe was a comparatively young man, whereas Dorchester was old and irritable and emptied of ideas. The new lieutenant-governor, like his superior at Quebec, was a soldier; but he had fought through the Revolutionary War as commander of the provincial regiment of the Queen's Rangers, which was mainly recruited by Loyalists. His plans for the future of that great "peninsular country" between Lakes Ontario, Erie and Huron were conceived in terms of the established British-American habits of settlement, agriculture and commerce in farming produce. Impatient of the fur trade, contemptuous of the laws and usages of French Canada, Simcoe eagerly adopted the new, the agrarian variant of the old design of the St. Lawrence. He frankly hoped to attract American settlers to his government and to win their loyalty by its excellence. He believed that Upper Canada, which jutted like a huge projection into the central waters of the continent, would be inevitably the focus of the trade in the new staples on the Great Lakes.

To Simcoe and to the merchants, who, at least in fundamentals, thought alike, the sense of new beginnings, the consciousness of the onrush of immense and unpredictable changes, must have been particularly acute in the last decade of the eighteenth century. The ideal boundary of 1783 had been drawn; but it was obvious in 1791 that the west was full of unsettlement and that its political future was uncertain. In all the long period of nearly two centuries in which the nations of West Europe had controlled the valley of the St. Lawrence, large settlements had never been established in the region of the lower lakes. But now, in the last two decades of the eighteenth century, the sudden, eager occupation of the area gave a new emphatic meaning to the old conception of the Canadian commercial state. Over in north-western New York State, while the speculators struggled for millions of acres of land, the pioneers moved in thousands into military tracts, the Phelps and Gorman purchase and the Holland purchase.[1] In the spring of 1788, migrants from the New England states founded at Marietta the first settlement in the Ohio purchase.[2] Before the turn of the century there were sixty thousand inhabitants in the new districts in north-western New York and the "Genesee Country" was gaining its reputation for superb wheat. In 1802 Ohio became the first of the new northern states beyond the Appalachians. The movement crossed the new international boundary and crept northward around the lakes. Settlers from New York, Pennsylvania and New Jersey followed the Loyalists into Upper Canada. In the last years of the old century and the first of the new, the Eastern Townships in Lower Canada were being slowly peopled by immigrants from New England and New York.[3]

Those great changes, which had been predicted by the merchants and foreshadowed by the coming of the Loyalists, were now visibly affecting the whole economy of the north. In the west there had arisen a new market which by 1821 was to displace completely the old market of the fur traders; and during the first ten years of the history of Upper Canada, from 1792 to 1802, the Canadian merchants began to revise the detail of their business system and to branch out into new commercial operations on a scale unknown before. At first the changes in organization were comparatively small. The new migrants were simply fitted into a strong commercial system which stood ready to receive them. The Eastern Townships formed a kind of extension of Vermont with which Montreal had already been doing business. In Upper Canada, the settlers established themselves along the river and the lakes; and Kingston, York, Niagara and Detroit, which became the centres of settlement, had been originally supply stations and stations of trans-shipment in the fur trade. In the far west, at Detroit, old fur traders like John Askin, William Robertson and George Leith still controlled practically all the business of the community. But in the central and eastern parts of the province, there were a few important newcomers, either Loyalists or later immigrants or merchants from Lower Canada. At Queenston were Robert Nichol, Thomas Clark, who sent one of the first Durham boats down the St. Lawrence, and Robert Hamilton, whom La Rochefoucault-Liancourt described as "an opulent merchant who is concerned in the whole inland trade of this part of America".[4] There were a few traders of importance, of whom Elias Smith of Port Hope was one,[5] stationed at the tiny settlements which were just beginning on the north shore of Lake Ontario and the St. Lawrence; and at Kingston, which was at first the commercial capital of the province, lived merchants such as Richard Cartwright, Thomas Markland, John Cummings and Peter Smith.[6] The two most important figures in this first generation of Upper Canadian merchants were Richard Cartwright and Robert Hamilton. Hamilton was a native of Scotland and Cartwright was a Loyalist from New York, a moderate, sound and able man, who built up the most important business in the province and founded a family distinguished alike in commerce and politics.

These traders inhabited a separate province, governed at first by a man who was vigorous in his insistence on provincial rights; but they enjoyed, nevertheless, no commercial independence at all.

Montreal had simply increased its western trading personnel; and although Mr. Grenville's new boundary was in so many ways a threat to what remained of the old unity of the St. Lawrence, it could not divide the trading brotherhood of Canada. "The principal merchants resident at Kingston", reported Isaac Weld, "are partners of old established houses at Montreal and Quebec."[7] Richard Cartwright, whose commercial importance gave his words an air of authority, amplified this generalization with more exact detail. "Not having a seaport in our Province," he wrote to a London house which was seeking his business, "it would be impossible or extremely inconvenient for any person here to import goods except through the medium of a Montreal house. . . . The merchant sends his order for English goods to his correspondent at Montreal, who imports them from London, guarantees the payment of them there, and receives and forwards them to this country for a commission of five per cent. on the amount of the English invoice. The payments are all made by the Upper Canada merchant in Montreal, and there is no direct communication whatever between him and the shipper in London."[8]

It was the role of the Upper Canadian merchants, who were thus financially dependent upon Montreal, to act as Montreal's western agents in effecting the great transition between the old economy and the new. They did not modify in the slightest the old territorial ambitions of Canada. In a revealing letter which he sent to Governor Simcoe, Robert Hamilton showed his knowledge of the geographic and historical foundations of the northern economy and his consciousness of its great tradition of western empire.[9] It was not the limits but the character of the northern commercial state which had changed. It was the coexistence of the fur trade and the trade in the new staples which made the task of the merchants so novel and so difficult. They had a dual role to perform. The north-west fur trade swept past, far above the Upper Canadian settlements, along the Ottawa river. But the first commercial interest of Niagara and Detroit was in the south-west fur trade; and when Isaac Weld arrived in Kingston in 1795, he found the merchants forwarding Indian goods up the lower lakes and trans-shipping packs of furs to Montreal.[10] Simcoe, who preferred agriculture to furs and frowned upon big monopolistic fur-trading companies, was delighted to find, when he visited Kingston late in 1794, that the merchants were already pretty deeply interested in other commercial projects.[11] They were trying to exploit the new market as well as to preserve the old.

As population in the new province increased, the little communities gradually struggled beyond the stage of mere subsistence. They began to buy and sell. The wants of the pioneer inhabitants were few and simple: tools, implements, fire-arms, liquors, tea, woollen cloth and printed calicoes. The province produced those staples which had always been characteristic of the north temperate colonies in the past, wheat, flour, peas, provisions, lumber and potash; but, of these, the production of wheat and flour was by far the more important. Agriculture in Canada was still subject to the old, violent fluctuations in yield. There were years, as there had been during the French régime, when the inhabitants could scarcely live upon what they produced; and in the autumn of 1795, due to a poor crop and much selling, Dorchester issued a proclamation forbidding the export of wheat and flour from the ports of Lower Canada.[12] But these were symptoms of a condition which was rapidly passing. In 1791 the traveller Campbell noted that 6,000 bushels of wheat had been bought and stored in Kingston;[13] and in the next decade production increased rapidly, with only few interruptions.

A good part of this wheat and flour was carried down the St. Lawrence, as the theorists of the new Canadian economy had always intended it should be, to swell the export from Montreal and Quebec. As in the past the principal exporters of wheat were Quebec firms such as Lester & Morrogh, Munro & Bell and Lymburner & Crawford; but it was significant that already fur-trading Montreal was taking a hand in the new business and in 1795 Forsyth, Richardson & Company were exporting wheat as well as furs.[14] Much of this wheat and flour was consigned to Spain and other foreign countries, since the Canadians lacked a good imperial market. But the French Revolutionary and the Napoleonic Wars, in which Great Britain was almost continuously involved for two decades, imposed unusual burdens on the resources of the mother country; and the war-time needs of the empire, which were soon to create the Canadian timber trade, began to encourage the export of wheat and flour. In 1795, when England experienced a scarcity, the home government appealed to Dorchester.[15] A proclamation was issued in the spring of 1795 which confined the export of wheat, flour and peas to Great Britain and the empire; and during the season some 370,000 bushels of wheat, more than half of which went by the special convoy of H.M.S. *Adventure*, were transported to England.[16] Upper Canada's portion of the Canadian export of wheat and flour was, of course, extremely small; but it grew rapidly during the first decade of the history of the province. In 1794, Cartwright estimated that 12,823 bushels of wheat and 896 barrels of flour, the produce of the Midland district, which was then the first agricultural region in the province, had been shipped from Kingston for Montreal.[17] In 1801, the Kingston merchants shipped down the St. Lawrence 13,963 barrels of flour and 350 bushels of wheat, the greater part of which came, as before, from the districts about Kingston.[18]

But export abroad was not the only outlet for the new staples of Upper Canada. There was a market within the province itself and immediately beyond its southern boundary. Back in 1760, in the days of the conquest, the needs of the British army on the shores of the St. Lawrence had first attracted the merchant adventurers to Canada. During the 1790's, the garrisons at Kingston, Niagara and Detroit constituted relatively an even more important market in the economy of the new province. Through the contract system, the valuable business of supplying the troops fell largely into the hands of the merchants. The Davison brothers, George and Alexander, the latter of whom was later sentenced to twenty-nine months in prison for taking unlawful commissions on sales, were awarded contracts for the supply of the troops in British North America. Alexander Davison appointed Munro & Bell and John Gray as his agents and these men were directed to employ Richard Cartwright at Kingston, Robert Hamilton at Niagara and John Askin and William Robertson at Detroit.[19] For some time after, these and other Upper Canadian merchants made the supply of the troops their most lucrative business. In 1794, Kingston furnished flour, peas and pork for the use of the garrison there to the value of £6,601, which was very nearly double the value of the produce exported from the district to Lower Canada.[20] The surrender of the western posts to the Americans in 1796 did not interrupt the trade: it may actually have increased it, for the British garrisons were simply transferred north of the boundary and the American garrisons occupying the old forts were at first dependent upon the produce of Upper Canada. Robert Hamilton reported that in the winter of 1797 the demand of the American troops had raised the prices of flour and peas in the Niagara district and had practically exhausted the supply.[21] Even the American settlements, so long as they remained in their first weak and dependent state, bought food-stuffs from Upper Canada; and in 1797 Cartwright claimed that the American garrisons and settlements on Lake Ontario and Lake Erie had been almost wholly supplied with Canadian bread.[22]

All this was evidence of the progress of the economic revolution, of the rise of new interests and endeavours which were slowly thrusting themselves up in the middle of the old commercial organization. The fur trade had been based upon a hunting society; but the new economy was agricultural and its basis was land. The novel interest of the merchants in landed property is one of the best indications of the great transition in the economy of the north. Up to 1783 the merchants had acquired land for social rather than for economic reasons. The arrival of the Loyalists had set them pondering the possibilities of land and the problems of land tenure; but during the first decade in the history of Upper Canada —and the coincidence of dates is significant—the merchants, for the first time, began land speculation upon a fairly large scale. There were, of course, no vast speculative purchases, no great capitalist attempts at community building such as those which were made during this period in New York and the new western American states. In British North America, land was an imperial concern, and the British decreed that the ordinary grant must be 200 acres and the maximum grant 1,200 acres to a single individual. But in Lower Canada and in Upper Canada as well, though to a lesser extent and for a shorter time, the promoters evaded these regulations through the system of colonization by "leaders and associates", a speculative technique for settlement which was already old in New England. The leader or capitalist, paying the fees and charges of survey, secured a large tract of land, preferably a whole township, for himself and the "associates" who were really his dependents. Legally the capitalist could only be granted 1,200 acres; but it was understood that the associates, in return for the services and expenditures of their leader, should convey back to him the greater part of their own grants.

Lured on by these handsome prospects, the bureaucrats, land-owners and merchants of Lower Canada, as well as some speculators from the United States, come forward *en masse* to request grants in the Eastern Townships and along the Ottawa. By two separate agreements in October, 1795, David Alexander Grant, Patrick Langan, Hugh Finlay and John Jacob Astor, the American fur trader, entered into a partnership for acquiring land in Lower Canada and looked forward, somewhat optimistically, to the possibility of dividing as many as twenty-four townships between them.[23] This grandiose scheme was dashed, of course. There were interminable delays. A quarrel between Governor Prescott and his council over the land-granting business still further postponed a settlement; and it was not until Milnes became lieutenant-governor that the administration began to grant land definitely by letters patent on a large scale. Though the most ambitious speculators failed in their schemes, the grants of land were still far larger than those customarily conceded in Upper Canada; and among other successful merchants, McTavish, McGillivray, Montour, Todd, Frobisher and Gregory, with their associates, each received a quarter of a township.[24]

II

The first stages in the Canadian economic revolution coincided with the beginnings of representative government in the two Canadas. Together these two great changes completely altered the basis of politics in the northern commercial state. New social groups appeared: old groups assumed a new prominence. The representative system opened a way of political action to the completely new class of agricultural frontiersmen in Upper Canada, as well as to the old and hitherto politically inactive group of French-Canadian farmers and professional men. And both groups, for reasons which had much in common, became politically opposed to the commercial class.

The dawn of democracy in the two provinces was appropriately greeted by electioneering, speeches, banquets and self-congratulation. In Upper Canada, D. W. Smith, the surveyor, was writing with energetic frequency to his friend John Askin, bespeaking advice and influence. "Should I be returned without an undue election or the appearance of party or bribery . . .", he wrote, "I beg an ox be roasted whole on the common, and a barrel of rum be given to the mob, to wash down the beef".[25] In Quebec city, in both the upper and lower town, there were banquets to celebrate the introduction of the representative system.[26] Veteran political campaigners like George Allsopp and Adam Lymburner sat down amicably to dinner with French Canadians in an atmosphere rarified with political idealism; and a toast to the disappearance of the odious distinction between old and new subjects was drunk with salvoes of applause, three times repeated. It was all very pleasant, reassuring and propitious. When the merchants contemplated the appointments to the new councils and the elections to the assemblies, they must have felt reasonably certain that at last they would begin to play a leading part in Canadian politics. One of their number, Adam Lymburner, had been made a member of the new executive council of Lower Canada. In Upper Canada, both Richard Cartwright and Robert Hamilton were members of the legislative council. And there was an impressive contingent of British-Canadian merchants to the first assembly in Lower Canada, for William Grant, James McGill, Joseph Frobisher and John Richardson, among others, had all secured seats. Lymburner, the Canadian agent at the time of the Constitutional Act, Grant, the erstwhile deputy receiver-general of the old province of Quebec, and Frobisher, the director of the North West Company, were all outstanding men in Canadian affairs; but the newcomer Richardson, who had arrived in Canada as late as 1787, was to excel them all in versatility of effort and solidity of achievement. He was a Scotsman, younger than most of his fellow parliamentarians, who had come to America in 1773 to join the firm of Phyn & Ellice at Schenectady. Like so many of his associates who abandoned the New York route during and after the American Revolution, he

came up to Canada; and in 1790, with his cousin, John Forsyth, he
founded the long-lived firm of Forsyth, Richardson & Company.
Honest, downright and intensely British, he combined a breadth
of interest and a readiness for experiment with his simple directness
of approach; and for forty years thereafter he was to live at the
very centre of all the affairs of the commercial state.

If, however, the merchants hoped to control and direct the new
forces in Canadian politics, they were very largely disappointed in
the event. The changes of the period profoundly altered the
position of the merchants in public affairs. It was not that they
became less "liberal" and more "conservative" in a political sense
at all: it was simply that the introduction of representative government and the changes in the northern economy made them new
political enemies and new friends. The feudal structure of society
in Canada had been completely undermined; a new social organism
had developed in which the merchants were clearly the dominating
economic and social group. In Canada, as everywhere else in the
English-speaking world, the new commercial middle class was
fighting its way upwards through society to a position of respectability and influence; and the British governors came slowly to
look upon the Canadian merchants, along with the churchmen,
professional men and landowners, as the pillars of society and the
natural support of government. The merchants, worried by a new
and powerful opposition from below, drew closer to the state which
every decade became more definitely commercial in spirit and
purpose. Slowly but in gradually increasing numbers they entered
the executive and legislative councils. In the days of the Quebec
Act they had seemed the defenders of popular rights; under the
new constitution they came to appear more and more like the
advocates of political privilege.

The most important feature of the new age was not, however,
the alliance between the merchants and the old governing class;
it was the growing antipathy between the merchants and the
small rural proprietors of both provinces. In Upper Canada, this
quarrel conformed in general to a type of political conflict which
was repeated regularly throughout the history of the Thirteen
Colonies and the United States. The whole capital equipment of
this pioneer agricultural community was in the hands of the

commercial class. The merchants owned the private vessels on the lakes and the *bateaux*, scows and Durham boats which plied between Kingston and Montreal. They controlled the marketing of wheat and flour. The shops, mills, distilleries and tan-yards were in their possession. It was a monopoly of economic power; it excited the customary opposition. But merchants and farmers in Upper Canada did not differ profoundly in their views of society and its proper organization. They both accepted the commercial organization of their economy and they looked forward with the same eager anxiety to a common prospect of material development. When they quarrelled, it was over the partition of the financial burden, the division of economic power and the distribution of the dividends of their labours. They fought over the tariff, the incidence of taxation, the expenditure of government money and governmental control of industry, commerce and banking.

In Lower Canada, the political struggle grew out of a deeper and more passionate social conflict. In the lower as in the upper province, there was, of course, the same division between the merchants and the farmers; but the dispute between the two groups was intensified by the lingering survival of the semi-feudal institutions of New France. The merchants were now its open opponents and the French Canadians became its last apologists. Their quarrel was more than a quarrel between two social groups within a single commercial economy; it was a struggle between commercialism represented aggressively by the merchants and a decadent semi-feudal society defended by peasants and professional men. The growth of the new agricultural economy, the rise of the new staple trades was slowly forcing the merchants to revise their old inadequate fur-trading business system. As they grasped eagerly after the new commercial opportunities which grew out of the economic revolution in the region of the lower lakes, they were caught and held in an almost unyielding tangle of laws, customs, habits and prejudices. The seigneurs were unable and the British governing class unwilling to defend the old system as they had done in the days of Carleton and Haldimand. But the Constitutional Act enrolled the scores of thousands of French Canadians in a last prolonged defence. Aloof, dogged and apprehensive, the French Canadians came to cling to the old ways of life both from conviction and from policy. Professional men, small tradesmen and farmers, who for generations had been accustomed to production for subsistence, they were distrustful of the ambitious programme of the commercial group. Like the farmers of Upper Canada, they preferred, in practice, to spend money on roads, bridges and locally useful public works; and, unlike the Upper Canadians, they were opposed in principle to rapid and intensive exploitation, to a greedy dissipation of lands and resources, which, in their opinion, ought to be conserved as the rightful inheritance of unborn generations of French Canadians. They wished to save their patrimony for the society of the future; and they soon came to realize that the laws and customs of their forefathers were the best protection against the domination of an acquisitive, speculative and alien race.

In Lower Canada, the opening of the parliamentary régime was attended by unexpected incidents which amazed and disgusted the commercial class. When in the past they had urged an assembly, the merchants had evidently entertained the expectation, or the hope, that they would guide the first faltering footsteps of the French Canadians in political democracy. Hugh Finlay, the astute postmaster-general, had always been sceptical of this comforting delusion; and it was completely exploded in the first session of the first parliament of Lower Canada. The French Canadians evidently arrived in a mood of suspicion, for there was a rumour about that Chief Justice William Smith and William Grant were a self-designated team of directors for the management of parliamentary business.[27] John Richardson, on the other hand, felt justified in asserting that "the session commenced with a determined spirit of Party amongst the French members".[28] The commercial group nominated James McGill and William Grant as its chief candidates for the speaker's chair; but while there were eighteen members who voted for the English nominees, there were twenty-eight French Canadians who preferred Jean Antoine Panet. The quorum was first set at 34—a number deliberately chosen, the English merchants insisted, to prevent their own triumph in a poorly attended house. "Everything is settled out of the House", wrote Richardson, "they come down with matters the most absurd, cut and dry. . . ." By one of the early rules of procedure, adopted in the face of the indignant opposition of the merchants and subsequently abandoned due to official disapproval, the French language would have been the enacting language for all legislation concerning property and civil rights.

"Nothing can be so irksome as the situation of the English members—", wrote Richardson, "without numbers to do any good—doomed to the necessity of combating the absurdities of the majority, without hope of success. . . ." This irritated feeling of political impotence, this disillusionment which grew mightily out of the successive frustration of so many hopes, must have become common to all the merchants during the first decade of representative government in Lower Canada. The commercial class was either unable or unwilling to elect as numerous and as capable a delegation to the later parliaments as it had to the first. The great scheme of reform which the merchants had developed before the Constitutional Act was shelved indefinitely in a mood of angry renunciation. The seigniorial system of land tenure continued unaltered. The new revenues were derived, not from taxes on land, but from duties on commerce. The organization of the courts was indeed thoroughly reformed;[29] but there was no fundamental change in the laws themselves and the legal compromise, won with difficulty as the old province of Quebec neared its end, was continued. The merchants seemed bewildered and numbed with disappointment. There was only an occasional utterance of those demands which in a few years became so insistent and imperative under the pressure of the economic revolution. In 1792, Phyn, Ellice & Inglis, Todd, McGill & Company and Forsyth, Richardson & Company concluded an abortive agreement for the establishment of a Canadian bank.[30] In the assembly of 1796 John Richardson introduced a bill for the construction of a Lachine canal and another for the building of a turnpike road from Montreal to Lachine.[31] But these premature proposals were dropped, in part because of a general lack of interest and in part because of inadequate and spasmodic support. The failure of the assembly, for which they had fought so long and upon which they had built so many hopes, left the merchants without any policy or any political enthusiasm. The economic changes in the region of the lower lakes had not yet proceeded so far as to convince them of the imperative necessity of immediate reconstruction. They could still afford to prepare half-heartedly for a future in which they would be compelled to act. Their vague general disgust for the system of the Constitutional Act had not yet been embodied, as it was soon to be, in a revolutionary programme; and the commercial class as a political force in provincial politics was at its weakest in the first decade of the history of Lower Canada.

In Upper Canada, the merchants and the governing class won a victory which was of considerable importance for the whole northern commercial system. It was essential that the Canadian provinces should remain a free-trade area despite the political division of 1791; and, although in Lower Canada the merchants had accepted customs duties for revenue as inevitable, the traders in the upper province were determined to resist this form of taxation. In the first two sessions of the provincial legislature, the Upper Canadian assembly, which was the political preserve of the farmers, passed legislation establishing a small duty upon all wines and spirits imported into the colony; and on both occasions the legislative council threw the bill out.[32] The assembly opposed a land tax as a burden on their own industry and as a check to immigration; but in the end they were powerless against Canadian geography and the commercial system based upon it. The great bulk of the liquors entering the province came up the St. Lawrence from overseas. It was evident that Lower Canada would lay duties upon these goods in the first place; and the imposition of another tariff by Upper Canada would duplicate machinery, embarrass trade and create misunderstandings and disputes between the two colonies. In the end these arguments prevailed. Upper Canada abandoned the idea of levying duties upon imports from the lower province and instead established a land tax.[33]

It was an important decision. In the interest of the unity of the northern commercial state, Upper Canada virtually gave up a part of its sovereignty; and Lower Canada, so far as trade on the Atlantic was concerned, was granted the approximation of federal power. This renunciation of Upper Canada's could not, of course, go uncompensated. It was generally agreed that of the total of duties collected at the port of Quebec there should be granted to Upper Canada a percentage corresponding to the proportion of the dutiable articles which she consumed. But it was one thing to admit the general principle of division and another to settle upon some method of determining the exact amounts. In the winter of 1795, when commissioners from the two provinces met first to consider the question, it was agreed that population was the "most eligible if not the most equitable" method of establishing a ratio, and that until the end of December, 1796, Upper Canada was to receive one-eighth of the net proceeds of the duties collected at the port of Quebec.[34]

This agreement, which was based upon the idea that Upper Canada would obtain all its supplies of the dutiable articles from the lower province, came to an end when the commissioners from the two provinces met again in the winter of 1797. In the meantime the Grenville-Jay Treaty had permitted a general inland commerce between Upper and Lower Canada on the one hand and the United States on the other. It was uncertain how far the upper province would make use of this alternative source of supply. Population was apparently no longer valid as a basis for the division of the customs revenue; and with some reluctance and misgiving the commissioners of both provinces agreed that an inspector should be established at Coteau du Lac, for the purpose of receiving accounts of all the dutiable articles passing from the lower into the upper province, with the exception of Indian goods which were simply in transit westward by the Ottawa river.[35] In order that the Americans might not obtain an unfair advantage in this market, the Upper Canadians consented to levy upon imports from the United States duties equivalent to those imposed upon the same articles by Lower Canada. It was this clause, clause 6, which led to the refusal of Upper Canada to ratify the provisional agreement of January 28, 1797. There were, as we shall see, good reasons for this refusal—reasons which were duly appreciated by the merchants of Lower Canada. For a short time the upper province was permitted to ratify the provisional agreement with a condition suspending the operation of clause 6.[36] But in the winter of 1801, when the provinces met once more in conference, it was decided that all the terms of the agreement of January, 1797, would henceforth be considered as binding and that the agreement itself was to continue for another four years.[37] Thus the financial disputes, which Lymburner had prophesied, were settled for the time being; but they were to arise again, and in an uglier fashion, in the not far distant future. Gradually, as the economic revolution proceeded, it became obvious how impossible it was to adjust the commercial state to the Constitutional Act, to maintain the unity of the St. Lawrence despite the political division of 1791 and to combine two provinces in a common defence of the northern commercial system.

III

The growth of settlement in the region of the lower lakes was appropriately accompanied by two events which seemed to symbolize the inevitable decline of the south-west fur trade. These events were the defeat of the Indians at the battle of Fallen Timbers and the British surrender of the western posts.

In 1792 western affairs entered upon the last brief crisis which was to precede a final settlement. The Indians had beaten the first American armies sent against them; and British policy, encouraged by this struggle and by the representations of Indians, fur traders and officials which accompanied it, moved out of the enigmatic reserve which had been its distinguishing characteristic ever since the peace of 1783. George Hammond was sent over as the first British minister plenipotentiary to the United States. He was still a young man, for he had been barely twenty when he had worked in Paris as David Hartley's secretary during the peace negotiations; and he came over with a policy in western affairs which was soon made more definite by instructions sent to him in the spring of 1792. Up to this point the British had merely seemed unwilling to carry out the old treaty. Now they were suddenly eager to negotiate a new settlement. They came forward modestly as peace makers. They would meditate between the quarrelling Indians and Americans. They would remove the cause of dissension by establishing, on the American side of the boundary of 1783, a neutral Indian reserve from which the settlers of the United States and Canada would both be barred.[38]

The project of the Indian barrier state assumed formidable proportions. The Montreal fur traders in their memorial to Simcoe in December, 1791, had put forward the old line of the Quebec

Act as their first choice for a revised boundary. The Indians had asked Dorchester to secure for them the line of the Ohio and the Muskingum. But the neutral Indian barrier state, as it was finally described in instructions to Hammond, was to extend the whole length of the frontier between British North America and the United States. Those individuals and groups whose collective opinion made up the body of British policy, were certainly solicitous of the Indians and apprehensive of their resentment. They were concerned for the security of Upper Canada and for British supremacy on the lakes. But these were merely the political aspects of that western imperialism which had been, from the very beginning, the deepest purpose of the northern commercial state. Geography and commerce were the basis of this imperialism, for the river system had made western dominion possible and the fur traders had first realized it. The neutral Indian state, which for all practical purposes would probably have become a British protectorate, was a typical adventure of commercial imperialism. It was the last rearguard action fought by the British to undo the Treaty of 1783 and to preserve the old unity of the St. Lawrence.

In the new diplomatic campaign, the merchants played an active, but clearly a very subordinate part. In the summer of 1791, before the defeat of the American general St. Clair, they wrote to the Indian superintendent, Sir John Johnson, begging him to use all his influence to induce the Indians to listen to peace and to secure for them a suitable boundary.[39] In December, 1791, and in April, 1792, they sent two long letters to Simcoe in which their whole case and their proposals for all contingencies were set forward.[40] "A new line of demarcation", they urged, was absolutely necessary. They suggested a number of different boundaries, in order of diminishing acceptability; and they assured Simcoe that they could not "sufficiently express the importance and propriety that we conceive are attached to the disputing the ground by negotiation, inch by inch. . . ". If all failed and the posts in despite of everything were transferred to the United States, they suggested that a "neutral reciprocity" on both sides of the border would still leave Canada considerable advantage in the trade. As usual the merchants employed what influence they had in London to the best of their ability. In March, 1792, when the project of the

Indian barrier state was being formulated in instructions to Hammond, William Robertson and Isaac Todd had several conversations with Dundas's secretary and came away cheered by the conviction that there did not seem to be any disposition to hand over the posts as yet.[41]

Although the Canadian capitalists flattered him to the best of their ability, Simcoe was not particularly friendly to merchants in general or to fur traders in particular. "The assertions of merchants . . .", he wrote, "are always to be received with great caution." But Simcoe was a born imperialist, ambitious, aggressive, truculent, with a strong bias against Americans in their corporate political capacity. The western fur trade, like so many similar commercial ventures in America, Asia and Africa, had been slowly ennobled by its political implications. It involved the conquest of territory; it implied the extension of empire; and its defence became a dignified object, worthy of the best attention of soldiers and gentlemen. Simcoe sent Captain Stevenson off to Philadelphia with the first memorial of the merchants and a map which they had drawn to accompany it.[42] He dispatched both memorials to London, with a letter in which he commended the merchants' analysis of British commercial interests in the west. And Dorchester favoured the Indian barrier state as the most acceptable alternative to British occupation of the territory.[43] The merchants, in fact, had done all that it was possible for them to do. Their case, drafted fairly cleverly and at length, was received and circulated by officialdom.

When Hammond first tentatively broached it, the project of British mediation between the Indians and the United States was received with cold disfavour at Philadelphia. At the end of September, 1792, the Indians, meeting again in general council, made that "unsolicited and voluntary" request for British mediation which Hammond had indicated might be of service; and the British minister renewed his proposal. But the Americans preferred to do their own negotiating with people who were, however ambiguously, their own subjects. A commission was appointed to negotiate with the Indians; and its three members, Messrs. Lincoln, Randolph and Pickering, disappeared into the wilderness and arrived eventually at Governor Simcoe's headquarters at Niagara. The British authorities, who were the only authorities on the spot, took complete charge of what was ostensibly a conference between two groups of American citizens on American soil. They arranged the meeting; they coached the Indians; they conducted the inexperienced commissioners. But in spite of all the advice of the British and the urgings of the Iroquois, the western Indians insisted upon the old boundary of 1768 which was much more than they had demanded a little while earlier in 1791. The American commissioners, who had no power to discuss such demands, at length unwillingly departed; and the last struggle for the old political unity of the St. Lawrence was at hand.[44]

In the autumn of 1793, General Wayne—"Mad Anthony" Wayne—began to advance northward from the Ohio. Up in Canada they were only too ready to believe that his advance was in fact a movement against the western posts and in form only a punitive expedition against the Indians. In February, 1794, Dorchester delivered his bellicose address to the Indians and a few days later he took Simcoe's advice and ordered the fortification and reoccupation of the "Old Miamis" fort on the Maumee river. Wayne's army started north from Fort Recovery in July, 1794. He reached the Maumee, travelled down it towards Lake Erie and at the foot of the rapids, only a few miles from the old Miamis fort, he came in contact with the Indians. The river was flanked here by low, swampy prairie, where the thick, tangled grass grew breast high, and by woods through which a tornado had rushed, tearing up the great trees and flinging them together in dense confusion. Behind these fallen timbers the Indians were waiting for their foes. But the position was outflanked by the mounted American volunteers; Wayne's infantry went in through the timbers with the bayonet; and down at old Miamis fort, where Colonel Campbell commanded, they could hear the firing slacken and cease as the Indians faded away in defeat. It was a tense, anxious moment for Campbell and his garrison. Wayne's army in its thousands practically closed in around the fort. The two commanders entered upon a brief correspondence, in which accusations, reprimands, boasts and defiances were exchanged in a spirit of dignified, manly valour.[45] But Wayne, having devastated the surrounding countryside, departed; and Campbell was left in possession, a little weak with anxiety and supremely happy with relief.

In 1794, Great Britain and the United States were perilously close to conflict, but they came together in a sober discussion, despite disputes not unlike those which set them at war in 1812. The Treaty of 1783 was an imperfect instrument imperfectly executed by both contracting powers. The British navigation acts, which had ruined the basic free-trade principles of the treaty, continued to restrict American commerce, particularly in the West Indies. And new disputes concerning the rights of neutral shipping had arisen between the two countries since Great Britain, in 1793, had declared war upon the first French Republic. In the spring of 1794, the American congress was making war by the approved methods of oratory, warlike resolutions and discriminating legislation, when the Federalists secured a great triumph and the reputed Anglophil, John Jay, departed for England as a special envoy. In England, Grenville was worried with the French war, with the evident disintegration of the First Coalition and with the unpleasant prospect of the armed neutrality of the north. In 1794 Great Britain could have fought a more successful war in North America than she fought in 1812; but as always, in every crisis in the relations of Great Britain and the United States which arose between 1778 and 1812, France appeared with exact and exasperating punctuality to divide British interests and weaken her demands. Both sides had no stomach for war; and in November, 1794, they signed the treaty of amity, commerce and navigation which is generally known by the name of the American gentleman who was received with disapproval at home for having signed it.

Jay's Treaty, as its formal title implies, was a commercial treaty.[46] It was entirely logical that the problem of the west, which was at bottom an affair of commercial imperialism, should be settled by a trade agreement. Although the British may have been apprehensive of Indian resentment and although they did not completely give up the idea of the barrier state, they let the Indians down with more thoroughness and less ceremony in 1794 than they had in 1783. The western posts were surrendered to the United States not in return for territorial concessions to the

Indians but in return for commercial concessions to the merchants of London and Montreal. By the treaty the traders obtained, what they had always requested, a period of nearly two years in which to wind up their affairs and withdraw their stocks from the American side if they desired. The treaty gave them that "neutral reciprocity of trade" which, as they had admitted to Simcoe, would still leave them great competitive strength in western commerce. The two nations granted to each other's nationals the right to pass freely over the border and to make free use of the lakes, rivers and carrying-places on both sides of the boundary for commercial purposes. And these privileges were precisely the privileges which the merchants had years ago demanded of Oswald and which they had insisted ever since were the irreducible, minimum payment in return for the surrender of the posts.

All this was gratifying. But there were other clauses in Jay's treaty which pleased the Canadian merchants less. Great Britain granted to American shipping free entry into the ports of the British East Indies and a limited entry into the market of the West Indies as well. Article 12. which dealt with the West Indies trade, was indeed suspended by the American senate; but article 13 was ratified and Montreal was soon to discover, to its intense annoyance, how effectively the Americans could compete in the marketing of East India goods. Worse still, there was no change whatever in the boundary between Canada and the United States. The fur traders had always insisted that the boundary beyond the Lake of the Woods must be pushed to the south, in order to give Canada an entrance to the Mississippi; for otherwise the right of free navigation, granted by the Treaty of 1783, would be a meaningless form of words. Grenville made the most of this argument; but all he was able to obtain was embodied in article 4 of the treaty which provided for a joint survey of the region and a deferred settlement by amicable negotiation. The political unity of the St. Lawrence was definitely at an end. Even the economic unity which the merchants had hoped to erect on the ruins of their political dominion, could never be completely realized now. The Americans agreed to levy no higher duties upon imports from Canada than would be payable on the same goods when imported in American vessels into the Atlantic ports of the United States.

But even this dissatisfied the Canadians, for they were obliged to make a similar concession to the United States; and it was annoying to be compelled to admit American goods into Upper Canada at the same low rates of duty which were applied to importations from Europe *via* the St. Lawrence. Above all, the mere application of duties, high or low, destroyed the old free-trade area of the west; and the new boundary had become a tariff barrier as well as a definitive political division.

In June, 1796, according to the terms of the treaty, the red-coats marched out from the frontier posts. It was the second surrender, for in the previous summer General Wayne had imposed the Treaty of Greenville upon the Indians and they had given up their rights to nearly two-thirds of the present state of Ohio. The Indians had been beaten in battle, and the British had been worsted in diplomacy; and under these two blows the old Canadian dominion collapsed in fragments. It might have seemed as if the very conception of the political unity of the St. Lawrence had been damaged beyond hope of revival. But the idea of the Indian barrier state, that modest, self-effacing brother of western imperialism, reappeared at intervals to haunt the minds of British statesmen like a wraith. And the Canadian merchants continued to hope for the resurrection of the old policy of western empire with the persistent fanaticism of a religious sect.

IV

In the meantime there was still, there was always, trade. Jay's Treaty and the Treaty of Greenville were essentially victories of settlement over the fur trade. Their effect on the commerce in the new staples was uncertain; but they seemed clearly to portend the eventual decline of the fur trade south of the lakes. A mere fifteen years ago, the trade of the north-west had been a novel and comparatively unimportant part of Canadian business, conducted by scarcely more than half a dozen traders. But, in the last years of the eighteenth century, with growing returns and with the rush of new firms into the region, it began, dimly but unmistakably, to take on the aspect of *the* Canadian trade. Frobisher and McTavish, who had hammered out the capital structure of their business by 1790, enjoyed only a few years' monopoly in the north, when their territory was suddenly invaded by successful firms of great strength and long experience in the south-west trade. The south-west trade, of course, was far from dead. For the first few years after 1796, it had, as we shall see, few evidences of dying. But it was obvious also that it was not destined to immortality. Jay's Treaty, the defeat of the Indians and the rush of settlers into the Ohio country were portents which no prudent man could ignore. The Montreal firms, Parker, Gerrard & Ogilvy, and Forsyth, Richardson & Company, as well as the Detroit firm of Leith, Jamieson & Company did not withdraw from the south-west trade, in which before they had been largely engaged. But, in combination with John Mure of Quebec and Sir Alexander Mackenzie, they formed the "XY Company" or New North West Company and frankly invaded the territory west of Grand Portage. There followed a conflict which differed only in duration and in the strength of the combatants, from the previous quarrels in the Saskatchewan and Athabaska districts. The first result of Jay's Treaty was thus a renewal of competition in the north-west. But this very competition foreshadowed the gradual shift north-westward of the Canadian fur trade under political and social pressure from the American side of the line. And, as it increased in numbers, the list of merchants engaged in the north-west trade began to look like a census return of the commercial population of Montreal.

In 1796, however, when the posts were surrendered, trade with the Indians south of the lakes continued undiminished and trade in the new staples showed a promising growth. Canadians hoped to keep the first and to gain the second. The western free-trade area, though Jay's Treaty had pronounced its certain end, remained in existence for a few years more. The United States established no customs houses upon its north-western boundary until 1799. The ordinances of the old province of Quebec, which regulated inland trade with the United States, remained in force in Upper and Lower Canada until they were expressly altered or repealed; but in fact, so long as the posts remained in British control, Upper Canada made no attempt to enforce these trade regulations and St. Johns, in Lower Canada, remained the sole legal port of entry.

Jay's Treaty and the surrender of the posts obviously created an entirely new situation. By an order-in-council of July, 1796, Lower Canada suspended the old ordinances regulating trade with the United States, declared the province open to American commerce by land or inland navigation and levied upon American imports the same duties as were payable by British subjects on importations into Canada from Europe.[47] Upper Canada, however, did not immediately follow this example. At the interprovincial conference of January, 1797, which was called to decide what proportion of the duties collected at Quebec was to be awarded Upper Canada, it was indeed agreed that Upper Canada would levy upon imports from the United States duties equivalent to those imposed by the lower province.[48] As we have seen, it was this clause, clause 6, which decided Upper Canada to reject the provisional agreement. The old trade ordinances were suspended, as they had been in Lower Canada, by proclamation; but there was no move made to set up customs houses and to enforce the collection of the Atlantic duties at the international boundary between Upper Canada and the United States.

Apparently the Upper Canadians were appalled by the mere physical difficulties of collecting duties along the thousand miles of open lake and forest which formed their frontier. But there was another and a deeper reason for their reluctance to accept the provisional agreement with Lower Canada and to establish a tariff on American imports. It was not Canada's part to begin the partition of the old economic unity of the west. It would be absurd for the upper province, by its own example, to induce the tardy Americans to take advantage of their treaty rights and to levy their Atlantic duties upon the north-western boundary. The trade in dutiable articles, in manufactures, fire-arms, spirits and wine was chiefly from Upper Canada into the United States; while the trade from the United States into Upper Canada was mainly in those raw products which, so long as Canada clung to the old doctrines of the northern commercial state, it would never tax at all. "Could the United States enforce the collection of their Atlantic duties on our inland commerce with them", wrote Cartwright, "they must necessarily operate as a bounty to take the trade from us and turn it into their own channels; or at best we should have to pay a pound where we could collect a penny."[49] Arguments such as these convinced the commissioners of Lower Canada. The upper province was permitted to postpone the establishment of a tariff; and the free-trade area of the west remained undisturbed for a while longer. But everybody knew that the unexpected and pleasing delay of the United States could not continue for ever. It had ended when the commissioners of both provinces met again in the winter of 1801 to renew their provisional agreement; and Upper Canada consented to implement clause 6 immediately. Eleven ports of entry were established. Duties similar to those imposed in Lower Canada were laid on American imports.[50] But, in fact, the Canadian tariff bore chiefly upon wines, liquors, sugar, tea, coffee and tobacco: and, as in the past, the two provinces remained open to the free importation of the raw products of the United States.

In fact, Montreal continued to dominate its old commercial dominion for a few years longer, despite Jay's Treaty, despite the surrender of the posts, despite even the imposition of the new tariff barriers. The prodigious diplomatic ability and the military strength of the Americans were contradicted by their curious commercial feebleness in the west. Evidently they had hoped that the provisions of Jay's Treaty would give them a chance to compete effectively with the Canadians in the western fur trade; but they did not venture north of the new boundary after 1796 and even the trade of their own territory was still exasperatingly withheld from them. John Jacob Astor was potentially the greatest American competitor in the trade; and for John Jacob Astor the chief immediate result of Jay's Treaty was that it permitted him to come north to Montreal and to buy from the Canadian traders furs which were very likely to have been secured on the American side of the line.[51] The south-west fur trade increased rather than diminished for the first years after Jay's Treaty; and Robert Hamilton estimated that in 1797 over 43,000 gallons of liquor and over £52,000 worth of manufactures had been carried down the Niagara portage and consigned to the merchants at Detroit on the American side of the line.[52] As we have seen, the Canadians were selling food-stuffs to the American garrisons and settlements in the first few years after the transfer of the posts. With the exception of some transient pedlars, American merchants had made no attempt whatever to enter the Canadián market; and Cartwright, who was probably the most important wholesaler and retailer in the upper province, reported in 1801 that he had never purchased any supplies from the United States.[53]

Those who believed in the future of the Canadian economy never doubted, despite all the reverses of the past years, that the St. Lawrence would remain the great channel for the developing commerce of the new west. "Sooner or later", wrote Simcoe, "those who shall settle on any of the Waters which flow into Lake Erie and Huron will find it advantageous to resort to Upper Canada as the Mart for British Manufactures, rather than to the Atlantic States."[54] There was hope, eager anticipation and almost unqualified assurance. But at the same time it was recognized that the new boundary, the opening of trade between Canada and the United States, the progress of settlement and the rise of the new staple trades had imposed upon the St. Lawrence a far greater burden than it had ever borne in the old fur-trading days. It is highly significant, therefore, that in the first few years after Jay's Treaty, both business men and politicians began to take a new interest in the Canadian canals.

The existing little canals, which had been completed in 1783 by Captain Twiss, had not been repaired for some time. This was a first and reasonable excuse for their reconstruction and enlargement. The unit of river transportation was changing as well. The boats were larger than they had been and the merchants were anxious to enlarge them still further. In 1801, Thomas Clark of Niagara travelled down the St. Lawrence from Kingston in a "Kentucky boat" which carried 340 barrels of flour.[55] In addition, the number of boats was increasing and the tolls taken on the canals in 1799 amounted to double those of 1795.[56] Plainly the route was defective and inadequate; and the prospect of renewed competition from the south increased the concern of the Canadian merchants for the weaknesses of their transport system. Jay's Treaty, as the London merchant Brickwood pointed out in a letter to John King, had in effect opened for Upper Canada another route to the sea beside the St. Lawrence.[57] This route was, of course, the historic competitive channel through the state of

New York. "Mercantile Competition", wrote Brickwood, "will now most probably place these two Communications with the Sea, more strongly in opposition to each other. The question will be by which Rout can the necessary supplies be brought up, or the superabundant Produce carried down, *on the best terms*, from these extensive Countries bounding the sides of the great Lakes." So long as the New York route remained unimproved, Cartwright considered it of no importance under the new conditions; but there was every prospect that New York would try to increase the competitive strength of its transportation system and the Canadian merchants watched their competitors from the south with a continued, suspicious scrutiny. In 1795, Brickwood reported that the Americans were improving their inland navigation by the Mohawk and in 1801 Sir Alexander Mackenzie communicated in some excitement the news that the New Yorkers were projecting a canal from Albany to Lake Ontario.[58] Both merchants argued that Canada could only meet this threat by means of a vastly enlarged system of canals. The engineer Gother Mann did indeed propose a series of improvements in the St. Lawrence; but the expense of the undertaking and the unlikelihood of repayment through tolls were strong deterrents which persuaded the British government to drop the scheme. The old canals remained, growing ever more antiquated and inadequate, as the changes of the period were accumulating. The problem of the northern transportation system, raised at the very beginning of the new century by the growth of the new staple trades, continued as one of the major problems of the commercial class for the next fifty years.

CHAPTER VI

THE CLASH WITH THE FRENCH CANADIANS

I

THE Canadian economic revolution, which had begun with the peace of 1783 and the coming of the Loyalists, reached and passed its half-way mark in the first decade of the nineteenth century. It was no longer possible to deny the changes which had taken place or to evade their implications. The new boundary, cutting across the old dominion of the St. Lawrence, was an established fact. The settlers had nearly encircled the lower lakes. Indian culture was failing in a last, losing struggle with the white invasion and the Canadian fur trade was in retreat north-westward towards the prairies. The society based on settlement and the new staple trades was no longer a dream or a hypothesis. It was a fact. Something definitive had taken root. It was growing slowly, but with purpose, with a kind of stubborn tenacity. It was visibly creating a new way of life in the Canadian commercial state. Unsettled problems were accumulating; basic contradictions remained unresolved. And the confidence which had survived even the Treaty of 1783 and the surrender of the posts began to be coloured by doubts and questionings. As Great Britain and the United States drew closer to the War of 1812, the sense of difficulty, of frustration, even of defeat, became ominously stronger.

In default of government statistics, observers estimated in the first decade of the new century that the population of the two Canadas was approximately 300,000.[1] Of these some sixty to eighty thousand lived in the upper province. The settlements straggled in a thin but practically unbroken line up the river and around Lake Ontario to Niagara. In Upper Canada the gaps left on the lake shore by the first Loyalists had been largely filled up; and in both provinces there were a few more distant and adventurous settlements. The frontier community in the Eastern Townships of Lower Canada was growing slowly. In the upper province settlement was pushing up Yonge Street on its way to Lake Simcoe; and westward, on the shore of Lake Erie, the first pioneers had established themselves at Long Point and Colonel Talbot had founded his little community in Norfolk county. The forest still broke, in wave after wave of green, over the greater part of the new province; but little by little, as the settlers cleared and sowed and tidied, the countryside began to take on something of that look of comfort and security that comes of human occupation. Down within reach of the lake, where ran the first row of townships, the wheat fields in the depth of summer ripened quickly under kindly skies where a few placid clouds pursued their indolent evolutions. Rough carts jolted over the execrable tracks and the white dust puffed and slowly subsided. In Cornwall (New Johnstown), Elizabethtown, Gananoque and Port Hope and in the other villages which were forming on the north shore of the lake, there was a little stir of life before the mills, the shops and the tanneries. Even at night, when the forest seemed to creep back upon the field whence it had been driven, there were yellow lights among the maple trees and voices unintimidated by the silence. Quebec and Montreal were growing towns, with possibly twelve thousand people each. At York, "persons who have formerly travelled in this part of the country, are impressed with sentiments of wonder, on beholding a town which may be termed handsome, reared as if by enchantment, in the midst of a wilderness".[2]

Under the pressure of this new agricultural community, the business organization of the country was changing. There was a slight, perceptible quickening of energy along the banks of the St. Lawrence. The life of the great river and its lakes was becoming fuller and more varied; and the traffic up and down the stream achieved a more regular and rapid beat. The canoe, by this time, had almost disappeared from the St. Lawrence system; and even the *bateau*, a small flat-bottomed boat carrying two to four tons of freight, was now supplemented by other and superior modes of water transport. The number of commercial sloops and schooners on the Great Lakes had greatly increased in the last two decades. The Durham boat, a large nearly flat-bottomed scow which carried from five to ten times the average freight of the *bateau*, was used more and more on the journeys up and down the river;[3] and the timber raft, guided by long sweeps and loaded with barrels of flour, was becoming a familiar sight. In 1809, the first steamboat on the river, John Molson's *Accommodation*, laboriously chugged its way down the St. Lawrence from Montreal to Quebec; and in 1813 Molson's new vessel, the *Swiftsure*, began making regular trips between the two chief Canadian towns.[4] By all these means of transport, the produce of the new Canadian community—squared timber, boards, staves, headings, potash, wheat, flour, biscuit and salted beef and pork—was floated down the river of Canada and dumped into the warehouses of Quebec and Montreal. It was estimated that in 1802 Canada exported 28,200 barrels of flour and 1,010,033 bushels of wheat.[5] This was so far the greatest export in the history of the country; and though it was not soon repeated, wheat was probably the most important of the new staples until the abrupt and dramatic rise of the timber trade.

The commercial class itself had altered. Its personnel was changing rapidly, as was inevitable, and as the old men died or crept away into retirement they carried with them that old-fashioned, almost heroic quality which had distinguished Canadian business in the past. The change was slow and almost unnoticed. The old society of the fur trade, the company of merchant adventurers whose simple code was made up of the virtues of bravery, enterprise, endurance and hospitality, appeared to be at the height of its career. "The North-west merchants", wrote one visitor to Quebec and Montreal, "live in a superior style to the rest of the inhabitants, and keep very expensive tables. They are friendly and hospitable to strangers who are introduced to them, and whom they entertain in a sumptuous manner."[6] The Beaver Club was more active than at any other period; and when John Jacob Astor came up to Montreal from New York in 1808, he was entertained in the good old style by Joseph Frobisher, William McGillivray and by the Beaver Club at Dillon's Tavern. One by one, however, the old-timers who had built up British-Canadian trade in the decades following the conquest, were dropping out from the round of dinners, dances and assemblies for which Montreal was famous in the winter. The survivors drew together in a little knot. They alone were acutely conscious of the changes and they watched them with the usual mixture of regret, bewilderment and resignation.

It was so long ago—nearly fifty years in 1809—that Alexander

Henry had listened to the French fur trader Leduc and had gone west to witness the horrors of Pontiac's rising. The old man wrote occasionally to his friend John Askin at Detroit; and his letters, brief and ill-composed, form one of the few personal valedictions of a disappearing generation. "your old friend Todd", he wrote on one occasion, "goes on in the same old way, complaining every morning, but a bottle of Mediera & a good dinner removes all his disorders. . . . Mr McGill is very well & Frobisher. there is only us four old friends alive, all the new North westards are a parcel of Boys and upstarts, who were not born in our time, and suposes they know much more of the Indian trade than any before them. . . . Montreal is much changed since your time. I meet twenty young men in the street in a day that I do not know."[7]

As the new young men crowded bewilderingly about them, the little group of veterans dwindled one by one. Isaac Todd died in 1819. Henry, the incredible old man who had lived through the entire rise and fall of the British fur trade from Montreal, lingered on until 1824. But William Grant, Nicholas Montour and James McGill all died within the first fifteen years of the new century. There was soon to be no occupant of Beaver Hall, for Joseph Frobisher, the last of the three fur-trading brothers, died in 1810. The great house which Simon McTavish had built at the foot of the mountain back of Montreal, stood empty. Its owner had been the commanding personality of the North West Company. When he died, in 1804, he was probably the richest man in Montreal. But McTavish, the "Marquis", as they sometimes called him, had the sentimentality as well as the astuteness of the Scotsman; and there were other things in his will beside the evidence of the wealth which he had amassed in the country of his adoption. Far back in Argyllshire lay the estate of Dunardarie, the seat of the chief of clan Tavish, which Simon, through some strong inner compulsion, had been moved to purchase; and in his will he tried to ensure that Dunardarie should pass intact from father to eldest son, and from the last McTavish to the McGillivrays or their descendants, who could succeed only if they assumed the name McTavish and bore the McTavish arms.[8] It was a curious will, suggestive of the clan and family spirit which had come to dominate the western trade, suggestive, too, of that mixture of qualities, that combination of simplicity and cunning, loyalty and acquisitiveness, emotionalism and ruthless energy, which had made the greatness of the vanishing generation of Nor' Westers.

In Montreal, Quebec, Kingston and York, a new commercial generation with new interests and different attitudes was assuming control. As Henry had gloomily noted, the change was already evident in the fur trade, for new men like the Gillespies and McGillivrays had taken over the direction once exercised by others. John Richardson, who had come to Canada as late as 1787, was already well on the way to becoming the dean of Canadian business. There were new commercial centres and new firms which dealt almost exclusively in the staples of farm and forest. In York, which had so recently become the capital of the upper province and still lagged behind Kingston, Niagara and Queenston in commercial importance, traders like William Allan began to build up a general importing and exporting business.[9] In 1800 the American, Philemon Wright, founded the settlement at Hull and a few years later he floated the first raft of squared timber down the Ottawa to Quebec.[10] At Quebec, which was to be the great Canadian centre for the trade in deals and squared timber, the "factors", or representatives of English importing houses, were opening branches in the first decade of the century.

Even Montreal, though still primarily a fur-trade city, was changed. There were more merchants there who had served only a brief apprenticeship in the fur trade and others who engaged directly in the commerce in the new staples without any previous fur-trade experience at all. In the first years of the nineteenth century, George Moffatt, who later managed one of the largest Montreal concerns trading with Upper Canada, was serving his apprenticeship in the firms of McTavish, McGillivrays & Company and Parker, Gerrard, Ogilvy & Company.[11] Horatio Gates came up from Vermont where he had gained his first experience in business, engaged in the trade in the new staples with the United States and eventually became one of the biggest exporters of agricultural produce in the old fur-trade city.[12] Down at the foot of St. Mary's current, below Montreal, John Molson in his plain homespun suit used to bargain with the farmers for their grain as they went to market past his brewery.

Undoubtedly, the country, its trade and its trading personnel had changed, were changing. But the revolution, which was transforming a fur-trading into an agricultural society, had not yet noticeably increased the size and consequence of the new economy which it had created. The new staple-producing dominion of the St. Lawrence existed; but its progress, after twenty years of plodding effort, was praiseworthy and unimpressive. A north temperate colony, producing staples which in many markets were unwanted and in others were better supplied by the competing American states, Canada had still to find its commercial justification within the British Empire, where lay its great chance of success. The corn laws still preserved the home market for the British agriculturalists. Through a variety of loopholes, American produce entered the British West Indies. And at home the fur trade, hostile to the last against settlement, pressed with the dead hand of the past against the effort of the colony. At the beginning of the century the agricultural community of the St. Lawrence had yet to find its place, to discover its real purpose and to gain its proper recognition. But to all these basic questions there came a sudden and apparently an amply satisfactory reply. By a combination of circumstances so fortunate as to appear to Canadians to have been directed by the guiding hand of a beneficent providence, the Canadian trade in timber was suddenly magnified out of all recognition by the necessities of imperial defence. And for a half century thereafter the trade from Quebec in deals and squared timber devastated the Canadian forests, whipped up Canadian business and populated the Canadian countryside with immigrants from the British isles.

The change came almost within a twelvemonth, in that hectic period when Napoleon overran Prussia, created the continental system and formed the alliance with Alexander.[13] Up to this time the colonies, though their export trade in wood had been encouraged by bounties and by free admittance into the British market, had never successfully competed with their Baltic rivals. The increase of duties on foreign timber during the Revolutionary and Napoleonic

Wars had at first no marked effect. In 1804 the duty on a load of foreign squared timber stood at twenty-five shillings; it had reached £1.7.2 in 1806. But St. Petersburg, Riga, Memel, Danzig and the ports of Sweden and Norway still monopolized the business, secure in their advantages of the short haul, cheap freight rates and long experience. Something more was needed and it came out of the storm which swept over central and eastern Europe in the wake of Napoleon. In 1806, from Berlin, the capital of his prostrate foe, the emperor proclaimed the continental blockade and closed the Prussian ports to English trade. In 1807 at Tilsit, Alexander and Napoleon staged the eminently theatrical performance of their first meeting on a raft moored half way across the river which divided an immense audience of two standing armies. The two emperors signed the Treaty of Tilsit; and that autumn Alexander joined the continental blockade. Sweden followed. And Denmark, furious with the British capture of her fleet at Copenhagen, blocked her own trade and that of her dependency, Norway. But the British fleet was built of Baltic timber; and the government realized with terror that this revered and venerable instrument of home defence and overseas expansion was endangered at the very moment when it was most vitally necessary.

The crisis, which lasted about two years, affirmed the wisdom of the old colonial system. The ancient mercantilist maxim "Ships, Colonies and Commerce" was clothed once more with the authority of a prophetic utterance. In rage and fear and desperation the British turned suddenly from the perfidious foreigners to the faithful colonies. The government took decisive action. It persuaded British merchants to do business in the Canadian market and it lavishly awarded contracts to cut timber in New Brunswick and Quebec. The Canadian timber trade sprang into being. It had been born of the war and the blockade; it was maintained and continued by all the devices of a reanimated and intransigent commercial imperialism. The preferential duties on foreign timber now became frankly protectionist. They were raised in 1810; in 1813 they reached the enormous height of £3.5.0 on a load of squared timber and £41.11.4 on a great hundred of deals. Canada, whose wood entered Great Britain free or nearly so, enjoyed a commanding preference. Just at the moment when action was most vitally necessary for Canada, the St. Lawrence and the British mercantile system combined to link the now expectant society of the Great Lakes with the rising industrial civilization of Great Britain.

For Canada this was the greatest single development of the years from 1800 to 1812. The timber trade, lifted almost overnight to a position of imperial importance, acted like a fresh and vigorous tide of energy in the social body of the St. Lawrence valley. Quebec was suddenly crowded with shipping. In 1807, 239 ships, with a tonnage of 42,293 were cleared. In 1810, the number of vessels had risen to 661, with a tonnage of 143,893. The timber and lumber exports soared upward. In 1807, Canada shipped 11,195 tons of oak timber, 3,333 tons of pine, 107,642 boards and planks and 1,783,890 staves and headings. In 1810 there were exported 33,798 tons of oak timber, 69,271 tons of pine, 312,423 boards and planks and 3,887,306 staves and headings.[14] Exports had jumped spectacularly upwards in every branch of the wood trade. The years 1810 and 1811 were the peak years, and thereafter, during the War of 1812, there was a steady decline.

Like the fur trade, the trade in deals and timber was rooted firmly in the geography and history of the country. Supplies were apparently inexhaustible. The river system of transportation was suited to the carriage of the buoyant softwood logs; and the commercial philosophy and system which had been elaborated to serve the fur trade could be transferred to support the commerce in the new staple. The Canadian commercial revolution increased in weight and consequence and perceptibly gathered speed. The timber trade, born of the war but continued by protection far into the nineteenth century, whipped up Canadian development, completed the great changes which had begun in 1783 and brought the strains upon the antiquated political structure of the St. Lawrence to the breaking-point.

II

It is, therefore, of considerable significance that, at this very point in the career of economic change, political controversies of deepened seriousness should break out in both the Canadian provinces.

In Upper Canada, the grievances of the small rural proprietors became unexpectedly articulate in the political agitation of a half a dozen disappointed men. Judge Thorpe, William Weekes, Joseph Willcocks, C. B. Wyatt and John Mills Jackson were a slightly raffish crew of mercurial adventurers and frustrated egoists; and their brief political protest was carried on in a spirit of tense theatricality and rhetorical exaggeration. Weekes, the first leader of the movement, was killed in a duel. Willcocks, who for some time lodged at the house of his patron, the wealthy ex-president of the province, Peter Russell, was a fortune hunter determined to exploit his opportunities. The mature Miss Russell was the obvious heiress of her unmarried brother; and Willcocks, who confided to his diary the sentimental reflection that "Beauty will not make the Pot boil", began to pay his addresses to the lady. The unsympathetic ex-president withdrew his patronage and terminated his hospitality. Willcocks found himself and his belongings in the street; and there was one more disappointed recruit for the cabal of opposition.[15] Robert Thorpe, who came to Upper Canada in 1805 as a judge in the court of king's bench, was yet another. Thorpe appears to have imagined that he was sent for the express purpose of conducting a kind of Domesday inquiry into the affairs of the province; and as he travelled about on assize he was accustomed to enliven the proceedings of his court with general observations on provincial politics.[16] These men did not emerge direct from the heart of agrarian discontent: they were a disappointed minority of the governing class. Willcocks was sheriff of York, Thorpe was a judge and Wyatt was surveyor-general. What they chiefly wanted was better government jobs or their old government jobs back again. In the main they were drawn together by a relish for controversy (Weekes, Willcocks and Thorpe were Irish), by desire for advancement and dislike for the unsympathetic local bureaucracy.

There was, however, something besides this in their agitation which reached its peak in the years 1806–1807. The group, particularly Thorpe, made a grandiloquent appeal to the small landowners and received a brief response. Thorpe may have been sincere and he may merely have attempted to invest his personal grievance with a kind of spurious social significance; but despite his incoherence, exaggeration and conceit, he showed a fairly shrewd sense of the deeper social conflicts in the province. His own interest, of course, dominated. Like many lawyers of the time he advocated the establishment of a court of chancery in Upper Canada, in order that the common law system might be rounded out by jurisdiction in equity.[17] He argued that land held in free and common soccage was not subject to simple contract debt and that means should be provided for the foreclosure of mortgages. If he knew that the London forwarders and the Montreal merchants were arguing much the same way and reaching a somewhat similar conclusion,[18] he remained unaffected. He saw a job and wanted it. It was only when Thomas Scott became chief justice and seemed likely to become judge in chancery if that court were established, that Thorpe and John Mills Jackson became aware of the sinister social consequences of an establishment which Thorpe himself had advocated. Jackson claimed that "much mischief may arise from an injudicious execution of its proceedings".[19] According to Thorpe, Scott was the erstwhile lawyer and submissive creature of the merchants of Montreal; and if he were given the chancery "then the property of half the inhabitants will be sacrificed to the Merchants".[20]

In other matters, where his own interests were not involved, Thorpe sounded the appeal to agrarian discontent with a loud persistence. He took an active part in the founding of the agricultural society, though, to be sure, some of the more studiously proper bureaucrats were associated with him. His fatherly charges to rural grand juries became notorious. In December, 1806, he was returned to Weekes's seat in York, Durham and Simcoe with a large majority and among his supporters were the Steckleys, Hoovers, Hyses, Borkholders and other sober Mennonite farmers who settled Markham and Whitchurch townships. He pleaded that more money be spent on roads and less on the expensive provincial marine. With a vigour unrestrained by lack of evidence, he attacked the whole conduct of the land-granting department—the vast tracts granted to the governing class, the arbitrary manipulation of fees and the niggardly treatment of the virtuous Loyalists. He not only criticized the individual policies of the provincial government; for the first time almost in the history of the province, he described and derided its fundamental character and purpose. To him it was a commercial state, governed in their own interest by a shopkeeper aristocracy. "Add to this", he wrote in his usual incoherent, effusive style, "the exertion and oppression of the Shopkeeper Aristocracy who rule British North America with a rod of iron, a voracious set, who are linked from Newfoundland to the Mississippi, with great interest in England, & even protegés in power, every man on his arrival becomes their debtor, and lest he should ever get extricated, they make every effort to defeat any project that might bring forth the energies of the people, they are universally the Magistrates & enforce the demands of each other, they make every exertion to make any expence in England from being curtailed, because every disbursement passes through their hands and finally becomes their acquisition, the land & produce is at their mercy. . . ."[21]

At almost the same moment that Thorpe and his associates were attacking the storekeeper administration in Upper Canada, a quarrel had broken out in the lower province between the merchants and the French Canadians. Thirty years later, in analysing the conflict in Lower Canada Lord Durham declared that he found "a struggle, not of principles, but of races". Obviously, Lord Durham and the historians who have repeated his aphorism, used the word race in its most general connotation; and it is evident that the French and English in North America were separated not so much by ethnological distinctions which can be summed up in the word race as by historical differences which are compacted in the word nationality. Race, language, literature, religion, laws, customs, ideals, and memories of successes and tribulations endured in common, are the normal constituent elements of nationality. But despite the protestations of the French Canadians, then and since, it is questionable if many of these elements of their culture were seriously in question. Canada, and North America in general, have proved curiously tolerant of peoples of different races, languages and religions, so long as the peoples so distinguished have been ready to accept and uphold the somewhat materialistic American variant of West-European culture. But, on the other hand, Americans have crushed out relentlessly the distinctive institutions, customs and habits of thought which have impeded their aggressive exploitation of the new continent, and the erection of a great, uniform material civilization. It was, in the main, for this reason, that the British-Canadian minority attacked French-Canadian culture at the beginning of the nineteenth century. A new and different society was slowly thrusting its way upward to the light; and the merchants could not hope to realize the new commercial opportunities with the primitive instruments of the fur-trading state. In their minds it was essential that the social and political structure of the St. Lawrence should be partly scrapped and wholly revised.

When, however, they turned impatiently to the task of reorganization, they found to their dismay that the French Canadians did not cherish their objectives nor share their enthusiasm. The fur trade, in fact, was the first and possibly the last great continental enterprise in which the French ever actively participated. In the direction of the new staple trades, in the banks, land companies, canal companies, in all the commercial projects characteristic of the new Canadian economy, they took, if any, a definitely subordinate part. As the old generation of French-Canadian merchants and *bourgeois* died off, the society turned inward upon itself and poured its brains and energy into the professions, the church, the petty trades and agriculture. Sullen, suspicious and unresponsive, the French watched the development of the commercial programme with an apathy which deepened into hatred. They refused to co-operate in the necessary adjustments. As the pressure upon them mounted, they organized their own defence, employed their most stimulating slogans and appealed to their sacred minority rights. The two groups were divided in their economic interests; but they were also separated by different creeds, languages, customs and habits of thought. And each side grasped its own appropriate weapons in a quarrel which became one of the central tragedies of Canadian history.

A clash was inevitable and it came. The opening encounter was an appropriate prelude to decades of strife. In 1805 the commercial minority in the Lower Canadian assembly made several attempts—such as they had been making intermittently ever since the parliamentary régime started—to reform the feudal system. Caldwell introduced a bill to enable seigneurs to compound with their tenants for feudal dues;[22] and Ross Cuthbert spoke in favour of the abolition of the *retrait lignager* which was a usage of the Custom of Paris permitting any relation of the vendor to repurchase sold property for the selling price at any time within a year and a day of the sale.[23] It was not, however, the rejection of these measures—they were solidly voted down, of course—but the passage of the Gaols Bill which provoked the merchants to wrathful protest. At the suggestion of the governor, the assembly took up the question of building new gaols in the districts of Quebec and Montreal and decided upon their erection.

Where was the money to come from? It was upon this point that the assembly divided, not as Frenchmen against Englishmen, but as farmers and professional men against merchants. The farmers and professional men, who paid no direct taxes and who had simply gone on increasing the tariff as occasion demanded, saw no reason why they should not continue indefinitely to make the merchants and the western Indians pay for their local improvements. The merchants, who simply wanted to avoid a new tax for revenue on their commerce, contended that local establishments should be paid for out of local rates on property. They argued that the new duties, which were relatively heavy, would embarrass the trade with England and the West Indies and would encourage the smuggling of goods across the boundary from the United States.[24] They took the controversy with portentous seriousness. Headed by John Richardson, the half dozen traders in the assembly fought the bill in its passage through parliament.[25] The commercial community as a whole petitioned the governor to disallow it. As in the past, the London merchants sent a written protest to the imperial authorities; and when the matter came up before the board of trade for discussion, the merchants Brickwood, Forsyth, Idle and Mills attended to give evidence.[26] In the end, however, all these protests were completely ineffectual and the new tariff bill became law.

Here perhaps the affair should have ended. But the merchants had been roused to a high state of moral indignation. Baffled, they felt that irrepressible need for a demonstration, for some significant gesture. Towards the end of March, they gave a complimentary dinner to the members of the provincial parliament who had supported the commercial case in the quarrel over taxation. The veteran fur trader Isaac Todd was in the chair; the band of the 6th Regiment attended and upwards of fifty sat down to dinner. Punctiliously, systematically, they paid their devotions to the different imperial shrines. They pledged the king, the empire, the lieutenant-governor and the navy and army to the accompaniment of such appropriate tunes as *God Save the King, Rule Britannia, The Roast Beef of Old England* and *Britons Strike Home*. Then they got down to the serious business of lauding the parliamentary supporters of the commercial case. A toast was proposed "To Our Representatives in Provincial Parliament who proposed a Constitutional and proper mode of Taxation for the building of Gaols, and who opposed a Tax on Commerce for that purpose as contrary to the sound practice of the Parent State". This was drunk to the strains of *Hearts of Oak;* and it was followed, after various similar sentiments had been pledged, by the pious aspiration "May the Commercial Interest of this Province have its due influence in the administration of its Government". All these matters were reported in considerable detail in the columns of the *Montreal Gazette.*[27]

Thanks to the kindly offices of this newspaper the impertinence of the merchants had been made irritatingly public. But the professional men and landowners, prudently remembering their strength in the assembly, delayed their revenge until 1806 when the provincial parliament was again in session and they were clothed once more with the formidable powers of a British legislature. Then they struck. With a blithe disregard for the liberty of the press which they were later to demand and the sacred rights of minorities which they were repeatedly to invoke, they began proceedings by appointing a committee to inquire into the false and scandalous libel of the *Montreal Gazette;* and in the end they voted that Isaac Todd and Edward Edwards of the *Montreal Gazette* should be taken into custody by the sergeant-at-arms.[28] When Thomas Cary, the editor of the *Quebec Mercury*, was moved by these proceedings to speculate upon the apparent connection between French influence and the oppression of the press, he was haled before the assembly and required to make an abject apology.[29] Finally, the house spent a considerable part of the remainder of the session in preparing a long address and memorial to the king, justifying its stand in the matter of the Gaols Bill. The executive, which was striving with worried earnestness for impartiality, took no part in the controversy whatever. It was a straight dispute between a commercial minority and a peasant and professional community which happened to be in control of the popular branch of the legislature.

III

The quarrel had its origin in the rivalry of agriculture and commerce. It was continued and exasperated by the economic revolution which was gradually accentuating the social divisions of the country. Even in Lower Canada, which in comparison with the upper province was relatively untouched by change, the evidences of the new economy were conspicuous and unavoidable. In Quebec and Montreal, which were the nerve-centres of the Canadian commercial system, lived a strong mercantile minority determined to break through all opposition and to realize the possibilities of the new age. The new settlements in the Eastern Townships, 5,000 strong according to the conservative estimate of Governor Milnes,[30] were infected with the energy and initiative characteristic of the typical American frontier community. Settled upon the basis of English freehold tenure which was in itself antagonistic to the feudal system, they were already demanding representation in the provincial parliament, the establishment of competent judicial machinery in the district and the improvements and expenditures which would enable them to progress.[31] The revolution had not only created the distant Upper Canada; it had also invaded the unchanging society of Quebec.

In such an atmosphere, the controversy begun over an incident of provincial taxation could not die. *Scaevola* began his attacks upon French-Canadian culture in the *Quebec Mercury*. In November of 1806, the year in which the assembly had arrested the editors of the *Mercury* and the *Gazette*, a group of French Canadians began the publication of *Le Canadien*, a frankly propagandist newspaper with the alarming but on the whole suitable motto "Fiat justitia, ruat cœlum". It was cause and effect. "C'est à l'occasion de ces discussions", wrote the editors of *Le Canadien* apropos of the disputes over the Gaols Bill, "que le Mercure a commencé à éclater en invectives contre les Canadiens de la Chambre d'Assemblée, ce qui . . . fit sentir plus que jamais la nécessité d'une presse indépendante des Marchands de Montréal et du parti ministériel."[32] The war of newspapers and pamphlets had begun.

It was the policy of the editors of *Le Canadien* to adopt an attitude of injured virtue, to protest their loyalty and defend their rights, to act strictly as if they were upon the defensive. But behind all this somewhat emotional obfuscation, they permitted more than a few glimpses of less unprovocative purposes. It is evident that one of the main movements in the campaign launched by *Le Canadien* was an attack upon the new commercialism, represented both by the merchants of Montreal and the settlers in the Eastern Townships. The new journal frequently published articles with titles as suggestive as the following: "Considérations sur la dépravation des mœurs Canadiennes occasionnée par la Commerce des Pelleteries"; and "Considérations succinctes sur l'utilité du Commerce en Canada".[33] Canada, according to the editors of *Le Canadien*, was definitely and finally an agricultural country. "Premièrement," wrote *Canadensis*, "je me crois autorisé de poser pour principe que le Canada ne peut être un pays ou un état commerçant."[34] Yet, despite this uncontrovertible truth, the commercial group was active and apparently influential in politics. "Quelques personnes", lamented *Le Canadien*, ". . . désirent . . . créer une aristocratie mercantile, le plus abominable, le plus pernicieux de tous les ordres, également préjudiciable à l'autorité de la Couronne, aux intérêts de Propriétaires, et aux Libertés du Peuple."[35] The incident of the gaols tax was simply an illustration of the power of this minority. "Cette circonstance ne sembleroit-elle pas montrer combien l'influence de la societé du Nord-Ouest est dominante dans le Pays?"[36]

The settlers in the Eastern Townships were subjected to a castigation which was even more pitiless. The settlers were Americans, "Yenkés", according to *Le Canadien*, and a low, vicious, turbulent and ungrateful lot. "Plus loin", wrote *Observator* referring to the Townships, "est un peuple demi-sauvage & dont les irruptions seront aussi à craindre, en Canada, que celles que firent, autrefois, les Goths & les Vandals en Italie."[37] These Americans were the same people, or their immediate descendants, who had revolted against the fostering care of the British government. On the other hand, the French Canadians—according to a bold historical reconstruction of *Le Canadien*—had leapt forward as one man to defend British sovereignty in Canada against the invasion of the American rebels. Unhappily, the chief characteristics of these Americans were "l'avidité & l'esprit d'accaparement". "Le Grand objet pour un Americain", wrote *Canadensis*, "est toujours d'acheter et de revendre."[38] It was the grant of land in free and common soccage which had persuaded these "Vandals" to enter the province; and the grant was an innovation supported by those commercially minded people who wished to "défranciser" and "Yankéfier" Quebec.

The essential grievances of the merchants and their supporters can be seen clearly in the body of criticism which they began at this time to direct against French-Canadian culture. It was not the different religion or the different language of the French which exasperated the merchants. A pamphleteer pointed out with some truth as well as some complacency that Great Britain had not been "the suspicious, reluctant Keeper, but the liberal Patron of the Catholic Church in this Province"; and on the subject of language he observed a little unctuously that "the British people have never made war on sounds. . . ".[39] "I have no particular personal friendship for the American;" wrote the editor of the *Mercury*, "still less have I any enmity to the Canadian; but I must be permitted to have an anxious wish to see so large a portion of the British dominions in a superior state to a wilderness. Before this, all minor considerations vanish."[40] This was the real purpose of the merchants and what goaded them to fury was the Canadians' lack of enterprise, their persistent failure to move with the swiftly moving times. "The Canadian", observed the *Mercury*, "moves in a go-cart, where his mind is more confined than his body"; and a pamphleteer, keeping with evident relish to the same metaphor, compared the Canadians to infants "withering in the cradle in which they had been rocked". To the commercial group, the chief sin of this spineless and unadventurous generation was its complete failure to conquer and exploit the country in the approved American way. As a settler and colonizer, the French Canadian was despised. "The population of this

Province", wrote the pamphleteer quoted above, "forms a small compact body inert in its nature, without one principle of percussion; and exhibiting its infant face, surcharged with all the indications of old age and decay. During a lapse of two centuries, little more than the borders of the St. Lawrence have been put under cultivation; in a few places only, have settlements slumbered forth, on the minor streams, with manifest reluctance and regret."[41]

This stubborn conservatism lay like a burden on the whole community; and, worst of all, it was an organized obstruction in the legislature. According to *Scaevola*, the French-Canadian members in the provincial parliament were "petty politicians; who are as much fitted to direct the measures of a commercial and enterprising people, as a church beadle is to be Chancellor of the exchequer".[42] They were blind "to the progress of the province, from a petty feudal state, to an important commercial one". Moved by absurd fears and by an undiscerning pride, they had made the defence of their moribund institutions a point of honour; and actually in the legislature "it has become indecorous to point out a fault, and a Legislative felony to propose a change".

To a very large extent therefore—and the contestants were quite conscious of the fact—it was a battle between the new commercialism and the stiffened feudalism of the St. Lawrence. There were, of course, other aspects to the quarrel—aspects which have been fittingly recognized in the pages of Canadian history; but the economic and social clash had appeared at the beginning and it remained obtrusively in evidence from that time on. Both sides wished to use the political institutions of the province, either to preserve an old society or to prepare the way for a new. Both sides met in the legislature, in conflict over the old institutions, laws and traditions of the province, which could be looked upon either as a rampart against dangerous innovation or as a check upon desirable progress. French-Canadian political writers descanted upon "la beauté, la sagesse et la majestueuse simplicité" of the unreformed Custom of Paris. To commercial sympathizers the edifice of Quebec law seemed to have been built by "the gloomy and wayward architects of the dark ages". Freehold tenure was in conflict with seigniorial tenure. The French-Canadian majority in the chamber objected to any legislation which would appear to confirm or extend the strange tenures and land law which had been regrettably established in the Townships. In 1808 the assembly actually voted "that this House will . . . resolve itself into a Committee of the whole House, to take into consideration the alterations it may be expedient to establish, touching the nature and consequences of grants in free and common Soccage. . . ".[43]

The quarrel had begun under the unprovocative rule of Lieutenant-Governor Milnes. It was continued during the presidency of Mr. Dunn, an undistinguished octogenarian resident of the colony, who enjoyed a temporary authority during the interval between the departure of one governor and the arrival of another. When in October of 1807, Sir J. H. Craig arrived in the province to assume the position of governor-in-chief, the dispute was already over two years old. Craig could not create what already existed; but he complicated the whole affair by dragging the government into what had been merely a quarrel between two groups of Canadians. A soldier of the old Murray school, as fiery and impetuous as his predecessor and with more dogged persistence, he simply could not watch, fretting impotently, while the battle raged. But when he did interfere he was almost inevitably compelled by events to take up a position diametrically opposed to Murray's. He left a country which was being revolutionized by industrial and social changes to become the governor of a colony which had been completely transformed by immigration and the rise of the new staple trades. To Craig, who cherished the nineteenth-century middle-class ideals of education, respectability and material progress, the French-Canadian legislators were simply a collection of illiterate, ignorant, oafish incompetents.[44] He turned from them to the merchants with evident relief. Many of the merchants were, as he said, "most respectable"; and he recommended that John Richardson be made a member of the legislative council on the ground that he had been "one of the most useful and intelligent Members of the Lower House. . . ".[45] The reversal of alliances, foreshadowed by the changes of 1783, was becoming a fact; and trade and bureaucracy drew together in what was beginning to appear more and more a typical American commercial state.

It was in the session of 1809, after Craig had been more than a year in the colony, that the French-Canadian majority decided to expel from the bosom of the assembly two members who were either known or suspected to be friendly to the impotent commercial group. Both men were vulnerable, for one, Ezekiel Hart, was a jew and the other, P. A. de Bonne, was a provincial judge. It was a rather odd prelude to their long advocacy of the rights of religious minorities when French Canadians solemnly decided that Ezekiel Hart, being a jew, could not sit or vote in the provincial parliament. As for Judge de Bonne, they came to the natural conclusion that judges were ineligible for election to the assembly. It was after they had spent some weeks in earnest discussion of these national affairs that Governor Craig, breathing the wrath of a disciplinarian, and the moral indignation of a patriot, descended suddenly upon them to castigate the assemblymen and dissolve the assembly. There was an election in the autumn of 1809; and when Governor Craig was confirmed in his early suspicion that the new assembly was as incorrigible as its predecessor, there was another election in the following year. Then the government seized the press of *Le Canadien*. Its editors were imprisoned; and the French-Canadian politicians, who a few years earlier had voted to take into custody the editors of the *Montreal Gazette* and the *Quebec Mercury*, suddenly discovered in a rush of emotional conviction how unequivocally they believed in the doctrine of the liberty of the press. This was Craig's Reign of Terror. He had envenomed the quarrel almost beyond alleviation.

But the merchants had begun it; and in spite of their defeat they saw now how it could be ended. It was at this time that they began to advocate the union of the two provinces,[46] for union, they hoped, would free them from the bondage of the Lower Canadian legislature. "The malady", declared the *Quebec Mercury*, "took root immediately on dividing Canada into two small legislatures; and would be totally eradicated by uniting them"[47]

IV

The original objectives of the merchants—the achievement of the commercial dominion of the St. Lawrence and the capture of political power at Quebec—remained precisely what they had been. But it was evident, as the consequences of 1783 and 1791 flowed remorselessly on, that the commercial class was failing in its attempt to gain the old aims under the new conditions. The political institutions, the laws and customs of the St. Lawrence had not been adapted to the new economy. The boundary of 1783, cutting through the old northern dominion, was becoming a commercial reality as well as a political fact. The creation of Upper and Lower Canada in 1791 had left each province to contribute independently to what should have been a common undertaking; and in Lower Canada, where reform was most urgently necessary, it seemed politically impossible. The commercial state was in the hands of lawyers and peasants at the very moment when its western territories were slipping into the control of the Americans. The decline of the first, the fur-trading unity of the St. Lawrence, continued without interruption. It was manifested in the ruin of the south-west trade. And even the grand rise of the North West Company symbolized the slow withdrawal of the old staple trade from the original dominion of the St. Lawrence to the restricted dominion of Canada.

In the decade which preceded the War of 1812, the North West Company attained its last and greatest period of success. It had both the weight of numbers and the strength of unity. Like all previous commercial rivalries between Canadians in the north-west, the rivalry of the XY or New North West Company on the one hand and the Old North West Company on the other had been ended by an amalgamation, which was effected in 1804. The old and new western traders, bringing with them the best ability and experience in fur-trading Canada, crowded into a single, great, transcontinental concern. Without a single Canadian competitor, it exploited the whole of the central and western districts of the future Dominion. But it was driven inexorably onward by the scarcity of beaver, the competition from Hudson Bay and the necessity of obtaining greater returns to support the unified and enlarged concern. Its destiny, like that of every other great Canadian company, was to cross the continent; and already Fraser, Thompson and other servants of the company were exploring and founding posts beyond the Rockies. But it was a sudden challenge from the Americans which made the advance into the Pacific slope more immediately and urgently necessary. Here, in the ultimate west, as in every other section of the long and uncertain boundary of the St. Lawrence trading system, the connection between commerce and politics was intimate and binding. The fur traders were commercial imperialists who alone of their whole generation could anticipate the territorial limits of their country. The race for the west was first of all a race for western trade. At the very moment when the Nor' Westers were slowly extending their business into the last available territory, they discovered that the Americans were likely to forestall them.

Ever since the Louisiana purchase—the most important land transaction in the history of the continent—both public men and private citizens in the new republic had been actively interested in the exploration of the far west. In 1804, with the support of the federal government, Lewis and Clark had led an expedition over-land across the prairies to the mouth of the Columbia river. John Jacob Astor, the business genius who in earlier years had come humbly to Montreal to buy his furs, organized the American Fur Company in 1808. Two years later, with a more ominously definite indication of his territorial ambitions, he formed the Pacific Fur Company and persuaded some veteran Canadian traders to join with him in it.[48] In the summer of 1810 two expeditions started for the Pacific coast. From Lachine went the first canoe-load of Astor's overland party; from New York sailed the unlucky *Tonquin* and its turbulent crew. Both expeditions were to co-operate in establishing the first of the Pacific Fur Company's posts on the Columbia river. The fact that Astor was partly dependent upon Canadian skill and experience did not blind the eyes of the Nor' Westers to the more important fact that they were faced by a strongly competitive American firm.

They hoped, of course, to persuade the empire to fight the battles of commercial imperialism on the Pacific slope. On January 23, 1810, while tongues were wagging in Montreal over Astor's amazing schemes, the agents of the North West Company dispatched an excited letter to their correspondents in London.[49] In March of that year a deputation from the committee of British merchants interested in the Canadian trade waited upon Lord

Liverpool, the colonial secretary, to discuss the proposed American expedition to the Columbia. He referred them to the Marquess Wellesley, head of the foreign department; and Nathaniel Atcheson, secretary of the British committee, sent letters and memorials to Wellesley in April and again in June. But when, after months of exasperating delay, it became amply apparent that the Marquess declined either to take their advice or to answer their letters, Simon McGillivray and the London forwarders renewed their direct application to Lord Liverpool.[50] They urged that the government should send a ship to the Columbia river and they declared that the company would at once dispatch an overland expedition to the same goal. The government remained irresponsively inactive; but the company was in dead earnest. Thompson, who was travelling back in 1810 to spend his year of rotation in Canada, was stopped at Rainy Lake and returned rapidly to the Rockies. It was perhaps still possible for him to repair the effects of his previous dilatoriness, to achieve the original Pacific objective of his company and to defeat the new challenge from the United States. But the hostility of the Piegan Indians whom he had helped to antagonize drove him to attempt the difficult Athabaska pass. His journey was toilsome and incredibly delayed; and when at last, on a July day in 1811, he reached the mouth of the Columbia, it was only to discover that the Pacific Fur Company's fort, Astoria, had already been established.[51] The commercial system of New York and the commercial system of the St. Lawrence had been brought face to face on the western edges of the continent.

Thompson, having reconnoitred, retired almost at once. The task which the company had set itself was evidently a formidable one. Thompson had not succeeded; and the appeal for direct governmental assistance had proved a failure. There remained the chance of enlisting indirect support. In 1811 there was published in London the anonymous, propagandist pamphlet *On the Origin and Progress of the North West Company*, a narrative which combined praise for the Canadian concern with solemn warnings of Astor's ambitions.[52] In the same year the company requested of government a charter of incorporation which would give the concern an exclusive right to trade within north latitudes 42 and 60 for a period of twenty-one years.[53] This unassuming petition was passed around in the usual leisurely fashion between the privy council, the board of trade and the law officers of the crown. But, in the end, it was refused, with significant references to American territorial rights. This was on the very eve of the War of 1812. It was the war, where all else had failed, which was to make the ambitions of the Nor' Westers an imperial concern; and British sea power, linked in the far west with the Canadian trading organization, was to drive the American fur company from the Pacific.

Thus, in the far west the Canadian merchants had shown strength and were to win eventual victory. But in the south-west, in the old dominion of the St. Lawrence, the whole history of the period 1800–1812 is the history of a slow, protesting retreat. Political suzerainty had been surrendered in 1796. The commercial dominion of the fur traders was only to survive it for two decades. The American government, emboldened by the Louisiana purchase, and American commercialism, personified in John Jacob Astor, combined to intimidate and finally to overpower the Canadians. The process began soon after the beginning of the new century. In August, 1805, General James Wilkinson, superintendent for Indian affairs in the new district of Upper Louisiana, issued a proclamation forbidding any but American citizens to engage in the fur trade of the Missouri region.[54] Traders must obtain licences at St. Louis, under conditions which it was impossible for British subjects honestly to accept; and these stringent regulations were justified on the ground that the territories of the Louisiana purchase were not subject to the terms of the Jay Treaty of 1794. The American government was busily extending its own factory system for trade with the Indians and posts were established at Chicago in 1805 and at Michilimackinac in 1809.[55] In 1808, at Niagara, there occurred an incident which filled the Canadian traders with fear and consternation. The spring brigade of twenty Canadian *bateaux* entered the Niagara river, bound for the south-west trade on behalf of the Michilimackinac Company. Unexpectedly the American officials required that the brigade make entry at their post and report for customs inspection. There was an altercation; and the Americans, deciding suddenly upon direct action, fired upon the brigade, seized eight *bateaux* and pursued the others, so the Canadians claimed, nearly thirty miles into the open waters of Lake Ontario.[56]

Driven together by their common need for defence, the majority of the important south-west traders had joined together in the Michilimackinac Company as early as 1806. At every move of the Americans, they protested loudly at Quebec. Their protests were relayed on to the British minister plenipotentiary at Washington and the government in England; and in March, 1808, the merchant Gillespie travelled down to Washington on the question of the embargo. Each of these cases was, of course, a problem in itself. But as time went on the Canadian merchants became convinced that all these difficulties were simply parts of a far more important general problem. The duties, regulations, seizures and embargoes appeared to be the various measures of a systematic scheme; and its evident object was the annihilation of the Canadian trade south of the lakes, "Your Memorialists", wrote the Canadian merchants, "have for some time seen progressing, with extreme concern, a systematic plan to drive the British Indian Traders from the American Territory, by every species of vexation; and they must soon succeed if His Majesty's Government does not take up their cause with decision. . . ."[57]

In the meantime Astor had begun direct competition in the trade from Michilimackinac. His entrance coincided neatly with the activities of the American government; and to the Canadians it must have seemed as if government and commercial capital were the two partners in a conspiracy for the ruin of their trade. As early as February, 1810, John Richardson and William McGillivray were in New York negotiating with Astor for a settlement of their rivalry in the south-west. Richardson wrote that only dire necessity had driven him to this extreme step.[58] He believed that partnership with Astor was the only way to avoid the total ruin of their property. But Astor, who must have realized that he had the Canadians at his mercy, was determined upon a larger measure of control. The conference broke up without result. The rivalry continued; and that summer, in disgust, the wintering partners in the Michilimackinac Company sold out their interests to the big Montreal firms. The merchants journeyed

down to New York again in the following winter and this time
they came to terms with Astor in the agreement of January, 1811.

A new concern, the South West Company, was established
and its control was divided equally between Astor and the Montreal
firms.[59] But this partition of what had once been a Canadian
monopoly was not the only significant feature of the agreement.
Back in 1806, when the Canadian Michilimackinac Company had
been formed, there had been a delimitation of trading territory
between it and the North West Company. By clause 11 of its
articles of incorporation, the new, half-American South West
Company was to accept this delimitation for the year 1811. After
that the North West Company agreed not to trade within the
territorial limits of the United States east of the Rockies and the
South West Company promised not to venture beyond the American boundary into Canada. Even in the fur trade, the political
boundary had become a commercial boundary. For thirty years
after 1783 trade had frustrated politics. But at last American
commerce was grasping the gifts of its inspired diplomatists.
All the Canadians could do was to hang on to a part of what was
essentially an American concern.

If the old fur-trading unity of the St. Lawrence were slowly
breaking asunder, what hope was there of replacing it with another
commercial unity based upon the new staple trades? From the
first rush of settlement to the lakes it had always been Montreal's
ambition to build up a new commercial system upon the solid
foundations of the old. This was the ideal of the entire business
generation which had grown up after the peace of 1783. And in the
eighties and nineties, when American trade and settlement in the
west were weak, it was still possible to be complacently optimistic
about the future, as Richard Cartwright and Robert Hamilton
had been. But now everything was changing. The Americans were
aggressively on the offensive. And, as the old unity of the St.
Lawrence broke in pieces, the prospect of the new receded
indefinitely into the future. The new west had arisen. It stood
waiting, expectant, for its markets and its commercial connections;
but the St. Lawrence was not playing to the full its destined role.

There were, of course, a fair number of the natural products
of the United States which were imported into Canada. Some

provisions, dairy products and a few thousand barrels of potash were yearly entered at St. Johns, Lower Canada, before the war. During the period of the Napoleonic Wars, when the differential duties suddenly magnified the Canadian trade in wood, there were considerable quantities of timber, deals and shingles imported into Canada *via* Lake Champlain and the Richelieu river. In 1810, 1,132,000 feet of oak timber and 1,975,000 feet of pine were entered at the port of St. Johns.[60] Indeed, the Baltic timber merchants asserted that the imperial preferences chiefly benefited the American timber contractors; and for some time after American imports had ceased to be of any real importance, this charge against the differential duties was repeated. Timber, like the other less important natural products, was admitted freely into Canada. The British preference increased the attractions of the northern route. Mercantilism and free trade were combining, as the Canadians had intended they should, to drive the natural products of the continent into the St. Lawrence system.

It was something, but it was not enough. It was only a part of the commercial programme which the Canadians had framed after the disruption of the first British Empire. To the merchants it was just as important that manufactures should be forwarded up the river to the new settlements as that the new staples should be brought down the river to Quebec and Montreal. But they could not realize their dual aim. From the few and unreliable statistics which exist for the period it is evident that the Canadian exports to the United States were becoming relatively few in number and small in quantity. In 1807, from St. Johns in Lower Canada there were exported the usual large quantity of furs, nearly a thousand barrels of fish and 13,670 bushels of salt.[61] There were a good many other oddments; but they were unimportant. There were few manufactures exported in any quantity. And yet, curiously enough, there was a considerable amount of manufactured goods coming into Canada from the United States. Hats, shoes, manufactured tobacco, sugar, chocolate and vast quantities of tea were imported, for the Americans were making the best use of Jay's Treaty. Their industries were slowly growing. The weight of their expanding economy was pressing in upon the stunted little colonies to the north.

V

It was only natural, with all these failures, that the Canadian merchants should make desperate attempts to change the conditions of their trade. During the first decade of the new century the familiar signs of commercial discontent began to multiply. Committees were appointed. Secretaries were nominated. There was a sudden spate of petitions and memorials; and over in England a number of pamphlets began to acquaint the public with the virtues of the Canadas and the enormities of the United States. In 1809, the committee of British North American merchants was formed in London.[62] John Inglis was chairman, John Bainbridge deputy chairman; and Nathaniel Atcheson, who had already displayed his disinterested patriotism in his pamphlet *American Encroachments on British Rights*, was appointed secretary. In the same year the Montreal and Quebec committees, headed respectively by John Richardson and James Irvine, dispatched the first of a series of representations to Castlereagh. This memorial and the petitions, letters and pamphlets which followed it presented, not a particular grievance, but a kind of commercial Grand Remonstrance.[63] The merchants reviewed the entire position of Canada in the imperial system and, on most counts, they found it profoundly unsatisfactory.

From their point of view, the era which had been inaugurated by the Constitutional Act and Jay's Treaty had been an almost unqualified failure. The commercial state had been divided. Its most important half lay in the dead grip of a reactionary peasantry. Great Britain, the centre of the empire and the guardian of its navigation laws, changed inexplicably from a praiseworthy care of her colonies to a deplorable neglect of their interests. The markets of empire, according to the good old fundamentals of mercantilism, should be opened to Canadians and closed to Americans, who had established a right to exclusion by winning a war of independence. But Great Britain, though she had fittingly crowned the edifice of mercantilism with the differential timber duties, had in other respects proved curiously neglectful of the ancient principles. By imperial orders-in-council American products had been admitted into the British West Indies when carried in British bottoms. By successive proclamations the governors of the islands had admitted American shipping itself. And this laxity, together with British preoccupation in the long French wars, had permitted the American trade in the West Indies to grow apace.[64] Moreover, by the Jay Treaty, the United States had secured an entry into the British East Indies as well.

In North America, the wayward American colonies had been treated with the same odd, unaccountable generosity. The Jay Treaty had given Canada few privileges and had left it unprotected to the assaults of American trade. It was true, of course, that Canadian needs, as well as general imperial interests, required the free entry of American natural products into Canada. But the impolitic Jay Treaty had allowed the United States to export its manufactured goods into Canada as well. Incredibly, it had even permitted the States to deal with Canada in imperial products— sugar, teas and cottons—obtained in the British East and West Indies. America had been granted much and had given little. The Jay Treaty had only in theory established a reciprocity, for the American tariff towered above the Canadian. Regulations, seizures, tariffs and embargoes had wrecked the Canadian fur trade south of the lakes. In the far west the Americans were disputing territory which the Canadians claimed was British by right of prior discovery.

These were the main commercial complaints and charges. But merchants are moved to lobby, as a people is moved to revolt, as much by the hope of better things as by the conviction of present injustices. The main reasons for the commercial propaganda were the disappointments of the past fifteen years; but its immediate occasion was the unexpected good fortune of the years 1807–1810. These were the years of the continental blockade in Europe and the American acts of embargo and non-intercourse. The blockade had directed the attention of Great Britain to her surviving North American colonies. The embargo had proved that the Americans were not quite so indispensable as they had imagined to the British West Indies. The merchants proceeded to press home this advantage. "Since the Northern Ports of Europe have been shut", they argued, "and the Embargo in operation, the Supplies of various kinds derivable from the British North American Provinces, and the Canadas in particular, have become objects of great national concern, and cannot but point them out as most valuable appendages of the Empire, meriting such a preference in the British & West India Markets, by Bounties, protecting Duties, or other expedients, as shall assure to the commodities they are capable of furnishing, decided advantages over those from the United States or from other foreign nations."[65]

In this confident and ingratiating spirit the merchants presented their scheme for the reorganization of British North American commerce. Their first major point was that the Jay Treaty was at an end. The United States, they argued, had itself invalidated the ten "permanent" articles of the treaty with its embargo and non-intercourse acts; and since this fiasco of British diplomacy was thus providentially laid to rest, Great Britain must never again enter into so inequitable a bargain. Trade between the United States and the British colonies in Asia and Africa must not be permitted without a real equivalent. American shipping should be excluded from the British West Indies. The North American colonies were capable of supplying the islands with fish and probably with lumber; and so far as other products were concerned, Great Britain should pursue a watchful policy of prohibiting their importation from the United States just so soon as it was reasonably certain that the Canadas and Nova Scotia could undertake supply.

In respect of direct trade between the Canadas and the United States, the merchants presented their old proposals, modified slightly by the bitter experiences of the past fifteen years. Mercantilist principles, which elsewhere in the empire should be applied rigidly to the disadvantage of the Americans, could be neglected on the boundary between the United States and Canada —in the interests, of course, of the empire as a whole. As in the past, the natural products of the States should be admitted freely into Canada, in order that the St. Lawrence might become the water boulevard for the trade of the whole northern half of the continent. Mere passage down the St. Lawrence should remove the alien taint from American produce and qualify it for all imperial preferences; and embarrassing certificates of Canadian origin, which were now required for potash shipped from Quebec, should be abandoned immediately. The idea of a western free-trade area, which was itself merely a debased form of the older idea of western political empire, was still embedded in the commercial philosophy of Montreal. Harking back to the project of the Indian barrier state, the merchants even proposed that an Indian trading zone, not subject to the American tariff, should be established in the great triangle of territory between the Illinois, Mississippi and Missouri rivers. Though the merchants did not say so, the imperial shipping regulations which they were so anxious to have applied against the Americans in the British West Indies had broken down completely in the Great Lakes. "It is certain", wrote J. B. Robinson, the attorney-general of Upper Canada, in 1823, "that vessels and boats of all descriptions, built in the United States, and owned and navigated wholly, or in part by American citizens were admitted to import & export merchandize & to carry from port to port in Upper Canada, until after the year 1814, without question, so far as I am informed, of their right to do so."[66]

Most of these proposals had been formulated long ago, immediately after the disruption of the first empire; and many of them had been accepted and acted upon. The real novelty was the anxious demand of the merchants for an effective tariff against American manufactures and goods from Europe and the East Indies which were coming into Canada in great quantities *via* the United States.[67] By the Jay Treaty the Canadas were prevented from levying duties upon importations by land and inland navigation which were higher than the duties upon the same articles imported by the sea. This placed the merchants in an impossible situation.[68] On the one hand they wanted to get their goods cheap from Europe, as the controversy over the Gaols Bill clearly showed: and on the other, they were eager to prevent the importation of similar exotic and manufactured goods from the United States. This was probably one of the main reasons for their persistent attack upon the Jay Treaty. It was their object to prohibit absolutely the importation of East India goods *via* the United States; and in all other respects they wished to use the high American tariff as a model. Here, in purely commercial matters, the Canadian merchants were able to persuade an imperial government still dominated by the old concepts of mercantilism. In 1812 the imperial parliament passed a statute prohibiting the importation into Canada by land or inland navigation of any commodities not the growth or manufacture of the United States.[69] This in theory, though not of course in fact, stopped the trade in East India goods. And in April, 1812, letters were sent to the governors in Upper and Lower Canada advising the adoption of the United States' tariff rates on all American imports, except, of course, those natural products which as in the past should be admitted free.[70]

This was on the very eve of the War of 1812. For years the scene of British-American affairs was sombre with accumulated resentments and lighted only by fitful flashes of temper. Once again, as so often in the past, the academic protests of the merchants were accompanied by a confused, angry murmur from the primitive west. As the first unity of the St. Lawrence crumbled in pieces, the two groups of its defenders in instinctive agreement moved forward for their last, their fruitless effort at defence. Tecumseh, the Shooting Star, rose from the obscurity of his Shawnee village to the moral leadership of the west. His brother, the Prophet, began to teach the austerities of his new religion. A great despairing breath of anger seemed to rise from the whole west. Even now, even after all that had happened, was it not possible to drive the frontiersmen beyond the Ohio?

CHAPTER VII

THE END OF THE FUR TRADE

I

THE War of 1812 was the final episode in the long struggle between settlement and the fur trade in the region of the Great Lakes. Ever since 1805, the Indians and the fur traders, the two elements in the old northern society, had been making their last, their belated effort to break through the Treaty of 1783, the Jay Treaty and the Treaty of Greenville; and it was the suspicion and fear of this alliance between the Indians and the fur-trading state which helped materially to provoke the American declaration of war.[1] There were, of course, other reasons for American resentment—grievances which no doubt assumed a greater prominence in the diplomatic interchanges which preceded the opening of the struggle. The *Chesapeake* incident, the British claim to impressment on the high seas and the British restriction of neutral commerce by the orders-in-council all rankled seriously.[2] But it is not without significance that the war to avenge these purely maritime injustices was opposed by maritime New England and hotly supported by the agrarian west. It was the drive of the west and the urgings of western men which largely committed the United States to war. Their purpose was, undeniably, to uphold the dignity of the United States in oceanic commerce; but, at the same time, their more immediate object was the free, secure and uninterrupted expansion of their western frontier at the expense of the fur-trading economy. Already, at Tippecanoe in 1811, the followers of Tecumseh had been broken; but behind Tecumseh was divined the vague, pervasive, sinister influence of northern fur traders and northern officials. The war, directed against this ambiguous union, promptly converted it into an open alliance. The Indians were not destined to fight alone for the St. Lawrence as they had fought at the battle of Fallen Timbers. At the last extremity of the long conflict between the seaboard and the St. Lawrence, the fur-trading society stood united in defence of the unity of the river and its lakes.

The merchants regarded the war with an enthusiasm which was only slightly tempered by anxiety. There had been little real doubt about their loyalty in 1775: there was none at all in 1812. For them the war was not a war of defence, but of reconquest. It was a war for the rectification of the incredible wrong of 1783. "Posterity will hardly believe," they wrote, "although history must attest the melancholy and mortifying truth, that in acceding to the Independence of the then Thirteen Colonies as States, their Territory was not merely allowed to them, but an extent of Country, then a portion of the province of Quebec, nearly of equal magnitude to the said Thirteen Colonies or States, was ceded, notwithstanding not a foot of the Country so ceded was at the time occupied by an American in Arms, nor could have been, had the war continued."[3] This treaty, with its unaccountable concessions, had been dishonoured in a dozen ways by the Americans. But now—thanks to their own foolhardy declaration of war—it was void at last. The United States had presented Great Britain with an opportunity of recovering the lost provinces, of redeeming *Canada Irredenta* for the Indians and the commercial state.

This, to the merchants, was the just cause of 1812. From the very beginning of the war they entered a period of feverish activity. They were advising the government, exhorting it to greater effort, assisting with their men, their experience in the west and their influence over the Indians. As early as January, 1812, in a long conversation with Gray, the acting deputy quartermaster-general for the British army in Canada, the representatives of the North West and South West Companies offered naval and military co-operation to the government on Lake Huron and suggested the capture of the American post at Michilimackinac as a first step toward the control of the upper lakes.[4] In March and again in August 1812, the committee of London merchants interested in the Canadian trade, approached the home government with urgent requests for the dispatch of larger imperial forces for the protection of Canada.[5] The Nor' Westers, evidently believing that the war would make government more sensible of the "national importance" of their Pacific ambitions, pressed their request for governmental assistance against Astoria and their demand for a charter granting exclusive trading rights on the Pacific. On August

18, the agents of the North West Company at Montreal wrote home urging that a vessel be fitted out in England for instant dispatch to the Columbia; and in October and November the London forwarders took the matter up with government.[6] An overland party had already been sent west for the Pacific. Donald McTavish had travelled over from Quebec with the summer fleet to conduct the naval expedition from England; and the London agents urged that their ship should be stocked with arms and ammunition, granted letters of marque and provided with a naval escort. The petition for exclusive trading rights was not forgotten; but the expedition to the Columbia was the immediate necessity and during December and January Simon McGillivray haunted the colonial office and the admiralty and besieged the government with his importunities.[7] At last, in mid-winter of 1813, the *Isaac Todd*, a twenty-gun ship bearing letters of marque, sailed from Portsmouth under convoy.

In the meantime, the campaign of 1812 had begun. With an eagerness which was in striking contrast to the apathy of the Canadian farmers, the merchants, the winterers, the canoemen and the Indians jumped into the war which was to right their wrongs and recover their territories. It was, characteristically, not through official sources, but *via* the speedy system of commercial communications that Brock first heard of the American declaration of war.[8] Robert Dickson, an old south-west trader and the real leader of the fur-trading offensive in the War of 1812, gathered together an odd little army of Indians and North West Company employees; and under the command of Captain Roberts, commandant at the British fort at St. Joseph's, they fell upon the American fort at Michilimackinac on July 17 and captured it without firing a shot.[9]

Brigadier-General Hull, who had retreated to Detroit, watched the fur-trading society rise around him with increasing trepidation, fearful that the forces assembling on the other side of the river would be suddenly augmented by the arrival of Indians and fur traders fresh from the capture of Michilimackinac. "I have", he wrote, "every reason to expect in a very short time a large Body of Savages from the North whose operations will be directed against this army. They are under the influence of the North and

South-West Companies and the interest of the Companies depends
on opening the Detroit River this summer. . . . It is the opinion
of the officers and the most respectable gentlemen from Mackinac
that the British can engage any number of Indians they may
have occasion for, and that including the Engagés of the North
West and South West Companies, two or three thousand will be
brought to this place in a very short time."[10] In fact, Dickson
and his party were advancing to co-operate with Brock for the
surrender of Detroit, but before their arrival Hull had already
capitulated. In the same month, August, the American garrison
evacuated Fort Dearborn at Chicago. And when, that autumn,
the Americans were driven from Queenston Heights, the fortresses
of the fur trade from Niagara to Michilimackinac were once again
in the control of the northern commercial system. The west was
united in confidence and exaltation.

From the beginning of the war, the merchants had stressed the
importance of the friendship of the Indians and the naval command of the lakes. In the winter of 1812–1813 Dickson was in
Quebec and Montreal, lionized by the admiring and grateful
merchants and honoured by Prevost with a commission as agent
for the western Indians. Then with great rapidity he travelled
westward bound for Prairie du Chien; and in the spring of 1813
the western Indians whom he persuaded to join the British appeared
at Michilimackinac and Detroit. But Procter's raids at the head
of Lake Erie, against Fort Meigs and Fort Stephenson, were
failures; and in September Perry defeated Barclay at Put-in-Bay
and gained the naval command of the lake. Procter's army trailed
eastward from Detroit, and at Moraviantown, in a wood yellow
with autumn leaves, Harrison's horsemen broke through the
British ranks and Tecumseh was killed. Detroit, the key to the
middle west, was once more in American hands. The long communications of the northern commercial system had been cut
in two.

This, for the British, was the lowest point in the western war,
in the war for the reconstitution of the first unity of the
St. Lawrence. That autumn and winter the merchants forwarded
their gloomy appraisals of the situation to the authorities and

again urged the government to greater exertions.[11] Michilimackinac had been left suspended and vulnerable by the American re-occupation of Detroit; and government determined to use that old alternative route, so often considered since 1783, the route from Toronto to Nottawasaga Bay. Lieutenant-Colonel McDouall, with reinforcements for Michilimackinac, left the bay in April, 1814; and his journey in deeply laden *bateaux* across waters which were thick with ice and whipped by violent winds, was one of the grandest exploits of the western war. In June Dickson arrived from the Wisconsin country with Indian reinforcements; and when in July 1814 the long-expected American raiding-party appeared at Michilimackinac, the fire of the Indians drove the attackers into confusion and in the end the American squadron withdrew in discomfiture. McDouall held Michilimackinac which was the fortress of the whole region of the upper lakes. And when news arrived that the Americans had taken Prairie du Chien on the Mississippi, William McKay, an old Nor' Wester, gathered together fur traders, *voyageurs* and Indians, travelled from Michilimackinac to Prairie du Chien enrolling more Indians on the way, and recaptured the fort.[12]

Thus, when the war drew to a close, the St. Lawrence had not only held its acknowledged territories; it had regained a substantial part of its lost empire. The main American attacks on Upper and Lower Canada had failed. On Lake Ontario, Yeo had finally forced Chauncey to retire to Sackett's Harbour. And although the Americans held Detroit and kept command of Lake Erie, they had failed to retake Michilimackinac and Prairie du Chien. The British had retained control of the upper lakes and the upper Mississippi valley; and the Indians of these regions had given a support which was practically unwavering if of dubious value. On the Pacific slope, in a region which was equally a part of the transcontinental system of the St. Lawrence, the North West Company had overcome its opposition. In October 1813 a strong party of Nor' Westers had arrived at Astoria, and with the prospective arrival of the *Isaac Todd* and its convoy staring them in the face, the Astorians finally agreed to sell out the property of the Pacific Fur Company to their rivals. In a war for which the west had waited thirty years, the fur-trading society had arisen in its primitive stubborn strength and had regained a large portion of the first unity of the St. Lawrence.

In the meantime, while fur traders fought battles and manipulated the Indians, the *bourgeois* back in Montreal and London gave their most prayerful consideration to the terms of peace. If the deplorable work of Oswald and Shelburne was to be undone, the British must first of all give up their attitude of negligent complaisance; and the merchants very properly concentrated upon this essential change of spirit. "We sincerely pray", they wrote as early as October 1812, "that the spurious and detestable philanthropy, which acts upon the principle of conciliation of enemies by the sacrifice of friends, may never more be heard of, in our relations or discussions with those who rule in the United States."[13] Great Britain must be realistic, unyielding and insistent in its demands of the Americans; and in a series of representations which began with the beginning of the war and only ceased in the spring of 1814, the merchants continued with unflagging zeal to state and restate these essential demands.[14]

There must, declared the merchants, be no treaty of "amity, commerce and navigation" as Jay's Treaty had been inaptly called. Great Britain and her colonies should regulate their trade with the United States unhampered by restrictions; and, as a sound beginning, Great Britain should prohibit American shipping from the ports of the British West Indies and exclude American fishermen from the waters of Newfoundland and the gulf. It was not these affairs, however, but the matter of the new boundary between Canada and the United States which concerned the merchants most deeply; and here, as in the past, they brought forward the two alternatives—that territory south of the lakes should be ceded outright to Great Britain or that it should be granted to the Indians as a neutral barrier state. The second proposal was, in the opinion of the merchants, an irreducible demand; and they insisted "it cannot be too forcibly impressed upon Government, as a *sine qua non* in any Treaty (if the Canadas are to be preserved from future aggression) that a *new Barrier or Line of Boundary for the Indians* must be obtained. . . ".[15] Possible boundaries were suggested with a fertility of invention which was equally the result of the merchants' optimism and their knowledge of the ground. The United States should not be permitted to erect fortifications or exact duties in the neutral territory; and Great Britain should, of course, become the guarantor of the Indian territory and Indian rights.

But in 1783 and 1794 Great Britain had acquired the habit of letting down her Canadian subjects and her Indian allies; and in 1814 she completed the process by an abandonment of conclusive finality. It is true that the British commissioners at Ghent included, among their original demands, the revision of the international boundary westward from Lake Superior and the creation of an Indian barrier state within the territorial limits of the United States; and, as the merchants had requested, this last was put forward as a *sine qua non*. But the American commissioners refused both proposals; and when the British sought to retain their conquests at Michilimackinac and Niagara by establishing the principle of *uti possedetis*, the Americans insisted upon the rival principle of the *status quo ante bellum*. Great Britain, whose problems in Europe were as serious as its interests in central North America were negligible, abruptly abandoned its entire position.[16] Each side agreed to restore its conquests; and the Indians had to be content with an article which provided for the restoration of their status previous to the opening of the Indian war in 1811. The war, which had been won in the far west by the old alliance of red-coats, fur traders and Indians, had been lost as usual by the British diplomatists in Europe. For thirty years after it had ceased to be a reality, the territorial unity of the St. Lawrence had lingered on as an ideal; but after this overwhelming disappointment of the war which had promised so much and had issued in nothing, the very conception of an enlarged northern empire was slowly effaced from the minds of Canadians.

II

At first there was a short period of stunned surprise and consternation in which, so Richardson and McGillivray declared, they were incapable of comprehending the full consequences of the disaster. Then, while their partially rebuilt edifice broke apart once more, the merchants set themselves a little weariedly to the task of gathering up the pieces. By an heroic but not very ingenious interpretation of the articles of the Treaty of Ghent, they made an unsuccessful, last-minute attempt to save Michilimackinac.[17] Over in London Inglis, Ellice & Company, worried over the possible effects of the treaty on the future of Fort George (Astoria), were writing to government, begging for official protection of the "colony" established in what they had always considered British territory.[18] "A British establishment on the shores of the Pacific", they wrote reproachfully, "has been heretofore looked upon as a national object, altho' it has now probably, like our connection with the Indians in Canada, ceased to be so considered. . . ."

The peripatetic Simon McGillivray saw Bathurst in England and Governor Drummond in Canada on the subject and even made an unsuccessful attempt to state his case to Baker, the British *chargé d'affaires* at Washington. The wrathful Astor was eager for revenge and the American government informed Baker in July 1815 that the United States intended to reoccupy the post at the mouth of the Columbia under the terms of the treaty of peace. It was not, however, until the autumn of 1817 that the American sloop-of-war *Ontario* sailed for the Pacific. The vigilant Simon McGillivray at once informed Bagot, the new British ambassador at Washington;[19] but the British government having argued for some time that Astoria had been acquired not by conquest but by purchase, agreed finally to permit the reoccupation, though without prejudice to the basic question of sovereignty. On October 6, 1818, the American flag fluttered over the fort. But the northern commercial state, while it had apparently lost political control, still maintained its commercial supremacy. Astor made no attempt to re-enter the competitive struggle on the Pacific slope; and the North West Company's hold on the post at the mouth of the Columbia was confirmed for another ten years by the Treaty of October 20, 1818.

On the other hand, the ruin of the south-west fur trade seemed absolutely assured. During the war, when the Canadians had returned to the region under the supposition that its political future was still uncertain, Astor had had all he could do to recover his portion of the furs at Michilimackinac which had been acquired for the South West Company during the season of 1811. But the peace, which restored so much to the United States, gave him back his confidence and his enormous political advantages. He still had his uses for the Canadians; but already he was looking forward to the time when the American government would regulate the trade in such a way as to shut out the northerners and make their co-operation impossible. In 1815 he agreed with William McGillivray, Forsyth, Richardson & Company and Pierre de Rocheblave to continue the old agreement of 1811 until the returns from the outfits of 1820 were complete. "I made an agreement with the Principles of them", wrote Astor in explanation to James Monroe, "to carry on that Trade for joint Acc[ount] for the Term of Five years, unless the Government of the United States should in the meantime pass such Laws or Regulations, which would render it incompatible for me or the American Fur Company to be so interested with them."[20] As early as April 1816, and probably, though not certainly, at Astor's instigation, the American congress, which was eager enough to mete out retribution to the Canadian fur traders, passed legislation providing that licences for the Indian trade within the territorial limits of the United States could be granted only to American citizens, except upon the personal direction of the president.

It was Wilkinson's old hateful order for upper Louisiana extended over the entire south-west; and as early as June of that year the Indians were congregating in hundreds at Drummond Island, complaining that the total exclusion of British traders from the Indian country in the United States was the greatest misfortune that had befallen them.[21] It was impossible, however, for either Indian importunities or their own interests to move the Canadians, for Astor at last had them completely at his mercy. In 1817 he bought out the South West Company at what was probably merely a nominal price, for the Canadians were in no position to haggle. The retreat of the fur trade to the north-west, which had begun as far back as the American Revolution, had become a rout and had ended in complete withdrawal.

The north-west trade, which a few decades ago had been merely a particularly enterprising branch of the general Canadian commerce in peltries, had thus become the only fur trade of the St.

Lawrence. The old dominion of the north had been irretrievably lost; but within limits which seemed narrow only in comparison with the grand boundaries of the past, the North West Company was laying the foundations for the future Dominion of Canada. The old rivalries had been reconciled and obliterated in a unified and enlarged concern. Carried forward in the rush of its own impetuous energy towards the inevitable goal of continentalism, the company had built up an organization which extended from the Atlantic to Pacific. It had achieved great things. And yet, at what seemed the very moment of its most solid achievement and assured success, the mere continuance of the concern became a matter of uncertainty. Burdened by its vast western commitments, which in the past had proved too heavy for the individual trader and the small company, the great monopolistic co-partnership became subject to a kind of chronic instability. From Hudson Bay, the huge inlet which cut into the centre of Montreal's transcontinental system, came a new and more efficient competition. The Canadians were restlessly avid for territory which Hudson Bay was more than ever determined to contest. The North West Company, troubled by its own infirmities and harassed by a more determined pressure from without, drew ever closer to a complete collapse or to an honourable surrender.

In this final struggle between the St. Lawrence and Hudson Bay, which like the struggle between the St. Lawrence and the Hudson river lay in the nature of geography and commerce in North America, the odds were weighted in favour of the bay. It had, in the first place, an immense initial geographic advantage; and from this flowed even more obvious advantages in lower transportation charges and general overhead costs. To counterbalance these weighty superiorities the North West Company had always had the driving energy of its personnel and the efficiency of its system, built solidly upon Indian custom and French experience and improved by decades of cunning adaptations. In the days when there was still room in the west, when beaver was still plentiful and when the Hudson's Bay men were content lethargically to watch their rivals take the initiative, this *élan* and this efficiency had sufficed. They had worn well; but they were nearly worn out now, for conditions in the west were radically changing. The two companies had divided the whole Canadian west into departments which were either competitive areas or monopolistic preserves of one or other of the concerns. Competition was infinitely more severe, for beaver was scarcer while at the same time the Indians were increasingly dependent upon European goods. Despite heroic efforts to reduce expenses by abandoning unproductive areas and cutting down transportation costs, the North West Company was probably headed for bankruptcy at least a decade before the amalgamation with the Hudson's Bay Company took place.[22]

It was at this unpropitious moment that that liberal philanthropist, Charles Douglas, fifth Earl of Selkirk, determined to found a colony in western Canada.[23] "The Bible Peer", as the Nor' Westers irreverently termed him, had already established two settlements, one in Prince Edward Island and one in Upper Canada, with scarcely more than indifferent success. But his passion for the social betterment of Scottish highlanders remained unsatisfied by these humane experiments; and with that genius for the inappropriate which is the frequent accompaniment of virtue, he decided that the Red River district was the place appointed for his next attempt. Selkirk's colony, no doubt, was conceived in all the simplicity of humanitarianism; but it developed under all the corruptions of commercial rivalry. Without the consent of the Hudson's Bay Company, it was impossible to secure a grant or to found a colony in the territory selected; and to make certain of this indispensable approval, Selkirk and his relations were obliged to purchase a considerable interest in the old fur-trading concern. The generous impulses of practical benevolence had involved the earl in a new and most engrossing connection; and both in his novel and minor role as business man, and in his major capacity as social benefactor, he began to take a lively interest in the claims and prospects of the Hudson's Bay Company. The jog-trot business methods which he found to be habitual provoked in him an unexpected concern in the company's efficiency; and the invulnerable title which he required for his land grant committed him to support the absolute legality of the company's territorial claims. When, therefore, Selkirk secured his ample domain of 116,000 square miles in Assiniboia, the success of his colony was inextricably bound up with the fortunes of fur-trading rivalry in western Canada.

The first two companies of settlers reached the Red River in 1812. With an ominous suggestion of future trouble, the formal ceremony of occupation was performed at "the Forks" of the Red and Assiniboine Rivers, in uncomfortable proximity to a North West Company post. The colony had, in fact, been established in the very centre of one of the main provision districts of the Canadian concern and it was already peopled by a mob of restless, reckless half-breeds who fetched and carried for their masters, the "winterers" from Fort William. With their usual brisk, unabashed efficiency, the Nor' Westers continued to take all the pemmican they wanted out of the district, while the new settlers went hungry and fought back their rage. Finally, in January 1814, Miles Macdonell, Selkirk's governor, issued a proclamation forbidding the export of provisions from the colony. This was just after the American victories at Lake Erie and Moraviantown had cut off the southern supply bases. Evidently the North West Company had a private war on its hands at the very moment when the south-west traders were winding up an official conflict on the upper Mississippi.

What followed was a contest in violence and intimidation, which occasionally degenerated into sheer savagery and was frequently relieved by incidents which were incongruous and delightfully absurd. When the news of Macdonell's prohibitions was brought down to the formal midsummer council of the North West Company at Fort William, it was decided that the ancient north-west spirit must exact revenge. In the campaign of 1815 the Nor' Westers carried all before them, even to the extent of deporting the greater number of Selkirk's settlers to Upper Canada. In 1816, when reinforcements had arrived to repeople the wrecked colony, the Canadian winterers returned with their half-breed mob; and a score of settlers lost their lives in the brief, savage little battle of Seven Oaks. Selkirk, travelling westward from Montreal with a company of mercenaries, heard the news of the disaster at Sault Ste. Marie and promptly decided to capture the North West Company's citadel at Fort William. In the two previous campaigns, Archibald Norman McLeod, who combined the powers of a justice of the peace with the partisanship of a

Nor' Wester, had dealt lavishly in warrants for the arrest of his enemies. Now Selkirk decided to use his own authority as magistrate for the Indian territories to arrest the mighty McGillivray and the other partners assembled at Fort William. McGillivray submitted with that profound reverence for the law which the Nor' Westers could assume on occasion. But when in a counter-attack, which was unoriginal but not inappropriate, the Canadians attempted to arrest Selkirk, the earl imprudently resisted. The whole affair, which had become a tangle of murders, assaults, arrests and seizures, at length became the prized possession of the commissioners, the judges and the lawyers.

The investigations and the trials pursued their involved courses for months. The affair broke Selkirk; but its effect upon the Canadian north-west trade was more important and equally profound. At every stage of the controversy—in English political circles, in Canadian courts and western prairies—the North West Company had shown its influence, its pertinacity and its brutal strength. But the war had been ruinously costly. It had exasperated an intolerable situation. And it brought the North West Company one great step nearer to surrender.

III

The decline of the fur trade in one region and its total disappearance in another served merely to accentuate the importance of the new staple trades. In Quebec and Montreal, the two little northern ports, with their odd mixture of Scottish dourness and French provincialism, the midsummer hum of activity became louder and more persistent. In 1814 the tonnage in the port of Quebec had been 38,605; it stood at 155,842 tons in 1819.[24] The bulk of this shipping was concerned in the new trades, particularly of course in timber; and despite continually falling prices the export of wood in 1819 exceeded that of any previous year. In 1819, 19,081 tons of oak timber, 75,124 tons of pine and 1,236,296 boards and planks were shipped from Quebec. The trade in wheat and flour was a much more modest affair. In 1818, which was a fairly good year for export, 30,543 barrels of flour and 401,791 bushels of wheat were shipped from the port of Quebec.[25] But both trades, despite their existing inequality, were of vital importance for the future of the new Canadian economy; and it was a matter of real concern that just when the old economy was in the last stages of disintegration, the new trades should appear threatened and insecure.

Partly, of course, the anxiety of the merchants was the result of the depression which lay like a dead weight on Canadian trade in the years 1819–1821. The depression was serious enough in itself; but it was accompanied by the first ominous beginnings of the great revolt against mercantilism in England. Now the Canadian merchants had always been stout, old-fashioned mercantilists. The navigation system, with its preferences for colonials and its prohibitions against foreigners, had been from the first one of the two main fundamentals in the plan which the merchants had evolved after 1783; and they had set themselves the task of winning protected imperial markets for the produce of the new society of the St. Lawrence and the lakes. They had had one amazing piece of luck in the timber duties. But in 1821, in the midst of the deep calm of the slump, they suddenly realized how inadequate was their protection on wheat and how uncertain was the future of the differential duties in timber.

The possible protected markets for wheat and flour lay in the other North American colonies, in the British West Indies and Great Britain itself. In the West Indies the struggle between the British and Americans for the carrying-trade continued unabated; and the Americans were so strong commercially in the islands that the Canadians complained that they found the markets glutted with foreign flour. By the new corn law of 1815, the Canadas enjoyed a small preference in the home market of Great Britain, for colonial wheat was admitted freely when the price reached 67s. a quarter, while foreign wheat could not be imported until the price stood at 80s.[26] From 1816 until 1820 Canadian wheat had regularly gained admittance; but the depression of 1819–1821, which sent wheat prices crashing down to a little over 2s. a bushel in Canada, suddenly and completely cut off the home market as well.

The group of Canadian grain merchants was now a stronger and more vocal body than it had been. Old fur-trading names like Richardson, Larocque, McGill and Gillespie appear together with those of George Garden, Samuel Gerrard, George Auldjo, the Blackwoods and other traders in the new staples; and in 1821, while Canada lay prostrate under the depression, these Canadian merchants and the usual London agents made a determined attack upon the corn laws.[27] The colonial preference, they claimed, was "nugatory". Canada already laboured under heavy disadvantages in the trade, for the long seasonal interruption of navigation and the great distance to England made it very difficult for Canadian shippers to cope with the fluctuating conditions of the British market. The obvious—the "just"—the truly imperial remedy was, of course, the free admittance of Canadian wheat and flour at all times. But, though the colonial preference was to be increased in the next few years, the whole course of the great movement in England was directed not towards the enlargement of imperial preferences, but towards free trade. And nothing in the power of the Canadas could stop it.

In 1817, the first proposal was made in the house of commons for the reduction of the timber duties. In the summer of 1820 the lords appointed a committee on the subject, which began taking evidence from experts and interested parties. The opposition to the timber duties in Great Britain was an odd collection of serious free-traders, "realistic" Little-Englanders and hard-looking Baltic merchants. Their arguments were chiefly economic with a faint flavour of moralizing. They insisted that the alleged "Canadian" timber was in fact American, that anyway it was bad timber and that the industry had the most deplorable moral effects on the population of the Canadas. It was the shipping interest, united as usual with imperialists of the old school, which defended the duties in England;[28] and in Canada public opinion was almost unanimously opposed to their modification. The two provinces were as one in the matter. Though Papineau, the speaker of the assembly, compared the timber trade unfavourably with the noble pursuit of agriculture, the two houses in Lower Canada agreed to a united protest;[29] and from the press, the merchants and the legislatures of the Canadas there came a great wail of remonstrance against changes in the timber duties during the years 1817–1821.[30]

Their protest, of course, was based upon the old philosophy of mercantilism which had been the commercial religion of Englishmen while they built up the greatest empire of modern times. Fervently imperialistic, the colonials believed in the old ideal of a self-contained empire, whose political unity and defence would be solidly secured by the close commercial interdependence of its parts. The protected colonial trade in timber was, in their opinion, the perfect example of how the old imperial philosophy worked in a practical fashion for the empire's good. It provided certainly for imperial defence. The long voyage across the Atlantic was a proper nursery for seamen. And because of their timber exports the Canadas were able to perform their appointed role of buying British manufactures. The differential duties safeguarded the capital already locked up in the industry in Canada. And the trade provided work for settlers during the winter and a market for the timber from their cleared land. So the merchants argued, with the usual mixture of fact, sentimentalism and invention; but they were powerless to prevent the first modification of the timber duties. In 1821, in the depth of the depression, the British parliament clapped a duty of 10*s.* a load on colonial timber and reduced the duty on Baltic timber to about 55*s.* a load.[31] Furthermore—and this was almost equally annoying—certificates of Canadian origin were required for timber entering under the colonial preferences.

This last requirement naturally brings up the whole question of the regulation of trade with the United States—the second of the great problems which the merchants had to solve before the St. Lawrence could become "the channel of Importation and Exportation in British Bottoms for the Trade of the Interior of North America". The Jay Treaty had been buried unregretted during the War of 1812. The Canadian merchants, who had a healthy respect for the Americans as negotiators, begged the British government not to get committed to a new commercial treaty;[32] and in fact the conventions of 1815 and 1818 between Great Britain and the United States did not affect the trade by land and inland navigation between the Canadas and America. In these circumstances, the British government might regulate Canadian trade by imperial statute: or the colonial legislatures might be permitted to do so with some paternal advice from home.

It was the second of these courses which was followed until the Canada Trade Act of 1822. And in the meantime it became amply apparent how unfitted were two separate legislatures to devise an effective trade policy for the economy of a great river system.

In some respects their problem, complicated as it was by previous imperial legislation, was quite incapable of solution. In 1815–1816, after Upper Canada had neglected the navigation laws during the entire period of its history, the collector at Kingston seized an American schooner for contravention of the old statutes of William III; and during the next few years the governor, the law officers, the courts and the legislature in the upper province were occupied with the question of whether the navigation laws could and should be enforced or whether the provincial parliament should substitute some less stringent legislation of its own.[33] Moreover, in dealing with the problem of the regulation of trade, the council and assembly in the two provinces were apt to be distracted by the exciting diversions of their private quarrels. In 1816, the legislature of Lower Canada broke up without renewing the act empowering the governor in council to regulate the trade with the United States;[34] and this automatically brought into force the old ordinances of the province of Quebec which, the merchants claimed, were totally inadequate in the existing conditions of the trade. In 1818, in Upper Canada, the legislative council attempted to amend the bill for regulating trade with the United States; and there immediately ensued a quarrel, the assembly protesting furiously that the council had no right to interfere with its sacred prerogatives in the matter of money bills.[35] Even when legislation was passed, there were differences in the statutes of the two provinces. Finally the governors complicated the whole problem by their interference and their scruples. In 1817, Sherbrooke refused the royal assent to a trade bill which had passed the legislature; and Maitland in Upper Canada was doubtful of the right of the province to regulate the trade at all.

Nor was this all. There was another issue involved in the regulation of trade with the United States—an issue which separated the interests of the merchants from those of the landowners and set the upper against the lower province. This was the question of how far the products of the United States should be admitted free. There was, of course, a pretty general agreement on the importance of the "National Carrying Trade" of the St. Lawrence. The fear of the proposed western canal through New York state—a fear which was voiced as early as 1816 by the executive council in Lower Canada—made it seem all the more advisable to increase the attractions of the St. Lawrence route for Americans. But the merchants went very far in their requests for the free admittance of American produce. They were satisfied with the declaratory imperial statute (52 Geo. III, c. 55) which forbade the importation of East India and European goods *via* the United States. They were quite willing to accept legislation which would prohibit the entry of the "finer" manufactures of the United States in leather, cotton, tobacco and paper—for, of course, it was their scheme that Quebec and Montreal should supply the people of the St. Lawrence with manufactured goods. Apart from this, they wanted free entry, not only for all natural products, but for goods "in the first stage of manufacture", such as flour, meal of all kinds and salted provisions.[36]

But would the free importation of these articles affect unfavourably the agricultural interest of the two provinces? The British government was beginning to think so. Bathurst, the colonial secretary, informed Governor Sherbrooke in July, 1816, that such an unlimited admission of American produce would operate as a check to Canadian and British agriculture and therefore could not be authorized; and Sherbrooke, acting upon this advice, declined to give his assent to the act of 1817.[37] In Upper Canada, the assembly and the council quarrelled over this very consideration in 1818. Maitland wrote: ". . . the unrestrained admission for home consumption into this province of articles which we do not want, and of which we raise more ourselves than we can dispose of to advantage must always impoverish this Country, render our lands of little value, discourage the farmer. . . ."[38] The board of trade proposed as a solution that flour and meal might be admitted for re-exportation only. But the merchants and the governors, weary of these fluctuations and fearful that the two provinces by conflicting regulations might throw the whole system of the St. Lawrence out of gear, were begging for a permanent imperial statute which would settle the problem. By 1821 it had been proved how difficult it was for the political system set up by the Constitutional Act to cope with the fundamental problems of the northern commercial state.

IV

In the internal affairs of both provinces the strains imposed upon the political framework of 1791 grew steadily heavier. The quarrel between bureaucracy and commerce on the one hand and agriculture on the other was, of course, the inevitable accompaniment of representative institutions in the St. Lawrence valley. But the Constitutional Act with its defiance of geography and commerce, added the disputes between the two provinces to the quarrels within each. By 1821 the old prophecy of Lymburner and the merchants had been fulfilled, for the two Canadas were completely at variance on the basic question of finance.

In Lower Canada, while the post-war boom sent the timber exports soaring upwards, actual material progress was only exceeded by the enthusiastic demand for further advance. The *Montreal Gazette* repeated with evident approval the remark of an American paper that the late war had "thrust Montreal forward thirty years";[39] and in the *Quebec Gazette* there were long letters demanding public improvements and complacent editorials on "The Progress and Prospects of Trade and Industry". By 1821 the St. Lawrence Steamboat Company ("the Molson Line") and a rival company had between them half a dozen steamboats on the run between Montreal and Quebec. When in August, 1817, the new Molson steamboat *Lady Sherbrooke* was launched, the *Quebec Gazette* concluded its report with an almost lyrical outburst: "This noble vessel moved towards her element and entered it in a majestic style, accompanied with the plaudits of a vast concourse of admiring spectators."[40] The growth of shipping on the lower lakes was watched with equal excitement; and in the same summer of 1817, the *Gazette* noted that over thirty schooners and other smaller vessels had cleared from the ports of York, Kingston and Buffalo within a fortnight.[41] There were already two large steamboats on Lake Ontario, others "were building" and it was expected that there would soon be one or more steam-propelled vessels on Lake Erie as well.

The agitation for a bank, which had been dropped shortly before the war, was revived again, for people supposed that the circulation of army bills during the war had helped to dissipate the prejudice of the *habitants* against paper currency. On May 18, 1817, John Richardson, for the committee, invited subscriptions to the stock of the Montreal Bank. In December of the same year the citizens of Montreal presented a petition for the incorporation of the city.[42] The merchants were demanding registry offices for recording transfers of property. In 1819 a pamphleteer estimated the population of the Eastern Townships at twenty thousand;[43] and year after year the townships approached the assembly, begging for improvements and reforms. A corresponding committee of agents for the Eastern Townships was appointed; and in 1819 Oliver Barker began a press campaign in the *Quebec Gazette*.[44]

As the economy developed, as the demand for changes increased, the pressure upon the local legislature grew steadily heavier. "Never, I believe, since the present constitution was granted to this Province," wrote a correspondent in the *Quebec Gazette*, "has the attention of the more reflecting part of the community, been so ardently and anxiously drawn towards our House of Assembly, as at this moment."[45] Unfortunately—or so it appeared to the merchants and their sympathizers, the assembly seemed so childishly unconscious of its responsibilities and so unwilling to take its proper place in the great march of improvement. The bill for the establishment of the Montreal Bank was indeed passed by the legislature in 1818. But in 1819 and 1821 bills for the enregistration of notarial deeds and acts were voted down by the assembly.[46] And in 1821 the petitioners from the Eastern Townships were bluntly informed that the cure for most of their troubles lay in their own hands and that the assembly had no intention of pampering them with special grants of public money for roads.[47]

In the meantime, the assembly had found a cause which was infinitely more to its liking than the cause of social changes and material progress. This was the financial issue.[48] It was a controversy which opened in 1817, and which remained for two decades the chief preoccupation of the French Canadians and of their new leader, Louis Joseph Papineau. For the merchants,

Papineau became—and not undeservedly—the very personification of the whole economic and social order which they wished to overthrow. He was a lawyer who had received the traditional seminary training at Quebec, a seigneur who was not indisposed to play the role of paternal overlord at his manor of Montebello. His fluent, rather empty eloquence was studded with the verbal commonplaces of early nineteenth-century reform; but this academic liberalism was an ornament rather than an essential element of his social and political thought. For him, change was desirable only within the limits of an existing culture, whose preservation it must always be his chief business to secure; and public finance was not so much a way to material progress as a path to political power.

In 1817 Sherbrooke, faced by a steadily mounting debt, was forced to admit that the permanent revenue, which was completely at the disposal of government, was insufficient to defray the ordinary annual expenditure of the province; and in 1818 he called upon the assembly to make good the deficiency. The steadily growing revenue derived from provincial statutes was in the power of the provincial legislature alone to appropriate; and steeled by confidence in its own power the assembly determined upon complete financial control. Public finance became a political football, kicked about by the two branches of the legislature, at a time when to the merchant it began to seem more than ever a necessary instrument in the advance of the commercial state. The assembly hardened its heart against expenditures proposed by its political enemies and spent its time in defending principles to the neglect of good works. "Without dwelling on the causes which have led to the unfortunate discussions between the different branches to the Legislature," wrote a correspondent as early as 1817, "it is too apparent how much the growing prosperity of the country has been impeded, for want of many necessary laws and regulations, either to stimulate industry where languid, or give private enterprise its most advantageous direction."[49]

In Upper Canada, where social divisions were not made more acute by different cultures and conflicting philosophies, the atmosphere was nevertheless a little more tense. 1818 was the year of the dispute between council and assembly over the trade bill; it was also the year in which Robert Gourlay's agitation reached its climax and its virtual conclusion. Gourlay was a Scotsman of some means and education, who might have enjoyed a life of reposeful obscurity. But he possessed an aptitude for quarrelling so remarkable in its consistency that it carried him on a long pilgrimage of disputation from Scotland to England, from England to Canada, and from Canada to the United States. In 1817, he arrived in Upper Canada, fired with the ambition of effecting its complete reform. He proposed to publish an elaborate statistical account of the province; he began a thorough investigation into its resources, disabilities and prospects. But he went on from social planning to political criticism, and from political criticism to violent personal abuse; and in the end, after many tribulations, he was banished from the province in virtue of a monstrous statute passed in 1804. His brief, tempestuous career in Upper Canada was certainly an ample revelation of the weaknesses of his own abnormal psychology and the absurd terrors of the local bureaucracy. But, on the other hand, it did not reveal a deep social division in the province or any serious conflict over fundamental aims. The farmers who replied to the 31st query of Gourlay's famous questionnaire, "What, in your opinion, retards the improvement of your township in particular, or the province in general; and what would most contribute to the same?" showed a spirit which Montreal could heartily approve. There was, of course, a good deal of criticism of the absentee landholders and the clergy reserves: but the requests for men "of capital and enterprise" were almost as frequent as the criticisms of the land-grabbers. There were demands for a bank, for canals, for the improvement of the navigation of the St. Lawrence river.[50] And it was later, when the "men of capital" had provided some of these desired improvements, that criticism was again focused on the powers of the commercial class.

On the whole the disputes within each province were less serious than the disputes between the two. The constitution of 1791 had made concerted action difficult, if not impossible. Yet, at this stage in the development of the new economy, concerted action was vitally necessary for the solution of its problems. The decline of the fur trade and the rise of the new staples had shifted the emphasis away from the Ottawa and the upper lakes to the lower lakes and the St. Lawrence; and if the river of Canada was to bear the new traffic to the sea, its navigation must be improved. It must be improved at once, for the certainty of revived competition from New York did not permit the northerners to choose their time. The Hudson river and Hudson Bay had been the two great trade routes which cut into the centre of the first fur-trading unity of the St. Lawrence; and was there not a chance—a probability—that the Hudson river and its projection, the proposed western canal to Lake Erie, would steal the trade of the new agricultural society from Canada?

It was Lower Canada which built the first of the new canals. During the war the difficulties of transport from Montreal to Lachine had become more evident; and as early as February 1815 the governor announced that the imperial government had in mind a canal from Lachine to the neighbourhood of Montreal and invited the assembly to make a grant in aid.[51] The assembly voted £25,000; but though Captain Samuel Romilly of the Royal Engineers prepared a report on the cost of a canal suitable for the transport of Durham boats, the imperial government gave up the project in favour of the Rideau canal. The Rideau, which was to connect Lake Ontario with the Ottawa river, was a military undertaking, intended to provide a safe, alternative, northern route for the St. Lawrence communication which might be blocked by the Americans in time of war. In the future, it was to become of considerable commercial importance in the transport of goods upward to Upper Canada; but, at the moment, it diverted imperial assistance from the projected Lachine canal. The burden of the new work was thrown back upon the province. At first, in 1819, after a debate of several hours, the assembly decided that the canal should not be built at public expense; but in 1821 came a long memorial from the Lachine Canal Company reciting its tribulations and the legislature decided to take over the work.[52] The state had committed itself to bear the enormous burdens of transportation under the new régime.

Old John Richardson was the chairman of the commission. It was decided to break ground on July 17, 1821; and since the canal was "a work of great public importance and expectancy . . . it was judged expedient that it should commence with appropriate form and ceremony. . . ". On that July day a little throng of people assembled at picket number 18, close by the Lachine turnpike. The commissioners were there, the engineer, the contractors and the band of the 60th regiment.[53] They distributed beef and beer to the labourers and the local farmers; and the band played marches under the bland summer sky. All around were the yellow wheatfields. The road ran down to the little huddle of wharfs and warehouses at Lachine. And beyond that was the river, sombre and glittering in the sunshine. It had reached its last obstruction. It travelled slowly, tranquil, unruffled, confident in its vast reserve of power, towards the final ordeal. And then at last it gathered itself in fury and leaped for the rocks.

The Lachine canal was, however, merely a small beginning. The navigation of the entire river, from Lake Ontario to the sea, would have to be improved; and if these improvements were to have their full effect, they must be built simultaneously by both provinces and on the basis of a general plan. In 1818 the council and assembly of Upper Canada joined in a memorial requesting the co-operation of the lower province in the undertaking. Lower Canada immediately appointed commissioners to investigate the problem; and next year George Garden and J. Papineau for the lower province and Thomas Clark and James Crooks for Upper Canada presented a joint report.[54] The fear of De Witt Clinton's great western canal dominated their findings. The commissioners urged that the proportions of the Canadian canals and locks should be not less than those of the canal in New York state. The width of the canals at the bottom ought to be 28 feet, their depth 4 feet; and the locks should be 90 feet long and 12 feet wide in the clear. It was a superficial report, but it was the first general review by Canadians of their greatest task in the achievement of the new unity of the St. Lawrence. There was, of course, no immediate action. Lower Canada became involved in the Lachine canal project and Upper Canada was oppressed by its poverty and the obvious magnitude of the undertaking. The commercial state, cut into two unequal fragments which possessed only a tithe of their united power, still hesitated before a task which was vital in the new economy and which acquired a fresh urgency with every year that passed.

The postponement of this co-operative enterprise was, however, less immediately serious than the disagreement which broke out between the two provinces over the matter of finance. Back in 1791, Lymburner had predicted that it was beyond the ingenuity of man to devise a financial settlement which would satisfy both provinces. For a while this gloomy prophecy remained unfulfilled, for the agreement of 1801 was regularly renewed. It was not until the confusion of the war that the settlement broke down completely; and in 1814, and again in 1816, the Upper Canadian legislature addressed the governor on the subject. The main claim of Upper Canada was that the inspector at Coteau du Lac, due to his own negligence and that of others, had not been able to keep a complete account of the dutiable articles entering the province from Lower Canada. During the war the commissariat had shipped goods for the army and navy to Upper Canada without ever rendering a proper account of its purchases; and what was even worse, the collector at Coteau du Lac had not been expeditiously informed of two revenue laws recently passed by the Lower Canadian legislature and for months he had failed to take account of the articles upon which the new duties had been laid. Manifestly, Upper Canada was being defrauded through the negligence of officialdom; and when the commissioners of both provinces met in May, 1817, the Upper Canadians modestly presented a bill of nearly £10,840 for arrears.[55] A fresh agreement, which settled the division of duties upon the altogether different principle of population, was to give Upper Canada one-fifth of all the monies collected at the port of Quebec in virtue of imperial and provincial revenue laws. The agreement was to run until July, 1819. But since the Lower Canadians claimed they were without powers, it did not settle the question of arrears and the matter of Upper Canada's little bill was left ominously in suspense.

Then came the real trouble. In 1819, the council and assembly in Lower Canada, pursuing their disputes with single-minded concentration, quarrelled over the appointment of commissioners to treat with the upper province. In the end no commissioners were appointed. There was no new agreement; and for two years Upper Canada could whistle for its money. Thus, when in 1821 negotiations between the two provinces were at last resumed, the

Upper Canadians arrived in a state of moral indignation, determined to take a high line. They presented their bill again with additions; and they demanded that for the period of the next agreement Upper Canada should receive one-quarter of the duties. Unfortunately the Lower Canadian commission, which was dominated by the "liberal reformers" Papineau and Neilson, was willing to make no reparation for the past and no concessions for the future. Population was "utterly inadmissible" as a basis for the division of the revenues: Upper Canada could collect its own duties. After two weeks of writing and replying to each other in this amicable fashion, the conference broke up having achieved precisely nothing.[56] Upper Canada was desperate for money. Maitland wrote home, begging the imperial government to intervene.[57] And in January, 1822, John Beverley Robinson was commissioned by the Upper Canada legislature to go to England and to present the case of the province.

The constitution of 1791 and the new commercial system of the St. Lawrence could not be reconciled. In trade, transportation and finance—in the three problems which were crucial to the development of the new commercial unity—the two provinces had either quarrelled or had failed effectively to co-operate.

V

In these circumstances, which promised so ill for the future of the new enterprises, the old fur-trading system came to an end. 1821 was a year of finalities, of drab conclusions; and the first unity of the St. Lawrence, based upon the fur trade, vanished before a second unity of the new staples had been erected in its place. The themes of the entire drama of change, which had been first stated far back in 1783, had been worked out now and exhausted. For 1783 had meant the establishment of the new, incomprehensible boundary and the coming of the Loyalists, the first settlers on the lower lakes. It had forecast the entire economic and social revolution which now at last in 1821 was finished and complete. The boundary stood. Despite all the repeated, desperate attacks against it, it stood immovably. White settlement had conquered the empire of the St. Lawrence; and the Indians had been driven before it, driven irresistibly through defeat and shame towards their final degradation—towards the reserve, the shapeless alien clothes, the crafts debased and meaningless in a new age, and the dull, uncomprehending, haunted search for something which had irrevocably vanished.

It was, however, the end of the fur trade which most fittingly marked the term of that old commercial empire which had been founded so long ago when the first little ships of the French crept up the St. Lawrence to trade with the Indians. The stand against Selkirk was the last great effort of fur-trading Montreal; and in the dull, disillusioning pause which succeeded the brave days of battle and the triumphs of the court-room, the North West Company was left alone with its own perplexities, with those tangled problems of its costs which could not be settled by a rush of half-breeds or ended by a court decision. By 1820 the winterers at Fort William had admitted defeat. William and Simon Mc-Gillivray, forced by this defection of their partners, hurried home to negotiate a union with the Hudson's Bay Company; and in London Edward Ellice had been persuaded to use his influence to end the everlasting savage struggle in the far west.

The agreement of 1821, by which the North West Company was absorbed into the Hudson's Bay Company, saved some of the pride of the McGillivrays; but the new agreement, negotiated in 1824, surrendered them to the mercies of their creditors. While the winterers were fitted smoothly into the enlarged Hudson's Bay Company, the pack closed in around McGillivrays, Thain & Company; and in 1825 the old Montreal house which McTavish and Frobisher had founded nearly forty years before went down in a last resounding crash. William McGillivray was dead. Thain was mad. Simon McGillivray's collection of pictures was sold; and as he toiled hopelessly through the muddle of the company's books and tried to settle the' long-delayed accounts, the last *bourgeois* of fur-trading Montreal beggared himself and his family in a final effort to make restitution.

The calamity, against which the two races, French and English, had been moved by the instinctive Canadian impulse to oppose, had fallen crushingly. The far west was lost to Montreal. As the French had feared and had foreseen, the seaboard and the bay had conquered in the end. The war with the United States, which had been partly won by the old society of the fur trade, had been wholly lost by the diplomatists in Europe; and Astor gathered up the last of the south-west trade and the North West Company passed from its final victory to its final surrender. The trade was dead and done with. The bustle died out in the North West Company's offices in St. Gabriel Street; and Montreal, the incredible little city which had won a half a continent, was now—what it had always seemed—a small provincial town. It had lost its country and its people. A future more homely and less adventurous awaited it. And many things would be forgotten: the way of the Indians, the tangled portages as spring broke in the woods around, the day dawning in fear and sorrow over one of the vast northern lakes and the unbroken, flowing desolation of the winter prairie. Pond, McGill, the Frobishers, Mackenzie and the aged Alexander Henry were all dead. The "Marquis", McTavish, was twenty years in his grave. And in obscure villages along the river the survivors grew old and tolerated, or struggled with poverty like David Thompson, borrowing a little money from friends and wondering miserably what had befallen them. A curtain was dropped, thick and impenetrable, over the heroisms and frivolities of the past, over the horrors of Pontiac's rising, the murders on the prairie, the solemn conclaves at Fort William and the deep potations of the Beaver Club. The strange, violent life of the fur trade, like the red blaze of one of its Indian camp-fires, died down in the grey morning of new endeavours and flickered out.

PART III

THE STRUGGLE FOR THE SECOND COMMERCIAL EMPIRE

CHAPTER VIII
THE FAILURE OF UNION

I

THE third, the final period in the history of the northern commercial state opened in 1821 and closed in 1850 with the abolition of the old colonial system and the achievement of responsible government. It differed markedly from the periods which had preceded it. Its economic bases lay definitely in the new staples, timber and wheat. It could not recover the primitive simplicity of the fur-trading days; and it did not repeat the striking contrasts which had featured the great transition from 1783 to 1821. A vastly increased population gave the period a number of subsidiary issues and minor problems which tended to obscure the grand lines of its commercial development. And yet, despite the confusion of these variations and interruptions, the original, historic theme of the St. Lawrence was maintained until the last. Under the new conditions the merchants continued to cherish the old continental objectives. Ultimately their reward was a final failure which drew relentlessly closer, as the inimical forces of the entire process gradually matured. In this period the weaknesses of the disunited northern state were revealed as they had never been before. The United States became far more formidable in western trade. And when Great Britain had abolished the timber duties, the corn laws and the navigation system, one of the fundamental bases of the northern commercial dominion was swept away. By 1849 the old commercial philosophy of the St. Lawrence was bankrupt.

Thus the three main themes in the last stage of Canadian commercialism are the increased competition of the United States, the slow ruin of the old colonial system and the intensification of economic maladjustments and social conflicts in Canada itself. Of these three, the revived competition of the United States came first in point of time and possibly first in point of importance. During the decade which followed the conclusion of the War of 1812, the port of New York had begun to capitalize its enormous natural advantages to the full. Its unconditional auctions for the sale of British textiles, its regular and rapid service of packet ships to Great Britain and its energetic exploitation of the American coasting trade, had all helped to put New York well ahead of its nearest rivals. But, in addition to its splendid harbour and the devices of its ambitious citizens, the commercial capital of the Empire State had back of it an inland country which was far greater than that of most of its competitors. The old western trade route from New York *via* the Hudson river had been weak during the first period of Canadian commercialism and little more than potentially powerful during the second. Now, with one great effort, it acquired a competitive strength which was unexpected and overwhelming.[1]

In July, 1817,—four years before the beginning of the Lachine canal—they first broke ground in the construction of the great western canal from Lake Erie to the Hudson. Late in October, 1825, a little fleet of vessels, decked with bunting and crowded with the dignitaries of the state, entered the canal at Buffalo and began its slow triumphal passage eastward. A long battery of guns, stretching five hundred miles from lakes to ocean, roared a prolonged, a repeated salute across the state. There were speeches, ovations, crowds, cheering—the crude, vigorous expressions of a new society in ferment—as the little fleet passed sedately along the canal. And on November 4, while appropriate speeches were made and a great procession wound its way through the streets of New York, Governor De Witt Clinton splashed a barrel of Lake Erie water into the ocean. The canal was completed; and its influence was extended and its enormous commercial pull strengthened, by the building of subsidiary canals—by the Champlain canal which was finished in 1822 and by the Oswego feeder which was completed three years after the Erie. The Champlain canal, which joined Lake Champlain with the Hudson river, re-annexed Vermont to the commercial system of New York; the Oswego feeder tapped the trade of Lake Ontario; and the main branch of the Erie led through the new agricultural districts of northern New York State to Lake Erie, Cleveland and the ports of the new west. The whole system became at once a success. In the first year, 1825, over 13,000 boats and rafts were cleared on the canal. Its tolls rose to over a million dollars in 1830. It was to help make

New York the commercial metropolis of America, to depress
Boston and Philadelphia and to frustrate the second unity of the
St. Lawrence imagined by the merchants of Montreal.

While pressure from the south came to weigh more heavily than
ever upon the commercial system of the St. Lawrence, the support
from Great Britain became weaker and more uncertain. The old
mercantilism, which had combined trade and politics, which
was at once a code for prosperity and a religion of conquest,
was worn by economic changes and exposed by intellectual attacks.
For three hundred years mercantilism had been the theory of
empire. It was born with the birth of world trade. But the very
territorial conquests which had been made under its inspiration
had now grown suspect; and the certainties which had seemed so
clear in the old days when Shaftesbury denounced the Dutch
before the lords were now ridiculed by the knowing. It was nearly
fifty years since the teachings of Adam Smith had excited the
interested, the truly "modern" curiosity of Lord Shelburne and
Mr. Pitt; and in the meantime, the rise of a great new industrial
civilization in England appeared to dictate the introduction of
free trade.

The new economic orthodoxy, interpreted by Ricardo, Malthus,
McCulloch and Mill, was hostile to the old ancestral myths. In the
pages of pamphlets and quarterlies, academic denunciations
rolled on sonorously in long, downright, antithetical periods; and
Cobden and Bright were soon to prove how easy it was to rouse
the new democracy by a skilful mixture of hard practicality and
moral earnestness. The Anti-Corn Law League, with its pamphlets,
its meetings and its bustling energy, was the most popular demonstration against the old commercial system, with its tangle of
duties, preferences, drawbacks and shipping regulations. Huskisson
and Peel, who typified the union between the new "industrious
classes" and the old oligarchy, were the appropriate instruments
of the new movement for free trade; and in the forties Peel completed what Huskisson had left undone twenty years before. By
1849 industrial Great Britain had abolished the old mercantilism
to which, until the very end, commercial Canada remained devoted.
It was the tragedy of the first empire that New England outgrew
the colonial system before Great Britain; and it was the misfortune

of the second empire that Great Britain outgrew the colonial system before Canada. To the Canadian merchants, who looked upon preferences and prohibitions with the eye of unquestioning faith, the action of Great Britain was just as unnatural, just as incomprehensible as had been the protests of New England to the world of George III.

The competition of the United States and the slowly approaching defection of Great Britain fell more heavily upon a country which was too weakened to defend itself. In this last period of its history, the Canadian commercial state was disturbed by economic maladjustments and distracted by social conflicts. The transition from furs to timber, and the further shift from timber to the new staples, wheat and flour, continued to keep the northern economy in a state of chronic disequilibrium. The immigrants who swarmed into Upper Canada and the new western states made possible a trade in agricultural produce on a grand scale; and the intensification of the agricultural interest, even more than the development of the timber trade, created new requirements, new commitments and new problems which unsettled the bases of the old commercial state. There could be no more delay in the reorganization of the crudely simple fur-trading system: the laws, the customs, the institutions of the St. Lawrence must be immediately adjusted to meet the pressing needs of the new economy. The search for new markets and new imperial preferences must be renewed with greater zeal. The state should make the way smooth for the commercial concerns, the banks and the land companies. The state should provide harbours, ship channels and canals. The state, in fact, must become the super-corporation of the new economy, dominated like any other corporation by commercial interests and used to its full capacity as a credit instrument in a grand programme of public works.

This commercial programme, which the merchants had devised for the conquest of the second empire of the St. Lawrence, was now confronted by the agricultural interests of the two provinces. The collapse of the fur trade and the rise of the new trades in timber, wheat and flour at once upset the balance of the northern economy and accentuated its existing social divisions. It was true that the French Canadians did much of the rough work of lumbering in the same cheerful, unquestioning spirit with which they had served the *bourgeois* of fur-trading Montreal. But the fact that individuals and whole groups found it natural and even congenial to give their services to the new trades, does not alter the more important fact that the new commercial system met with the stubborn resistance of the society of the lower St. Lawrence as a collective whole. The new trading system required more than the simple services of individual *habitants*. It demanded planning, revolutionary legislation, heavy expenditures. And these demands were made of a society which, in the mass, was rural and sedentary in character, which gave its best brains to the priesthood and the professions and which was spiritually so little attuned to the new commercialism that it had practically no influence whatever in its direction and control.

The great migration from Great Britain, which occupied the quarter-century from 1825 to 1850 and peopled the western part of Upper Canada, extended this social conflict territorially and deepened its import. Though at first the frontiersmen had been only intermittently critical of the commercial system, their attitude of deepening hostility came in time to differ comparatively little from that of the peasants and the professional classes of the lower province. It was the belief of the agrarian leaders in both colonies that the institutions, projects and expenditures desired by the commercial class would either divert attention from rural needs or would impose intolerable burdens and inflict definite injuries upon the countryside. To a large—though an indefinitely large—extent, the approaching conflict in the Canadas was a conflict between agriculture and commerce, farm lands and trade routes, North American parochialism and the old colonial system. The merchants conceived of the St. Lawrence simply as the great channel of imperial trade from America to Europe. The farmers looked upon the river and the lakes as the centre of a homeland with a life and an importance of its own. Satisfied, because of the benefits it gave them, with imperial control in trade and politics, the merchants' sole major contribution to Canadian political theory was the idea of centralization, expressed politically in the demand for the union of the two provinces. It was the farmers and their leaders who fumbled with current democratic notions in their blind, instinctive search for a greater measure of popular local control. In 1840–1841, with the establishment of the union of the provinces, the merchants won. But it was a late victory, a victory delayed so long that it was followed almost immediately by the downfall of mercantilism, by the grant of responsible government, and by the end of the second commercial empire.

II

In the early twenties, when the Canadian commercial system was just entering upon this final period of its history, the new interests and the new trends were already clearly discernible. The first great immigration from Great Britain to Canada lay still in the future—in the very near future; and the migrants numbered only a few thousand each year. But the country was growing rapidly. In 1825 the population of Lower Canada was estimated at 479,288 and that of Upper Canada at 157,923.[2] The depression of 1821 was over; 1823 and 1824 were years of increasing prosperity which had its climax in the boom of the next year. White pine reached the price of 85s. a load, red pine 110s.; and from 1823 to 1825 the export of timber and deals from Quebec rose without interruption. In 1825 Canada shipped 33,152 tons of oak timber, 128,078 tons of pine timber, 1,679,000 boards and planks and 3,950,000 staves. The export of ashes had risen in 1825 to 65,502 barrels, which was 10,000 barrels larger than the shipments of either of the two previous years. Between forty and fifty thousand barrels of flour were exported annually during the period 1823–1825; and in 1825, when Huskisson made the first really generous concession to Canadian agriculture, 671,801 bushels of wheat were shipped from the port of Quebec. In 1822, 612 vessels were cleared and in 1825 the number had risen to 832.[3]

The enterprises which were to feature this new era in the Canadian economy were rapidly growing in number. There were now four chartered banks in the two provinces—the Montreal Bank, the Quebec Bank, the Bank of Canada and the Bank of Upper Canada. The Lachine canal was completed in 1825. Dalhousie declared that the locks were "of the finest masonry I ever saw"; and even William Lyon Mackenzie grew enthusiastic over the work and praised John Richardson "as the life and soul, the very De Witt Clinton of the Lachine Canal".[4] William Hamilton Merritt—persuasive, energetic, robustly optimistic, the born promoter of a frontier society—had fired the imagination of the two Canadas with his project of a canal from Lake Erie to Lake Ontario. The Upper Canadian legislature made a loan and bought shares in the undertaking; Lower Canada contributed £25,000; and in 1824 and again in 1825 Merritt was selling shares to the merchants of Quebec and Montreal.[5] In 1824 the editor of the *Montreal Gazette* was rejoicing over the rumour that a land company had been formed in England to take over the crown reserves in Upper and Lower Canada. The merchants of Quebec and Montreal proposed the formation of a Lower Canada land company. Stock was subscribed. Though the Canadian gentry would have "nothing to say to it", Richardson, Gerrard, Forsyth, McGillivray "and all the most respectable folks here are favourable to the plan. . . ".[6] W. B. Felton, who had sponsored the venture, went to England to enlist the support of English capitalists; and in September, 1825, in London, Ellice, Gould, Usborne, Gillespie and the other merchants interested in the Canada trade, agreed to join the concern.[7] Actually, the Lower Canada Land Company was abandoned during the depression which followed; but in 1826 the Canada Company acquired the great Huron tract in the upper province.

The new trades, the new commercial and financial undertakings were to prosper the fortunes of York and Kingston and a dozen little places along the St. Lawrence and the shores of Lake Ontario. The trade in timber was to give a last fillip to the declining commercial importance of Quebec. But Montreal, the river city, was inevitably becoming the metropolis of the commercial state. It was to be the forwarding centre for the trade in manufactures with the communities of the new west; it was to be the depot of trans-shipment for western wheat and flour and provisions on their journey towards the protected imperial markets of the Atlantic. The island lay like a great wedge in the middle of the river. The whole quickening life of the St. Lawrence, the traffic which fought its way up against the current and the traffic which was carried eastward to the sea, the sailors, boatmen and immigrants, the *bateaux*, ships and steamboats, the lumber and grain were creating the one city which could serve their purpose. The town stirred uneasily, growing with difficulty, reaching out after its new opportunities. Its smallness, for a place so long established, seemed "inconceivable" to an American visitor. But beyond the old walls, in the Recollet, St. Lewis, St. Lawrence and Quebec suburbs, a new town had arisen; and the population was perhaps 20,000 souls.

At the beginning of this third, this crucial, period in the history of the northern commercial system, Montreal still preserved to the eyes of occasional visitors, the aspect of a small old-country seaport. The sombre grey stone, quarried in the vicinity, was still used in the majority of buildings, though Montrealers proudly took care to point out the bright, new brick houses of a few of the merchants. In St. Paul and Notre Dame streets, the close-packed shops and houses, built of grey stone, roofed with sheet iron or tin and sealed with iron shutters, presented an appearance which even the citizens admitted was forbidding. From the river, as one came across from Longueuil or Laprairie, the long blank walls of convents and the towers and spires of churches recalled the piety and devotion of an earlier day. As it lay in the spring sunshine, with the fields and market gardens about it and the lofty greenness of the mountain in the distance, the little town had an odd, old-fashioned gravity, a faint flavour of staid Scottish seaports and French provincial towns.[8]

While the city seemed touched with a kind of old-world sobriety, it showed all the rawness and all the interest in material improvements which were characteristic of North America. Some streets were well paved with flagstones and at night there were a few lights in the principal thoroughfares. In 1819 the defunct water-works company, which had attempted to run water from beyond the mountain in wooden pipes, handed over its unexpired charter to Thomas Porteous; and to the admiration of the citizens a new system of cast-iron pipes was laid down. Dillon's Tavern, of course, had disappeared. Down by the river, there was a "superb" new hotel, the Mansion-House, with an assembly room and "elegant" appointments. A theatre had been built in College street; and on summer evenings the Champ de Mars was crowded with people who were "partial to a lounge in company assembled".

The city, in its slow growth towards metropolitan power, was impeded by a dozen handicaps. It was not incorporated; and the impulse to municipal reform was felt indirectly, for Montreal, like the hamlets and the countryside about it, was a charge upon the paternal solicitude of the provincial legislature. It had not yet been made a port of entry. A hundred and eighty miles away, in the rival port of Quebec, sat the board of the Trinity House, in which was entrusted the ultimate control of Montreal harbour; and the Montreal merchants were forced to repair to Quebec for the settlement of marine disputes before the court of vice-admiralty. "Quebec", declared the *Montreal Gazette* indignantly, "affords an example of centralization of Military, Civil, Financial, Clerical, Commercial, and Marine power, worthy of the policy of the late Napoleon Bonaparte. . . ."[9]

The number of ocean vessels which ventured up the river from Quebec to Montreal was still comparatively small. The *Montreal Gazette* informed its readers that during the season of 1824 only 55 vessels out of the 613 entered at Quebec had made the ascent up the river.[10] The ship channel across Lake St. Peter was treacherous—the merchants were pressing for its improvement; and the notorious St. Mary's current, racing past the island of Montreal, sometimes kept the baffled sailing-ships at a standstill for days and even weeks. In the main, the transport up and down the river was still maintained by the ordinary small river craft and by the steamboats. The speed and regularity of the steamboat service had so improved that by the end of 1827 the Montreal merchants were able to get replies to their Quebec letters within forty-four hours. In the early twenties, John Torrance's Tow Boat Company, closely followed by the Molson Line, began to employ steamboats to haul the sailing-ships up the river past St. Mary's current to the harbour of Montreal.[11] It was, for the time, almost a revolutionary experiment, watched with interest and anxiety by the merchants, and destined within the next few years to alter the traffic on the river considerably.

The harbour itself and its approaches still remained neglected. It was not until 1824 that a commission was set up for the improvement of Montreal harbour; and next year, the commissioners, Messrs. Blackwood, Forsyth, Moffatt, Larocque and Auldjo, presented a report urging that the harbour, its regulation and proposed improvements should be vested in the control of a corporation independent of Trinity House.[12] The construction of the new docks was to be long delayed; and in the early twenties, when the "spring fleet"—a mere half dozen sailing vessels—had worked its way laboriously through the narrow channel and had cast anchor in the deep water between Market Gate Island and Montreal, it faced a kind of long natural quay which would have done credit to a country village.[13] At one point, where the bank ran south-west between Callière's Point and the shipyard, there were two irregular wooden wharfs. In places the abrupt shore was strengthened by "revêtements". But in the main the gentle arc of the shoreline which ran westward along Commissioners Street past Callière's Point to the Grey Nunnery and the shipyard, was merely "natural bank", littered, muddy and treacherous.

Montreal was the logical centre of the new commercial system. "It is the heart of the country", wrote Dalhousie, "and from it circulates the life blood of Canada." It illustrated all the requirements and the difficulties of the new commercial unity of the St. Lawrence. There was so much to do, so few resources, so many obstacles. And when in 1822 the merchants learnt that Great Britain proposed to unite the two provinces of Upper and Lower Canada, they gave their almost fanatical support to what they thought was the only possible political solution for the problems of the commercial state.

III

It was highly appropriate that the breakdown of the constitution of 1791 should occur at the moment when the fur trade disappeared and the new commercial system took its place. The climax of economic change revealed the basic contradiction between trade and politics. The constitution had been a hindrance to the old commercialism of the fur trade: it could not help but be a positive barrier to the new commercialism of wheat and timber. As soon as the two provinces approached the really vital and significant problem of their corporate existence as a commercial state, the inadequacy of the political system of 1791 was made manifest. They had boggled the regulation of trade with the United States.

They were angrily at issue over the division of duties collected at Quebec. And their first tentative attempts to grapple with the problem of water communications had suggested how difficult it would be for them to collaborate in a great programme of public works. Divided into two separate quarrelling political entities, the commercial state could not borrow heavily, build effectively, grow into the great capitalist concern which the merchants desired it to be.

The crisis of 1821 forced the intervention of the British government. Appealed to by the governors, the merchants and the legislature of Upper Canada, the home authorities decided upon a general reorganization of the affairs of the two provinces; and the proposed union of the legislatures was merely one part of a general settlement which was designed to embrace the questions of land, commerce and finance. The crisis had been a revelation of the weaknesses of the commercial state. The solution was largely financial and commercial in inspiration and was sponsored and supported by the merchants and their sympathizers. Ever since they had recovered from the numbed dejection of the 1790's, ever since their gloomy prophecies had been confirmed by the operation of the Constitutional Act, the merchants had fixed upon the panacea of union with undeviating concentration. In 1819 they had been cheered by the happy rumour that the Duke of Richmond had written home advocating their favourite remedy.[14] John Caldwell, the receiver-general of Lower Canada, a man who was deeply interested in the new trades in flour and timber and who had been almost ruined by the depression of 1821, was in London at the time when the Union Bill was being prepared. John Marshall, the solicitor-general of the province, drew up the first draft. And Edward Ellice, who had just helped to bring about the union of the two Canadian fur companies, transferred his attention briskly from commercial to political amalgamations, used his considerable influence to the full at the colonial office and was one of the few people who spoke in favour of the bill in parliament.

The Union Bill, as it was originally drafted, was designed to accomplish three principal purposes: it regulated the trade between the Canadas and the United States, it set up an arbitration system for the division of the duties collected at Quebec, and it united the legislatures of the two provinces of Upper and Lower Canada. In its first form the Union Bill was thus a jumble of not too closely related elements; and what was more important, it was a vulnerable bill, one of those unfortunate measures which subject a good scheme to criticism by faulty execution in general and by offensive, superfluous clauses in particular.[15] It did not completely unite the two provinces; it merely joined the two legislatures into one provincial parliament which was to make laws for the peace, order and good government of either or both. As the terms of the scheme were worked out, each province, irrespective of population, would eventually have a representation of sixty members in the united legislature. There were clauses providing high property qualifications for membership in the assembly and permitting the governor to summon two executive councillors to participate in the assembly's debates. The use of the English language was made immediately compulsory in the written proceedings of the legislature and it was to be ultimately compulsory in debate. Although the previous religious concessions to Roman Catholics were confirmed, the governor's approval was to be necessary for the appointment of new clergy.

During the summer, the British passed the commercial and financial sections of the original bill in a separate statute, which became known as the Canada Trade Act; but the question of political union remained disquietingly in abeyance. The details of the whole comprehensive scheme of legislation became public property in the two provinces towards the close of the year; and during the autumn and winter of 1822–1823 every official and unofficial body in Canada felt called upon to express its opinion on what was easily the most important political issue of the time. From councils, assemblies, towns, townships and districts there came a great mass of resolutions, petitions and memorials. Full of the reproaches of injured virtue and the indignation of belittled loyalty, Papineau and his party organized the Constitutional Society to protest against the union; and committee men travelled through the highways and by-ways of rural Lower Canada collecting those signatures and those not infrequent crosses by which the French Canadians were accustomed to signify their mature intellectual convictions. Petitions against the union bearing the names of 60,642 Lower Canadians and 8,097 Upper Canadians were carried over to England by Papineau and Neilson.[16] James Stuart crossed with a less impressive collection of requests that the bill be passed. A pamphlet controversy broke out, the opponents of union going the unionists one better by advocating a general federation of the British North American provinces; and the agitation, both by its duration and its acrimony, revealed how crucial was the question of the unification of the Canadian commercial state.

Naturally, therefore, the controversy provided a brilliant revelation of the nature of public opinion in the two Canadas. The division over the Union Bill was not primarily a division between two races, or two provinces or two political philosophies, such as liberalism and conservatism. It was, in the main, a division between those who thought commercially in terms of the commercial system of the St. Lawrence and those who thought in terms of rural and parochial interests and who instinctively distrusted centralization and control. Apart from the Eastern Townships, which definitely favoured union, the bill found its chief support in the towns; and from Quebec to Niagara, there was scarcely a town or an aspiring village which did not contain a commercial minority actively interested in the measure. Rural French Canada, of course, was solid in opposition; for union, to the French Canadians, meant the slow submergence of their own peculiar culture, as well as the rapid exploitation of lands and resources which in their opinion ought to be developed only at the rate of the natural increase of the population of Lower Canada. The town of York, where the job-holders naturally believed in the doctrine of local autonomy, disliked the measure; and in the rural communities of Upper Canada the opposition grew stronger as one travelled westward away from the river and its commercialism. It was on the St. Lawrence and on the shores of eastern Lake Ontario, where the commercial system really dominated the lives of men, that the bill found its heartiest support. "From what I have heard", wrote J. B. Robinson, "I gather that some of those in U. Canada resident near Montreal, or rather nearer to it than to the seat of Government in Upper Canada are in favour of the Union, while those in York and above are with very few exceptions against it."[17]

In a long series of meetings which were held in the Eastern Townships, along the Ottawa and in Quebec, William Henry, Montreal, Cornwall, Prescott, Kingston and Niagara, the merchants and their sympathizers presented the old case for the unification of the commercial state. They paid, on the whole, extremely little attention to the details of the measure. Unlike the French Canadians, who grew incoherent over the clauses relating to religion and language, and unlike the Upper Canadians who had the typical frontier dislike for high property qualifications and councillors deliberating in the assembly, the merchants scarcely troubled to deal with clauses which they probably realized were unwise and which, in any case, interested them comparatively little. It was the mere idea of union which thrilled them. Mercantilists could always talk with propriety and conviction on the subject of imperial defence; and the merchants spoke patriotically of how the union would save Upper Canada from the clutches of the Americans and fortify the two provinces against the attacks of the United States. In the main, however, they showed an incurable tendency to regard the project, not as a political union, but as a kind of commercial merger. "It is most true", wrote J. B. Robinson, "that the advocates of the Union in Lower Canada, chiefly Merchants, did organise corresponding committees in Upper Canada with the same activity, and much after the same system as committees are organised for advancing Canals, or urging objects connected with trade and speculation. . . ."[18] The merchants, as always in the past, were thinking chiefly of their commercial system. They saw in union a measure which would solve the particular economic problems of each province and promote the commercial prosperity of both.

Union, in the first place, would break the bondage imposed upon commercial Lower Canada by the "anti-commercial" French. The assembly which could block progress indefinitely by sheer inertia, was practically a monopoly of the rurally minded French Canadians; and hence "all commercial enterprise and improvement have been crippled and obstructed". The province was lethargic and legislation had not helped to galvanize it into activity. The statute book, declared W. B. Coltman, was "filled with various trifling enactments, but containing fewer important Regulations for the good Government of the people, than is perhaps to be met with in any other Body of Laws of the same length whatsoever".[19] "It might be considered indelicate and improper", said Walker at the same Quebec meeting, "to tax any portion of His Majesty's Subjects in this Province with anti-commercial principles and feelings, but it may not be irrelevant to notice the great imperfection of our Laws affecting that important interest, and the number of fruitless propositions that have been made to improve them."

The merchants had failed every time they approached a body which was uninterested in change and unwilling to effect it. "During Thirty Years", declared the *Montreal Herald*, "Commercial Men have been engaged in unavailing efforts to obtain from that anti-commercial branch of the Provincial Legislature various salutary Laws and Regulations, particularly a Bankrupt Law and a Law establishing Register offices, for the enrolment of all conveyances of Real Estate and of all burthens thereon. . . ."[20] There had been no reform of the seigniorial system and no lessening of the burdens of the mutation fines. The complaints of the Eastern Townships to the provincial assembly had always been treated with "contempt or indifference"; and their lack of courts and representation in parliament was a positive discouragement to immigration. "One marked consequence of the present state of Lower-Canada", wrote a minority in the legislative council of the lower province, "is, that respectable Emigrants from the Mother Country are discouraged from coming to or remaining in it, seeing themselves, on arrival, considered as if they were strangers, although in a British land."[21]

From the point of view of Upper Canada the merchants argued that the union would make possible an improved system of communications and cheaper transport. Down at Niagara, Robert Nichol complained that the profits of production in Upper Canada were swallowed up by the enormous transportation charges eastward.[22] "The greatest difficulties now exist", asserted the citizens of Cornwall, "regarding the transportation of produce from the interior parts of this district to market, there being no direct land communication with Montreal, this being the consequence of the interested conduct of those persons holding seigniories near the line, and of the inattention of the Legislature of the Lower Province to the internal improvement of that portion of Canada, notwithstanding repeated applications have been made to the House of Assembly of Lower Canada, to open the different communications. . . ."[23] In fact, far from lowering the charges of transportation, the lower province had actually increased them, by clapping a tax on scows and rafts descending the river, without the consent of Upper Canada.

The problem of cheap and rapid communications by land and water could obviously not be solved by Upper Canada alone. Even if the western province beggared itself in the construction of magnificent canals, the works would lose most of their value if they were not followed immediately by similar improvements east of the interprovincial boundary. Moreover the province was not free to raise its revenue to meet the great expenditures of public works. In the establishment of duties on sea-borne commerce at the port of Quebec, Lower Canada was still to have the positive and Upper Canada merely the negative voice, according to the Canada Trade Act of 1822; and at a meeting at Kingston, C. A. Hagerman pointed out that if the parliament of Great Britain accepted a proposed new revenue law, the miserable negative of Upper Canada could be overridden.[24] In other words, the amount of the customs revenue was to be decided outside of the upper province; and its division, in case of a dispute, was to be determined by three arbitrators of whom Upper Canada appointed only one. "She has been, and must continue to be, therefore," wrote Stuart of Upper Canada, "incapable from the want of pecuniary resources, at her disposal, from entering upon many measures of public utility that she would otherwise advantageously adopt, and from the fluctuating and uncertain amount of her revenue, depending on the will of the legislature of Lower Canada, must be injuriously shackled in all her legislative provisions for the public good."[25]

Obviously the measure would have particular benefits for each of the provinces. But the main effort of the merchants was to prove that union would create a common prosperity, and confer a general benefit greater than all its particular gifts. "It was . . . to consolidate", declared the *Upper Canada Gazette & Weekly Register*, "*not to scatter and destroy*, the liberties, energies, and power, of a Free People into one efficient whole, with a view of enlarging and reaping the full benefit of every source of domestic wealth and improvement . . . that, in our mind, the measure was proposed. . . ."[26] Separated, the two provinces could not help but be backward, argued the merchants; and the superior prosperity of the United States, which was frequently mentioned in the discussions, would continue as long as the separation of the Canadas endured. But union would create a new temper and a new energy. It would link the financial strength of Lower Canada with the enterprise of the upper province. "It is a fair presumption . . .", declared Macaulay at Kingston, "that in the event of a union, some portion of the noble spirit of improvement evinced by our Parliament would be transferred into the breasts of the Lower Canadian Members. . . ."[27] And in Lower Canada John Richardson was ready gratefully to embrace the Upper Canadians as men who "were possessed of enterprize and a spirit of traffic which might be beneficially exerted for the good of the country. . . ".[28]

Geographically the provinces were one. The River St. Lawrence which bound the commercial state together seemed to dictate political union with all the imperative force of a heavenly command. The river gave the provinces common interests and saddled them with joint responsibilities. "That these Provinces have common interests which cannot be provided for by separate legislation and local expedients is indisputable", wrote a correspondent in the *Montreal Gazette*;[29] and among all the objects which were of "joint utility though of separate locality" the improvement of the St. Lawrence was the most vital and most immediately necessary. The approaching completion of the New York canal allowed the Canadas no time. It was impossible to believe "that, with distinct Legislatures, the two Provinces could ever agree upon the apportionment of the expense to be defrayed by each in accomplishing such works". Only a unified country could effectively complete the task. "The united energies of the Canadas, if judiciously directed," said Macaulay, "might soon form a most magnificent and commodious channel of communication with the ocean, which, aided by natural advantages, would quicken the advance of the United Provinces to a proud eminence of commercial prosperity, and deprive foreign states of the many advantages they expect to reap from our present inert condition."[30]

Nor was this all: Transportation and public works were inseparably associated with finance and fiscal power; and in the matters of revenue laws and public money the union offered a complete solution where the Canada Trade Act would lamentably fail. The old system, by which Lower Canada imposed duties and "impartial" arbitrators divided the proceeds, must not continue. The commercial keys of the St. Lawrence—the control of customs and ocean ports—were in the hands of anti-commercial Lower Canada, while Upper Canada had an equal right in equity to use them and a better will to use them well. Would the most scrupulous arbitrators be able to still jealousies and disputes? "Will perpetual arbitration not increase rather than remove the causes of Provincial discord about Revenue," inquired a correspondent in the *Montreal Gazette*, "and is it possible with one common Port of ingress, to continue a system for imposition of Import duties, which will not give to the one or the other Legislature an unfair influence?"[31] In the Upper Canadian assembly, the speaker, L. P. Sherwood, argued that the checks and balances created by the Canada Trade Act, the appointment of arbitrators and the negative voice given to Upper Canada, was cumbrous machinery which promised discord and infringed upon the constitutional rights of the provinces.[32]

Thus, by 1822, the merchants had roughly worked out the only significant political philosophy which existed at that time in Canada. It was unfortunate that there was no Canadian Alexander Hamilton to give coherence and form to the views of the commercial class, to organize the scattered ideals of practical men into a complete and impressive political theory, to exalt the interests of a particular group into the aspirations proper to the Canadian nation as a whole. But, like the views of Hamilton, the ideas of the merchants were based on the economic interests of their class. They had the same belief in a strong political unity, in government by the commercially minded, in institutions which would protect and advance their interests. They showed the same impatience for local views, rural predilections and the ineptitudes of democracy.

Some points in their philosophy remained undeveloped, for upon these issues public opinion continued unformed and the opposition inarticulate. But the case for union had been made. The merchants had specifically rejected the idea of a larger federation, for they realized that a federal union of all the British North American provinces was impractical at the moment and would leave the difficulties of Lower Canada unsolved.[33] Fifteen years later Lord Durham travelled by much the same route to reach a similar conclusion.

The merchants could argue, but they could not persuade the imperial parliament to legislate. When the Union Bill was first introduced into parliament, Sir James Mackintosh, who, according to the irate Dalhousie, "acted like a childish boy to get his will", virtuously advanced the unimpeachable democratic argument that the Canadian people should be consulted before a measure so seriously affecting their welfare was passed. This objection may have accounted, in part, for the original delay; and according to Bathurst and the permanent under-secretary, Wilmot Horton, it was the unexpected whig opposition—and still more, the confusion which followed Castlereagh's suicide—which induced the government to give over the union temporarily and to pass the unobjectionable remainder of the Canadian legislation as the Canada Trade Act of 1822.[34] The year's delay revealed how violent was the opposition of French Canada to union; and the British government, faced by the confused and acrimonious controversy in the Canadas, decided to abandon the bill. After all, some of the most pressing Canadian problems had been settled by the legislation of 1822. The Canada Trade Act provided machinery for the division of the customs revenue collected at Quebec; and it established regulations—which can best be considered in connection with the general commercial reforms of Robinson and Huskisson—for the trade between the Canadas and the United States. But the idea of political union had been dropped. And it was the tragedy of the merchants that its achievement was delayed for another eighteen years.

IV

After the great campaign of 1822-1823, the commercial class
was left in that state of depressed, unhappy lassitude which follows
a great expenditure of energy in a cause which has been lost.
The merchants had only one policy and it had failed. All they
could do in the years which immediately followed 1823 was to
discover a possible substitute for union—a substitute which would
be almost as satisfactory to themselves and possibly more acceptable to the waverers. This was the proposal for the annexation of
Montreal and a strip of the surrounding country to Upper Canada.
The island of Montreal lay just below the confluence of the Ottawa
and St. Lawrence rivers; the province of Lower Canada extended
westward to include a triangle of territory between the two great
rivers; and although the schemes for annexation varied in detail,
they agreed in demanding that this triangle of territory and the
island of Montreal immediately below it, should be annexed to
Upper Canada. Annexation would give the upper province a
seaport. It would rescue Montreal from "the feudal barbarisms and
withering prejudices" of Lower Canada. When in 1826 the legislative council of Upper Canada actually passed resolutions advocating the annexation of the island, the editor of the *Montreal Gazette*
openly rejoiced. "Let the lower province enjoy its St. Petersburg;"
said he, alluding a little tactlessly to the city of Quebec, "but
the other might by this means justly boast of her Liverpool."[35]

In the meantime, Montreal remained in "bondage" and the
two provinces continued their independent existence. The new
economic and social system, which had now completely emerged
from more primitive forms, was blocked; and the commercial state
had to get along as best it could with the antiquated and unsuitable
political machinery of 1791. The Canada Trade Act of 1822 had,
it is true, removed some of the obvious causes of friction. The
imperial parliament was regulating colonial trade; and the arbitration system, set up for the division of duties collected at Quebec,
was working with a minimum of difficulty. But the problem of
transportation—a provincial problem, which could be solved by
the two provinces acting in unison—remained. As the Erie canal
neared completion, the popular demand for the improvement of the

St. Lawrence increased. The St. Lawrence Association was formed; and during 1824–1825 it developed branches in the river towns from Quebec to Cornwall, began taking unofficial surveys and petitioning the legislatures for action.[36] At regular intervals requests arrived at Quebec from Upper Canada—requests for roads in the western part of the lower province, for the more vigorous improvement of the St. Lawrence, for higher duties which would increase the revenue available for public works—all intended to goad Lower Canada into action and all without effect.[37]

For the Lower Canadian assembly maintained an irritatingly judicious calm on the subject of canals. It was true that John Richardson and his commission were able to complete the Lachine canal as far as the harbour of Montreal. But the work was more expensive than anybody had anticipated, since, as Richardson said, "substance had been preferred to show"; and when the commissioners approached the assembly for more funds, the assembly accompanied its grudging grants with long moralizing lectures on the subject of extravagance.[38] The Chambly canal, which would connect St. Johns with the River Richelieu, was the only other project undertaken in this period. Commercially it would benefit Quebec alone; and a correspondent in the *Quebec Gazette* inquired sarcastically, "What impression may we expect to find made on the minds of the people of Upper Canada on hearing of this munificent Grant for the attainment of a bauble, whilst the great Interests of one of the finest countries in the world, and which is, or ought to be considered as part of our own soil, is, comparatively speaking, altogether neglected?"[39] On occasion the assembly would appoint a committee to consider the general problem of the navigation of the St. Lawrence; and the committee, having considered, would reach the profound conclusion that the improvement of navigation was a difficult subject which required a great deal of deliberation and research. Moreover—and this was the vital difference between feudal Quebec and the normal American community—Lower Canada shrank back aghast from heavy expenditures and particularly from loans.

Upper Canada had no such inhibitions. While Lower Canada hesitated, the upper province committed itself with blithe enthusiasm to the enormous project of the Welland canal. On June 28,

1823, the original promoters held an organization meeting at Beaver Dams, where Hiram Tibbett delivered his absurdly optimistic report; and from that day on, the canal from Lake Erie to Lake Ontario *via* the line of Twelve Mile creek, the Welland and the Grand rivers, was to assume ever more grandiose proportions and to weigh ever more heavily upon the people of Upper Canada.[40] The depth of the canal, as originally planned, was to be only four feet; but in 1825 a canal for sloop navigation was projected, the depth was increased first to $7\frac{1}{2}$ feet and then to 8, and the canal was to be 34 feet wide at the bottom and 52 feet 6 inches at the surface. At first the directors were contented with an extremely modest capitalization; but in 1825 they asked and obtained from the legislature the permission to increase the capital stock to £200,000, and the zealous Merritt, assisted by H. J. Boulton and J. H. Dunn, departed enthusiastically for a raid upon the money markets of Lower Canada, New York and London. Only a meagre amount of stock was sold in Upper Canada; but while it was financially weaker, the party in the upper province which believed in expenditure for prosperity's sake, was politically stronger than it was in Lower Canada. J. H. Dunn, the receiver-general of the province, became president of the Welland Canal Company. Robinson, the attorney-general, approved of the project, and H. J. Boulton, the solicitor-general, was commissioned to sell stock in England. The venerable Archdeacon Strachan, momentarily interrupting his labours in behalf of the exclusive pretensions of his church, penned a glowing pamphlet in which the virtues of the Welland canal were exalted above those of any other similar work, ancient or modern, in Europe or Asia. The governor, Maitland, was converted to the scheme after the northern terminus had been shifted to the mouth of Twelve Mile creek. Moreover, the tie between trade and politics, between the canal company and the government, was strengthened and tightened by the legislature itself. It made a loan of £25,000 in 1826: in 1827 it bought stock to the value of £50,000. Yet a good part of the stock remained unsold, the estimates increased, the company neared the end of its resources; and, at the end of 1827, it faced the really herculean job of the "deep cut"—the passage through the watershed of the

Niagara peninsula. The company approached the government; and Maitland sent off a letter home begging for an imperial loan of £50,000.[41] The Welland Canal Company was less than four years old; but already it was well on its way down that now wearisomely familiar road which begins with government assistance and ends in government ownership.

In Lower Canada, the defeat of the Union Bill had left the conditions of political strife unchanged and had only altered—for the worse—the temper of the political parties. The old moves were made: they were met by the old counter-moves. And, as they viewed this futile stalemate, men drifted rapidly from a feeling of impotent fury to an irrepressible demand for direct action. Decked out in the repellent garb of political reaction, the merchants fought to prosper and extend their commercial power. The French Canadians, masquerading in the fashionable hues of liberal democracy, were heart and soul in the defence of the *ancien régime*. When, by clauses in the Canada Trade Act and by the Canada Tenures Act of 1825, the British government made possible, though not obligatory, the commutation of feudal tenures in the province, the assembly protested in the name of its priceless heritage of feudalism which had been secured for all posterity by the Quebec Act.[42] Year after year, in regular petitions which were answered by habitual refusals, the commercial class made its requests for the improvement of the channel through Lake St. Peter and the establishment of registry offices for recording transfers of real property. It was pointed out that registry offices were merely intended to safeguard purchasers from the frauds of "clandestine mortgages". Why—said the supporters of the measure hopefully—registry offices had even been established in France! But M. Viger observed that it had taken two hundred and fifty years of effort to establish registry offices in France and apparently implied that it ought to take two hundred and fifty years of effort to establish them in Lower Canada.[43] As for M. Berthelot, he knew that it was only "les amis de l'union", "quelques marchands et quelques spéculateurs", who wanted registry offices. In M. Berthelot's mind registry offices were mysteriously mixed up with such oddly extraneous subjects as the Union Bill, the probable confisca-

tion of all French-Canadian property, the intended suppression of
the French language and the oncoming attack upon the Roman
Catholic religion.[44]

Meanwhile, the merchants gave some support to the cause of
the Eastern Townships which in some ways was closely allied to
their own. At the beginning of the century it had been the official
theory of French-Canadian leaders that the inhabitants of the
Townships were a kind of cross between prehistoric men and
historical Goths and Vandals. It seemed prudent, as well as
morally gratifying, to leave them severely alone. They had been
left severely alone for a total of twenty-five years. Naturally, they
were a little restive. Their appeals for roads, registry offices,
courts and, above all, for representation in the provincial legislature, kept pouring in upon the assembly. In 1824 and the years
that followed, the assembly took up seriously the problem of
representation; but to the indignation of the council, the merchants
and the "tory" press in Quebec and Montreal, the assembly
wanted more representatives for the entire province, not merely
new representatives from the Townships. "The inhabitants of
the most intelligent portion of the Province", raged the *Montreal
Gazette*, "feel the want of proper representation, and a Canadian
House of Assembly in granting them the desired boon of *four*
members, requires THIRTY FOUR additional Seigneurial members to counteract the dreadful effects of admitting into the
Lower Branch of the Legislature, these few individuals."[45] The
council and the newspapers were in a distinctly uncomfortable
position, for the assembly had the censuses of 1825 and 1827 to
fall back on. But the council resolutely threw the representation
bills out and the newspapers searched feverishly for arguments.
"In the work of regeneration, heads alone have been counted . . .",
observed the *Quebec Mercury*. "Multitudes, no matter where or
how cooped up in nooks and corners, were to furnish representative
multitudes, without reference to local wants, advantages, disadvantages, or capabilities of territory."[46]

But all issues were confounded in the financial issue. While the
French Canadians desired financial control for the sake of political
power, the merchants desired it for the sake of commercial
prosperity. They saw in the provincial treasury a golden hoard

which would speed the rush for expansion and prosper the fortunes of the commercial state. And yet, while they planned what might be done with money, the revenue and borrowing power of the province remained locked up as in a strong box while the governor and the assembly quarrelled for its possession. The march of progress has been brought virtually to a complete standstill. The unyielding opponents were locked together in a kind of furious immobility. Only in 1823, when Papineau and Neilson were away in England, and in 1825, when Dalhousie was absent himself, did the three branches of the legislature agree upon a revenue bill. Dalhousie, who was governor from 1820 until 1828, was determined to persuade the assembly to co-operate in establishing a permanent civil list, without surrendering the control of the permanent revenue of the crown. The assembly, on the other hand, insisted upon its claim to appropriate the permanent as well as the provincial revenue, in annual grants and item by item. Driven almost completely from the assembly, the remnant of the commercial group had taken refuge in the legislative council, where they were led by John Richardson. The old man was getting on for seventy; but he had lost none of his varied interests, his immense vitality and his pugnacious downrightness. He leapt into quarrels with all the unabashed zest of a novice; and in 1822, when he declared that a secret committee was operating in the assembly, the assembly readily took time off to declare his words "false, scandalous, malicious", and to request his dismissal from all public employments.

In 1827 Dalhousie dissolved the legislature. There was a general election, in which Montreal passed definitely into that mood of tense, explosive excitability which was to last through the rebellion of 1837 and on to the riots of the forties. In Montreal West Ward, where McGill and Delisle were contending with Papineau and Neilson, the election bullies assaulted the voters, stones broke some of the windows of McGill's house and an unhappy, faithful magistrate was beaten. On the evening of the poll, when it was gloriously certain that all the "popular" candidates had been successful in Montreal, Papineau, Neilson, Heney, Quesnel, Leslie and Viger set off in triumph through the West Ward in two "elegant barouches", while a long line of beribboned *calèches* followed and the ladies fluttered handkerchiefs from the street windows.[47] It was a grand triumph for liberal democracy. Fired by their victory the French Canadians would certainly propose Papineau again as speaker. But Dalhousie, who had passed beyond all sense and moderation, was determined to refuse him.[48] Papineau was elected. The governor declined his approval. After a moment of stunned consternation, the assembly returned to its familiar exercise of passing resolutions; and then the governor ended the deadlock by a prorogation. "Here I sincerely hope", wrote Dalhousie at the height of the crisis, "will be an end of Parliament in this Province."

CHAPTER IX

THE REFORM OF THE OLD COLONIAL SYSTEM

I

THE Canadian commercial state was left unprepared and vulnerable at the very moment when threatening changes began to multiply beyond its borders. The failure of the Union Bill meant the continuance of a political system which helped to prolong futile disputes and to postpone desirable capital expenditures. In Canada the merchants stood arrested in frustration before a programme of reorganization which was a necessary preliminary to the solution of their problems; but all the while, the gravity and complexity of those problems were steadily increasing as a result of dynamic changes in England and the United States. The American Revolution, which undermined the British colonial system and created the basis for a great, independent commercial organization in the new world, was at length having its inevitable results. New York, the destined leader of the commercial Atlantic seaboard, built the Erie canal and laid a sudden, imperious claim to the trade of the north-western American states. The old colonial system, which had lost its own best justification with the wreck of the first empire, was now judged and condemned by men who had grown up in the new industrialism, who held the hope of world commerce and believed in the doctrine of free trade. The basic principles of Canadian commercialism, which seemed to the merchants to have all the consoling immutability of the mechanics of the solar system, were now being questioned and denied. The decade of the 1820's was a decade of reforms and changes which unsettled the whole trading system of the St. Lawrence and foreshadowed its disintegration within the next decades.

In 1822, after the Union Bill had been dropped, the British parliament passed the Canada Trade Act—a kind of mediocre substitute for union, in the opinion of the merchants—which regulated the financial relations of the two provinces and their commercial relations with the United States.[1] It was the year which ended the absolute domination of mercantilism and began the era of free trade; and thus, by an unhappy coincidence, the

231

failure of union occurred at the same time as the first successful attacks against the old colonial system. The new commercial theories grew rapidly, luxuriantly in the thick, torpid atmosphere of the depression. The clamour against the corn laws and the timber duties mounted. And in the colonial world it began to seem as if mercantilism was no longer worthy of the desperate efforts which were necessary to maintain it. The struggle between Great Britain and the United States for the West India carrying-trade was being fought in a spirit of greater truculence and with fiercer retaliations. When in 1818 and 1820 the Americans hit upon the novel expedient of passing navigation laws of their own, which closed the ports of the United States to British ships from the West Indies and from the British North American provinces as well, the wretched islands, cut off by both British and American prohibitions, sent up piteous cries that they were being starved to death.

Already in 1821 the timber duties had been reduced. A new corn law appeared in 1822; and in the same year, Wallace and Robinson, president and vice-president of the board of trade, pushed through the first really serious changes in the old colonial system.[2] In the cabinet shake-up which followed Castlereagh's suicide, the liberal tories, who were to do half the work and incur most of the odium of the reform measures in the next decades, entered the administration in numbers. Robinson became chancellor of the exchequer and Huskisson was moved up to the presidency of the board of trade. It was he who completed the first radical revision of mercantilism in 1825 by a series of great reforms which altered tariffs, imperial monopolies and shipping regulations.[3] Huskisson was a tory by political association, a gradualist in principle and an imperialist in sentiment; but the revolution which he worked in the commercial system of the empire was as much as Great Britain was willing to accept until the time of Peel.[4] Thus the Canada Trade Act, which regulated inland commerce between the Canadas and the United States, was only one measure in a new commercial code which changed the trade relationships of the entire empire.

The general purpose of the Wallace-Robinson legislation of 1822 and the Huskisson legislation of 1825 was to open the British colonies to a direct import and export trade with foreign countries in a list of specified commodities which could be carried in British or foreign vessels. It was true that these unparalleled privileges were only available to foreigners at certain designated "free ports"; but there were a number of these in the West Indies, and Saint John, N.B., Halifax and Quebec were listed as well. At first, by the Wallace-Robinson code, this direct trade in foreign ships between the British colonies and foreign countries was only extended to states or colonies in North or South America which were not under the British crown; and while trade between Europe and the British colonies was permitted as well, it still had to be carried on in British ships. In 1825, however, Huskisson abandoned the distinction between Europe and the Americas and opened the ports of the British possessions to the goods and ships of all foreign countries who were prepared to reciprocate adequately.

At the beginning, when the British made their first timorous, tentative breaches in the navigation system, the list of enumerated articles which could be imported into the colonies from foreign countries in British or foreign shipping, was brief and niggardly. The Canada Trade Act, which regulated trade by land or inland navigation between the Canadas and the United States, and the Wallace-Robinson statutes which adjusted ocean commerce between the British possessions on the one hand and the Americas and Europe on the other, permitted the exportation of all the products of the colonies. But very cautiously the statutes did not allow the import of more than natural and semi-manufactured commodities, which had to be carried directly from the foreign countries of origin. It was again the more daring Huskisson who escaped completely from the inhibitions of his ancestors and who opened the colonial free ports to the entry of an almost unlimited number of foreign products. There were only a few articles— fire-arms, ammunition, sugar, rum, salted fish and fresh and salted provisions—which could only be imported into the American possessions from the United Kingdom or from other British colonies.

To Robinson, Huskisson and the other commercial radicals of the 1820's, it was enough—it was perhaps more than enough— to admit the produce of foreign countries into the British possessions. Intellectually they may have been convinced that tariffs were the bane of the world's trade; but, as practical politicians who were members of the tory party, they were forced modestly to interpret the grand doctrine of free trade as freedom to import and not freedom from duties. There were, of course, a number of colonial warehousing ports, of which Quebec was one, at which foreign goods in transit between the Americas and Europe could be landed without the payment of duty. But upon commodities imported into the colonies in the ordinary fashion there were duties; and to the Montreal merchants, accustomed as they were to the old spacious days of inland trade between Canada and the United States, the duties were unexpectedly stiff. There was a tariff on lumber, cattle and grain. A duty of 5s. was levied on a barrel of flour and 1s. on a bushel of wheat. The free list was insignificant; and upon all articles not enumerated a general tariff of 15 per cent. *ad valorem* was imposed. Thus, after more than thirty years during which the Canadian merchants had enjoyed the advantages of protection in imperial markets and the benefits of free trade on the Great Lakes, the British parliament had stepped in to impose a new, uniform commercial code, a single system of regulations and tariffs, upon the trade of the whole empire, including Canada. The very uniformity of the new code was, in the eyes of the Canadian merchants, its chief defect. There had been no recognition of the peculiarities of the St. Lawrence trading system and no special provision for its interests. And the natural conclusion of the Canadians was that the legislation of Wallace, Robinson and Huskisson gave far too little commercial freedom on the lakes and far too much commercial freedom on the ocean.

Moreover, this inept reform of the old colonial system, which brought strange weaknesses and novel rigidities into the Canadian trading system, was accompanied by a steadily increasing pressure from the United States. The revival of vigorous competition from the Atlantic seaboard was, like the decline of the old colonial system, one of the main themes in this last period in the history of the old commercial empire of the St. Lawrence; and it is highly suggestive that the Erie canal was completed by a pat coincidence in the very year in which Huskisson's revolutionary laws were passed. The interests of the St. Lawrence were subjected to diplomatic as well as to economic pressure by the United States; and the Canadian merchants tried desperately to prevent Great Britain from accentuating Canada's commercial weakness under the new régime by signing away commercial privileges to the Americans. In the West Indies, where the reformed colonial system reduced the protection for imperial traders, the United States was attempting by diplomacy and intimidation to shoulder its way into greater freedom. In the interior of North America, where the new tariffs had raised novel obstacles in the way of the northern carrying-trade, the Americans had provided a competitive route in the Erie canal and were ready to take advantage of the embarrassment of the Canadians. Gloomy and apprehensive, the merchants felt themselves attacked on the one hand by naïve British free-traders and, on the other, by ambitious American merchants and cunning American diplomatists. They no longer felt comfortably adjusted to the British colonial system. The St. Lawrence was no longer a unique advantage. And to the Canadians it seemed as if the new colonial system and the new canal were combining for the ruin of the northern commercial state.

II

During the 1820's, which in so many ways was a period of successive shocks, the Canadian merchants were worriedly trying to understand their altered situation and to prepare for their defence. In all essentials their commercial philosophy was unchanged. In 1822 there remained precisely what the geographical fact of the St. Lawrence and the political fact of the American revolution had forced them to become as early as 1783. They were mercantilists on the Atlantic ocean and free-traders on the Great Lakes. They had fashioned two completely different policies for two widely separated markets. And it was, therefore, one of their main tasks to break down this imperial protective system which the British began to apply to the trade of the Great Lakes, commencing with the Canada Trade Act of 1822.

At first these restrictions were not so serious as they became later. It was true that the Canada Trade Act listed only a relatively small number of articles which, subject to duties, could be imported into the provinces in American as well as in British shipping. But it said absolutely nothing about the importation of other commodities in *British* bottoms; and the provinces very naturally took the line that, in the absence of positive imperial legislation to the contrary, the products not enumerated in the Canada Trade Act could be imported as before, subject to the duties imposed by previous provincial statutes. The major restriction, apart from the new imperial tariff contained in the act, concerned the navigation laws. By the general terms of the Canada Trade Act and by its eleventh clause in particular, it seemed perfectly clear that American ships could only enter Canadian lake ports with cargoes of the articles enumerated in the act. Faced by the apparent obligation of enforcing ancient legislation which had never been properly enforced before, the provinces quailed and muddled their impossible task. There were seizures by the customs officials, releases by the governors, long discussions in the executive councils and frenzied appeals home for advice.[5]

The new trade act of 1822 did not merely create annoyance for the Canadian merchants and trouble for the Canadian officials; it also had frightening repercussions in the United States. The new duties and shipping regulations imposed on American produce entering Canada by land or inland navigation, were almost as distasteful to the New Yorkers as they were to the Canadian merchants, for the Erie canal was not completed until 1825. The American congress declared that the new regulations were severe and unprecedented in the Great Lakes trade; and Richard Rush, the American ambassador at London, was instructed to demand the free navigation of the St. Lawrence by American citizens as a "natural" right.[6] This was a novel and a disturbing demand. The navigation laws had been virtually forgotten on the Great Lakes, it was true; but, in the opinion of the Canadians, the St. Lawrence was still mercantilist territory, and time had to elapse and many things had to happen, before they saw any advantage in surrendering the British monopoly of the through traffic down the river.

Huskisson's comprehensive legislation of 1825, which was supposedly so modern and so magnanimous, merely completed and systematized the new and irksome régime upon the lakes. The great reforms of 1825 opened the Canadian lake ports, as well as the "free ports" of the ocean, to the entry of an almost unlimited number of products, whether carried in British or American shipping. But, at the same time, the statutes imposed a complete tariff upon the trade. There was nothing new in the entry of American produce by land or inland navigation. There was nothing new in the suspension of the navigation laws, for the two Canadas had suspended them for decades without imperial permission. In fact, so far as the trade on the Great Lakes was concerned, the chief novelty of the Huskisson legislation was the tariff, which was as stiff as it was comprehensive. To shut out American manufactures by high duties was perfectly all right, argued the merchants; but to tax American natural products would ruin the carrying-trade of the commercial state. The merchants were aggrieved; but the Canadian farmers looked at the matter very differently. Between the merchants and the farmers a controversy broke out over the new trade laws—a controversy which was simply one more symptom of the increasingly divergent economic interests in the two Canadas.

On May 18, 1826, in an editorial review of the reception accorded to the various trade acts, the *Montreal Gazette* informed its readers that Upper Canada had expressed decided approval and that Lower Canada had disliked the heavy duties on American lumber and agricultural produce. Indeed, as early as the legislation of 1822, the *Upper Canada Gazette & Weekly Register* had declared that "the Trade Act, which exacts a duty on American produce, holds out great, nay, *every* advantage to this Province".[7] Even in Lower Canada, which the *Montreal Gazette* implied was united in its disapproval, there were agricultural interests strongly in favour of the acts. From the Ottawa valley and from the district of Montreal there came memorials praising the acts of 1825 for the protection they afforded Canadian agriculture against an avalanche of American supplies.[8] Even in the columns of the *Montreal Gazette* itself a correspondent pointed out that the urban population of Lower Canada numbered probably only 39,000 out of an estimated total of 400,000; and asked why Great Britain should oppress 361,000 farmers for the sake of the Canadian merchants.[9]

The Canadian merchants, in the meantime, were busy on their own account. It was an indication of how completely the new staple trades dominated the old fur-trading city that Montreal took a strong lead in the protest. And on January 23, 1826, the merchants flocked to a meeting held in the exchange room in St. Joseph Street, where George Auldjo was called to the chair and Peter McGill presented some very moving resolutions.[10] With a readiness born of long practice, and an enthusiasm undimmed by countless repetitions, the merchants presented their old case for the free-trade area of the St. Lawrence.[11] To them the river was the natural outlet for the raw produce of inland North America; and the fact that misguided politicians had divided the river's dominion by an absurd international boundary should not be allowed to mislead the British into regrettable tariff blunders. The prohibition of American beef and pork—they were on the brief list of articles which could not be imported into the British possessions from foreign countries—was unfortunate, for these commodities were essential both in filling up the cargoes for the West Indies and in supplying food for Canadian lumbermen. American potash was subject to the 15 per cent. *ad valorem* duty which was placed upon all articles not enumerated in the tariff acts of 1825. It was impossible for the merchants importing American flour by land or inland navigation to take advantage of the warehousing facilities at the port of Quebec, for before the flour could reach Quebec, duty had to be paid upon it at the inland port of entry. The trade acts, in short, were simply helping to drive the produce of inland North America down the new American canals. If, argued the Canadian merchants, the principles of free trade were so noble and so salutary, why had they not been applied to the commerce of the Great Lakes?

The British, who had restricted free trade on the Great Lakes, were thus—in the opinion of the merchants—open to serious criticism; but the Americans, who wanted free navigation of the St. Lawrence, must be resisted at all costs. The doctrine that American shipping had a natural right to a free ride down the St. Lawrence left the Canadians completely unmoved. They were still ready to accept the high freight rates inseparable from the British shipping monopoly, for the sake of the monopoly itself and for the colonial system of which it was a part; and in 1824 the legislative council of Lower Canada protested vigorously against the American claim.[12] Free navigation of the St. Lawrence was inadmissible; but possibly those who voiced it could be satisfied with other and more acceptable policies. The Canadians, confronted by American international lawyers on the one hand and by imperial free-traders on the other, tried to use the demands of one to frighten concessions out of the other. It was the new tariff, they said, which had put the evil thought of free navigation in the minds of the Americans. Grant them freer trade and they would forget free navigation.

Everything, then, pointed to the necessity of modifying the new colonial system on the Great Lakes and restoring the old western free-trade area. According to the merchants, the best and simplest solution of the whole problem was to admit American timber, lumber, potash, grain, flour and provisions free, without payment of duty. But if the opposition of the farmers made the simplest solution politically impossible, then these natural products might be admitted freely and bonded through to Quebec for exportation only. In either case, whether they entered the province by the first or second method, American goods should be shipped abroad as though of Canadian origin. For the merchants this was a complete solution. They had criticized the uniform regulations of 1825 in the light of the old peculiarities of the St. Lawrence; and the British government, influenced in part by these criticisms, began to alter their new standard imperial laws in favour of the northern carrying-trade. By the imperial statute of 1826,[13] salted beef and pork could be imported into Canada without payment of duty, for exportation only to Newfoundland, *via* the free warehousing port of Quebec. Foreign flour warehoused at Quebec was to enjoy a marked imperial preference when shipped direct to the British West Indies; and by supplementary instructions of the board of trade, American flour could be bonded through from the inland ports to Quebec without payment of the regular duty.[14] The act of 1827 confirmed and extended these privileges.[15] American timber, lumber, tallow, ashes, fresh meat and fish were to be admitted into Canada duty free when brought by land or inland navigation. Foreign beef and pork, along with some other articles, could be warehoused at the free warehousing ports for exportation anywhere. Kingston and Montreal were named warehousing ports for goods brought into Canada by land or inland navigation; and American goods entered at the western frontier ports could be bonded through without payment of duty. Finally, by the acts of 1826 and 1827, timber, all kinds of lumber and potash imported into Canada by land or inland navigation were to be deemed the produce of British possessions upon importation into the United Kingdom.

Thus, only a relatively short time after they had been passed, the new trade laws were modified in respect of the Great Lakes trade, as the Canadian merchants desired them to be. Some American commodities entered Canada duty free, others escaped the new tariff through the bonding system; and in addition there were a few important products which acquired Canadian status by the mere passage down the St. Lawrence. In the very near future, moreover, the British were to remove the last duties upon American natural and semi-manufactured products imported into Canada; and so far as imperial legislation could make it so, the international carrying-trade of the St. Lawrence would soon be completely free. The new colonial system was being loosened on the Great Lakes where the merchants desired relaxation. But could it also be tightened in the imperial markets of the Atlantic, where commercial Canada desired the rigidity of the old mercantilism to be maintained?

III

Ever since 1783, this had been the second objective of the commercial group. They must keep or secure protected markets for all the new staple products which were to be attracted to the St. Lawrence route by cheap transportation and free trade; and they instinctively sought these markets within the empire and looked to mercantilism for their protection. Even the shipping regulations were acceptable—in the West Indies they were a useful check upon American competition. But undoubtedly it was upon the preferential tariff that the merchants chiefly relied. If Canadian exports "deemed colonial" as well as those really colonial did not have real preferences in imperial markets, then the attractions of the St. Lawrence as an outlet for western American produce would be radically reduced. Preference had been the great redeeming feature of the old colonial system. Preference might be the sufficient compensation for the new reforms. And so during the early twenties the merchants redoubled their efforts to obtain what they considered adequate protection in the markets of the United Kingdom and the British possessions overseas.

The West Indies were still, from the Canadian point of view, among the most important of these overseas possessions. It was a difficult market; but its difficulties merely increased the ardour with which the Canadians clamoured for the protection of navigation laws and imperial preferences.[16] If the islands were freely opened to American shipping and supplies, it would become impossible to force the provision trade of the West Indies through the imperial route of the British North American colonies; and this defeat of mercantilism seemed the object which the British free-traders and the American diplomatists were conspiring to achieve. In the early twenties, the American ambassadors Rush and Gallatin were negotiating in London with the British government for the settlement of the outstanding commercial disputes between the two countries. Probably the main objective of the American negotiators was to obtain the right for their ships and goods to enter the ports of the British West Indies upon virtually the same terms as the ships and goods of Great Britain and her other colonies.

As has been seen, the trade acts of 1822 permitted the United States to trade direct with the West Indies in a specified list of commodities; and for the next few years the Canadians watched the Americans monopolize the commerce of the islands in gloomy resentment. In the end, however, Canada was saved from what it considered the absurd generosity of the British by the over-reaching self-confidence of the Americans. The United States had accepted the concessions of 1822 as if they were only a part of her right and had failed to place the commerce and navigation of the British Empire upon the footing of the most favoured nation—a condition laid down in the imperial statutes of 1825. The British, after waiting a while until these diplomatic misdemeanours had reached proportions which could be stigmatized as criminal, abruptly closed the ports of the West Indies to American shipping by an order-in-council of July, 1826.[17] It seemed as if—temporarily at least—right had triumphed in despite of the deluded free-traders; and over in Canada the editor of the *Montreal Gazette* was congratulating his readers upon the folly of the Americans.

Though the merchants hoped this prohibition would continue, they suspected that it was the work of a spasm of indignation and that it could not possibly last. In fact the discussions over the West Indies trade were renewed in London. Rumours of these negotiations, rendered still more ominous by American over-confidence and optimism, reached the Canadian merchants by the newspapers of the United States; and periodically they urged that on no account should Great Britain conclude a new commercial treaty which would sacrifice the imperial preferences in the markets of the West Indies. These urgings were scarcely necessary, for the reforming tories had no intention of surrendering more than the shipping monopoly. In Huskisson the austere principles of the new political economy were modified by a faintly old-fashioned enthusiasm for the empire. It was no part of his or his colleagues' policy to abolish the preferences on colonial goods entering the United Kingdom or to wipe out the preferences on British and colonial goods entering the colonies. The negotiations over the West Indies trade were not yet concluded; but when the United States stuck to its incredible demand that American produce be admitted into the West Indies upon terms of equality with the produce of the other British colonies, the British kept reiterating an unshakeable refusal.

Great Britain was, however, a far more important market for Canada than the West Indies; and, as the Canadian merchants had realized long ago, their real task was to secure preferences in the home market for timber, lumber, potash, wheat and flour—for all the staple products characteristic of the new agricultural economy of the St. Lawrence and the west. After the detested reductions of 1821, the differential timber duties remained unaltered and the Canadian timber trade continued to prosper. There was a preference for colonial potash in the home market, though the Canadians were doubtful of its sufficiency. But the most important preference —the preference which might make the success of the new commercial system—was the preference on wheat. And it still eluded the merchants. It was true that the new British corn law of 1822 continued the old, moderate colonial preferences and reduced the price level at which colonial wheat might be admitted. But in the early twenties the price of wheat in the United Kingdom was still fairly low; and in 1824 there was a considerable amount of Canadian wheat lying idle in the warehouses of the English ports.[18] In 1825, Huskisson proposed to admit colonial corn at all times, irrespective of prices in the United Kingdom, at a flat rate of 5s. per quarter. But the lords demurred; and a substitute measure, extending this privilege to the colonies until the end of the next session of the imperial parliament, was passed instead.[19] It was a concession which tantalized rather than satisfied; and the merchants' disappointment almost overcame their gratitude.

In Upper Canada, the traders were chilled by the reflection that the new concession applied only to wheat and not to flour; and they argued that Upper Canada, owing to the dangers and expense of transportation, was almost forced to convert its wheat into flour for shipment down the St. Lawrence.[20] Moreover, the grant was so very temporary. The merchants concentrated feverishly upon the task of removing those absurd delusions from the British mind which had prevented the prolongation of the act.[21] Since the lords apparently feared that a perfect inundation of American wheat would descend upon England via the St. Lawrence, the merchants pointed out the sad fact that American wheat was now going regularly eastward by the Erie canal. The admission had its value as an argument; but it must have been extremely painful for the Canadian merchants to make. At that moment, their state in general was low, for the depression of 1826–1828 was upon them and business failures were numerous. While the future of the wheat preference remained uncertain, they were, as Dalhousie expressed it, "awfully gloomy under the present suspence".

The next imperial parliament was to decide the fate of the preference. In their agitation the merchants were convinced that they must be represented at home. But the assembly, with a characteristic refusal, turned down their request for a special, official agent to represent Canadian commercial interests in England; and in their deep need the merchants decided—with Dalhousie's unofficial approval—to send W. B. Felton again to England to watch over their affairs.[22] This was in the winter of

1827; but despite all that Felton and anybody else could do, the wheat preference was only renewed for a year. The new act, which was due to expire in the spring of 1828, was more acceptable than the first, for its terms were more generous and it extended the colonial preference to flour.[23] During the winter of 1828, the merchants made one more effort; and this time their uncertainty was almost immediately ended, for the imperial parliament passed a new, general corn law in 1828 and incorporated in it the special, temporary concessions to colonial wheat and flour which had been made in 1825 and 1827.[24] Canadian wheat continued to enter the United Kingdom at a duty of 5s. per quarter when the price of British wheat remained below 67s.; and when the home price rose above 67s., the duty was to be only 6d. A barrel of colonial flour weighing 196 pounds was to pay a duty equal in amount to the duty payable on $38\frac{1}{2}$ gallons of wheat. It was, on the whole, an important concession; but it did not—or at least in theory it did not—admit American wheat and flour to the preference, and it was very far from being that free entry to which the Canadian merchants imagined themselves entitled.

Such as it was, the wheat preference appeared to be established; but concerning other protected markets there was uncertainty and some dissatisfaction. The British and Americans had not yet extricated themselves from their pleasing impasse over the West Indies trade; and who could be sure that Great Britain would not be persuaded suddenly to make lamentable concessions to the United States? If the Baltic merchants and the free-traders made another assault on the differential timber duties, would it not mean ruin to the Canadian trade? As timber prices and exports declined during the depression of 1826–1828, the worried merchants began to believe that they could not compete with Europe under the preference as it had been revised in 1821.

IV

The year 1828, which saw the passage of the new corn law, was also the year in which Andrew Jackson, "the people's choice", was elected to the presidency of the United States. The failure of President Adams, and of his ambassadors, Rush and Gallatin, to settle the acrimonious disputes with Great Britain concerning the West Indies trade had played a considerable part in Jackson's election. The new president was expected to do something about the West Indies; and the new president was naturally anxious to live up to expectations. Louis McLane was sent over to England to renew the negotiations late in 1829.[25] He was placatory, accommodating—even a little repentant about the past. But the British now hesitated where before they had denounced the hesitations of the Americans. There were the colonies to be considered—the colonies which had rejoiced when the United States was excluded from the West Indies by the order-in-council of 1826; and in fact, as soon as they heard about the negotiations, there was a great indignant wail of protest from the British North American possessions. "The whole and entire opposition", declared the *New York Morning Courier*, "to the just expectations of the United States, that the West India trade will be again opened to them, comes, as we have occasion to know, from a little contemptible interest, which has grown out of the exclusion of the United States from the West India ports, seated in Canada and the neutral Islands. A few Merchants have established themselves in these places, inspired with the ambition and the hope of becoming the carriers of the United States! Our readers will smile, but so it is— and such are the delusions of narrow-minded self-interest. . . . They are few in number, but, as is usual in such cases, make up for their insignificance by the vehemency of their clamours."[26]

The clamours, in fact, were as loud as the Canadians could make them. News of the negotiations reached Montreal by private letter in December, 1829, and as early as December 23 the Montreal merchants held their protest meeting.[27] In the following months there were angry remonstrances from the newspapers of both provinces, memorials from the committees of trade in Quebec and Montreal, meetings in Kingston and Hamilton, and a protesting address to the king from the assembly of Upper Canada.[28] The Canadians argued that the United States could not conceivably compensate the British for the immense boon of the West Indies trade; that the Americans grew practically all the products of the islands and that they had completely lost their taste for good Jamaica rum by drinking bad whiskey made in their own distilleries. On the other hand, ever since the Americans had been excluded from the islands and some of their raw products freely admitted once more into the Canadas, the St. Lawrence had become the perfect, the ideal imperial channel for trade between North America and the West Indies. Canada had sunk money in the trade; and the projected canals—so the Canadians implied— were dedicated to the hope of the Canadian-West Indian commerce. Moreover, the trade was great: it was rapidly growing. And thus, with the usual exaggeration and the customary appeal to the ancient doctrines of mercantilism, the Canadians sought to maintain their privileged position in the difficult market of the West Indies.

But despite all the protests of Nova Scotia and the Canadas, McLane and the Americans seemed to be making alarming progress by the sheer virtue of magnanimity. The United States trustingly repealed its navigation acts against British shipping; and confronted by these multiplied evidences of good faith, Great Britain at length, in November, 1830, revoked the order-in-council of July, 1826. But the surrender was not unconditional; and, among other things, the British expressly stipulated that they reserved the right to impose whatever duties they saw fit upon the trade of the islands in order to protect the commercial interests of the British North American colonies. Discriminating duties were accordingly imposed. Imperial shipping monopolies might be modified; but the old colonial system lived on by virtue of imperial preferences and its old age would continue to be honoured, so long as the preferences endured.

The attacks upon the mercantile system did not cease, however. It had to be watched with a jealous fervour and an unceasing vigilance. The imperial preferences in the West Indies had barely been saved, when the timber preference in the home market was attacked once more by free-traders and Baltic timber merchants. In 1831, Viscount Althorp, the chancellor of the exchequer, brought down a budget containing a reduction in the duties on foreign timber, which would have left the imperial preference at a mere 30s. a load.[29] The committee of trade in Quebec reacted automatically. The council and assembly in Upper Canada joined in a protest to the king, while over in England the shipowners and imperial timber traders held a meeting at the City of London Tavern to concert action, and Nathaniel Gould was indefatigable as chairman of the colonial and shipping committee.[30] All these forces were able to defeat the bill to reduce the timber duties; and in the early spring of 1831 the British merchants and the Canadians uttered a great sigh of relief. But the encounter left them worried for the future. In fact, from then on, the attacks upon the timber preference recurred with alarming frequency; and it was partly in anticipation of these approaching crises, that the British merchants trading to Canada founded their special lobbying union, the North American Colonial Association.

This not entirely reassuring vindication of imperial preferences in both the timber trade and the trade of the West Indies had an immediate sequel which was equally important for commercial Canada. The retention of preferential treatment in the markets of the Atlantic was enhanced in value by the restoration of free trade on the Great Lakes. The change came in the same session of the imperial parliament—the session of 1831—which saw the defeat of the new timber duties; and it was the almost complete answer to incessant urgings and appeals. For commercial Canada had never been satisfied with the amendments to the Huskisson tariff on inland trade between the United States and Canada; and the opening of the West Indies to American shipping merely increased the dissatisfaction. The appeals of the merchants of Quebec and Montreal were now strengthened by the pleas of the Welland Canal Company, for the Welland was a part of the Erie canal system as well as of the St. Lawrence, and only through free trade in American natural products could it take its place effectively in either route. Already, by the tariff adjustments of 1826 and 1827, American timber, lumber, potash and fresh meat entered Canada free of imperial duties. American flour could be bonded through to the free warehousing port of Quebec; and, if shipped direct to the British possessions in the West Indies or South America, could be entered at a duty of 1s. a barrel, instead of at the usual duty of 5s. on foreign flour. This was all very acceptable; but if the carrying-trade was to continue—if the St.

Lawrence was to draw in American natural products despite the opening of the West Indies to the shipping and products of the United States, then these privileges must be extended still further.

In 1830 the merchants of Quebec and the directors of the Welland canal proposed that the duties on American wheat, coarse grains, corn meal, rice, and salted provisions brought into Canada by land or inland navigation should be radically reduced.[31] They asked for much; but they got more than they had asked or hoped for. The British, having opened the ports of the West Indies to the United States by the "reciprocity" of 1830, immediately attempted to guard against those ill effects which might fall upon the North American colonies as a result of the action. They had claimed the right to juggle with the tariff. They proceeded to do so. An attempt was made to force the trade between the West Indies and North America through the northern colonies. By the act of 1831 the duties on certain foreign goods imported direct into the islands were increased; but American produce was to enter the Canadas free[32] and it could be trans-shipped to the West Indies as though of British colonial origin. At one stroke the imperial tariff on American wheat, flour, meal and salted provisions imported into Canada by land or inland navigation was swept away. The duties of the Canada Trade Act and the Huskisson legislation ceased to trouble the merchants. The old free trade in natural products was re-established on the Great Lakes; and at least in this one respect the St. Lawrence and the British colonial system were reconciled and harmonized once more.

V

Under these successive changes, which followed each other so rapidly, how was the trade of the St. Lawrence prospering? The dozen years which followed the withdrawal of the Union Bill and the passing of the Canada Trade Act had been filled with changes which unsettled the entire organization of the Great Lakes trade. The collapse of the North West Company presaged the development of a commerce in the new staples; and as immigration peopled the western American states and the province of Upper Canada, the Canadian merchants sought to build a new international commercial empire upon the bases of the staples, wheat and timber. They were checked by the grand reorganization of the British mercantile system which at first made no provision for the peculiarities of the St. Lawrence trade. In their search for protected imperial markets, they had met a partial defeat in the West Indies. They had failed to gain in Great Britain the ideal wheat preference—free entry—which would cover both American and Canadian produce exported from the St. Lawrence; and although the differential timber duties still remained upon the books, they were subject to ominously frequent attacks.

Thus the shift from the old to the new staples was complicated in the region of the Great Lakes by an alarming tendency towards fiscal change within the empire; and while the Canadians struggled with problems created by the liberal mercantilists in England, New York, the empire state, dramatically reasserted its ancient claim to the western trade. The Champlain canal, the Erie canal and the Oswego feeder combined to form a transportation system unequalled in the north-west. Though it was and remained a barge canal, though its tolls were relatively high, the Erie offered what the St. Lawrence could not possibly duplicate in this period, unbroken navigation from the lower lakes to the sea. Moreover, New York kept and continued to keep its old advantages over the port of Montreal. Its freedom from the ice which clogged the St. Lawrence would alone have made it the envy of its northern rival; but, even when compared with its more normal competitors, the harbour of New York was one of the finest in the world. The ships which arrived twice yearly, in the spring and autumn fleets, to Quebec and Montreal, could not approach the fast and frequent service maintained by the packet boats which plied between New York and Liverpool, London and Le Havre. New York's charges for wharfage and pilotage were lower than they were at Montreal; and finally, in the extremely important matter of ocean rates for freight and insurance, the American route was definitely cheaper than the Canadian. The regions which had once been tributary to the St. Lawrence—Vermont, the shores of the lower lakes and the Ohio country—were falling rapidly under the commercial control of New York. The Hudson river had always bit deep into the very heart of the geographic empire of the St.

Lawrence. And now the long, relative inactivity of the New York route during the days of the fur trade was revenged by its sudden, imperious grasp of the new staple trades.

These stubborn facts contradicted the theories upon which the St. Lawrence trading system was based. It was the hope of the new generation of Canadian merchants, as it had been the practice of the fur-trading generation of the past, to exchange the manufactures of Great Britain for the staples obtained in the hinterland of North America; but the rise of American industry, the American tariff, the Erie transportation system and the aggressiveness of the American merchants combined to defeat this naïve hope. While the Erie canal was transporting thousands of tons of assorted "merchandize" to the new communities in northern New York state and on the shores of Lake Erie, the exports of British manufactured goods from the Canadas to such American ports as Oswego, Buffalo and Cleveland, were trifling or non-existent. Indeed, as had been evident at the port of St. Johns two decades before, the tendency was all the other way; and both by smuggling and by legitimate entry the Canadian provinces imported considerable quantities of teas, tobacco, manufactures and luxury goods from the United States.[33]

But though they were compelled to modify their ambitions in some respects, the Canadian merchants still clung with tenacity to their old view that the St. Lawrence system was a capacious funnel into which the natural produce of mid-western North America would inevitably be poured. In the twenties and early thirties, when production was rapidly increasing in northern New York, in Upper Canada and in the western states, there was undoubtedly a good deal of American produce which found its way down the river to Montreal. To a considerable extent, the Canadas were dependent upon the United States for their supplies of fresh and preserved meats; and thousands of barrels of American beef and pork were annually imported for home consumption and for re-export to the other British American colonies and the West Indies. In the export of wheat and flour, which increased so enormously in the early thirties, supplies from the United States were certainly an important element. Certificates of colonial origin were required to obtain the preference in the United Kingdom;

but the Canadians found various ways of partly overcoming this difficulty, and it became established that American wheat milled in Canada could qualify as colonial flour. The year 1831 was the peak year in the wheat and flour trade during the first four decades of the century; and it was estimated that of the total of 81,144 barrels of flour exported from Quebec during that year, 41,856 barrels had come from the United States by inland navigation.[34] During 1834, the Welland canal carried 22,170 bushels of wheat destined for Montreal from American ports, as well as 18,464 bushels from Canadian ports.[35] And in 1835, the western states, and chiefly the port of Cleveland, shipped 18,917 bushels of wheat to Montreal *via* the Welland.[36]

It is when these figures are brought into comparison with those for the New York route that the relative failure of the St. Lawrence as a system for the export of North American commodities becomes immediately apparent. In 1834, when the Welland canal carried 40,634 bushels of wheat for Montreal, it also transported 224,285 bushels for the American port of Oswego, on Lake Ontario; and in 1835 the wheat shipped from Cleveland to Oswego was an even larger proportion of the whole. In many ways the Welland canal was simply an auxiliary of the Erie system. The wheat shipped by it re-entered the Erie at the Oswego feeder; and within ten years of its completion the New York route was dominating the trade of the new agricultural west. The Lachine canal, which was the bottle-neck of the entire St. Lawrence system, carried only 91,862 barrels of flour and 293,968 bushels of wheat during 1832, which was a better than average season.[37] But in 1834, which was a relatively poor year, 977,027 barrels of flour and 748,433 bushels of wheat were transported by the Erie canal to tide-water.[38]

The St. Lawrence was a trade route to Great Britain; but the Erie found its outlets in the markets of the eastern states as well as in the export trade of the city of New York. The pull from the Atlantic states, the demands of the populous and growing commercial and industrial centres in the east, were so strong that the new agricultural west was occasionally overtaxed by them; and during the 1830's, which were unsettled by crop failures and periods of scarcity, the North American continent was driven for the last time to import wheat from Europe. In these circumstances, there was little likelihood of large American exports by the St. Lawrence; and in fact, in 1834 and 1836, Upper Canada was actually exporting wheat to the United States, despite the tariff. This condition was inevitably temporary in character. As production increased in the west, the exportable surplus of wheat in the United States would be re-established; and of this export trade, the St. Lawrence would probably get its share.

But the fact was that the United States was beginning to appear as a possible market for produce, as well as a source of supplies for export to Great Britain. On occasion, the United States had taken Canadian wheat; and, what was more important, it began slowly but in increasing volume, to import sawn lumber from the Canadas. The imports of timber from Vermont, which used a few decades before to come through St. Johns to swell the exports at Quebec, slowly decreased in volume during the eighteen-twenties and early thirties. There was a period of indecision; and then, after 1835, the trade began to flow the other way. In the thirties, the Canadas were exporting timber, sawn lumber and staves *via* the Welland canal to American ports; and before long Kingston actively began to export lumber to Oswego.[39] The capacious markets and the higher prices south of the border began to fascinate the Canadians; and out of this small, restricted commerce to the south, which was a deviation from the original theory of the St. Lawrence, there developed later the idea of reciprocity with the United States.

For all these reasons, as well as many others, the old and majestically simple design of the Canadian merchants remained an unrealized conception. In itself the Canadian economy was weak enough. It suffered from all the chronic infirmities inherent in an economy which produced and traded staples; and it was disturbed both by the erratic movements of the trade cycle in Great Britain and by the still recurring crop failures in the new west. These disabilities of the St. Lawrence commercial system were ineradicable. But it was the frustration of its promised greatness, and not the persistence of its inherent infirmities, which made the tragedy of the River of Canada under the new régime. Insufficiently supported by the preferences and monopolies of the old colonial system, the export trade of the St. Lawrence was faced both with the competition of the American canals and the distractions of the American markets. The northern trade route had lost some of its last advantages. Its weaknesses were exposed as they had never been before. And it was the Erie system, and not the St. Lawrence, which was realizing that idea of commercial dominion in the new staples which had inspired the Canadian merchants since the peace of 1783.

This failure was revealed in the last, crucial test—in the exports overseas from Quebec and Montreal. Though Canada did some business with France, Spain, the Netherlands and other European countries, the vast bulk of its trade was carried on within the imperial markets of Great Britain, Ireland, the British North American colonies and the West Indies. Due to the old obstacles— distance, seasonal interruptions to navigation, and the relatively small Canadian demand for West Indian goods—the West Indies remained for Canada a difficult and secondary market. The attempt to force the provision trade of the islands and the British North American colonies through the St. Lawrence by dint of imperial preferences was a relative failure; and it was chiefly when the low price of bread-stuffs in England forced up the imperial prefer- ence to its maximum, that Canadian wheat and flour were diverted to the markets of Nova Scotia and the West Indies in any quantity. The tonnage employed in the outward trade from Quebec to the other North American colonies rose slightly from 9,153 tons in 1830 to 12,784 tons in 1835;[40] but this rise was more than balanced by the decline in the amount of the West Indies trade. In 1828, when American shipping was excluded from the islands by the order-in-council of July, 1826, the tonnage outward from Quebec was 7,373; but in 1835, under the régime of imperial preferences, it had declined to 3,874.[41] These insignificant totals bore no comparison with those employed in the trade between the United States and the West Indies; and during the period 1824–1826, which was just before the United States was excluded from the islands, the yearly average tonnage of American ships alone, leaving the continent for the British West Indies, was 96,849.[42]

The trade of the Canadas to Great Britain and Ireland, which formed the great bulk of Canadian commerce, recovered after the depression of 1825–1827 and acquired an increasing prosperity. The tonnage employed in the outward trade from the St. Lawrence to the United Kingdom rose from 176,484 tons in 1828 to 254,891 tons in 1832; and the great majority of the ships which sailed from Quebec and Montreal were freighted with the bulky article of timber. In 1828, 110,779 tons of white pine timber were exported to the United Kingdom; by 1832, the total had climbed to 192,944 tons; and the trade in deals and other forms of sawn lumber showed a steady improvement. According to estimates made in Canada, the value of wood exceeded the value of all other commodities exported to Great Britain during the late twenties. But in 1830 the export of bread-stuffs began to approach the previous peak established in 1825; and for the next few years the quantities of wheat and flour exported to Great Britain increased enormously.[43] The wood shipped to the United Kingdom in 1831 was valued at £465,074, all other goods at £786,114; and the total export of the St. Lawrence to all countries for the same year was estimated at £1,411,493.[44]

It was in these years, while Quebec and Montreal were making this deliberate progress, that New York began its rapid advance towards the commercial leadership of North America.[45] It had outdistanced its old rivals, Boston and Philadelphia; and it monopolized the import and export trade of its own state, which in 1831 was valued at $82,000,000.[46] The Empire State was becoming a reality; and the commercial empire of the St. Lawrence remained a remote ideal. The Canadian merchants, as they contemplated the marvels which were wrought in part at their expense, were goaded by envy and ambition into an unremitting agitation for the improvement of their own route. The demand for the canalization of the St. Lawrence became a persistent chorus; the clamour for capital expenditures and radical reforms increased in volume; and a note of worry, of urgency, almost of desperation, crept ominously into the merchants' political campaign. They had held and lost the first dominion, the dominion of the fur trade; and out of its wreckage there had now arisen a second commercial empire, which they could not hold, which they could not even grasp, and which was falling, despite ineffectual strivings, into the control of their most ancient enemies.

CHAPTER X

COMMERCE *VERSUS* AGRICULTURE

I

THE year 1828 marked a momentary and uneasy pause in Canadian affairs. A concurrence of several events, which was partly but not wholly accidental, implied that the commercial state had finished one stage of its development and was hesitating on the edge of another. The worst of the depression of 1825–1827 was over; and this slow upturn of the business cycle was accompanied by the beginnings of the first great migration of British peoples to Canada. In England, that stoically conservative bureaucrat, Lord Bathurst, left the colonial office; and the new governors, Sir James Kempt in Lower Canada and Sir John Colborne in Upper Canada, were more accommodating in spirit and more politically adroit than Dalhousie or Maitland had been. The colonial office became benignantly liberal. And 1828 was the year of the Canada Committee, a British parliamentary committee which heard a mass of ill-assorted evidence concerning the Canadas and penned a report which combined a few wise suggestions with a lot of liberal ambiguities and futile benevolence.

This investigation, which was the first serious attempt made by the imperial parliament since the Union Bill to review the Canadian problem, was brought on by Dalhousie's rejection of the speaker and the "constitutional crisis" which followed. There was immense excitement in the province; and though a few of the merchants looked doubtfully at Dalhousie's inflexibility and ineptitude, they took an active part in the meetings which were called in Quebec and Montreal to give moral support to the governor.[1] With a newly exalted moral fervour, they spoke of the "prerogatives of the crown" and the "British connection"; and already they were beginning to denounce the assembly as a body which was despotic in spirit and revolutionary in intention. "Every democrat is at heart a Tyrant", wrote a correspondent in the *Montreal Gazette*, "and when he attains office, invariably proves it. Of all tyrannies a popular tyranny is the most hopeless and unrelenting."[2] The merchants, though they posed as the defenders of the constitution, were exclusively concerned with the constitutional powers of those whom they supported; and their own intentions, which were just as revolutionary as the assembly's, were now expressed with a new frankness and vigour. "There is indeed no course short of annihilating the assembly", wrote one ultra-tory merchant indignantly, "or a thorough modification of the constitution and junction with Upper Canada that can preserve the connection with Great Britain, for any useful or creditable purpose."[3] The increasing identification of government and business and the rising protest of both feudal and frontier agriculture had completely altered the political philosophy of the merchants; and the *bourgeois* who had fought bureaucracy, militarism and feudal privilege, had now become politically conservative, suspicious of democracy and resentful of the opposition of the fourth estate.

John Neilson, D. B. Viger, and Austin Cuvillier departed for England to place the cause of the popular party before the government. Samuel Gale was deputed to represent the Eastern Townships. But no special representative was sent by the merchants, who were content to rely upon Gale, the London forwarders and the Canadians who were almost certain to cross the ocean during the season. In the spring and summer months of 1828, when the parliamentary committee held its sittings, the inevitable little group of commercial sympathizers appeared. There were old fur traders—Edward Ellice, Simon McGillivray and Robert Gillespie; and the new staple trades were appropriately represented by William Hamilton Merritt, the eager, pushing, incurably romantic promoter, who happened to be in London negotiating for an imperial loan in aid of the Welland canal. In the background hovered Nathaniel Gould, who was just beginning his long career as commercial correspondent to government and who now helpfully submitted a character study of the three delegates of the Canadian popular party.[4] Cuvillier, he informed the colonial office, was an auctioneer, head over ears in debt, who had just barely managed to get clear of Canada. D. B. Viger was—it was true—a man of "a certain degree of respectability". But unwisely he had studied the *Edinburgh Review*. He was steeped in the "Malthusian and Macullochian" principles of what was commonly

—and erroneously—called the "science" of political economy. And it was plain that Nathaniel Gould regarded these errors in much the same way as a medieval lawyer would have looked upon the sins of witchcraft and diabolism.

It was quite characteristic of the merchants that, when they came before a committee concerned with the problems of Canadian civil government, they talked almost exclusively about the problems of Canadian trade. Untroubled by doubts, fortified with the ancient orthodoxies of mercantilism, they took for granted that a happy colony was a prosperous trade route and that reform of the constitution meant the removal of all barriers to commercial development and prosperity. They reviewed the old arguments against the land-holding system of Lower Canada, the feudal law and the "transit duties", as Simon McGillivray called them, which the British parliament had laid upon inland trade between the Canadas and the United States. They restated the old case for the development of the St. Lawrence; for the union of the two provinces or the annexation of Montreal to Upper Canada; and for a system which would give ascendancy to British views and "security to British capital". To all this the Canada Committee listened with a certain measure of detachment. And its report was a perfunctory and evasive document, its benevolent generalities interspersed with a few positive suggestions which were distinctly unpalatable to the commercial class.[5]

To be sure, the committee approved of the Canada Tenures Act, urged the colonial government to take the lead in the commutation of seigniorial tenures, and suggested that representation in the Lower Canadian assembly should be based on territory as well as on population, so as to give the Eastern Townships a fair voice in provincial affairs. But the question of union was raised— and dropped—in a hurry of obvious embarrassment; and the report, which recommended that the receipt and expenditure of the whole public revenue should be placed under the superintendence of the house of assembly, found an enthusiastic reception only in the ranks of the popular party. The merchants were depressed and disappointed. They realized that the imperial authorities were fallible and human; but their commercial and political views still kept them to the old idea that the British parliament was the true œcumenical council of the empire and that, if it were properly constituted and fully informed, it could not err. It was reports such as that of the Canada Committee which began to educate them out of this comforting delusion; and the time was not very far away when the process of education would be complete.

II

The report of the Canada Committee was, therefore, a very unpromising basis for a peaceful settlement. Where it satisfied the merchants it disgusted the radicals; and where it raised liberal expectations it dashed commercial hopes. English politicians were, however, insufficiently acquainted with Canadian party divisions; and the report served to guide the reforming tories and the whigs in various ways, although its recommendations were never embodied in a general statute. By the Howick Act of 1831, the crown revenues, apart from the casual and territorial fund, were handed over to the control of the provincial legislatures; and the imperial authorities endeavoured to reform the executive and legislative councils, which were supposed to be too much dominated by government officials to keep their independence or to merit respect. Without altering the Canadian system in any of its essentials, the British tried cautiously to correct it. In the brief, uneasy lull which followed the crisis of 1827, they pursued conciliation and harmony with a virtuous earnestness; and under the soothing ministrations of colonial governors and colonial office officials, even the Canadian parties were persuaded to grant a few concessions and to make a few compromises.

But Canadian political disputes grew mainly out of Canadian conditions; and although the strife could be enlivened by affronts from the governor and the imperial authorities, it could not be finally pacified by their blandishments. To a considerable extent at least, the conflict in the Canadas was a conflict between commerce and agriculture, between the directors of the old commercial state and the inhabitants of the new agricultural Canada. In the years which followed 1828, at the very moment when the politicians were trying to re-establish harmony, the balance of the Canadian economy was upset and the relative weight of Canadian social groups was altered by a new movement, which became the greatest feature of the period. This was the migration of British peoples to Canada. It began to gather its impetus, its unprecedented volume at this time; and it did not reach and pass its climax until the troubled period of the thirties and forties was over. It stands out, along with the coming of the Loyalists and the immigration of 1900–1910, as one of the three greatest movements of peoples which Canada has ever seen.

Its causes lay in the periodic depressions which lasted from 1815 until the middle of the century, in the apparent chronic instability of British agriculture and industry, and in the pervasive, mounting unrest which affected every phase of English political and social life in the years which followed the conclusion of the general European war.[6] As unemployment and distress continued in England, Scotland and Ireland, as the poor rate rose and as the monster petitions for relief descended upon parliament, it began to seem to both the authorities and the people that over-population was a fact and that emigration was one of its few practical remedies. Theorists and bureaucrats began to consider plans for assisted migration; and, while they considered, the unassisted migrants collected in bewildered thousands in the ports. The migration became a mass movement. It was driven onwards by the actual evils of the depression, by the public consciousness of these evils, by the vague hope of better things, and by that contagion of restlessness which helps to inspire the collective units of history. During the decade from 1815 to 1825, some 50,000 unassisted migrants crossed the ocean from the British isles to Canada. The total for the year 1827 was 12,648. It reached 15,945 in 1829, 28,000 in 1830 and 50,254 in 1831.[7] In the eyes of Canadians, the migration of the 1830's was an acknowledged epic. And in fact, though the Canadas were already settled and a system of transport already established, the migration of masses of people was still half a breathless adventure and half a horrible ordeal.

In the ports of England, Scotland and Ireland, the migrants crowded into the timber ships which were ill-adapted for their accommodation and carelessly inspected by the authorities. Jammed together in narrow, unventilated quarters, ill-prepared for their journey, badly fed and inadequately cared for, they endured a voyage which was at best a stern discipline and which at worst became a savage test of mere survival. In the steerage of the rotten ships that sailed from Ireland, the voyage became a nightmare, lurid with the horrors of sickness and privation, the outrages of undue proximity, the quarrels brought on by boredom and hunger, and the incessant, violent noise of talk and argument and drunken singing. All this lasted for weeks, for interminable weeks, in close quarters which seemed as if suspended in space and time; and then at last, in the first months of spring and summer, the ship sailed into the immense estuary of the St. Lawrence and the uplands of the Shield drew gradually closer as the days went by.

At Grosse Isle, a little distance east of Quebec, there came the first halt. A quarantine station was established there in 1832; and during the great epidemics whole boatloads of people, ill and well, were flung ashore upon the island to recuperate or die from cholera. At Quebec there were more delays and disembarkations; and then the tow-boats, owned by John Torrance and the Molsons, began to drag the emigrant vessels up the St. Lawrence to Montreal. In those first weeks of summer, the river cities were crowded with immigrants. They filled the hotels, the taverns, the quarters provided by the emigrant societies, and the hospitals. Many of them were emaciated, poverty-stricken, without funds or prospects. But they had just escaped from the long imprisonment of the voyage; they were excited by a thousand crowding novelties; and they wandered restlessly up and down the town and filled the taverns with their clamour. Then by carriages and carts they left the city for Lachine. There the steamboats waited for them; and alternately by steamboat and by stage, as the river transport was interrupted by the rapids, they passed up to Cornwall and Prescott and around the lake to Kingston, York and Niagara.

It was deep summer when the steamboats carried them westward, up the river, into the heart of the country. At times the air was close, languorous, curiously oppressive; and the brief, violent thunderstorms seemed merely to saturate the atmosphere without cooling it. Then, while the wind blew steadily from the west, the air cleared, the sunlight became bright and hard, and for days the sky maintained its undisturbed serenity. Around them, as the panting steamboat followed the slow curves of the river, the landscape spread out like a gay mirage. Moving slowly between the wooded shoreline and the wooded islands, they watched the cottages, the orchards, the wide promising wheatfields emerge out of the green forest and close into the green forest again. They slipped out from the river into the open lake; and as they stopped before the different settlements, they saw the continual rearrangement of the picture and the continual renewal of its bright colours. And the intoxication which was a mixture of hope and regret and wonder and fatigue, sustained them and drove them onwards. The stops and disembarkations, the jolting rides over the narrow bush roads, the nights spent in the hot, close rooms of crowded taverns and the days of interminable passage up the lake—all these passed rapidly like the unreal and disconnected episodes of an exciting dream. Then came the final stop. There was a journey through the bush; and then the forest closed around the migrants and the land appropriated them for its uses.

"Emigration" had effected its final delivery. It was a trade like any other, prosecuted and exploited like the timber trade, and closely allied to it. The two trades, in fact, strengthened and supported each other; for the transport of timber had meant a heavy outbound cargo and a light return; and the immigrants were gladly packed away in space which had been previously occupied by ballast. Immigration helped to solve the problem of "unused capacity" in the timber trade; but, though its immediate effects were in favour of balance, its long-run consequences implied disequilibrium.[8] For the Canadian commercial state it had potent and disturbing results: it emphasized agriculture at the expense of the old commercial undertakings. The migrants, coming in great, successive waves, occupied Canada like an army. The population shot upwards. In 1827, the number of inhabitants in Upper Canada was 177,174; but by 1834 the total had climbed to 321,145.[9] Immigration meant settlement, increased production, the strengthening of the agricultural interest and the intensification of agricultural convictions and grievances.

Thus the quarrel between settlement and commerce, which had begun with the beginning of the Canadian fur trade, was inevitably aggravated under the régime of the new staples. There were those who looked upon the Canadas simply as a great imperial trading system: there were those who regarded the St. Lawrence as the centre of a new homeland, of future North American communities. And the issue between these two groups was already joined in Lower Canada, where social peculiarities added a touch of archaic misunderstanding and hatred to that dislike of commercial wealth and privilege which was natural in a frontier community. Immigration, which emphasized agriculture and multiplied the agricultural population of Upper Canada, upset the balance of Canadian affairs; and thus the very trades which prospered the fortunes of the new commercial system, helped also to bring on the crisis of the Canadian commercial state. After 1827, the murmur of protest gradually increased in volume all along the river and the lakes, from Quebec to Detroit. In Lower Canada, the French Canadians consolidated their position in the assembly. In Upper Canada—and here immigration had its greatest, most obvious effects—the party of protest became more distinct, more conscious of its identity, more determined and purposeful. Men like Marshall Spring Bidwell, William Lyon Mackenzie and Egerton Ryerson arose to lead it and it won the general election of 1828.

Bidwell, Ryerson and Mackenzie were three clearly contrasted reformers who represented the three different sources of Upper Canadian rural life. Ryerson was of loyalist stock; Mackenzie was an immigrant from Scotland; and Bidwell's father was an American who had come to Upper Canada just before the War of 1812. The distinction which they shared in common was gained in conspicuously different ways; and their characters, and the contributions which they made to the Canadian protest movement, varied as widely as their origins. Bidwell, who became recognized as the virtual leader of the reform party in the province, was distinguished rather by his moderation and his general capability than by any unusual brilliance. Ryerson, who was a clergyman in the Methodist Church, attained the intellectual leadership of a religious community which was largely agrarian in character and radical in spirit; but, though he possessed the real political capacities, of drive, of organizing ability and controversial skill, he used them mainly, if not exclusively, in attacking religious inequalities rather than abuses in general.[10]

Mackenzie, who dramatically broke with the more cautious

Ryerson in 1833, was a very different man. If Ryerson did not carry politics into religion, Mackenzie certainly carried religion into politics; and it has been appropriately said of him that at heart he always remained a Puritan with a mission.[11] To him government was a trust which must be fearfully undertaken and meticulously discharged; and he denounced abuses and rebuked defaulters with an unyielding sternness and a passionate sincerity. Emotional, impetuous, eager for controversy and burning with party spirit, he first gained notoriety as the editor of the *Colonial Advocate;* and his career as a journalist probably encouraged his tendency to invective, his concern for concrete abuses and his disorderly verbosity. He had many apparent inconsistencies. He never clung to one sovereign political panacea. But he had a shrewd, censorious eye for the hard realities of Upper Canadian life. He made it his chief business to defend the interests of the "mechanics and freeholders of Upper Canada", whose integrity and solid virtues he loved to celebrate. And his interest in social values and his hatred of commercial exploitation made him a natural leader of the insurgent group.

In both provinces, the reformers drew inspiration and guidance from contemporary European revolutionaries and English radicals, as well as from the Jacksonian democrats of the United States. In both provinces, their grievances were partly political and partly religious; and these grievances, which in many cases had an origin independent of economic conditions, formed a large part of the stock-in-trade of the reform parties. But, at the same time, the radicals represented the frontier and semi-feudal agriculture of the Canadas—the economic and social problems and grievances which were characteristic of it. They came to view the commercial class as a body which was seeking to control the government, as well as the business of the country, for the sake of its own private interests; and this conception of a dominating commercialism grew slowly more coherent and defined, without ever losing all its cloudy and emotional vagueness. The undertakings and policies of commercialism began to arouse suspicions. The malign influence of banks, land companies and canal companies was discovered. People began to talk about the burdens which debt and tariffs laid upon the farmers. And, on one occasion, a radical journalist, attempting vainly to get hotel accommodation on a visit to Niagara, was moved to brood upon the secret and sinister influence of commercial Montreal.

"We entered another room", he wrote, of his experience at one tavern, "which was occupied by 11 Lower Canada Merchants and their runners. They were busily employed writing mortgages and cognovits, in the hope of getting some of those in their debt to sign them! They reminded us of the artifice and activity of Spiders preparing their murderous web in the silent hour of night, in order to enable them to allure, capture and prey upon their innocent and unsuspecting victims!"[12]

III

The governing class, which now faced an organized and angry opposition in both provinces, derived most of its wealth and economic power from the Canadian commercial system. Men entered the governing class from the lower ranks of the bureaucracy; from commerce and the institutions which it had created; and from the professions which served both government and business. It would be absurd to imply that the merchants, and those who consciously sympathized with them, inevitably monopolized the control of government. The bureaucrats and professional men, who had the assurance of training and prestige, formed a distinct and important element in the governing class; and, since their tenure of office under the old colonial system was infinitely more secure than it would ever be under the régime of responsible government, it was at least possible for them to keep clear of the entangling alliances of business. But, whatever their independence and their incalculability, the civil servants and the professional men were obliged to live in a provincial society, which was nourished in certain definite ways. The country was incapable of supporting a landed aristocracy; it was still unfitted to create an industrial capitalist class; and it was only natural that the trades of the St. Lawrence should form the main economic basis for the controlling political and social group. While the merchants were anxious enough to use the strength and seek the favours of government, the professional men were often ready to accept directorships in commercial companies and to promote commercial projects; and the "Family Compact" in both Upper and Lower Canada was less a company of blood-relations than it was a fraternal union of merchants, professional men and bureaucrats. The group was relatively small; and the names of a few dozen persons turn up again and again, with almost equal regularity in the affairs of business and of government, until the extent of their monopoly control suggests the practical identification of the political and commercial state.

The personnel of the commercial group in Montreal altered considerably during this and the following decade. It was John Richardson's death, in the spring of 1831, which perhaps suggested the changes more forcibly than anything else could have done. His life had linked the fur trade with the trade in the new staples. He had inherited from the merchant adventurers of the eighteenth century and passed on his authority to the respectable business men who were to dominate the life of early Victorian Montreal. The whole long, difficult transition of the northern commercial system was written in the crammed pages of his career; and when the man who had fought the North West Company gave place to bankers like Peter McGill and dealers in the new staples like George Moffatt, the process of transformation was finished and complete. The new men had never known the country north-west of Michili-mackinac or preserved only the memories of apprenticeship for the fur trade. They differed in character from Richardson, just as Richardson had differed from the simplicity and directness of Simon McTavish and the Frobishers. And George Moffatt, who was the senior partner in the firm of Gillespie, Moffatt & Company, could stand as the type of the new commercial generation of Montreal. Sober, conservative, inclined to moderation in policy and formality in manner, Moffatt succeeded naturally to the moral leadership which Richardson had just laid down.

Montreal was commercially far more powerful than York; but it stood isolated in a province which had never accepted its materialist philosophy, and it had not been able to acquire open control of the apparatus of the state. The merchants and their sympathizers had been almost completely driven from the assembly; and in the councils they were faced by the survivors of the seigniorial class and the French-Canadian professional men.

But though they were thus checked and circumscribed, the merchants played openly a part in provincial politics which was only less important than their indirect influence at London and Quebec. John Richardson had been regularly appointed to government commissions and committees and had sat in both the executive and legislative councils. Bell, Forsyth, Moffatt, McGill, Molson, Harwood and Gates all became members of the legislative council; and these men represented the banks, the transport companies and the chief wholesale merchandising houses of Quebec and Montreal. The presence of the merchants and their professional friends in the administration of government suggested, though it inadequately suggested, the extent of the commercial influence. That influence reached beyond the limits of the merchants' business and professional connection; and their programme, the wisdom of which seemed evident and irrefutable to most of those who came from England, became the basis for tory policy in Lower Canada.

York may have been commercially weaker than Montreal, but it was unified as Montreal was not, for no essential conflict of views and interests separated the merchants from the professional group. Usually they both helped, and seldom either hindered, that amicable co-operation of business and politics which was one of the features of Upper Canadian life. In the assembly and in both councils there were merchants, headed by William Allan, who became the dean of Upper Canadian business after the manner of John Richardson, but who lacked Richardson's pugnacity and fiery party spirit.[13] The judges, lawyers, clergymen and civil servants were not too proud to advance the interests of commerce, nor too disinterested to accept the honours it awarded them. J. H. Dunn, the receiver-general of the province, became president of the Welland Canal Company. H. J. Boulton, who was appointed attorney-general, was solicitor for the canal company and the Bank of Upper Canada. William Allan and Archdeacon Strachan, who were both legislative councillors at the time, were among the first directors of the canal company, and Strachan composed an enthusiastic pamphlet in favour of the undertaking. Allan became president of the chartered Bank of Upper Canada; and twelve of the original fifteen directors were then—or soon became—executive councillors, legislative councillors or officers of government.[14] By statute, the province was empowered to purchase £25,000 of bank stock—a quarter of the original capitalization. But in 1830 it was a fact—accepted apparently with complacency by everybody but the radicals—that the directors appointed to represent the government holdings were chiefly government officials who already owned hundreds of shares in their capacity as private investors. "Civil and military officers of the government," wrote Mackenzie angrily, "executive councillors, reverend clergy of the sects paid by government, legislative councillors, or their partners, or brothers, sisters or mothers; in short, all persons interested in and profiting by the present system of rule" held stock which he estimated at $192,856; and the province, the board of education, the law society and the York hospital held most of what remained.[15]

The Canadian commercial machine, like the trading system upon which it was based, had its terminus in the metropolis of London. The British merchants had always worked in the closest co-operation with their Canadian correspondents; and the London group was stronger now than it had been, for timber was a far more important staple in the imperial economy than furs, and back of the timber interests lay the still enormous influence of the shipowners. But, in the new period, the philosophy of free trade was gaining converts; the attack upon the imperial timber preference was renewed; and in 1831, a sub-committee of that formidable body, the general shipping and colonial committee, recommended that separate British associations be formed to represent the different colonial interests. In April, 1831, the Canadian traders held a meeting at No. 13, America Square.[16] The North American Colonial Association was established; and Nathaniel Gould—the second Nathaniel to devote his talents to the cause of Canadian commercialism—became the really pushing member of the permanent committee. He was informed, assiduous, energetic and persuasive. He wrote letters to the colonial office. He wrote more letters to the colonial office. He never missed a chance or neglected an opportunity. And under his guidance and that of his associate, Robert Gillespie, the North American Colonial Association fought to keep the Americans out of the West Indies, to maintain the timber preferences, to defend the interests of the colonies against imperial tariff standardization, and to win the union of the two

Canadian provinces or the annexation of Montreal to Upper Canada.

That these British and Canadian merchants, in co-operation with the wealthy professional men and civil servants, should combine so consistently and so smoothly, is only difficult to explain upon a superficial view. Physically they were separated by hundreds of miles of ocean, river and lake; they were divided into different occupational groups; and yet, despite all this, they were united by common interests and common purposes which bound them together almost as tightly as articles of incorporation would have done. Canada was a staple-producing commercial state. The institutions and enterprises which government and commerce had created between them—the banks, the public works, the loans, the tariff, the canals and the land companies—were all related to and finally dependent upon the staple trades of the St. Lawrence river. And this staple-trading economy was still relatively simple, comprehensible; the pattern of its activities was regular, unvaried, unspoilt by serious contradictions. It was possible—it was normal—for a merchant to know the entire Canadian economy, to know it unconsciously through the conduct of his own typical business, to understand it consciously through discussions, meetings and appeals, and to stand for it, in his own person, whole-heartedly and without reservations.

There were, of course, some differences. The anger and ambition of Montreal were not felt so strongly in other places; and the timber factors at Quebec, who managed an older trade and got along well enough with the French Canadians, were not inclined to meddle with provincial politics. But as time went on and the pace became more furious, even Quebec became intransigent in the tory cause; and, in general, the commercial philosophy of Canada was like the creed of an establishment untroubled by dissenters. It was a concord created by the simplicity and uniformity of hopes and actions; and it grew out of the great, unifying fact of the St. Lawrence. The river was closer to them, closer physically and spiritually, than it would ever be again to Canadian business men and politicians. A few yards away, beyond the ships and houses, beyond the cobbled streets and narrow jetties, lay the water whose movement was a perpetual accompaniment of all their actions, which flowed through all their most prosaic concerns and all their most romantic aspirations.

Thus the governing class, a small and fairly compact body, inspired by a common purpose and speaking a common language with great conviction and authority, stood ready for its final battle with the agricultural interest of the two provinces. In sharp contrast with the opposition, it was, as it had always been, the party devoted to the realization of the commercial empire of the St. Lawrence; and this connection with big business, with the economic development of the country by private capital and public expenditure, was the strength as well as the weakness of the group. Colborne believed that the defeat of the reformers in 1830 was due in part to the opposition of people who had gained influence in the constituencies by their loud advocacy of public works; and in 1834, Vankoughnet was writing to the civil secretary of the province, urging that the St. Lawrence canals must be pushed forward as the best security for his party's success in the approaching election.[17] The tories mocked the reformers for their opposition to public improvements and derided Papineau as the defender of a feudal system which had been abolished even in France itself.[18] They made no effort to conceal their basic interest in the country's commerce; and this interest was now heavy with doubts and forebodings and irrepressibly demanding action. These were the years of the opening of the West Indies trade, of the attacks upon the timber preference and the triumphs of the Erie canal; and the merchants were driven onwards by a desperate urgency towards agitation and conflict.

IV

The antagonism of agriculture for commerce, of farm lands for trade routes, of North American parochialism for the old imperial trading system, became articulate in a dozen different squabbles in the years from 1828 to 1834. Naturally, the canals were one of the chief objects of controversy. In Upper Canada, they had been undertaken light-heartedly, in an unthinking spirit of general agreement; but so far the chief result of effort appeared to be a mounting pile of obligations which inspired fears and aroused suspicions. The expenditures for the Welland canal exceeded the estimates with mechanical regularity. The original estimate for the entire work had been £147,240. In 1830, J. B. Yates admitted an expenditure of £272,795;[19] in 1833, the total amounted to £360,000, and the estimates were once again shoved up, this time to £400,000.[20] The canal company was deeply indebted to the Bank of Upper Canada. By 1831 the province had sunk £100,000 in the undertaking, either through loans or purchase of stock; and Merritt, during his visit to England, had been obliged to mortgage the entire property to the British government, in return for a loan of £50,000. Rapidly the canal company was settling down upon the comfortable support of government; and it became therefore a legitimate and favoured subject of debate.

It was not long before the two parties differed markedly in their attitudes to the canal. Though in theory the radicals favoured "public improvements", they became suspicious of big enterprises, for big enterprises always seem to mean big expenditures of public money, by speculators and political opponents whom they heartily distrusted. As early as 1828, Mackenzie was coldly critical of the canal; and after 1830, when the tories, who were now in control of the assembly, proposed fresh loans to carry on the undertaking, the reformers voted against the proposals. Mackenzie was suspicious—he grew increasingly suspicious—of the candour, honesty and good management of the directors. For him the project came to be largely the pet, private interest of the merchants and capitalists; and he laid great emphasis upon the fact that the canal, which was being paid for out of the hard-earned cash of the Upper Canadian farmers, would encourage the importation of American wheat, flour and pork, which would compete with Canadian supplies in the protected markets of Great Britain and the West Indies.[21] When, in the session of 1834, the tories introduced resolutions recommending the purchase of the entire property as a provincial work, the reformers denounced the resolutions in particular and the canal in general. According to Bidwell, the canal was a "great overgrown concern which is consuming the life's blood of this young province"; already it had devoured thousands of pounds which ought to have been spent on roads for the real benefit of the Upper Canadian farmers. "My opinion is", declared Perry, "you would injure the agricultural interest of Upper Canada, which ought to be guarded by a protecting duty, and I never will give up the interest of Upper Canada for the Welland Canal. Is all to be subservient to this great Moloch, and everything bow to it?"[22]

The St. Lawrence canals were another and a more serious matter. It was during this period that the pressure for the thorough reorganization of the whole northern trade route became irresistible; and a number of significant changes indicated that the country would inevitably commit itself to the great project of a ship canal from the ocean to the Great Lakes. At length Montreal was made a port of entry for general purposes. The Montreal committee of trade employed Captain Piper of the Royal Engineers and Peter Fleming to prepare plans and estimates for the improvement of the harbour of Montreal; and in 1830, chiefly at the instance of the merchants, the provincial legislature set up the Montreal Harbour Commission.[23] In 1832, the imperial government at length completed the Rideau canal from Kingston to Bytown, and the Ottawa canals which were to connect it with the St. Lawrence. The Rideau system was of some commercial value, though it had been planned as a military route; but it could not compete with the Erie canal and it probably encouraged, rather than checked, the demand for the improvement of the St. Lawrence, which was now voiced by the river towns, the commercial associations and the tory press. It was not, however, until 1833, when both provinces appointed commissions for the improvement of internal navigation, that the work was really undertaken in dead earnest. The canals which were projected during the summer and autumn of 1833, were virtually all part of a single scheme, planned under one direction, for the American, Benjamin Wright, advised both commissions, and J. B. Mills made the surveys on both sides of the interprovincial boundary. The canals were to be 9 feet deep throughout: the locks 9 feet deep, 55 feet wide and 200 feet long. The gross estimate for the works in Upper Canada came to £350,000; and the cost of the improvements in the lower province was expected to total £235,782 at least.[24]

The clash between commerce and agriculture was apparent once more in the reception accorded to this programme by the different parties in the two legislatures. In Upper Canada, the reformers, led by Bidwell and Perry, talked gloomily about debt, predicted that Lower Canada would not co-operate and advised a ten years' delay.[25] But the commercially minded tories were in control of the assembly, as well as of the council; and in the session of 1834, a bill was passed authorizing a public loan of £350,000 at not more than 6 per cent. In Lower Canada, where agricultural and professional interests swayed the assembly, no action was taken at all. In February of 1834, Stuart moved, in accordance with the terms of the report, for a loan of £240,000 which would be expended to make the St. Lawrence navigable for steamboats from Lachine to the province line. He spoke with that florid rhetoric and robust optimism which were characteristic of all speeches on the St. Lawrence by the members of the commercial group. "Was it nothing", he asked, "to open a free communication with the great internal seas of our continent; those seas which Providence had bestowed upon us as a source of inexhaustible wealth. . . . Our natural advantages exceeded those of all other countries whatsoever. Our ancestors knew the value of them, and their visits into the interior are proofs of it. . . . The waters of this continent had but two great outlets, the St. Lawrence and the Mississippi and Montreal and New Orleans, must be the greatest marts of trade on the continent. . . ." He explained to the apathetic French Canadians that debts were not always burdens. "The question was", he declared, "whether by borrowing we did not enrich ourselves."[26]

These reflections were repeated and amplified in the British press by eager editors and fervent correspondents. But even when a writer prophesied that the American union was destined to break up and that the proposed improvements on the river would help to "knit the basin of the St. Lawrence into one vast confederacy", he failed to inspire the reformers; and no amount of economics or cajolery would remove their prejudice against debts. The debates on the proposed loan dragged on through the session of 1834 until a good many of the members had departed; and then their absence was used to justify another year's delay. Both Bourdages and Papineau advised caution and deprecated loans;[27] and early in March the merchants were morosely certain that the plan was lost for another year at least.

The disputes over the canals were one feature of the rising conflict between commerce and agriculture. But there were other controversies, which were inspired by other enterprises of the merchants and the commercial state. Immigration and land settlement had now become big businesses. In Upper Canada, William Lyon Mackenzie protested against the monopoly of the Canada Company in the north-western part of the province; but disputes over land and its settlement were more serious in the lower province, for a variety of reasons. The French Canadians were determined to resist immigration, for immigration would rob their children of the land which was their rightful inheritance. Immigration would inevitably affect the law, the agricultural system and the static culture of the lower St. Lawrence. The *patriotes* preferred to save subsistence agriculture on feudal lines at the expense of large-scale trade in the new staples. Their professional and bureaucratic tendencies made them naturally suspicious of land companies. As for the law of the province, it was indisputably perfect; and its apparent defects—so Papineau could argue with serene complacency—were to be attributed largely to the ignorance and prejudice of the English judges, who were incapable of appreciating the virtues of the old laws and made misguided efforts to improve upon their majestic simplicity.[28]

To the British a free tenure seemed the obvious basis for successful settlement on a large scale; and in their eyes a free tenure meant the English form of free and common soccage. But the French Canadians were determined to resist the introduction of new tenures in the seigniories and were even disposed to question the validity of English land law in the Eastern Townships.[29] Whenever a proposal was made in the Lower Canadian assembly for the commutation of seigniorial burdens, it was received with apathy or cold disfavour. "As trade was increasing", said Stuart in the assembly of 1834, "our laws ought to be modified so as to favor it. The old tenure was against the progress of trade."[30] These arguments left the assembly completely unmoved. The British statutes—the Canada Trade Act and the Canada Tenures Act—which permitted the conversion of feudal tenure into tenure by free and common soccage, were considered revolutionary innovations. They had remained almost completely inoperative, but the assembly had regularly protested against them in the twenties; and it continued to do so, though the Canada Committee had recorded its approval of their terms.[31]

In addition, the question of immigration became unfortunately connected with the problems of public expenditure and taxation. Great numbers of the immigrants arrived bewildered, penniless, enfeebled and ill; and they became immediately a charge upon the immigration authorities and upon the local immigration societies which were formed in the different towns at this time. In June, 1831, the "Emigrant Association" of Montreal was founded by a group of citizens, among whom the merchants were prominent; and during the first year of its operations, it expended over £750 in sending 4,022 immigrants to various places in Upper and Lower Canada.[32] But far more was needed. Even the conservative papers in Montreal raged against the captains and their treatment of the wretched, defrauded immigrants; and the *Montreal Gazette* itself suggested a light capitation tax upon immigrants, to be paid by the captains of vessels, which would create a really useful "Emigrant Fund". This suggestion coincided with the views of the imperial authorities; and in 1832, at the suggestion of the governor, the assembly passed a bill imposing a poll tax of $1 upon immigrants who sailed with government authority and $2 upon those who did not.[33]

Immediately there was a chorus of remonstrance in which the Upper Canadians lustily joined. In Lower Canada, the merchants, led by Moffatt, vainly tried to block the bill in council. Then the Quebec traders petitioned the governor to disallow it.[34] It was, they said, unjust, it questioned the right of free Englishmen to settle wherever they pleased in the empire and it would infallibly divert immigration to the United States. As Colborne said, there was considerable opposition to the bill in Upper Canada. The legislature, as well as the York society for the relief of the sick and destitute, petitioned against the bill;[35] and the tory press of Upper Canada joined the *Montreal Gazette* in denouncing it. The tax, declared the Upper Canadian editors, was "an open and glaring attack" upon the constitutional rights of Upper Canada; and it had been adopted, not in fact to provide for British immigrants, but to protect French-Canadian culture from inundation. "We have for some time past", wrote one editor, "enjoyed a valuable influx of Emigrants, or as it might be termed, a valuable import trade of the nerves and sinews of prosperity—of the true wealth of the country, an industrious peasantry; and now that this influx is visibly enriching this Province a tax has been laid on it, ostensibly for the support of pauper Emigrants; but in reality to obstruct that influx of Europeans which by increasing the number of English inhabitants, threatens soon to merge the preponderance of the French Canadians in Lower Canada."[36]

The year 1832 marked the real crisis of the great immigration. The petty disputes over the immigrant tax were followed rapidly— revengefully—by the real calamity of the cholera epidemic. From Grosse Isle, where a quarantine station had been newly established to cope with the expected arrival of infected ships, the plague reached Quebec; and during June it travelled with sinister and incredible rapidity up the river and into the heart of Upper Canada, killing settlers and immigrants indiscriminately, paralysing all activity and producing an atmosphere of apprehension and hysteria. Immigration, which the French Canadians had always disliked, became suddenly in their eyes a fearful and loathsome abomination. It not only peopled the countryside with foreigners; it massacred "les enfants du sol". At a meeting held at the village of Debartzch, in the parish of St. Charles, towards the end of July, immigration in general was attacked and Great Britain was censured for permitting the destructive immigration of 1832.[37] In August, Neilson's *Quebec Gazette* ran a series of editorials against immigration; and from Papineau down, the *patriotes* denounced the movement with a new intensity of moral fervour.

Of all these men "who tortured God's scourge into a political grievance", M. Rodier obtained probably the greatest notoriety for the most magnificently affecting effort. "When I see my country in mourning", M. Rodier declared, "and my native land presenting to my eye nothing but one vast cemetery, I ask, what has been the cause of all these disasters? and the voice of my father, my brother, and my beloved mother,—the voices of thousands of my fellow-citizens—respond from their tombs, It is emigration. It was not enough to send among us avaricious egotists, without any other spirit of liberty than that which could be bestowed by a simple education at *the counter*, to enrich themselves at the expense of the Canadians, and then endeavour to enslave them;—they must also rid themselves of their beggars and cast them by thousands on our shores; they must send us miserable beings, who, after having partaken of the bread of our children, will subject them to the horrors following upon hunger and misery; they must do still more, they must send us in their train pestilence and death."[38]

The tory press leapt upon this sublime utterance with fury and venomous contempt. One editor, seeking desperately for a suitable comparison, declared that M. Rodier's harangue exhibited "as extravagant a superabundance of impudence and folly, as any that has yet escaped the lips of Ambassador Mackenzie. . . ". It was unthinkable and revolting that Great Britain should actually be accused of infecting French Canadians—of "introducing disease and pauperism among their high mightinesses, the wealthy Monsieurs of the Lower Province, a people steeped in seignorial barbarism, ignorance and beggarliness to the very eyes".[39] In their pitiable weakness, they had never been able really to occupy the country; and now they actually sought to prevent the intrepid sons of Great Britain from doing so. "So Mr Rodier will oppose 'a dam to the torrent of emigration', eh!" enquired one journalist dramatically. "Villainous conception!! Let us look to it: the crisis seems at hand *everywhere*. . . . Let us foster emigration, and swell the 'torrent' more and more, and let its opponents beware lest it overwhelm them."[40]

It was at this distinctly unfavourable time, when people were still quarrelling over the immigrant tax, when the country had barely recovered from the cholera, and when the tory press was baying furiously after Monsieur Rodier and his kind, that the new Lower Canadian land company at last began to get under way. For some time, the members of the North American Colonial Association had been interested in the scheme; and the enormous immigration of the last few years appeared to make its success a certainty. A meeting was held at the London Tavern in February, 1832, where Nathaniel Gould addressed the gathering, and it was decided to establish the British American Land Company, with a capital of £500,000.[41] G. R. Robinson, M.P. was made governor, Nathaniel Gould deputy governor; and George Moffatt and Peter

McGill were later appointed resident commissioners in Canada.[42] The company, moved not so much by the sordid hope of profit as by the "laudable and patriotic design" of directing immigration to Canada, began a long negotiation with the colonial office; and in the end it acquired over half a million acres in the Eastern Townships.

In the meantime the mere news of the company's formation had created a furore in the lower province. As early as April, when the first reports were published in the province, the press began to argue about the land company; and during the summer the county of the Lake of the Two Mountains and the assembly at St. Charles reasserted the claim of the province to a control of its waste lands and denounced the cession of a part of this patrimony to rich and grasping English capitalists.[43] In the next session of the provincial parliament, the session of 1832–1833, the assembly passed an address to the king, protesting against the land company.[44] Papineau did not merely attack the land company as a dangerous monopoly. He warmly defended the home-loving French Canadians who were unwilling to put a price upon the land of their forefathers; and he was led on to criticize the frontiersmen in the Eastern Townships who welcomed the sale of land to an enterprising concern. "They who had quitted the land of their birth", said Papineau, referring obviously to the American settlers, "were willing to sell that of their adoption—to sell for dollars—all they had, and part with the asylum they had chosen for themselves for dollars—dollars appeared to be their only aim."[45]

These pleasantries merely increased the ardour with which the supporters of the company campaigned in its favour. For the merchants, the British press, and the men of the Eastern Townships, the British American Land Company became, rather oddly, a symbol of the whole energizing revolution which they were anxious to effect. It meant immigration and progress: it threatened feudalism and stagnation. The legislative council drafted resolutions in support of the company;[46] and at a meeting held at Sherbrooke the men of the Townships appointed an agent to carry their petitions in favour of the land company to England.[47] Ralph Taylor, one of the members for the Eastern Townships, was moved publicly to repudiate Papineau's "base imputation" against his constituents. For this offence he was promptly voted guilty of "malicious libel" by the assembly, jailed in the assembly's usual summary fashion; and for a day he became a kind of martyr to the cause of frontier agriculture and the British American Land Company.

Immigration and land companies were matters of debate chiefly in Lower Canada; but the banks and their alleged misdoings were a favourite theme of the radicals in both provinces. There were three chartered banks which had survived the early, experimental stages of Canadian banking—the Bank of Montreal, the Quebec Bank and the Bank of Upper Canada. They were controlled by merchants, executive and legislative councillors and officers of government; and in Upper Canada, where the province was itself a shareholder in the Upper Canada Bank, the tie between banking and the governing class was particularly close. The banks had now been in existence about a decade; and during the early thirties they were intent upon the renewal of their charters and the augmentation of their capital. It was an unfortunate time. In the United States the bank war was at its height; and in Canada the whole problem of banking had become an object of speculation, criticism and party politics.

Papineau and his followers looked upon the banks with that instinctive distrust for all things commercial which had its roots in the simple, agrarian character of their society. In 1830, when the Montreal Bank petitioned for the renewal of its charter and an increase in its capitalization, the leaders of the popular party took advantage of the occasion to conduct a kind of general review of the banking system of the province. Papineau objected to the limited liability of the shareholders and to the increased capitalization demanded by the bank. He wished to limit its power to issue small notes; and he complained about its reluctance to grant information to the assembly. The theme, however, upon which he harped most frequently, was the enormous and sinister political influence of the bank. "Another most weighty consideration", he said, "was, whether, by the controul of £600,000 of the capital of the country, the Directors did not possess an alarming political influence. In fact that political influence had been felt in Montreal at the last election. The President of the Bank, accompanied by a

Member of the Executive Council, had gone round to solicit votes
. . . almost all the Directors had interested themselves in that
election. . . ."[48] In the end, the charters of the old banks were
renewed, and a new bank, the City Bank of Montreal, was given a
charter as well. But the assembly tightened its restrictions and the
reformers continued to display hostility. Bédard complained that
the banks were useful only as offices of discount and that the
directors and shareholders absorbed all the money available for
discounts themselves. He concluded that "the Banks had done
great harm"; and Bourdages magnanimously modified this by
declaring that they "had done more harm than good".[49]

In Upper Canada, Mackenzie was easily the outstanding critic
of the banks. He had received his early training in a counting-house
in Scotland. He evidently knew a good deal about the Scottish
banking system, and he became well read in the history and
practice of the banks in the United States. He was relentless,
voluminous and informed in his criticism. When in 1830 the reform
assembly in Upper Canada appointed a select committee on the
state of the currency, Mackenzie was appointed chairman and
his ideas are obviously reflected in the report.[50] Like all the
reformers, as well as many of the tories, he hated the monopoly
power and the political connections of the Bank of Upper Canada;
but he and the small group of radicals which he led were no
advocates of many banks and easy money. In fact, Mackenzie
heartily disliked the American system, with its numerous banks
and floods of paper currency; and he would have preferred the
establishment of a limited number of local, independent banks,
unconnected with government, yet strictly regulated by the
legislature, with a view to enforcing the responsibilities of the
directors and shareholders, the stability of the institutions and
the soundness of their paper money.

The committee on the state of the currency had both increased
Mackenzie's stock of banking information and heightened his
suspicions of the banks. From then on, in his paper, in the assembly
and at the colonial office, he pursued Upper Canadian banks in
general and the Bank of Upper Canada in particular, with a tireless
and avenging zeal. He stormed over the limited liability of the
directors and shareholders, their laxity in fulfilling obligations and

responsibilities, and their brusque refusal to disclose the full state of their business. Repeatedly he informed his readers of what was in fact the truth—that the Bank of Upper Canada had invested its fairly large note issue and the greater part of its capital fund in discounts, leaving only a comparatively small reserve in funds and specie.[51] It gave him great pleasure to point out that the directors appointed by government in virtue of its stock were invariably government officers and councillors who already had a personal interest in the bank. "No one individual", he declared, "who possessed the confidence of the people in so great a degree as to be returned to this house [the assembly] . . . has ever been thought worthy of a seat on the board of directors by the Lieutenant Governors of Upper Canada. . . ."[52] The bank was dominated by the government and the governing class; and they had used their power to advance their own interests and to defeat their critics and opponents. A bank, if properly regulated, might be a good thing; "but in the hands of our irresponsible governing faction, it becomes a political curse of the first magnitude—a prostituted instrument of corruption, of all others the most powerful and insidious".[53]

The local merchants, who were strong in the new assembly elected in 1830, wanted more banks. The Bank of Upper Canada, which dominated the council, wanted both its monopoly and an increased capitalization. In 1831 each side revenged its own disappointment by a denial of the other's request. But the unwisdom of fighting each other instead of the radicals was soon realized by the official group and the local merchants; and in 1832 the assembly amiably helped to increase the capital of the Bank of Upper Canada while the council magnanimously chartered the Commercial Bank of the Midland District. In 1831, in the last assembly he attended before his expulsions, Mackenzie had vowed that if the bank bills were passed he would carry his opposition to the foot of the throne. In April, 1832, when he at last departed for England, he had more and better reasons for a pilgrimage to the colonial office; but he did not forget the banks, for he never forgot anything. In his letters to the colonial office, which were distinguished by their acuteness and vehemence as well as by their incredible detail, Mackenzie found plenty of space to expose the villainies of the bank monopoly; and in his letter of March, 1833, he was able to discover nearly twenty-five separate objections to the Upper Canada Bank Act of 1832.[54] He did not toil in vain. His criticisms found a sympathetic reception in the colonial office and the board of trade, both of which were inclined to view North American banking practice with frigid disapproval. And in the spring of 1833, Stanley notified Colborne that the bank acts were to be disallowed.[55]

This blow was the last of a shattering series of rebukes and punishments which had been administered to the Canadian governing class by a strangely altered colonial office, acting— apparently, though incomprehensibly—at the dictation of that disreputable demagogue, "Ambassador Mackenzie". Messrs. Boulton and Hagerman, the attorney-general and solicitor-general, had been dismissed; the bank acts were to be disallowed; and actually the news of this intended disallowance was first communicated to the Canadians by Mackenzie himself, in a complacent letter. The governing class, in 1833, was in a state of befuddled indignation. The two banks concerned, the merchants of York, Belleville and Kingston, and the North American Colonial Association in London, petitioned against the disallowance, lamenting its probable commercial consequences and refuting the arguments on which it was based.[56] While Mackenzie and the radicals extolled the wisdom of the colonial office with a strangely novel enthusiasm, the tories bewailed the ineptitude and injustice of its interference in the purely internal concerns of the province. ". . . We defy all men in the world", wrote one tory editor with a large gesture of indignation, "to produce, in any country or age, an act of folly more egregious than the puerile meddling of the Lords of Trade with our tills and money-chests. . . . The Lords of Trade must not be permitted to meddle with our money concerns. . . . Our money is our life's blood, which ought not to be committed to other keeping than our own, and *must not.*"[57]

In the session of 1834, this loyal, tory assembly rebuked the home authorities for their maladroit and tyrannical act.[58] It became clear once again that tory loyalty and tory interests were intimately connected, and that submissive devotion to the "parent state" was regarded as payment for real favours and tangible support.

V

These were provincial affairs. But most of them were common to both provinces; and even when they seemed peculiar to one, their settlement inevitably affected the whole community of the St. Lawrence. The disputes over immigration, emigrant taxes and the land company in Lower Canada excited the Upper Canadian tories just as much as they did the merchants of Montreal and Quebec; and the problem of the canals was as indivisible as the river which they were intended to improve. In these circumstances, when provincial issues assumed an interprovincial significance, when a movement by one province provoked or necessitated action on the part of the other, it was natural that the system of government itself should become subject to strain once more. The constitution of 1791 had been patched up by the Canada Trade Act; but repaired or not, it was no vehicle for the commercial state. The friction between the two provinces began again; and as soon as it did so the agitation for the removal or the alteration of the interprovincial boundary was at once revived.

Most of the troubles between the provinces were directly or indirectly connected with finance. The Canada Trade Act was supposed to deal with inequalities of revenue; but it had nothing to say about inequalities of expenditure. And almost at once these became disturbingly pronounced. While the richer province sternly refused to borrow, the poorer province proceeded rapidly to acquire a large debt. In the autumn of 1821, Upper Canada had begun to sell debentures on a modest scale; and by 1833 the amount of government debentures outstanding was slightly over £203,000.[59] It was not a very terrifying total; but in itself it did not reveal all the disquieting features of Upper Canadian finance. It did not include, for example, the unprecedentedly large loan which had been sanctioned by the legislature in 1833–1834, for the construction of the St. Lawrence canals; and it gave no indication of the difficulties which Upper Canada had already experienced in respect of its credit. In the summer of 1833, the receiver-general, J. H. Dunn, admitted that he had not been able to dispose of the first block of debentures in either Canada or the United States, at a rate which he considered the province could bear.[60] He departed for London, where eventually he persuaded Baring Brothers & Company and Thomas Wilson & Company to underwrite the new Canadian issues. But this was merely the beginning of Upper Canadian financial difficulties. The fact was that the resources of the province —its inelastic taxing and borrowing powers—were simply incapable of supporting the ambitious project of public works which had been planned. Within a few years it became clear that Upper Canada was headed either for bankruptcy or absorption in an enlarged concern; and union became financially necessary as the only possible fiscal basis for the support of the St. Lawrence transportation system.

The crisis of expenditures, however, still lay in the future; but in the meantime the squabbles over revenue had broken out once again. In 1828, when the commissioners of both provinces met to determine Upper Canada's proportion of the Quebec duties for the next four years, the conference went off fairly amicably, though, indeed, a third arbitrator had to be appointed. But in 1832 the negotiations opened very inauspiciously; and when George Markland demanded that Upper Canada should receive one-third of the duties, Pothier, the Lower Canadian commissioner, flatly refused. Among all the claims and counter-claims, which were repeated wearisomely in a long series of statements, replies and rejoinders, one really serious disputed point stood out.[61] While Pothier maintained that Quebec was strictly a Lower Canadian port in which Upper Canada could have merely the right of entry for her goods, Markland insisted that Quebec was common to both provinces and that its mere geographical location in Lower Canada did not confer any special privileges or advantages upon that province. The question was basic, for it involved the interpretation of the constitution; and both commissioners returned to it with zest and conviction. They could agree upon nothing. They could not even agree upon the appointment of a third arbitrator. And it was not until 1833, when the Crown selected Ward Chipman as the third commissioner, that Upper Canada's claim was finally accepted—Pothier dissenting to the last against the award.

In the meantime a number of things had happened. Once more, as in 1820–1822, the quarrels over the division of revenue inspired a campaign for the political unification of the St. Lawrence.

From the assertion that Upper Canada had a right in equity to the Lower Canadian ports, it was an easy, natural step to the demand that Upper Canada should in fact be put in territorial possession of a port of her own. It was a demand which had been made before; and the tories in both provinces were ready to take advantage of an occasion for asserting it again. In October, 1832, when the abortive negotiations in Montreal had barely finished, a public meeting was held in York; and William Allan, the president of the Bank of Upper Canada, H. J. Boulton, the attorney-general, C. A. Hagerman, the solicitor-general, W. H. Draper and George Munro were appointed a committee to draw up a petition to the king for the annexation of Montreal to Upper Canada.[62] In December, a similar meeting was held in Kingston; and immediately the legislatures in both provinces took up the question. In December and again in February, 1833, annexation was debated in the Upper Canadian assembly, with Boulton, Hagerman and Merritt making speeches in its favour.[63] Down at Quebec, John Neilson sponsored resolutions censuring George Markland and protesting against the dismemberment of Lower Canada, while Papineau declared, for the benefit of both provinces, that "the conclusion to be drawn from the whole must be that the only principle actuating the government of Upper Canada, is that which actuates a highway robber. . . ".[64] As for the newspapers, they had never really ceased to discuss the subject; and beginning with October, 1832, the entire tory press in the two provinces was filled for months with news reports, letters and editorials on the subject of annexation.

Annexation, as the reformers were never tired of pointing out, was a substitute for union. It was simply another scheme for adapting the political system of the St. Lawrence to the needs of the commercial state. Naturally, its support came from the governing class, from the groups which were related to or dependent upon the commercial system; and this support was so unanimous that Mackenzie could argue, in a letter to Lord Goderich, that the annexation of Montreal was in effect a "government measure".[65] Just as during the controversy over the union of the provinces, the commercially minded governing class argued almost exclusively in economic and geographic terms. "The omnipotent interests of commerce", wrote one partisan rhetorically, "which have ever swayed the destinies, not only of Kingdoms and empires, but of continents, will usurp their dominion over this. Individual men, and little political juntas, in the infancy of population, may project schemes, and imagine boundaries, and set their hearts on the success of the former, and the integrity of the latter; but at last, nature, whose laws are imprescriptible, and ever finally Triumphant, will settle all."[66]

In detail, the arguments for annexation differed from those which had been advanced for union only in so far as the latter had been modified and developed by the experience of the intervening years. It was argued, as it had been for union, that annexation would end the stupid quarrels over the division of duties. It would liberate the Montreal merchants from the baneful domination of the anti-commercial French; and it would remove Upper Canada from the thraldom of the lower province—from hateful emigrant taxes and other burdens. Lower Canada, which held the ports merely as a trustee, had abused its trust; and Upper Canada, which was the really commercial province, had a right to one of them. Upper Canada had shown the energy and initiative to build the Welland canal and to attack the enormous problem of the St. Lawrence; and it should be given the power and the opportunity to do what the other province refused to do—to complete the whole navigation system upon one uniform and consistent plan. These, in the main, were old arguments, refurbished for the occasion; but they were advanced with a kind of angry peremptoriness which was new and not entirely assumed. ". . . If any opposition was exhibited to the present imperative demand upon His Majesty's interference", declared J. S. Cartwright, president of the Commercial Bank, at Kingston, "that such should be treated as a territorial assumption, that would be settled by a *vi et armis* recourse by the people of Upper Canada."[67]

These bursts of temper, these threats half serious and half rhetorical, were brief flashes which lit up a sullen atmosphere charged with fear and anger and frustration. The quarrel between commerce and agriculture, merchants and farmers, centralization and particularism, the old colonial system and Canadian autonomy, had now become a chronic and rancorous dispute. The agitation was at its height in the two legislatures. It was breaking out in a dozen different places, in town meetings and rural assemblies. In Upper Canada the extreme reformers were being driven into desperation by their political impotence and helplessness; and, as the tide of immigration and commercialism closed in around them, the French Canadians hysterically realized its threat to their culture and political supremacy. Nothing in its past had equalled the violence of the tory party in the Upper Canadian assembly during the session of 1832; and the British in Lower Canada, with the Eastern Townships and the governing class of Upper Canada behind them, "assumed a bolder tone and now exhibit a determination no longer to submit to the domination of the French party". Both sides were moved by vindictive anger to the most extreme reprisals. The regularity with which the tories expelled Mackenzie from the Upper Canadian legislature was equalled by the persistence with which the reformers ejected Robert Christie from the assembly at Quebec. The repeated elections in York county, which repeatedly returned Mackenzie during the session of 1831–1832, were the scenes of great popular demonstrations; and in May, 1832, there was violence and rioting at a by-election in the turbulent West Ward of Montreal.

The merchants, and the professional and governmental groups with which they had become associated, looked upon all this with rapidly increasing perturbation. The main purpose of the merchants was to maintain the historic commercial empire of the St. Lawrence; and this interest, from its very nature and extent, was connected with other and more emotionally potent loyalties. The St. Lawrence was an imperial river. The northern trading system stretched from the centre of North America to Great Britain; and the idea upon which it was based was the historic mercantilist conception, ennobled by all the struggles, defeats and victories of the British Empire. Both in theory and in practice, by its loyalties as well as by its interests, the Canadian commercial state was linked inseparably with the motherland; and the merchants, when they rushed to protect their own concerns against Canadian agrarianism, believed that they defended a whole empire and a great imperial tradition. As the old commercialism was questioned and disputed, as a second American revolution grew more probable in the very provinces which had shunned the first, the merchants and their sympathizers became more emotionally aroused, more militant, more prepared to fall back upon direct action. They still depended —for their old philosophy impelled them to depend—upon Great Britain for a final settlement; but they were coming gradually to the belief that they might have to do for the empire what the empire would be slow to do for itself.

"We must not, however," wrote one 'loyal agitator', "look to His Majesty, His Majesty's Ministers, or the House of Commons, for emancipation. We must look to ourselves. Upon us is the burthen imposed and we must free ourselves from it. . . . We are capable of righting ourselves, we must right ourselves, we shall right ourselves. I do not mean that the British of this Province shall arm themselves and make war on the followers of the 'Assembled Demagogues', and put them down by main force, which, with the assistance of our Upper Canada friends, could be done in one campaign; but I mean, that we shall assume such an attitude that there will be no mistaking it:—*then*, . . . should the British Government not perform the needful; why *then*, we shall be prepared to perform it for ourselves."[68]

CHAPTER XI

BREAKDOWN

I

THE two provinces passed from the mood into the act of violence through a few intermediate stages of rapidly increasing militancy. After 1833, the drift towards revolt increased definitely in speed; and this acceleration became noticeable in 1834, which was a year marked by an ominous combination of commercial distress and political excitement. The difficulties under which the Canadas struggled—the strains imposed by their relations with Great Britain and the United States, and the stresses created by their own internal contradictions and disputes—were combined in this year to impose an almost intolerable burden. The Canadian parties, driven on by their angry sense of deadlock, were now led to form associations, draft manifestoes and fight elections in a more determined spirit. In England the year 1834 witnessed a new and disturbing attack upon the timber preference; and in the United States the speculative and already unstable prosperity, which had developed since 1830, was shaken by the war between President Jackson and the Bank of the United States.[1] When, in the late summer of 1833, the federal deposits were withdrawn from that institution, there followed a financial and commercial panic which invaded Canada as naturally as it spread through the United States. In the autumn of 1833 there were failures in Quebec, Montreal and Kingston; and in the first months of 1834 the Montreal merchants looked back upon a dismal season and forward, in apprehension, to a year which appeared likely to be still more gloomy.[2]

The slump was accompanied and followed by political definitions and the organization of political hatreds. In Lower Canada, where the commercial programme was at a standstill and the civil government rested in uneasy suspense, the two parties were led by their very sense of impasse into that penultimate stage of drafting manifestoes and striking morally indignant attitudes. The assembly, which could spare no time for the consideration of the commercial programme, was ready to lavish its attention upon the attractive subject of grievances; and during the session of 1834, it produced that formal codification of provincial discontents, known as the *Ninety-two Resolutions*. It was a definitive and provocative document. Its clauses attacked the merchants, their interests, their loyalties and their one source of political power, the legislative council. From then on the tories held, as an established article of faith, that the popular party was in fact disloyal and republican. The resentments and frustrations of years found expression in the emotional appeal for the defence of the British connection and British institutions. The Resolutions, wrote one indignant Montreal merchant, "are the most insolent, disloyal, insane and ridiculous productions that were ever submitted to the consideration of a deliberate body".[3] In Canada and in England, the merchants began to argue that the crisis was at last at hand, that the imperial parliament must interfere and that troops should be sent out for the preservation of the North American empire.[4] In April a "great constitutional meeting" was held in Montreal and loyal addresses were sent to the governor from Quebec, William Henry, and the Eastern Townships.

In Upper Canada, where the conservative assembly elected in 1830 was approaching its end, the tories made a similar attempt to resolve provincial politics into a simple controversy between loyalty and republicanism. In May, 1834, Mackenzie published in the *Colonial Advocate* that unfortunate, notorious letter from his radical mentor in England, Joseph Hume. In this effusion, Hume referred, with evident complacency, to "that crisis which is fast approaching in the affairs of the Canadas, and which will terminate in independence and freedom from the baneful domination of the mother country. . . ". In delighted astonishment the tories appropriated this sentiment as a revelation of the real aims of the perfidious radicals; and the "baneful domination letter" enabled editors to play with infinite variations upon the popular theme of republicanism hypocritically disguised as reform. "It is seldom conspiracies succeed", wrote one editor in a moralizing tone, "because some of the wretched conspirators are almost certain to disclose the views of the cabal before the maturity of their infamous designs; and now we have it from the great Mr.

Hume himself, and published by Mr. Mackenzie that the design of these worthies is neither more nor less than to separate this Country '*from the baneful domination of the Mother Country*', and thus are they gibbeted together, TRAITORS IN THE FIRST DEGREE. "[5]

In this mood of exalted patriotism and outraged loyalty the tories marched into the general elections of 1834. That autumn there were elections in both provinces; and while in Lower Canada the merchants could hardly look forward to more than a few morally consoling victories in the towns, the Upper Canadian constitutionalists had a fair, fighting chance to rule the next assembly at Toronto. Their election programme was a typical mixture of sentiment and practicality. The tories stood upon their record as builders of commercial prosperity and as defenders of the British connection. At Toronto the younger politicians and the journalists founded the "British Constitutional Society of Upper Canada" upon the pure and unimpeachable principles of loyalty and constitutionalism;[6] but other and more materialistic considerations were not forgotten. In the eastern part of the province the candidates tried to capitalize the popularity of the new St. Lawrence canals, which the tory party had started;[7] and of course the journalists attempted to prove that British control was, in a very real sense, the blessing, not the bane, of Canada. "I would now inquire", wrote one correspondent, "in what consists the '*baneful domination*' of the Mother Country, of which these heartless demagogues complain. Is it shown by her paying for our protection and government . . . ? Is it shown in the preferences accorded to our productions in the British markets?— And, finally, is it shown in the constant influx of British capital and enterprise, which is adding incalculably to the value of every man's estate?"[8]

The Upper Canadian reformers, who had been four years in angry opposition, had now a long and crowded list of tory jobs, monopolies and offences to denounce. There were the clergy reserves, the bank monopoly, the Welland canal, the mounting provincial debt and other matters about which one could hardly be sufficiently vociferous; but in addition to all these, there was the question of the tariff, which had come up once more since the last general election. The duties placed by the Canada Trade Act and the Huskisson legislation upon American natural products entering Canada, had been repealed—as has been seen—during the past few years by the imperial parliament; and, with the hope of a victory at the polls before them, the reformers renewed their criticism of the commercial system of the St. Lawrence and raised a great indignant cry for the protection of Canadian agriculture. They argued that the virtual free trade, maintained by both the British parliament and the local legislature, was a completely unequal arrangement, for the American tariff prevented the Canadian farmer from seeking a market in the United States. Canada was drained of its specie and loaded with competitive products merely to satisfy the merchants and their satellites. "If", wrote Mackenzie, "an additional quantity of wheat, flour, pork, beef, and other produce belonging to the people of the United States go down the Welland Canal from Ohio, *via* the St. Lawrence, upon equal or better terms than ours, and swell the exports at Quebec, what advantage is that to us? . . . The proprietors of a few frontier flouring establishments may profit by this law; Messrs. Chisholm, McMillan and a few more of our forwarding merchants and owners of schooners may gain temporary advantages; the government officers by their bank monopoly, and the lawyers and sheriffs by their exorbitant fees, may contrive to keep down the spirit of the people, by the present expensive system, but, unless some miraculous and unforeseen event should occur in their favour, the farmers must be deeply injured, and the progress of the colonists retarded."[9]

In the weeks which preceded and followed the general election, the tories worked their hardest to refute this case. They argued that it was absurd to think that the Canadian market was a domestic market which could be effectively protected. Canada was essentially a country of trans-shipment, its markets were world markets, governed by world prices, which no amount of tinkering with the inland tariff could alter in the slightest. The import of American goods simply increased the export stocks, brought more British shipping to Quebec and Montreal and consequently helped to reduce freight rates. In these ways, the tories tried to refute the reformers' economic arguments; and they endeavoured, also, to disparage Mackenzie's class appeal. "It has of late been the fashion in this Country", wrote one editor, "to cry up the Farmers as all in all—they are spoken of as everything, and all else as nothing. This silly and invidious practice was introduced by Mackenzie, who had a design upon their votes, and others have caught from him this nonsensical jargon. The Farmer is undoubtedly a most useful link in the great chain of civilization, but not more so than the Blacksmith, the Clothier, the Builder, the Merchant, and the Capitalist, nor more worthy to have his interests considered in the great scale of Legislation."[10]

The election followed. The Upper Canadian farmers, revealing a presumptuous over-estimate of their own importance in provincial society, proceeded to fling the tories out of power. The defeat was bad enough in the eastern part of the province, where the river towns could still be counted upon to return a few commercially minded citizens to the legislature; but in the west, in the new agricultural districts, the election was a rout.[11] In a period of increasing political tension, the governing class had lost its hold upon the one assembly which it could reasonably hope to control; and the election in Lower Canada, which followed in November, was a doomed failure. The most the merchants and the British party in general could expect was a few victories in the Eastern Townships and the towns. But it was characteristic of a period, when the conflict of interests was resolving itself into a conflict of emotionally charged political principles, that the merchants fought their minor engagements with increased fervour. They put up good candidates—Andrew Stuart at Quebec and Walker and Donnellan in the West Ward of Montreal; and in Quebec there were public meetings during every night of the election. "I began to ask myself whether I was really an Englishman", wrote one tory rhetorically, "my conscience answered in the affirmative then I said now is the time to prove myself a worthy member of that great nation. Consequently I entered the field and have been in active service from the beginning."[12]

Like the tories, the reformers were becoming more militant; and, as the conflict neared its climax, they made a more strident appeal to the farmers and the small shopkeepers and a more direct attack upon the merchants and the institutions of the commercial state. In his long address to the electors of the West Ward of

Montreal Papineau suggested the policy of non-consumption of British goods and urged a run upon the banks of Lower Canada. The banks, said Papineau, were the preserve of the big merchants and capitalists, the monopoly of a dangerous political and financial coterie. "The most efficacious and most immediate means", he declared, "which the Canadians have to protect themselves against the fury of their enemies, is to attack them in their dearest parts—their pockets—in their strongest entrenchments, the Banks."[13] In Quebec city, in the early days of November, a run began on the Quebec Bank and on the local branch of the Bank of Montreal.[14] The merchants began to argue, in horrified tones, that nothing so immoral and antisocial had ever been seen during the French revolution; and a tory paper compared Papineau to "a well-drugged Malay running a-muck". But the hysterical efforts of the conservatives were as fruitless in Lower as they had been in Upper Canada. Andrew Stuart was defeated in Quebec; and after an excited election, the returning officer announced that Papineau and Nelson had won in the West Ward of Montreal. At a time when their loyalties were aroused and their resentments dangerously increased, the merchants had suffered a crushing defeat. Would they accept it? And if not, what were they going to do?

II

The eighteen months which followed the general elections of 1834 saw the development of a militant tory counter-offensive in both provinces. Its spectacular climax was to come in Upper Canada, in the spring months of 1836; but it had its first beginnings in Quebec and Montreal. On November 17, just as soon as the election in the West Ward was officially declared ended, some representative Montreal citizens wrote to the governor charging grave irregularities in the conduct of the election;[15] and three days later, a great public meeting of protest was held in Tattersall's or Jones's "Long Room" in St. James Street.[16] Meetings were a normal part of commercial activity in Montreal; but the assembly in November was unusual and significant. This time the tories were moved by a compelling sense of outrage to generalize their criticism and to create a permanent organization for their party.

They declared that they would no longer "submit to the domination of a party averse to Emigration, to commerce, to internal improvements, and to all those interests which may be regarded as British. . . ".[17] A "Loyal and Constitutional Association" was proposed; and a committee was appointed to correspond with the British and Irish in both provinces. Two days later another and similar meeting was held in Quebec city, in the Albion hotel. Like the British in Montreal, the Quebec tories agreed unanimously that the present position was intolerable and that a "Constitutional Association" should be formed to protect their rights and property. Committees were appointed; and three weeks later, at a general meeting held on December 12 and attended by more than 400 citizens, a lengthy declaration setting forth the causes which had led to the formation of the association and the objects it intended to pursue, was read, debated and approved.[18]

Though they had been founded almost simultaneously, the two constitutional associations remained distinct and autonomous; and the Quebec and Montreal tories did not talk an identical language, though they spoke together and with almost equal vigour. It was asserted, of course, in the manifestoes[19] of both societies, that a crisis in the affairs of the province was fast approaching, that the omnipotent French-Canadian party was mercilessly persecuting all other classes in the community, and that the British and Irish must unite in the constitutional defence of their property, their political rights and their imperial connections. The two societies could agree to denounce the transformation of the legislative council into an elective body, and to argue in favour of a reform of the laws, a better representation of the British minority in the assembly and the maintenance of the imperial tie. But for a variety of reasons, local and personal, the Quebec tories were apt to be more moderate, more really "constitutional" in their agitation. Andrew Stuart, who believed in the full commercial programme, was, it was true, the first chairman of the Quebec society; but John Neilson was one of its most outstanding members, and John Neilson had opposed the Union Bill and had broken with Papineau only as late as 1833. There was no unanimous support for the union of the provinces in Quebec; there was naturally complete opposition to the annexation of

Montreal to Upper Canada;[20] and it was left to Montreal to urge the old commercial objectives with the old eloquently materialistic arguments. Though at times it modified its demands in deference to the wishes of Quebec, Montreal—the focus of the whole northern system—was in general more radical and intransigent; and its chief purpose was still to effect the union,[21] to break through the feudalism of the anti-commercial French and to realize the commercial empire of the St. Lawrence.

In the spring of 1835 the newly formed constitutional associations sent their first formal deputation to the colonial office in England. The last session of the legislature, terminated in March, had proved that political rivalries had brought the affairs of the province to an utter standstill. Once again the assembly made no grant for the support of civil government. Once again it neglected that part of the commercial programme which it did not actually oppose. The legislative council threw out the bills of the assembly and the assembly those of the council; and the whole machinery of government was visibly disintegrating. "Under these circumstances", wrote Governor Aylmer to Hay, "there is no room for hope left, but in the measures of the Imperial Parliament."[22] The tories fervently agreed with this sentiment. The Quebec society appointed John Neilson and the Montreal association nominated William Walker; and both departed together on a pilgrimage to the colonial office.

When they arrived in England, the delegates discovered that the British government had already decided to send a commission of inquiry to Lower Canada. Their representations were a little ill-timed and superfluous; but they were permitted to make them up until the time when the commissioners sailed; and they had various interviews with Glenelg, the colonial secretary, and even, on one great occasion, with the prime minister, Melbourne, himself.[23] They argued the "inadmissibility" of an elected legislative council and pleaded for other reforms upon which both were agreed; but in all these interviews no mention was apparently made of union or the annexation of Montreal to Upper Canada, though in fact the Montreal petition carried both proposals as alternative suggestions. The Montreal committee, in one of its accommodating moments, had instructed Walker not to press these proposals; and it was not until the mission was really ended, that the Montreal delegate felt free to point out that his city's petition contained other and more drastic remedies. He even proposed a third plan by which the unity of the Canadian commercial system might be achieved.[24] The St. Lawrence, he suggested, might be taken out of the hands of a legislature which was uninterested in its commercial future and transferred to the control of the imperial government. If union and annexation were alike objectionable, if the Canadian political system could in no way be adjusted to the needs of Canadian commercialism, then let the imperial trade route of the St. Lawrence be removed from Canadian politics and entrusted to the fostering care of the empire itself.

Meanwhile, the British government, despairing of solving the problems of Lower Canada by parliamentary committees, had transferred its hopes to royal commissions of inquiry. Lord Aylmer, who had governed Lower Canada from 1830, was to be recalled. His successor was to be invested with both the ordinary powers of governor and the extraordinary powers of commissioner for the investigation of grievances; and after having shopped around a little, unsuccessfully, the British persuaded the Earl of Gosford to accept the post. Lord Gosford was an Irishman whose amiability was hardly a sufficient compensation for his lack of distinction. The tories, who regretted the departure of Lord Aylmer, watched the first actions of the new governor and his two equally undistinguished associate commissioners with misgivings which soon deepened into angry dismay. Lord Gosford did all the wrong things with all the cheerful heartiness of a convert to a new religion. He lavished social attentions and political concessions upon the French Canadians. He promised to issue his warrants for the contingent expenses of the assembly. He spoke affably, with respectful admiration, of the seigniorial system. And the tories, who had hoped to gain a leader for their counter-revolution, gasped with amazement and indignation, as they watched His Majesty's commissioner betraying the empire with all the deferential obsequiousness of a lackey.

That autumn, some of the constitutionalists, particularly in Montreal, began to take up a definitely threatening attitude. Towards the end of September, Adam Thom commenced the publication of the *Anti-Gallic Letters*, which impartially attacked the new governor and the "French faction". In November, the *Montreal Gazette* printed a justification of an appeal to force; and a Canadian correspondent of Robert Gillespie was talking already in terms of a civil war, which, he declared, was due soon, if something were not done to curb the assembly and to give scope for British capital and commerce.[25] "Your lordship may have been led to believe", wrote Adam Thom in one of the more extreme passages of the *Anti-Gallic Letters*, "that the avowed determination of the constitutionalists, to resist the extension of French domination, was merely an empty threat; but they have not forgotten, that the glorious fields of Cressy, Poictiers, Agincourt and Minden were won by 'miserable' minorities of Englishmen over vast majorities of Frenchmen."[26]

As early as March, 1835, Lord Aylmer had predicted that the British party would soon be driven to politics of force. ". . . If something is not done", he wrote, "to curb the unbounded pretensions of the House of Assembly, I shall indeed begin to fear that the English portion of the Population will take the Law into their own hands.[27]" The "pretensions" had been encouraged; the assembly, in session once more, was particularly provocative; and towards the end of 1835 the move which Aylmer had predicted was made. On December 16, about three hundred of the younger citizens of Montreal assembled to constitute a "British Rifle Corps"; and at a second meeting, held a few days later, it was decided to request the governor's permission for the formation of the corps.[28] The affair produced a mild sensation at Quebec. Through his secretary, the governor wrote to the riflemen, paternally correcting their mistaken notions of the critical state of the province; but the unabashed riflemen met once more and passed an address and resolutions correcting His Excellency's too sanguine view of the existing security of British rights and the British connection.[29] Since the corps would not yield to persuasion, Gosford issued a proclamation on January 15, 1836, dissolving the Rifle Corps and prohibiting the formation of similar associations. But the persevering riflemen promptly rechristened their society the "Montreal British Legion". There was a final meeting in January; and when Gosford's proclamation had at last been read, "three rounds and one round more, of real groans succeeded". Then the corps took to the streets for its customary parade; and this was, apparently, the largest on record, for a thousand men were said to have taken part in it.[30]

This brave gesture was, however, the end of the British Legion. There were, Gosford noted, advertisements in the papers for targets and promises of rifle practice; but in the end the association was discreetly permitted to dissolve. These frank preparations embarrassed the older constitutionalists, who seem, at least in some cases, to have been genuinely perturbed by them. Whenever anything really happened, tory Montreal could be assembled for action just as effectively and far less ostentatiously than by these obvious methods; and in the meantime the constitutionalists could continue their unexceptionable programme of building a party and concerting action. At Quebec, a day after the British Legion had held its last parade, a meeting of the local constitutional association was held, which was attended by Messrs. Walker, Penn and Holmes from the Montreal society.[31] It was decided to make preparations for a meeting of a "select general committee" of the constitutionalists, to be arranged by the two big associations in consultation. It was to be a kind of little provincial convention; and Walker of Montreal followed this up with the suggestion that a general congress of the British North American provinces should be held.

III

In Upper Canada, toryism responded rather differently to the victory of the reformers in 1834. The British party in the lower province had been driven to action by the repeated defeats of the past and the hopelessness of the future; but the Upper Canadian tories, who had suffered less frustration and could entertain greater political hopes, were not yet ready for an aggressive programme of organization. The new assembly met; Marshall Spring Bidwell was chosen as speaker; and the reformers plunged eagerly into the task of reviewing grievances and correcting abuses. The entries in the assembly journals respecting Mackenzie's expulsions were solemnly expunged. There were laws passed for the sale of the clergy reserves, for the abolition of primogeniture, and for the establishment of vote by ballot. The committee on grievances, over which Mackenzie presided, completed its vast labours of interviewing witnesses and collecting materials, by the publication of the notorious *Seventh Report*. This, like the *Ninety-two Resolutions*, concentrated criticism on the appointed legislative council and tended to favour the "elective principle" in government; and although it differed considerably in form and content from the *Resolutions*, it deserves also to be regarded as a kind of provincial Grand Remonstrance.

This formal codification of grievances, this general critical attack upon the political system of the province, was accompanied by some even more direct hits at its commercial foundations. The reformers, who had denounced the free admission of American produce into Canada, proposed to establish relatively heavy duties on imports of American grain, flour, meal, provisions and leather. In the assembly, the commercial sympathizers deplored the bill, protesting that such legislation could not protect Canada's products from the operation of world prices and therefore could only ruin the carrying-trade of the St. Lawrence and wreck the prospects of the Welland canal. The bill was, declared Thomas Dalton, the editor of the *Patriot*, ". . . a Bill to destroy Canadian internal navigation, to impoverish the Canadian Farmers, depopulate our Towns and Villages, to raise the Commercial prosperity of the City and State of New York, destroy the commerce of Montreal and Quebec, and injure as much as in us lies the interests of British Shipping. . . ".[32] These frightful consequences were either discounted or lightly regarded by the reformers. The bill passed the assembly. But the legislative council, justifying itself with a recital of the arguments which had already appeared in the press, threw the bill out; and this veto, along with many others, was to exasperate the relations between the two houses and to create an approximation of that legislative impasse which had existed for so long in the lower province.

Some of the main commercial enterprises appeared, at least temporarily, to be beyond the reach of the reformers. The credits for the St. Lawrence canals had been voted by the tory house; the work was actually in progress; and, as for the Welland canal, it had been granted one more provincial loan of £50,000 by the tories in the session of 1834. After the depression of that year, the boom continued exuberantly as if it had never been interrupted. In 1835 the tolls from the Welland reached the modest but promising total of £5,807; and the American Yates, who was the principal private stockholder, even hoped that it might soon be possible to buy out the provincial holdings completely.[33] But in the meantime the connection with government continued; new "reforming" government directors were appointed in 1835, and among them was William Lyon Mackenzie. Poor Yates expressed the fond, deluded hope that the old promoters might get along pleasantly with the new director. But Mackenzie proceeded with great energy to ransack the records of the company and to accumulate a mountain of evidence in support of a pile of accusations. Eventually he became so fired with the import of these discoveries, that he could neither wait for the opening of the legislature to make his denunciations, nor could he entrust them to the columns of an ordinary, common newspaper. He founded instead *The Welland Canal*, a weekly periodical which began to appear in December, 1835. In voluminous detail it dealt with the entire history of the canal company, with its dangerous political connections and with its financial operations down to Merritt's expenses in London for clubs, theatre tickets, cigars and gin.[34] The tory editors were overwhelmed by this detailed and comprehensive indictment; and Thomas Dalton wrote hastily to Merritt, begging for anything he had to say in rebuttal.[35] Mackenzie continued to carry everything before him; and when the legislature met, he preferred thirty charges against the canal company and obtained the appointment of a select committee of investigation.

Though repeatedly he overreached himself, Mackenzie struck with skill and force at the fundamentals of the commercial system. Above all others in the reform party, he inspired and directed the radical agrarian movement in the province; and his passionate localism occasionally associated him with other strong local interests. The session of 1835 had barely opened, when he moved for an address to the king, requesting him to negotiate with the government of the United States for the free passage of Upper Canadian goods, both exports and imports, *via* the New York route. The proposal, though it was a natural development of

Mackenzie's own views, was not original with him; for a few weeks previously, towards the end of December, the merchants had held meetings at Toronto for the purpose of considering the advisability of petitioning for the free transmission of British and European goods to Upper Canada *via* New York.[36] Thus, when Mackenzie declared that "we had a right to go to Oswego with our produce; to buy our Tea wherever we could buy it best", he had, amazingly enough, the support of his old inveterate enemy, solicitor-general Hagerman.[37] The fact was that the failure of the campaign for the annexation of Montreal, the obvious reluctance of Lower Canada to co-operate in the building of the St. Lawrence canals—the utter collapse of all efforts to solve the fundamental problems of the commercial state—were driving even some of the tories into changes and disavowals. A few of the papers even began to write of the St. Lawrence as the "unnatural highway" to the sea; and although some of the key tory journals, notably the *Patriot*, denounced the whole idea of the New York route savagely, its sudden rise in popular interest created consternation in Montreal.

The fact was that the whole political system of the St. Lawrence was cracking under the strains imposed upon it. The two provinces were almost continually at issue; and each provincial government was divided within itself. The division of legislative authority between council and assembly was the provincial counterpart of the division of territory between Upper and Lower Canada; and both together paralysed the activities of the provinces, singly and collectively, and blocked the recapture of the commercial empire of the west. In Upper Canada, the tory council threw out the bills of the new reform assembly with the same systematic thoroughness which had become habitual in the lower province. "God help us!" wrote one tory piously, "if we had not a Legislative Council to resist the fury and madness of radical legislation the country would speedily become a desolate waste."[38] But this resistance, while it gratified the tories, provoked the assembly to long protests; and very rapidly the Upper Canadian radicals developed that sense of impasse, that angry feeling of frustration which had by now embittered politics in Lower Canada. "I expect", wrote Mackenzie, on the eve of the session of 1836, "to meet my fellow representatives next month to pass a few monopoly bills, borrowing bills, supply bills, and so on—debate and send up to the council two dozen of other bills prayed for by the assembly, there to be thrown under the table by dependent persons clothed with legislative power—resolve so many things, quarrel with the governor, report on grievances, and go home—to meet no more until the riots and disturbances of a new election shall have removed many and returned others to go thro' the same absurd routine of useless and expensive duties."[39]

The deadlock, however, though it appeared irremediable, was in fact relatively new. It had not yet driven either party to vigorous action—to politics of force; and the tory "counter-revolution" was inspired, not by the tories themselves, but by the accidental arrival of a new and crusading leader. This was the new lieutenant-governor, Sir Francis Bond Head, who arrived in January, 1836, at the beginning of the legislative session. He was an odd, almost an inexplicable, choice. His lack of political experience was uncompensated by any native capacity for statesmanship. It was as a soldier, as a traveller, as a gentleman adventurer that he had spent his life. He journeyed on a romantic pilgrimage around the Mediterranean; he galloped across the plains of South America; and in between these picturesque excursions he produced graphic and popular travel books. This faintly Byronic combination of literature and adventure must have gratified Sir Francis; and there ran, through his entire career, a strain of imitative romanticism and second-rate theatricality. He judged life, or liked to think he judged it, upon the simple principles of the gentleman soldier of fortune. He tried to settle hard situations with big words, full of cloudy and grandiose associations; and he governed Upper Canada by mouthing rhetoric, striking heroic attitudes and making melodramatic gestures. For him the governorship of the little frontier province became a kind of romantic lead. He saw himself as the protagonist in a dramatic conflict between monarchy and republicanism, civilization and anarchy, good and evil. And from the very moment of Head's arrival in the province, the confused conflict in Upper Canada developed a simplification of theme, a new intensity of moral fervour and a rapidity of movement which was superbly enlivened by stage effects and dramatic surprises.

It was the first task of the governor to recruit the membership of the executive council, which had been reduced to three; and after some protracted discussion he persuaded three supposed moderates, Robert Baldwin, Dr. John Rolph and J. H. Dunn, the receiver-general, to join the council board. But Robert Baldwin and his father, Dr. W. W. Baldwin, though they ostentatiously dissociated themselves, both socially and politically, from the common radicals, were great believers in the whiggish doctrines of responsible government, which they defended on all occasions, in cumbrous language and with unalterable conviction. According to their view, the executive council was to be responsible to the assembly and hence to the people for all the executive acts of government; and when the new councillors found that in fact they were not consulted about executive acts for which they were popularly held to be responsible, they joined with the old councillors in a protest to the governor. Sir Francis replied with a few of his literary productions, defending his own responsibility with the manliness of cavalier defending his own honour. The councillors resigned; and the quarrel was transferred to the legislature, where the assembly sponsored the principle of responsible government, declared its lack of confidence in the new council and stopped the supplies. But Sir Francis went one better. He engaged in his "moral struggle" with the spontaneous and unquestioning bravado of a knight-errant. He refused the assembly's contingent expenses. He stopped every single money-bill which the legislature had passed. He dissolved the house and appealed to the country.

It was this stand which rallied the tories and transformed them into a united, aggressive and triumphant organization. Already they had suffered, in two sessions, and in both their interests and their principles, from the policies of the reform assembly; and although the Welland canal was, indeed, acquitted by the investigation inspired by Mackenzie, it was very plain that the reformers were hostile to the commercial projects and the vested interests of the governing class. These interests the tories had sought to defend in the legislative council and the press; but it was the paladin Sir Francis who changed this sullen resistance into an attack à outrance. It was he who succeeded supremely, where the tories had been only moderately successful, in transforming a confused struggle of groups and interests into a grand conflict of political loyalties. "The rallying word", declared the tories, "is the maintenance of the Union with the Mother Country—if need arise, it shall be the battle cry." In the spring months of 1836 the tories were founding constitutional associations, pledged to the undying defence of the British connection and British institutions;[40] and their spirit was that of the governor, who plunged ahead, shouting defiances like a cavalry leader. They mocked the disloyal principle of responsible government and denounced the reformers as "revolutionists" and "destructives". "British subjects, of whatever clime, of whatever faith, of whatever opinions . . .", shouted one editor, "charge in a firm and irresistible phalanx! rally round Sir Francis Head—and save the British Constitution by a bloodless victory."[41]

In the election which followed in June, the tories swept the radicals before them. The stand taken by Sir Francis, as well as the ominously increasing agitation in the provinces, had strengthened the old political loyalties and constitutional convictions among people who were tories neither by habit nor interest. The leaders of the Methodist Church, a body possessing great strength in the countryside, assumed a definitely conservative attitude in the crisis. Egerton Ryerson, the first editor of the Methodist organ, *The Christian Guardian*, had broken with Mackenzie as early as 1833; and although this breach had been followed by some political dissension and a definite religious division in the church, the Wesleyan Methodists, who formed the main Methodist communion, now ranged themselves on the constitutional side. Ephraim Evans, the new editor of *The Christian Guardian*, urged his readers to support the governor; and Ryerson, who was in England at the time, was moved to admonish his countrymen in several epistles, one of which defended the Constitutional Act as a solemn compact between the British Crown and the inhabitants of Upper Canada, while another was reprinted as an election broad-sheet under the journalistic title, *Peter Perry Picked to Pieces by Egerton Ryerson*. The adhesion of the Wesleyan Methodists, as well as other temporary accessions, converted the tory party into a kind of constitutional coalition; and, in the June election, it swept the radicals to defeat. Bidwell, Perry and Mackenzie all went down in the general rout; and the reformers, who less than two years before had won a general election, were left a crushed, humiliated and desperate party.

IV

Thus, by the summer of 1836, the governing class in both provinces was in full career of a vigorous political offensive. In Lower Canada, this movement had gathered momentum spontaneously, under the unrelenting pressure of circumstances; in Upper Canada it had abruptly developed under the reckless manipulations of a political adventurer. Sir Francis, who had galvanized the tories of the upper province into action, helped also to reanimate the political movement in the east. He gave power to the clique in Toronto and the hope of power to the constitutionalists of Quebec and Montreal. In the eyes of the merchants of Lower Canada, Head possessed all the virtues which they believed a colonial governor ought to have and which they were sure the Earl of Gosford conspicuously lacked. In July, 1836, the Quebec constitutionalists held a great banquet in honour of the triumph of truth in Upper Canada; and the *pièce de résistance* of the dinner was a great baron of beef, from which fluttered four bannerols of white silk, tastefully inscribed with the mottoes, "The King", "The Constitution", "Sir F. B. Head" and "The Men of Upper Canada".[42]

Sir Francis, however, encouraged the constitutionalists of Lower Canada in other and more direct ways than by the ostentatious display of his own pattern virtues. Indirectly but none the less effectively, he had already contrived, during the winter of 1836, to undermine the position of Lord Gosford and to change the whole state of affairs in the lower province. In one of his characteristically decisive actions, he had made public the instructions which he had received from the colonial office, *in toto*. These instructions were composed, partly of special recommendations for Head alone, and partly of general recommendations on subjects agitated in both provinces, which had also been issued to Gosford and his associates. When, therefore, Sir Francis made his own position clear, he also unfortunately disclosed some of the restrictions with which the commissioners in Lower Canada had been hedged about. Lord

Gosford was practically precluded in advance from recommending an elected legislative council or from suggesting the surrender of the waste lands of the crown to the assembly. Lord Gosford, in short, could talk, but his hands were tied. He could be affable, condescending, genially acquiescent in small things; but he could make no substantial concessions.

The constitutionalists were pleasantly surprised. The Quebec society, which held more modest aims, declared itself, in March, 1836, largely satisfied with the intentions of the British government.[43] But the radicals were discomfited and disillusioned. It began to seem to them that Head's intransigence and Gosford's affability were simply two different, but equally objectionable methods of obtaining the same fell aims. The constitutionalists, particularly those in Montreal, rejoiced over the disillusionment and anger of the radicals and joined eagerly in the revengeful pursuit of the governor. What the extreme tories wanted was the recall of Gosford—the recall of the man who had "virtually banished from his presence, the whole of those respectable, intelligent and wealthy men who compose the great body of the Constitutionalists of Lower Canada". They agreed with the excited radicals that Gosford had dealt merely in disingenuous cajolery and intrigue for the mere purpose of obtaining funds from the assembly. "The mission of the Commissioners, together with that of Lord Gosford, is in my judgment ended", wrote the editor of the *Montreal Gazette* in June. "The sooner they leave Canada the better for all parties. . . ."[44]

By this time the "constitutional" movement had acquired fairly large proportions; and during the winter of 1836 the different societies held meetings in various parts of the Eastern Townships, in Beauharnois, in the town of Three Rivers, as well as in Quebec and Montreal. The Montreal society remained the most aggressive; and when the "convention" of the assembled constitutionalists met in that city late in June, 1836, it was probably the Montreal delegates who proposed a petition for the recall of Gosford and who argued for a declaration in favour of the union of Upper and Lower Canada.[45] But the petition, though it was agreed upon, was never apparently composed and presented; and the delegates, evidently unable to reach a decision on the matter of union, were referred back to their constituents for further instructions. During the summer there was evidence of dissension between moderates and ultras in the Montreal society; and the disagreements between Quebec and Montreal did not entirely cease. But in November, 1836, the "Select General Committee of Delegates of the Constitutionalists of Lower Canada" met once more and reported an "almost unanimous" resolution in favour of union.[46]

Thus the "owners of Property", the "commercial and loyal" part of the population, those who, in the words of the manifesto of the convention wished "to extend the range of commercial civilisation", were united and aggressive in both provinces and had been victorious in one. Their activities, their violence, their injuries, which were inspired by the campaign of the radicals, in turn provoked the radicals to more desperate efforts; and both sides were driven inexorably onward by a movement which they had helped almost equally to create and which they could no longer scarcely control. The electoral defeat in Upper Canada, the revelation of Gosford's "duplicity" and the apparent refusal of the colonial office to grant major reforms, all left the reformers in both provinces in a state of disillusionment and desperation. But the first move was not necessarily expected from the radicals; and although people talked a lot about "rebellion" and "revolution", they talked even more about a "civil war". ". . . We are hurrying fast onward to anarchy and confusion", wrote the editor of the *Montreal Gazette*, "and a civil warfare cannot but ensue, if a people, strong in their attachment to the institutions of their forefathers, are to be degraded and insulted in the land acquired by the blood and treasure of their ancestors. . . ."[47] The truth is that both sides were militant, at least in spirit and occasionally in intention. And, as the manifestoes, speeches and writings increased in violence, each side found in the other's menace a justification for its own readiness to appeal to force.

The political excitement was accompanied and accentuated by a rising economic tension. The crisis in politics, which had issued so largely from the fundamental, long-term contradictions in the Canadian commercial state, reached its climax at the very moment of a sharp turn in the business cycle of the British-North American world. The boom, which had suffered a momentary interruption in 1834, now reached its conclusion in a final and excitable speculation. Already, earlier in 1836, the British speculative movement had reached and passed its climax; and in the autumn, just as the constitutionalists were departing triumphantly from their convention, the last period of hectic prosperity was at hand in the United States. The proliferation of banks since 1830, the great increase in banking capital and circulation, the brusque expansion of credit had given support to an exuberant activity which invaded every sphere of business life.[48] The craze infected individuals, companies and governments alike; and the insatiable demand for banks, canals, railways and other "public improvements" galvanized the legislatures of the United States into further expenditures and greater activity.[49]

In the Canadas, as the boom neared its peak, economic conditions became obviously abnormal and disquieting. In the lumber and square-timber trade, 1835 and 1836 were relatively prosperous years, years which in quantities exported to Great Britain and Ireland surpassed even the previous height reached in 1825.[50] The glut of wheat and flour, which had forced down prices during 1834–1835, and compelled the Canadians to turn to their secondary market in the West Indies, was now succeeded by a sudden and appalling scarcity; and the harvest of 1836 was an almost complete failure in Lower Canada and the north-western American states. Upper Canada, despite the tariff, disposed of most of its surplus wheat and flour south of the border; and before the end of the year was reached, Montreal was actually importing wheat from Europe.[51] Flour had opened, at the beginning of the year, at 28s. 6d. a barrel; and late in December it was selling in Montreal at 42s. 6d. Prices of all provisions were to rise still higher, and with violent sharpness, during the first months of 1837; and Gosford, with distress and actual starvation around him, was forced to help certain parishes with money grants.[52]

The financial crisis was at hand. The two provinces were totally unprepared to meet it. The northern commercial system was dangerously weakened, both by the continuous neglect of the lower province and by the injudicious extravagance of tory Upper Canada. The legislature of Lower Canada had met once more in the early autumn of 1836 and had quickly been prorogued, without having passed a single measure. The state of the province was unimproved and unrepaired. The canal projects had been thrown aside, the works in the Montreal harbour had been abandoned for lack of money, the bank charters were running out. In Upper Canada, where the boom spirit lasted until the very end, everybody was still talking "public improvements"; and, as soon as the election of 1836 was over, little knots of business and professional men began to prepare in secret for a pleasant legislative session of capital expenditure and commercial expansion.[53] In the winter of 1837, when the new parliament met for its first session, the capital structure of the Welland Canal Company was completely reorganized and the provincial holdings actually increased by £245,000. The province plunged enthusiastically into the Trent navigation scheme, as if the burdens of the Welland and St. Lawrence canals were insufficient. The capital of the Bank of Upper Canada was increased. There were bills for new banks, for the establishment of loan and trust companies and for the building of a "Great Western Rail Road".[54] The confidence of Upper Canada was as unthinking as the caution of Quebec was narrow-minded; and both provinces, in their different ways, were rending, distracting and weakening the whole structure of the commercial state.

Even after Head had reserved the banking bills, Upper Canada had completed a formidable legislative achievement. And the winter session of 1837 was to pass into history as one of the last prosperity sessions of the period in America. For the boom had now become ominously abnormal and precarious. In the United States, the transference of the federal deposits from the Bank of the United States was followed by the distribution of the federal surplus revenue among the different states. The government, still pursuing its campaign against the bankers and speculators, issued the notorious "specie circular", which demanded payment in specie for all the public lands of the United States. These financial raids and forays, these ponderous governmental manipulations, helped to upset an already perilously unsteady prosperity; and in the meantime, in England, retrenchment had been followed by financial unsettlement and unsettlement by failure. Burdened as they were with heavy credits in America, the London and Liverpool houses were in no position to meet the demands of the English bankers; and, in their desperate efforts to avoid collapse, they applied what in the circumstances was an intolerable pressure to their debtors in the United States. North America passed abruptly into an acute financial panic at the very moment when the Canadas had almost reached the angry culmination of their quarrels.

V

The two things came together. The impact of the political crisis was driven home by the dead weight of the financial and commercial collapse. Canada was at once a member of the British Empire and a minor partner in the system of British and North American trade; and she had as little chance of escaping the influence of the American business cycle as she had of avoiding the interference of the imperial authorities. Late in the winter, when commercial failures were already imminent in the United States, the Gosford commission of inquiry published its conservative report; and early in March, at the instance of Lord John Russell, the imperial parliament passed the notorious *Ten Resolutions*, which declared an elected legislative council to be inexpedient, affirmed the title of the British American Land Company and permitted the governor of Lower Canada to appropriate provincial revenue without the authority of the legislature. The uncompromising demands of the *patriotes* were met by an uncompromising refusal. Great Britain, as the stronger of the contending factions, ended the angry political deadlock in the Canadas; and, at almost the same moment, the financial tension broke in the United States. In March and April the eastern American commercial houses began to fail in numbers; and on May 10, the New York banks suspended specie payments.

The end, towards which the two Canadas had been travelling for a generation, was now at hand. These two brusque movements, political and financial, precipitated the crisis in Canadian affairs. While in both England and Lower Canada the tories praised the manly firmness of Lord John Russell, the *Ten Resolutions* goaded the radicals into a renewed and fiercer activity. During the spring and early summer months, they held crowded and excited meetings in both the Montreal and Quebec districts. Lord John Russell was denounced as a master robber who had ordered his hireling Gosford to filch the pockets of the defenceless patriots; and since the greater part of the provincial revenue came from customs duties, the radicals decided to abstain from using dutiable articles as far as possible and solemnly asserted that smuggling was a "perfectly honourable" activity. "HENCEFORTH", wrote one radical journalist, "THERE MUST BE NO PEACE IN THE PROVINCE—*no quarter for the plunderers.* . . . Agitate! *Agitate!!* AGITATE!!! Destroy the Revenue; denounce the oppressors. Everything is Lawful when the fundamental liberties are in danger."[55] The tories, adopting an attitude of mingled contempt and moral indignation, regarded this crusade as a final and complete revelation of the perfidious purposes of the radicals. "The scenes which are now, or have lately been enacting", wrote the editor of the *Montreal Gazette*, "form but one act of the great drama that may be denominated—'The Canadian's Road to National Independence'."[56] Lord Gosford now began to share the same view.[57] Rapidly the radical leaders were becoming committed to the doctrine of an independent republic and involved in a tempestuous agitation which they could no longer control.

In the meantime the banking crisis went from bad to worse. The bankers feared for the safety of their institutions, the merchants for the continuation of their loans; and it was argued everywhere by commercial men that the suspension of cash payments was the only means by which the Canadian banks could stop the drain of metals to the United States. In Lower Canada, where the banks could suspend without forfeiting their charters, the bankers, with the unanimous support of the mercantile community, took immediate action and within a week of the suspension of the New York banks the payment of gold and silver had been stopped throughout the province.[58] In Upper Canada, the merchants confidently expected suspension and Mackenzie dramatically urged the farmers and mechanics to get their gold and silver while they could; but, in the end, they were all disappointed by the amazing attitude of the governor. Sir Francis characteristically decided an economic problem by a point of honour. In his mind, the maintenance of specie payments meant, not a paralysing contraction of credit, but a consoling affirmation of a moral principle. The banks had promised to pay out specie on demand; therefore, in spite of everything they must fulfil their obligations. "Upper Canada", declared the governor rhetorically, "would prefer to lose its specie rather than its character. The principle of Monarchy is honor and from that principle the Lieutenant Governor will never consent to depart."[59]

The financial crisis, however, did not merely involve the banks, the merchants and the province generally: it also directly involved the government. Not a single tender was received for the loans which the legislature in its last session had so blithely sanctioned for the construction of public works; and, what was infinitely worse, the security of the loans already contracted became suddenly uncertain. The province had not yet drawn for the full amount of the £600,000 loan which J. H. Dunn, the receiver-general, had negotiated in London; and in April, when the rumours of the impending failure of Thomas Wilson & Company and Baring Brothers became really alarming, there was an estimated balance in favour of Upper Canada of £147,000 in the hands of the two London firms.[60] If Dunn's latest bills of exchange were protested in England, it would mean the bankruptcy of the province; it would mean, at least temporarily, the stoppage of the ambitious programme of public works. W. H. Draper, a member of the executive council, was hurriedly dispatched to London by the governor; J. H. Dunn followed him immediately, advising that government expenditures be narrowly contracted during his absence;[61] and back in Canada, where they faced realities closely, the authorities wondered whether they could afford to continue operations sufficiently to prevent a riot among the disappointed labourers.[62] During the summer, Messrs. Glyn, Halifax & Company took up the bills of exchange drawn upon the bankrupt house of Thomas Wilson & Company.[63] But it was estimated that the province had lost £53,000 in the crash; and for a while there was no money, or very little, available in England. The commissioners for the St. Lawrence canals struggled with difficulty to keep the works going; and at one point, during September, when the province and the banks alike could give it nothing more, the board was £10,000 in debt to the contractors.[64]

These crises in private and public finance exaggerated the commercial depression which came to lie like a blight over the two provinces during the summer of 1837. The Lower Canadian banks, by their prompt suspension of specie payments, had averted a serious contraction of credit; but in Upper Canada, where the bankers prudently obeyed the exhortations of their gallant governor, the financial stringency became intensified. To preserve their specie, the banks contracted their loans and discounts; and the merchants, defrauded of their usual "accommodation", began to agitate for the immediate suspension of cash payments and for a special session of the legislature to deal with the financial crisis. The governor, whose popularity in commercial circles had descended with a crash, yielded a little regretfully to this last demand; and towards the end of June the provincial parliament met. The assembly, which was dominated by the commercial element, was determined to break the contraction of credit. The members derided Sir Francis as an economist and made irreverent jokes about "the art of banking on monarchical principles with empty vaults". Their solution was to permit the banks to suspend specie payments and to make bank notes and provincial debentures legal tender.[65] But Sir Francis refused to sacrifice the honour of monarchy to the avarice of shopkeepers. With the help of the council he defeated the assembly's bill; and by the statute which eventually passed the legislature for want of a better, the banks could suspend payments and continue business only under the terms which the governor in council imposed.[66]

The rigid contraction of credit continued. The Bank of Upper Canada, which enjoyed a large part of the government business and hoped to profit from dealings in specie and foreign exchange, practically abandoned its ordinary loans and discounts and withdrew in complacent austerity from the troubles of the commercial world.[67] The other Upper Canadian banks either followed its example or, if they tried to suspend specie payments, found enormous difficulty in meeting the onerous terms imposed by the governor. When the desperate merchants turned from their own provincial institutions, which were unable or unwilling to give them credit, they were met by similar refusals elsewhere. "We all here feel the importance of affording facilities to the purchase of wheat in Up: Can:", wrote Peter McGill, of the Montreal Bank, to W. H. Merritt, "—but the Banks of L: Can: cannot give them, and but few Individual Houses will be able to supply their Correspondents with the needful from hence, because their Capital is already in Up: Canada Credits, and nothing coming down.—In my day such times, have never been experienced."[68]

Thus the tightness of the money market in both provinces helped to intensify and to prolong the inevitable commercial slump. In Montreal and Quebec the spring business was pitiable; and it was reported late in May that affairs in Upper Canada were virtually at a standstill.[69] Throughout the season the depression continued; and it reached its nadir during the late summer, when the market reports asserted repeatedly, with a kind of shocked amazement, that there was literally nothing doing. "An excessive languor pervades nearly every branch of commerce", wrote one Montreal journalist, "and our streets have, so far as relates to business, the appearance they are wont to exhibit on a close holiday or a Sunday."[70] In a long, dull, weary season, which showed only a moderate flurry of activity towards the end of September, the exports in the timber trade were alone comparable to those of the preceding year; and there were no shipments of wheat, for Montreal was importing until late in the summer to feed the impoverished farmers of Lower Canada. A winter of high prices, scarcity and aggravated distress was followed by a financial panic, a commercial slump and a partial interruption of the public works. ". . . During my residence in this province", wrote one observer to the governor of Upper Canada, "I have not witnessed so much absolute distress at any period as now exists."[71]

The financial breakdown and the commercial collapse combined to create an atmosphere of irritable tension, in which political passions grew rapidly to their maturity. In July was held the last session of the parliament of Lower Canada, for the imperial authorities had decided to act cautiously upon the *Ten Resolutions* and Gosford was instructed to make one more effort for conciliation. But his request for supplies was met by a blunt refusal and an uncompromising restatement of popular grievances; and the abrupt prorogation which followed removed the last hope of peace and released the irrepressible drift to agitation and disorder. The radical meetings were repeated, multiplied. A rudimentary organization of several counties developed. And while the threats and injuries of the radical papers took on a note of hysteria, rumours of overt action, of intimidation, of physical violence began to filter in to Montreal and Quebec from the countryside.

In Upper Canada, after the emergency session of the legislature, the left-wing radicals, led by Mackenzie, at last determined upon decisive action. As early as July 5, the editor of *The Constitution* had entitled an editorial "Will Canadians declare Independence and Shoulder Muskets?"; and late in July, the extremists held a meeting in Doel's brewery, in Toronto, where an address to the reformers of Upper Canada was adopted and plans were prepared for an immediate organization throughout the province. The rebellion which ended ingloriously in a tavern, began, appropriately enough, in a brewery; and early in August, Mackenzie departed from Toronto, to preach agitation and to promulgate the "Convention of the Canadas" in Newmarket, Lloydtown, Cooksville and other places "north of the ridges". Though the Upper Canadian reformers naturally obtained their heartiest support in the countryside, Mackenzie could never count upon that unqualified ovation which attended Papineau on his travels; and at the reform meetings, which were held north of Toronto and in the western part of the province during August and September, the magistrates, shopkeepers and Orangemen assembled uninvited and tried to dominate the assemblies and to pass their own "loyal" resolutions.[72] The tories were supposed to be equipped with clubs and leaded whips; the radicals took to coming armed "each man with a solid oak or hickory stick". There were contests, scuffles, minor affrays; and at Churchville, the second-last meeting in Mackenzie's first series, the Irish broke up the reform assembly completely. Mackenzie's writings took on a shriller, more hysterical note. "Sir Francis may find", he wrote after the violence at Churchville, "that an opinion is gaining ground that deeds are doing among us, which will have to be answered by an appeal to cold steel."[73] In the autumn the reformers were drilling at Lloydtown, Gibson's farm on Yonge Street, and other places; and their leaders passed finally from the idea of a militant, massed demonstration to the idea of open revolt.

This intensification of extreme radical propaganda was accompanied by a rapid contraction of extreme radical support. As the crisis drew near, the constitutionalists in both provinces were heavily reinforced by reformers who kept breaking with the radicals in increasing numbers and by that great mass of bewildered, unhappy people who would infallibly remain inert in the first shock of the revolt. The Roman Catholic Church in Lower Canada and the Methodist Church in Upper Canada were the two churches which had the largest following among the simple people of the countryside; and while *The Christian Guardian*, the organ of the Methodist Church, preached against violence and disorder, the Roman Catholic hierarchy now turned its full influence against revolt. Political convictions, religious affiliations, loyalties and sentiments—the whole intellectual and emotional heritage of a people—exerted their potent influence in the final hour of decision. The devotion to the old imperial connection, as well as the respect for constituted authority, maintained the loyalty of the bulk of the people, at least in Upper Canada. But for the actual rebels, and for the more militant tories, there were other interests—compelling interests—which had helped to create the quarrel and to bring on its explosion.

In one important respect, the rebellions were the final expression of that hatred of the rural communities for the commercialism of the St. Lawrence; and the defence of constituted political authority was an exciting incident in the ceaseless effort to protect the interests of the Canadian commercial state. The rebellions came, and had to come, from the countryside; but the existing order found its most violent supporters among the magistrates, the civil servants and the merchants. The towns were the citadels of the governing class; they were, in particular, the strongholds of the powerful and determined commercial group; and it was appropriately enough in Montreal, the focus of the whole northern trading system, that toryism found its most provocative and violent expression. Even in the tiny villages of the countryside, as Mackenzie found to his cost, the local shopkeepers were energetic in opposing the radicals. "It is provoking", wrote Mackenzie, "to see the Storekeepers continually against Reform. . . . At Equesing who were more indefatigable in raising recruits to put down the voice of the town and its 5000 inhabitants than Squires O'Reilly, Brown, Chalmers, and Chisholm, and Mr Salisbury, all Merchants? So it was in Caledon, Albion, and Chinquacousy."[74]

In the last few weeks before the outbreaks, the tories maintained their accustomed attitude of mingled indignation and contempt. Their two opinions, which they never troubled to reconcile, were, first, that frightful rebellions were about to break out, and, secondly, that the radicals were too few and too contemptible to attempt to rebel. The Montreal papers talked of the *patriotes'* "wretched impotency of moral and physical courage"; and it was complacently asserted that "the faction of the smuggler is too dastardly, too full of braggart bluster, to do anything more than show its teeth". In Upper Canada, the papers derided the ignorance, illiteracy and youth of the crowds which attended Mackenzie's meetings; and the "atrocious little monster of Radicalism" was pictured attempting to impose upon the credulity of illiterates and half-grown boys.[75] The unfortunate meeting in the brewery inspired an endless stream of raillery at the expense of the radicals. Mackenzie became "the doughty hero of the spigot and bung", his journal "The Mash Tub", and the great convention which the reformers hoped to assemble was pilloried derisively as the "Bung-hole Convention, or Small Beer Parliament of Upper Canada". At times the papers scorned even to imagine a rebellion in Upper Canada; and when the troops were actually sent to the lower province, it was claimed by the *Patriot* that full reliance could be placed upon the militia.

At the same time, the tories dealt in other things besides raillery, derision and abuse. They were defending British institutions, British principles, the British connection; and the protection of this venerable inheritance ennobled the defence and transfigured it with moral fervour. The constitutionalists were defenders of empire; but were they not also, and by natural association, the defenders of order, civilization and religion? Was there not, for example, inquired one correspondent solemnly, a disquieting resemblance between Mr. Mackenzie and that irreligious, ultra-democratic maker of utopias, Mr. Owen of Lanark?[76] It was the purpose of all these utopian agitators to cast all the graces and the solid achievements of civilization "into the burning fiery furnace of democratic experiment. . . ". Their object was "to ridicule, weaken, and cast down religion. . . ". They could not be checked by derision and contempt alone. They were dangerous. They must be strenuously resisted by those who refused to permit all they held dear to be sacrificed "before the hideous many-headed Hydra of Revolution". "Then let them throw aside inglorious ease, *and stand to their arms* . . .", wrote one tory in a moment of exaltation. "*Words* are well enough in their season; but the period for acting will sooner or later arrive, and then *acts* alone will be found of use or value."[77]

Up on Yonge Street Mackenzie's farmers were going through their primitive manœuvres. In Lower Canada the *patriotes* were forming "Sons of Liberty" associations, while the tories in Montreal reorganized their own militant society, the "Doric Club". There was drilling going on in and around Montreal; the press campaign reached a crescendo of violence; and the public meetings swelled into great assemblies, semi-military in character, which were lashed by furious speeches and passed provocative resolutions. On October 23, the *patriotes* held their great rally of the six confederated counties at the village of St. Charles; and on the same day the Montreal tories staged a great mass meeting in the Place d'Armes.[78] There were supposed to be over 7,000 people present. The square was decked with flags and bunting. And the processions from the different wards advanced to the assembly like the regiments of an army, heralded by drums and music, headed by standard-bearers and troops of horsemen. "There is no mincing matters now—", wrote a tory editor a few days after the meeting, "the period of action has arrived, and a collision must inevitably take place soon, in spite of government. . . . There are not any visible means of preventing a hostile collision, as both parties appear to be aware of each other's intentions, and are prepared for the worst. . . . Both are anxious for the coming conflict, and are equally confident of success."[79]

This prophecy was made on November 2. On the 4th, which was a Saturday, there were persistent rumours that the *patriotes* intended to hold a demonstration on the following Monday in the Place d'Armes. The constitutionalists frankly prepared to oppose them; and on Monday the long-expected clash occurred.[80] Though the radicals abandoned their public meeting, they assembled to drill in a private yard; and there they were discovered and provoked to action by a few over-zealous constitutionalists. When the *patriotes* rushed from the yard to punish the marauding tories, they carried everything before them at first. Then the Doric Club mustered to assist their brothers. The streets were suddenly full of men armed with clubs and sticks; and the resulting battle raged up and down the city until the British drove the *patriotes* into the St. Lawrence suburb and sacked the offices of one of the chief radical newspapers. It was this clash which hurried on affairs to a crisis. It heightened the apprehensions and hastened the decisive action of the executive. It forced the hand of the radicals. They had been beaten in Montreal; and when in prudence their leaders left the city, the executive, misinterpreting their equivocal movements, abruptly issued its warrants for their arrest. Then the countryside resisted; and the resistance swelled into open revolt at St. Denis and culminated in the serious affray at St. Eustache. This was not a revolutionary offensive, deliberately begun by insurgents in their own way and at their own time; and the radicals had merely been goaded into a series of *jacqueries*, unplanned, sporadic, hopeless.

While the movement in the lower province was drawing haphazardly to its conclusion, the extreme radicals in Upper Canada were about to begin their deliberately planned revolt. There were reformers in Toronto: the campaign of militant organization had been started there during the summer. But in the end the revolutionaries in the capital of Upper Canada were not willing to test their strength in the city as the *patriotes* of Montreal had done. It was Mackenzie, Lount, Matthews, Anderson and the farmers from "north of the ridges" who made the last effort of that protest movement which had always been so largely agrarian in character. Their aims, which were social as well as political in character, were set forth not inaccurately in Mackenzie's draft constitution for the state of Upper Canada.[81] Incorporated trading companies were to be outlawed from the new republic and labour was solemnly declared to be the only means of creating wealth. The draft constitution expressed in final theoretical form the old rural attack upon the institutions, powers and privileges of the commercial state. It was as much to establish a simple Arcadia of freeholders as it was to win political independence from England, that the angry farmers revolted; and in the blunders and absurdities of the rebellion can be seen the tragic inexpertness of a farming population, goaded onwards by distresses towards the achievement of impossible ideals.

And so, in the oppressive atmosphere of rebellion, defeat and political chaos, the year of crisis closed. The country had not been able to endure the grinding stresses imposed upon it; and now at last its breakdown was complete. The finances were in disorder, the public works were suspended, the commerce of the country had dwindled away under the pressure of renewed competition and the stagnation of the slump. The population, still suffering from the effects of the financial crisis and the depression, was now divided by the rancorous political hatreds of an abortive civil war. Upon the weaknesses inherent in its economy, its political structure and its social composition, the commercial state had piled the burdens of ambition. Its strength had not sufficed; and it now lay wrecked in moral and material disintegration.

CHAPTER XII

THE LAST RECOVERY

I

The half dozen years which followed the collapse of the rebellion and the advent of Lord Durham were years of reorganization and recovery. The establishment of the long-desired union, the flotation of the indispensable loan, the work of a few men of constructive genius and a brief burst of material prosperity, all combined to reinvigorate the prostrated colonies. For the first time—and also for the last time—in its history under the régime of the new staples, the commercial state acquired a measure of inward harmony and outward adjustment. The interlocking commercial and political ideas, which made up the doctrine of the second British Empire as it was understood on the St. Lawrence by the possessing classes, were worked out more fully and applied more completely than they had ever been before. For a few years, under favouring conditions which a quarter-century before might have altered its whole existence, the commercial state progressed. It was a brilliant period, as full of energy and accomplishment as it was brief in duration. For the forces which were inimical to the success and to the very existence of the old Canadian system continued to develop in the Canadas, the United States and England; and before a half dozen years were out, the entire, newly repaired structure was exposed once more to strains from within and from without.

In 1838, when the rebellions had failed, and the reforming party lay prostrate in both provinces, all these repairs were still to be made. The country had passed through an emotional as well as a material upheaval. The air was heavy with a sullen sense of defeat and a feeling of vindictive triumph; and the emotions engendered by the crisis were kept alive by the hope, or the fear, that the defeated rebels, with the aid of the Americans, would invade the country from the south. Mackenzie, Duncombe, Rolph, Papineau, Brown, Lafontaine and the other leaders of the popular party had fled the country. Bidwell, who had had nothing to do with the

321

rebellion, was hounded out of Upper Canada by Sir Francis Bond Head. The jails in both provinces were crammed with hundreds of political prisoners; and although Lount and Matthews were the only two men who were hanged for their complicity in the revolt, the penalty of death hung over a good many others during the first months after the rebellion. For a while the reaction, fed by fear and hatred and outraged loyalty, became a positive campaign of retribution. The authorities acted with instinctive sternness and suspicion, while the tory press clamoured for revenge and in Upper Canada the loyalists formed vigilant committees to harry suspected reformers. Gosford wrote that the violence of the English party in Montreal "exceeds anything you can well form an idea of";[1] and the *Montreal Gazette* assured its readers that the British would sooner reconquer the province than restore any of its old power to the French-Canadian faction.[2]

While these emotional conflicts agitated the provinces, their material structure lay in complete disorder. The financial stringency and the commercial depression continued; and the legislatures of both provinces, by the operation either of economic or political brakes, had been brought virtually to a complete standstill. While the British government suspended the constitution in Lower Canada and entrusted a limited, temporary authority to a special council, the legislature of Upper Canada was held down almost as effectively by the dead weight of the provincial debt. By the end of 1837 the obligations of the province had reached a grand total of £1,083,218;[3] and, what was still more ominous, it had exhausted both the capacity of the provincial money-lenders and the patience of the bankers in London. During the previous summer, when the government was at its wit's end for funds and the stoppage of the public works was almost daily expected, the Upper Canadian executive had decided to sell to the local banks a series of debentures, valued at £138,650, the interest and principal of which were payable, not in Canada, but at Baring Brothers in London.[4] This extraordinary manœuvre, which was undertaken without the knowledge or consent of Baring Brothers, provided the province with a temporary supply of funds at the expense of damaging its reputation with the great English firm. The rebellions, which made provincial bonds virtually unsaleable on the London market,

completed the disgust of Barings and the discredit of Upper
Canada.

The province could borrow neither in England nor in the Canadas
upon anything like acceptable terms. Its enterprises, which had
moved with jolts and interruptions during the past twelve months,
slowed down rapidly and came to a dead stop. In March, 1838, the
receiver-general Dunn notified the commissioners for the St.
Lawrence canals that there was no more money available for the
works. The protests of the commissioners and the contractors only
sufficed to persuade the government against an abrupt and total
stoppage; and it authorized two last grants which were made on
the express stipulation that the money was to be used to pay up
arrears and to put the works in as fit a state as possible for a
suspension of operations.[5] By the middle of the summer progressive
development had slowed down to mere preventive measures; and
the trade of the St. Lawrence, which had dwindled under the
commercial depression, passed by a series of unfinished and
abandoned canals.

The bankruptcy, both moral and financial, of the two provinces,
was apparent in the attitude of the British-American world. The
Canadas were shunned both by the poverty-stricken and the
wealthy. London capitalists and Irish immigrants turned their
eyes elsewhere; and the distracted provinces were abandoned
even by the Canadians themselves. Migration, which had brought
scores of thousands of British settlers to Upper Canada in the early
thirties, now carried hundreds of frightened and discontented
frontiersmen beyond the boundary into the new west of Ohio,
Indiana and Illinois. "Emigration to the States is the fever of the
day", wrote William Ryerson from Toronto, "& is going on to an
extent truly alarming & astonishing."[6] During the spring and
summer of 1838 the piled waggons of the escaping migrants jolted
by hundreds into Detroit and Buffalo. The steamboats carried
hundreds more from half-depopulated Canadian villages to such
ports as Lewiston and Cleveland. And the movement became so
general and so compelling that Peter Perry, Francis Hincks and
other well-known radical leaders formed a company for the
transportation of persecuted Canadian reformers to the free
soil of the territory of Iowa.[7]

In these first few months after the rebellion, as they faced a ruined commerce and a stricken country, the tories held tenaciously to their old programme of reform. Every merchant in Canada could agree with the assembly of Upper Canada when it resolved in February, 1838, that "the chief causes of the evils under which these Provinces have suffered, may be traced to their unwise division into separate and distinct Colonies in 1791. . . ".[8] Montreal, of course, had always favoured union. Early in 1838, the Constitutional Society of Quebec endorsed a resolution of its committee favouring a legislative union of the provinces.[9] The assembly of Upper Canada, by a majority of 29 to 4, supported the idea of union, though with the most exacting conditions, including a demand that a decided majority in the united legislature should be given to the upper province. Union or the annexation of Montreal to Upper Canada—these old proposals of the commercial group—were urged for the same old reasons, which had simply grown weightier since the rebellions and the financial collapse. For the merchants and the governing class it was more than ever essential that the unruly and anti-commercial French should be submerged in a political union which would make certain the supremacy of British peoples and British institutions, and which would leave the way clear for the progressive development of the St. Lawrence commercial system by British capital and British enterprise.

Only one definitely new recommendation was introduced into this venerable programme as a result of the experiences of 1837. People began to wonder, where before they had been certain, whether the union would be in itself sufficient, whether the canalization project and the credit of Upper Canada could both be salvaged by a political amalgamation alone. Out of this anxiety arose the demand that the British government should carry through a financial as well as a political reorganization and fortify the weakened credit of Upper Canada by a guaranteed imperial loan. The idea took shape in the finance committee of the Upper Canadian assembly, over which W. H. Merritt presided, during the session of 1838;[10] and the legislature passed a statute, permitting the executive to issue debentures to the value of £1,000,000, bearing interest at 3 per cent. only, providing the British government would support the venture by guaranteeing the interest. The imperial loan, the interest of which could be insured by a slight increase in the customs duties, was to be used to convert as much as possible of the original debt and thus to reduce the heavy interest charges which absorbed so much of the Upper Canadian revenue.

These ideas of political and financial reconstruction were urged all the more forcefully in the months which followed the rebellions, for the tories knew that the crisis would infallibly bring on an imperial investigation and that the investigation might result in imperial reforms. The Quebec Constitutional Society nominated Andrew Stuart as its agent in Great Britain; and George Moffatt and William Badgley departed for England as the representatives of the British of Montreal. Their expectation, which was common to all Canada, that an important imperial investigation was imminent, was fulfilled during the early months of 1838. In January, John George Lambton, first Earl of Durham, accepted appointment as high commissioner for British North America; and towards the end of May, in the full flush of the brief Canadian springtime, he landed at the port of Quebec.

II

Lord Durham, the author of the greatest report in British colonial history, occupies an accepted, a renowned, but none the less a slightly ambiguous position in the evolution of the Canadian provinces. He proposed responsible government, a political device which became the hope of the Canadian radicals; but he also advocated the union of the provinces, which for two generations had been the objective of the Canadian commercial class. When he discussed the affairs of Lower Canada, he appeared almost to write under the inspiration of the Montreal merchants, while what he had to say about the upper province might have been composed under the direction of western radicals. He performed the remarkable feat of joining the Lower Canada merchants and the Upper Canadian radicals in approval of his measures and of uniting the French Canadians and the Toronto tories in outraged disapprobation.

Lord Durham's report, which fitted so imperfectly into any of the categories of Canadian political thinking, can perhaps best be understood in relation to its author's character, interests and environment. Born into a whiggish family, brought up in an atmosphere of liberalism, Lord Durham put the full force of his impetuous character into the struggle for the first Reform Bill. He was a builder of the new democracy; but also, and not unnaturally, he was a protégé of the industrial revolution which had preceded it and made it necessary. The pupil whom the scientific and utilitarian Dr. Beddoes instructed in elementary economics, inherited the ownership of some of the most important collieries in the Newcastle district. The young "king of the coal country", who became known as "Radical Jack", spent the early years of his career not merely among the members of the whig political coterie, but also with the merchants and industrialists who were laying the basis for British supremacy in world trade.[11]

The energy, the enthusiasm, the creative imagination which were peculiarly Lord Durham's, could find congenial scope in materialistic enterprises as well as in purely political plans. The man who personified the whig union between landed property on the one hand and commerce and industry on the other, was ready for the impact of North American materialism; and the whole design of the St. Lawrence trading system was brought home to him, directly through his own appreciative understanding and indirectly through the contacts that he made. He saw little enough of Upper Canada as a province, or of the French Canadians as a national group. But while his knowledge of the Upper Canadian tories appears to have been gathered chiefly from their enemies, he managed, in one way or another, to have a good many direct contacts with the merchants of Montreal. Before he left for Canada, Messrs. Gould and Gillespie of the North American Colonial Association were providing him with a good deal of carefully selected material; and Moffatt and Badgley, who had come all the way to London for the purpose, presented the petitions of the constitutionalists and drove home the point that the political union of the provinces was the only way to remove the French-Canadian obstruction to the supremacy of British institutions and the advance of British enterprise.[12]

In Canada, these contacts were renewed, at the instance of Lord Durham himself and his associates as well as of the Canadian merchants. Before Durham left Quebec, Charles Buller went on in advance to Montreal to consult with McGill, Gerrard, Pothier and Moffatt, the leaders of the British party; and with the exception of Moffatt, whom he described as a "stern proud" man, he found the members of the commercial group almost unexpectedly lenient and reasonable.[13] Early in July, when Durham at length arrived in Montreal, he laid his scheme for the federation of the British North American provinces before a committee of seven, selected by Peter McGill, of the Montreal Bank. The high commissioner not only invited the general support of the members of the tory party; he also sought the direct assistance of its supposedly most violent and provocative publicist. Late in August, he appointed Adam Thom to his commission on municipal government. Thom had been the editor of the *Montreal Herald;* he was the author of the abusive *Anti-Gallic Letters.* And yet, despite his damaging notoriety, he was taken into the councils of the Durham mission, "acted as though he were the Dictator's minister", and played the part of the principal liaison officer between Lord Durham and the commercial community of Quebec and Montreal.[14]

These contacts and associations were not the artificial arrangements of men seeking with deliberate magnanimity to understand two strange and alien points of view. They were natural associations, based rather upon common respect, common assumptions and common objectives. Lord Durham was notoriously an extreme whig; the Canadian merchants were reputed in London to be bigoted and ultra tories; but these misleading political labels could not conceal a considerable similarity of views. It was not strange that Buller should remark the moderation of "these old tories" and the general wisdom and acceptability of many of their demands. It was not unnatural that a good deal of the ancient gospel of Montreal found its way into Durham's dispatches and into the greatest liberal report in British colonial history. Lord Durham took over, practically in its entirety, the philosophy of union and eventually the idea of legislative union itself; and the eloquent prose of the report echoes the phraseology of countless commercial petitions and repeats the arguments which had been heard for decades in Quebec and Montreal.

From his dispatches and his report, it is plain that Lord Durham looked upon the St. Lawrence not only as the centre of communities whose conflicts must be quieted by British statesmanship, but also as the focus of a great commercial system whose collapse could be repaired by British institutions, British capital and British enterprise. Like the merchants, he was oppressed by the financial instability, the impoverishment and the depopulation of the two provinces; and, like the merchants again, he saw in the energy and material prosperity of the United States an example which might be followed and a rivalry which must be met. He believed that Upper Canada was suffering politically from the domination of a selfish and exclusive oligarchy; but he also saw those economic disabilities, inherent in the financial and commercial position of the province, which had driven the tories to agitate for union or the annexation of Montreal. He pierced beneath the "liberalism" of the French Canadians and the "toryism" of the British, to the real cultural conflict in Lower Canada; and he realized how the dispute over immigration, land tenure, finance and public works, had blocked the development of the country. The language in which he described the obstructive, unprogressive and anti-commercial French Canadians excelled in majesty of style, though scarcely in vigour of expression, the talk which had been common in Montreal for a generation; and his basic conviction that the Canadas must necessarily and inevitably be anglicized had been the cardinal principle of Lower Canadian toryism since the turn of the century. Lord Durham hoped to make the Canadas preponderantly British, to improve their fiscal and commercial position and to make the way clear for the completion of the canals. The commercial future of the St. Lawrence appealed to him so strongly that he devoted an entire dispatch to it.[15] He was prepared to support the canalization project, as the Upper Canadians had come to believe it must be supported, by an imperial loan. "I believe, my Lord," he wrote extravagantly to Glenelg, "I am not too sanguine when I assert that such a step taken would at once put an end to all discontents and disturbances in the Canadas."

From the first, therefore, there was much implicit and outspoken in Lord Durham which attracted the tories of Quebec and Montreal. But their general approval of his programme was qualified, nevertheless, by one extremely important reservation. In London, Durham had derived from Arthur Roebuck, the agent for the radicals of Lower Canada, the idea of a general federal union of the British North American provinces; and it was this plan which he presented to Peter McGill and the other leaders of the British party in the conference in Montreal early in July. Fifteen years before, in the arguments over Wilmot Horton's Union Bill, the theorists in Canada had explored the whole question of a federal union. In Upper Canada they were still willing to consider it as a solution; but the assembly had decided, in 1838, for legislative union, under conditions. The Lower Canadian tories still held to the view that the ambitious federal project was impractical, unnecessary and incapable of removing the crucial difficulties in the lower province. It was this belief which estranged the merchants from the man to whom otherwise they would have been irresistibly attracted. When Adam Thom attended a meeting called in September by Peter McGill, he found that "the best possible spirit was evinced on every point, but the general scheme, which seemed altogether distasteful, not so much, I am convinced, on account of any demerits of its own, as on account of its interference with the grand hobby of the union of the provinces.—"[16] The *Montreal Gazette* declared that it objected to a few of Lord Durham's measures, though it expressed complete approval of his general policy; and late in November it carried an editorial on "this wild and unconstitutional project of a Confederation of the British North American Provinces".[17]

But Lord Durham was gradually and reluctantly converted from the scheme of federation, which had been conceived in London by British statesmen, to the plan of legislative union which had been matured in Canada by the directors of the commercial state. Adam Thom, among others, suggested some changes in the original federal scheme which would probably have made it more acceptable to the merchants; and their steady opposition to the whole measure was perhaps responsible for an even more important alteration which had crept into the project by the autumn. Lord Durham, developing and revising the old idea of the annexation of Montreal, proposed to create between the two original Canadas a third province, which would include the Eastern Townships, the island of Montreal, and a part of eastern Upper Canada.[18] He was prepared to hive the French Canadians on the lower St. Lawrence to liberate the city of Montreal; but he would not yet yield to Montreal's plans. And, although there are indications, which even crept into the newspapers, that he was changing his views before his departure, he apparently left Canada still holding to the federal scheme.

It was the programme of anglification, the general refusal to submit again to French-Canadian domination in the lower province which finally undermined Lord Durham's academic federalism. As Charles Buller put it "the great argument against a federal Union is that it does nothing to attain the main end which we ought to have in view. That end is the keeping Lower Canada quiet now, & making it English as speedily as possible".[19] Late in the year, when Lord Durham was returning to England, the renewal of rebellion appeared to prove that the lower province needed drastic remedies which must be immediately applied. In London the merchants interested in the Canadian trade renewed their desperate protest against any federal scheme, which must of necessity leave to the French Canadians the management of their local concerns; and the prime minister, Melbourne, had declared in December, 1838, that "it is laid down by all as a fundamental principle that the French must not be reinstated in power in Lower Canada".[20] These considerations, which summed up the habitual arguments of the Canadian merchants, sufficed to overcome Lord Durham's federal plan; and the historic commercial scheme of union took its place as the logical conclusion of the commercial philosophy which pervaded so much of the report.

Thus, partly because of their own exertions and largely because the events of the rebellion had convinced British statesmen of the justice of their views, the Canadian tories had seen their doctrine almost in its entirety elevated to the dignity of a great imperial report. Their one objection to the programme of Lord Durham had been removed; and they had apparently no anticipation whatever that the report would contain another recommendation, more objectionable even than federal union, and ultimately more destructive of their fundamental views. In fact, Lord Durham proposed that the executive government of the united province should be entrusted, in the same way as it was entrusted to the cabinet in England, to a ministry possessing the confidence and support of the majority of the provincial parliament and hence of the Canadian people. This was the political device which came to be known, in Canada and in the British colonial world generally, as the doctrine of responsible government.

In Canada the effects of Lord Durham's recommendation were profoundly disturbing. It reanimated the beaten reforming parties and made their union possible. It gave them a neat political programme to substitute for the visionary social and political philosophy by which, in the past, they had been chiefly known, and which had gone down to defeat in the rebellions. In the "Durham meetings" which were held in Upper Canada during the summer and autumn of 1839, the radicals appropriated the magic word "Durham" as an impressive synonym for the adjective "reform". And thus, as it was inevitably interpreted in terms of Canadian politics, the great report on the affairs of British North America contained a major contradiction. On the one hand, it implied, through the union, a programme of anglification, of reconstruction, of practical reforms. On the other hand, it invited a renewal of that party warfare which had been the curse of the Canadas for the past decades. The first would fulfil the desires of the merchants; the second might permit the reformers, including the solid *bloc* of French Canadians, to recover power.

Naturally, therefore, the Canadian tories read Lord Durham's report with mingled feelings of exasperation and gratitude. In Upper Canada, where anger triumphed over every other sentiment, the conservative press bespattered the high commissioner with abusive epithets. In Lower Canada, the *Montreal Gazette*, expressing a fairly general attitude, described the report as "laboured" and "overwrought" and declared that "we are not the indiscriminate approvers and panegyrists of the Report before us. . . ".[21] The tories in Quebec and Montreal could heartily approve of Lord Durham's general picture of the affairs of Lower Canada. The Upper Canadians had a number of acid criticisms to make of the report's inaccurate, superficial and radically inspired analysis of their own province.[22] But, whatever their individual strictures and complaints, the tories of both provinces could write in unqualified denunciation of the principle of responsible government.

Their attitude to the new theory of colonial government was logically consistent with the political philosophy they had professed for decades and with the part they had played in the crises of the rebellions. Their loyalties and their interests were bound up with the old imperial system. They sided instinctively with those who defended it; and, in the matter of responsible government, they took their stand upon the pronouncements of Lieutenant-Governor Arthur and upon the principles set forth in Lord John Russell's dispatches of 1839. A committee of the legislative council of Upper Canada declared that it was impossible to maintain the existing colonial relation on such a plan as that of responsible government.[23] The North American Colonial Association observed that responsible government was inconsistent with the dependence of the colony upon the parent state.[24] This "insane principle of Colonial Government", this "Chartism of the Colonies", would, declared the *Montreal Gazette*, "render the authority and intervention of the Mother Country as unnecessary as they could not fail to be impotent. . . ".[25] In the past the governor and the imperial parliament had used their power to preserve British interests in the colony and to moderate its bitter factional disputes. But if Great Britain abandoned this "umpirage", if she permitted her governors to be "the shuttle between colonial parties", then the result for Canadians would be the destruction of "the equilibrium and practical utility of their own local governments. . . ". From then on the tories rang the changes upon the benefits of the imperial connection and the evils of party warfare; and their concern with these two ideas was all the greater since they identified their own interests with the first, and the menace of their opponents with the second. They were determined to save the programme of anglification, practical reform and progress, which was implicit in the legislative union of the province, from the sabotage of the reformers and the French. And they concentrated determinedly upon the defeat of responsible government and the achievement of union.

III

It was fortunate for those commercially minded people in Canada who desired reorganization and hoped for prosperity, that the man who came from England to carry out the great scheme of reconstruction was not a mere benevolent and self-effacing liberal, but an immensely practical man of affairs. Charles Poulett Thomson, who was soon raised to the peerage as Baron Sydenham, was a vigorous personality who brought the aggressiveness of the new British business into the chaos and torpidity of Canadian affairs.[26] He was born into one of the old merchant families engaged in the Baltic trade. He had spent the first years of his career in the company of business men, utilitarian theorists and free-traders. It was Manchester, the capital of the new industrialism, the city which had given its name to a new school and a new philosophy, which sent him for ten years to parliament; and it was his "arithmetical" genius, his easy dexterity with facts, statistics and finance, which kept him for five years in the Melbourne cabinet as president of the board of trade. He had the plausibility and the engaging address of a promoter, the drive and energy of a captain of industry and the instinct of the efficiency expert for order, system and quick returns. The doubts and objections which were voiced by Canadian merchants and the North American Colonial Association at the appointment of a Baltic timber merchant and a professed free-trader to the governorship of the Canadas, died away in an astonishment of gratification; and within less than two years this coolly complacent, self-opinionated little man had completely changed the position of the Canadian commercial state.

Sydenham came to Canada with a vast plan of campaign in which the first strategic move was necessarily the accomplishment of union. In Lower Canada, where the old constitution had been suspended and a special council entrusted with provisional legislative power, it was easy enough to get agreement to the plan of union which the British authorities proposed. But Upper Canada was a distinctly different matter. For nearly twenty years now the Upper Canadian tories had wavered about union. The annexation of Montreal to Upper Canada was, of course, a device by which the tories hoped to gain all the economic advantages of union without incurring any of the political disabilities with which it appeared to be involved; and they agreed to union in 1838 only on the basis of onerous conditions, which were intended to safe-guard the political "rights" of the province. Upper Canada was sick of its economic solitude, while at the same time it recoiled in horror from the company of the Canadian French. Experience had proved that the two provinces could not live economically apart and instinct warned that they could not live politically together.

In December, 1839, when Sydenham proposed legislative union to the parliament of Upper Canada, it was economic facts which triumphed over racial and political prejudices. The general terms of the union, as Sydenham proposed them, were a permanent civil list, equal representation for each province in the united legislature, and the charging of the Upper Canadian debt upon the general revenue of the new province. The second of these conditions, which removed some of Upper Canada's political fears, may have helped to persuade the legislature; but it was undoubtedly the third term which won them, for the third term provided the only really possible solution for their financial difficulties. In both the council and the assembly, the speakers harped upon the incompleted canals, the ruined finances and wrecked credit of the province;[27] and very significantly the assembly's fourth resolution, which affirmed the idea that Upper Canada's debt should be charged upon the united province, was passed without a division. "Our case every Hon. Member must admit", said Morris, "is a desperate one, and I am not prepared to deny that the remedy proposed may be looked upon as desperate also; but, Sir, something must be done and that speedily—" Tories like Cartwright and Hagerman, who had campaigned for union or annexation in the past, now voted against a measure which would tie them to the rebellious French; but for the majority of the members the cogency of the facts triumphed over these emotional aversions. In the minds of the Upper Canadians as well as for the merchants of Montreal, the union was largely a fiscal measure—a business arrangement undertaken a little regretfully—by which a bankrupt company could be salvaged in an amalgamated concern.

Once the consent of the Canadas had been obtained, the union bill could be pushed through the imperial parliament. It was, said the enraptured Montreal tories, "the *Magna Charta* of Canada", founded alike on Canadian welfare and imperial unity. For Sydenham, as for the merchants who had advocated it for so long, the union was to be the starting-point for a series of practical reforms; but it was not to be, as Francis Hincks and some of the radicals hoped, the first step in the realization of responsible government. Against the full doctrine of responsible government as it was finally conceded under Elgin, Sydenham and the colonial secretary, Lord John Russell, set their faces resolutely.[28] The executive council, according to Sydenham, was a council for the governor to consult, and not a ministry to use the governor's signature to validate its own decisions. Sydenham declared that it was impossible for him to get rid of his own responsibility, which meant that he had no intention of abandoning his own powers. There were times when he hankered after the power of a dictator; but as a parliamentary man faced with the government of an enormous province, he was really satisfied to be his own prime minister. It was his intention to gather about him at his own discretion a group of able administrators who would be influential parliamentarians without being party men. In council and in their respective departments, they could work out the details of a policy which must be largely the governor's in inspiration. In the legislature and before the people they could stand for the government's programme, which was designed to quiet party strife and win general popularity by its practical appeal.

It was, in all essentials, Montreal's conception of reconstruction. It was the tory theory of how the union could at once serve the material needs of Canada and satisfy the ancient principles of the second empire. Moreover, in the disgust and apathy which succeeded the rebellions, it had a good chance of winning popular support. "Languor, for the moment", wrote one editor, "seems to be felt in almost the whole circle of Provincial controversy. Men in general are sick and tired of the whole thing."[29] There were many, who, in disgust for their burnt-out political passions, turned in relief to the practical needs of the province; and Lord Sydenham expressed a general sentiment in his famous, his repeatedly quoted aphorism, "avoid useless discussions upon theoretical points of government". Here was a governor who wished to carry out a constructive programme and who was quite prepared to play the role of Patriot King; and encouraged by these favourable circumstances, the tories returned with relish to their colonial adaptation of Bolingbroke's eighteenth-century theory. "Canada", said the editor of the *Patriot*, "has been half ruined by political agitation . . ." It was unthinkable that with this experience, she should jeopardize the noble promise of union by a revival of party strife. Governors were instructed to keep ever before them the grand maxim "*That Canada cannot and will not be governed either* FOR, BY *or through* A PARTY".[30] The populace was advised "to shun as they would a pestilence the contaminating presence of an itinerant preacher of grievances—the self-named patriot spouting from the stump or the barrel about the vices and tyranny of men in power . . . to cast politics to the winds and devote themselves as sedulously to their farms and their warehouses as if the name of an Agitator or the turmoil of an election had never been heard by their peaceful firesides".[31] The tories, as they were never tired of pointing out, stood for measures, not men—in part through self-interest and in part through conviction. In obedience to their principles they were willing to follow Lord Sydenham, who was a whig, a free-trader and a Baltic timber merchant, and who ought, on all three counts, to have been anathema to them.

The trouble was that Sydenham, though he appealed for non-partisan assistance in a great programme of reconstruction, indirectly invited the renewal of party strife. The flexibility and strength which he and Lord John Russell imparted to the provincial executive inevitably focused all political agitation into a struggle for its control. By making the governor's council the visible centre of the administration, he made it the target for all the political ambitions of the time. In the past, in the days before the rebellions, executive authority had been limited rather than sovereign, divided rather than concentrated, remote rather than publicly exposed. Under the old dispensation the executive had not been composed of heads of departments who were members of the legislature. The secretaries, the law-officers, the inspectors-general and receivers-general were not invariably members of the executive council; and neither they, nor the councillors, were always members of the legislative council or the assembly. There was no single body of departmental experts who together concerted government policy and sponsored it in the provincial parliament; and most of the public works and other provincial undertakings were proposed, not by the executive, but by the members of the assembly, and carried out, not by the heads of departments, but by parliamentary committees. It was this disordered system which the Sydenham measures were designed to correct. By the Union Act of 1840—and this was a fundamental alteration—the executive was provided with a permanent civil list and the assembly was prevented from voting any tax, or any appropriation, for any object, which had not been recommended by the government.[32] To bear the weight of the burden of initiation Sydenham created a board of works and an administration composed of heads of departments; and these men entered the legislature to sponsor and defend government policy.

Lord Durham had recommended both the union and responsible government. It was Lord Sydenham's purpose, as it was in the main the purpose of the tories, to achieve the first and to defeat the second. But the union, as it was in fact established, was not merely the basis for a great programme of reforms, but also a challenge to party warfare. The executive, which contained a monopoly of power, might be won by majorities, and majorities created by party organization; and for this purpose responsible government was the ideal slogan and the post-rebellion reform party the ideal instrument. For nearly two years before the first union parliament met in June, 1841, the adroit and insinuating Francis Hincks worked away in secret with the French-Canadian leaders to perfect a coalition of the reformers of both provinces.[33] It was an alliance based, first, upon the doctrine of responsible government and, secondly, upon the idea of amicable and unconditional co-operation between the two races. It was not associated with any common programme of political action, for it was not based upon any unanimity of political and social views. Lord Elgin's opinion that it was an unnatural and factitious union was common long before he uttered it. "What", asked one editor, "is the bond of union between Mr. Robert Baldwin and Mr. Louis Hypolite Lafontaine as leaders of the Western and Eastern Reform or Radical parties?

We think that a gold medal might with great propriety be offered to any one capable of giving a satisfactory solution to this question. . . ."[34]

In the days before the rebellions, the simple agrarianism of the reformers of both provinces had helped to link them spiritually, though politically they were separated by the interprovincial boundary. But this inflexible anti-commercial policy had gone down to defeat in the fiasco of the revolts; and while the new reform party was led by such conservative landowners as Robert Baldwin and such constructive financiers as Francis Hincks, there was little chance of its revival. The reformers of the forties were less clearly distinguished from their tory rivals and less closely associated among themselves than their predecessors had been. It was not necessary to accept the tory dictum that the Upper Canadian radicals had "as little in common with the habitans of the Eastern division of the Province as the modern Yankees with the inhabitants of Japan".[35] But there would obviously be enormous difficulties in combining men who understood reform to be the progressive development of the entire country with men who identified it as the defence of their peculiar sectional culture. In the meantime, however, there was responsible government, which was a parliamentary device for the establishment of an executive. It implied no social philosophy and suggested no programme of reforming measures. The radicals in both provinces could unite most enthusiastically to promote by their joint endeavours the national interest upon the particular principle of responsible government, which committed them to nothing but a political mechanism by which they might all get into power. Thus, at the very beginning of the united province, the programme of union and anglification was met by the revival of the French, and the idea of non-partisan reconstruction was challenged by party.

The completeness with which this opposition was overcome is a tribute to Lord Sydenham's incomparable political finesse as well as to the solid virtues of his reforming programme. At first the triumph of the united reformers appeared certain. Robert Baldwin had accepted office as solicitor-general in the belief that responsible government was about to be conceded; and in February, 1841, he became a member of the first executive council of the united

province, though with the somewhat curious proviso that he had
no confidence in half his colleagues. In the general election which
followed in the early spring, Sydenham gerrymandered the urban
electoral districts in Canada East and the Montreal press clamoured
for the defeat of the ex-rebels; but in spite of everything Lower
Canada returned a compact group, which was opposed to government. If Hincks' coalition of the French and the Upper Canadian
radicals could be kept together, it would dominate the new
assembly; and with this apparent majority at his back, Baldwin
now demanded that the entire ministry should be reconstructed on
reform lines. The governor peremptorily refused and Baldwin
resigned. The tories rejoiced over the withdrawal of "the Achilles
of Reform—the Atlas of popular grievances—the 'Jack the Giant
Killer' of the Radical nursery tales. . . ". According to the
Montreal Gazette, the devious conduct of the "insidious and designing" Mr. Baldwin was capable of two explanations, both of them
indicating an almost equal amount of treachery. Either he had
betrayed his idolized party in the first place by accepting office
or he had betrayed the governor by resigning it.[36]

In opposition, the numerically superior reformers carried the
election of the speaker; but thereafter the coalition rapidly dis-
integrated. The bulk of the Upper Canadian reformers, showing
an odd preference for the progress of their country over the
advancement of Mr. Hincks's political machinations, were to be
found voting steadily for the progressive measures of the government; and before the end of June, the tory papers were triumphantly proclaiming that "the so called Reform party has been
split up—we trust the rupture is an eternal one. . . ".[37] Mr.
Baldwin, affirming his single political principle with a kind of bovine
fixity of purpose, was left practically alone, a martyr to the cause
of co-operation between the two races, in the midst of an almost
solid French-Canadian opposition. Even Francis Hincks, the
strategist of the great coalition, deserted the field with most
realistic alacrity after the rout of his western wing. At the beginning
of the session he had been rebuking the Upper Canadian reformers
for the desertion of their eastern colleagues; but before parliament
was ended, he was jibing the French Canadians for their reactionary
tendencies like any tory.[38]

Hincks may have been converted by the intrinsic excellence of the governor's programme. He may have been seduced by the pleasing prospect of the job which was eventually given to him by Bagot in the following year. The "marvellous facility of apostacy" which he displayed during 1841–1842 was, declared the tories, comparable only to that of Charles James Fox when he joined with Lord North to form an administration; and for years afterward they found it a delightful intellectual exercise to speculate upon the motives of this pattern reformer. "The exact period and nature of the inducements offered", wrote one tory editor, "—whether it was a compliment to Mr. Hincks on the amiability of his manners—or the sweetness of his temperament, the rigidity of his principles, or his peculiar fitness ('that's your failing, Mrs. Jiniwin') for managing a Bank of Issue—will probably never be known. The victim in such case is not always conscious of the process of seduction. All that can be said is, that Mr. Hincks was gained, that he deserted his friends, that he was first suspected, then known, to have sold them, and a bargain was begun which was afterwards matured. . . . There must have been a peculiar gratification to a man like Lord Sydenham, in detaching him from Mr. Baldwin; exchanging pieces, as it were, on the political chessboard; and damaging Mr Hincks irretrievably, so as literally to leave him no party, and make him the most dependent tool, and create what would have happened with men of ordinary honour and feeling—an irreconcileable quarrel between him and his former allies."[39]

IV

The collapse of the united reform party meant the failure of any attempt to upset the union and the frustration of any drive for party government. The great reorganization of the new province which was at once the desire of the commercial class and the promise of the Durham report, could now be carried forward—free of interruptions—by an able governor and a composite executive of moderate party men. The years which followed the arrival of Sydenham and the establishment of union were years of confidence, activity and achievement. "*We are destined*", wrote one correspondent enthusiastically, "*to become a wealthy and powerful country,*

at no remote period." Carried forward by the crusading ardour
of the governor and by the general inspiration of returning prosperity, the commercial state entered the last great period of its
existence.

This buoyant confidence was, to a considerable extent, a result
of the return of good times. The country recovered, though not too
rapidly, from the financial panic and the scarcity of bread-stuffs
which had unsettled it during 1836–1838. In 1838–1839, exports,
except of timber, were inconsiderable, money was still tight and
real estate extremely depressed;[40] but before the end of 1839 the
trade of Upper Canada had begun to pick up and real estate values
were rising.[41] Up to 1842, when the British preference was once
more reduced, the wood trade steadily improved; and the price
of wheat in Great Britain, which, on the yearly average, was well
over 60s. the quarter during the period 1838–1841, encouraged the
export of Canadian bread-stuffs. The tonnage of vessels cleared outward from Quebec rose from 354,739 in 1838 to 478,906 in 1840.[42]
Traffic and tolls on the Welland and the Lachine canals increased
steadily; and the recovery was so sudden in 1840 that shipping
was at a premium, freights rose and the ports above Montreal were
choked with supplies of wheat and flour.[43] The collapse of the
western trade had been succeeded with characteristic abruptness
by an impressive revival. For a few years produce poured in
from the United States; and imports of American wheat and flour
for 1840 were estimated as equal to over two million bushels of
wheat.[44] Exports overseas from Quebec and Montreal in 1841
were valued at over two million pounds; and they were supposed
to have included 356,210 barrels of flour and 562,862 bushels of
wheat.[45]

The commercial revival, moreover, was accompanied by the
recovery of provincial finance. The dead weight of its contractual
obligations was the basic problem of the commercial state; and the
almost magical solution of this ancient question was probably the
greatest achievement of the reconstruction under Sydenham.
During 1838 and 1839 the unfinished or imperfectly completed
public works had been suspended for lack of funds; and yet the
interest on the loans which they had already occasioned was
almost equal to the revenue of Upper Canada.[46] In both provinces,

and necessarily in the united province also, the income, which was principally derived from an extremely low tariff, was patently inadequate; and in 1840, the last year before the union, Sydenham estimated that the combined deficit would amount to nearly £60,000.[47] At the same time, Canadian credit had been seriously shaken on the London market. Sydenham asserted that the 5 per cent. provincial debentures, if saleable at all, could only be disposed of at a discount of 25 per cent.; and he believed that a new issue, if it were sold at par, would have to bear interest at 8 or 9 per cent. The two provinces went into union with an inadequate revenue, a broken credit and a combined debt of £1,325,000 currency.[48]

The remedy, or rather the main remedy for all this, was the imperial loan. It had been recommended by Lord Durham; and the pessimistic Sir George Arthur, the last lieutenant-governor of Upper Canada, had pleaded for it in gloomy and impressive dispatches.[49] The British authorities, eventually though reluctantly convinced, agreed to base the new political union upon the solid basis of a financial guarantee. Sydenham was instructed to use the promise of the imperial loan as an additional inducement to persuade Upper Canada to enter the union;[50] but the case of Upper Canada was so desperate that he found it unnecessary to employ the bribe. It was not until the opening of the first session of the united parliament, in a speech which confidently sounded the theme of constructive planning, that Sydenham first publicly announced the news of the £1,500,000 imperial loan. It was the most brilliant example of that easy, irresistible magic by which the amazing governor conquered human opposition and swept aside material obstruction. It confirmed the tories' belief in the union and reinforced their conviction of the value of the imperial tie. "These, truly," said the *Montreal Gazette* in a rapturous editorial, "are not the partial and stinted gifts of a step-dame, but the natural and spontaneous offerings of a kind and affectionate parent, anxious to protect and foster those whom she loves, and to afford them such assistance as will enable them to secure their own future happiness and prosperity."[51]

There was, indeed, some disappointment, for it was plain that the British authorities intended that the loan should be used to retire as much as possible of the original debt. Sydenham proposed to improve the financial position of the province by increasing the general tariff on manufactured goods from 2½ to 5 per cent. and by converting the greater part of the old debt at a lower rate of interest with the proceeds of the imperial loan. He hoped then, on the basis of this improved financial position, to obtain a second imperial loan of £1,400,000 and to complete the public works. He picked out Francis Hincks, whose financial abilities conspicuously outweighed his gifts for political intrigue, and apparently intended to make him his chief agent. But the governor's abrupt, unfortunate death delayed this arrangement; and it was not until the summer of 1842, during the régime of the new governor, Sir Charles Bagot, that Hincks was made inspector-general of the province. In the same year the imperial loan became available. The colonial office refused to extend the British guarantee to fresh Canadian financing; but, in recompense, it agreed that the £1,500,000 loan might be used, not to convert the original debt, but to complete the public improvements. The Canadian government closed with this offer in the autumn of 1842; and under Francis Hincks, who reformed the whole financial system of the province, completed the arrangements for the new loan and established a sinking fund for its redemption, the long-delayed plan for the transportation system of the St. Lawrence could at last be pushed forward to its completion.[52]

The demand for it, in the meantime, had become practically unanimous. In the face of business conditions in 1840–1841, it was obvious that the canals were necessary not only to encourage prospective trade, but also to cope with the trade which actually existed; and the discussion of freights on lake, ocean and river which filled the press during these years, was an indication of how expensive and unsatisfactory the Canadian route was felt to be. By now it had become established that transport up went largely by the Ottawa and Rideau route and down-traffic by the unimproved St. Lawrence.[53] There were half a dozen big forwarding companies on the two routes, of which McPherson and Crane (the Ottawa and Rideau Company) was probably the most important; but the companies had fallen down badly before the inrush of supplies in 1840, and, at the same time, they were repeatedly criticized for their high freight rates.[54] The distance from Montreal to Kingston by the Rideau was about half that from New York to Buffalo by the Erie canal; but, according to a report of a committee of the Canadian legislature in 1841, the Canadian charge on a ton of merchandise approached very closely to the American rate of $13–$15.[55] Transport down, by the St. Lawrence, was as cheap, or cheaper, than anything the Americans could provide; but it was hoped to reduce the charge further, to reduce it radically, in order to compensate for the abnormally high ocean rates which obtained from Quebec to Great Britain.

The St. Lawrence transportation system had almost ceased to be a political question. The last serious protests of agrarian opposition had died away in the wreck of the rebellions; and the new, united Canada was committed almost unanimously to a project which the commercial class had regarded for decades as the chief means by which the province could express its fundamental character and achieve its real destiny. In the session of 1841, when Harrison submitted the Sydenham government's programme of public works, there were only a few echoes of that old antagonism to debt and expensive public improvements; and Baldwin and the French-Canadian Viger, intent upon safeguarding the sectional interests of Canada East, supported the motion for the immediate completion of the St. Lawrence canals.[56] During the summer of 1842, drawing upon the British treasury in anticipation of the imperial loan, Bagot recommenced the works on the St. Lawrence system. The Cornwall canal was now practically completed; and the government plunged at once into the improvement of the Welland and the preparation of plans for the new Beauharnois and Lachine canals.

For the next few years, the works were driven forward with persistent energy. In the Niagara country there were hundreds of labourers working at the reconstruction of the Welland canal. Down by Ellice's old seigniory of Beauharnois, where the river raced in a white fury over its obstructions, the big ditch was slowly pushed through the earth; and in Montreal and Lachine the journalists and citizens used to wander out to measure the progress of the mammoth operations of the board of works. "Huge mounds of earth rear their sombre-hued crests where the barges from Upper Canada once floated—excavations of mighty dimensions open themselves where formerly the citizens promenaded—" The hundreds of labourers—Irish Roman Catholic "Repealers" and Protestant Orangemen—added all their violence and unruliness to the excitement of the great constructions. In 1844, in a by-election in the West Ward of Montreal, the "Repealers" were brought in in hordes to bully the British tories into submission; and in the summer of 1842, at St. Catharines and along the line of the Welland, the men of Cork and the men of Connaught plundered property and terrified householders in the brief intervals between fighting each other.[57]

The improvement of the St. Lawrence, though it was one of the most important, was, after all, only one of the several means by which the northern commercial state could be protected and improved. The St. Lawrence was an imperial river which connected far markets with distant depots of supply; and it had always been the purpose of the commercial class to keep the depots open by free trade and to safeguard the markets by imperial preferential tariffs. The colonial preference on wheat and flour which had been finally established by the imperial act of 1828, had never really satisfied either the Canadian farmers or the Canadian merchants; and after Canadian agriculture had recovered from its collapse in 1836–1838, they joined together in agitating for freer entry into the British market. From 1839 to 1842 the high prices for corn in Great Britain made it frequently possible for Canadian wheat to enter at the merely nominal duty of 6d. per quarter; but the ever present fear that a decline in prices would drive the colonial tariff up to its maximum, helped to stimulate the old agitation for free entry. The legislature of Upper Canada, in its last session, petitioned for a reduced tariff on bread-stuffs; the Montreal merchants and their London correspondents renewed their appeals; and late in 1841 they were forming agricultural committees in Canada West to petition for the free entry of Canadian wheat and flour into the British market.[58]

The reduction of the British tariff on Canadian bread-stuffs was not, however, the only demand of the new agricultural Canada. During 1840–1841, when the imports of American wheat and flour again became heavy, the old agitation for the protection of Canadian agriculture was renewed. Before the rebellions, this had been one of the questions which had set the agrarian parties against the upholders of the commercial state. Canada, a staple-producing country, worked by producers and merchants, could, of course, agree upon a low tariff, for revenue purposes only, upon most articles of import; and the one major disagreement which marred this concord had been, and remained, the demand for protection against the influx of American staples for export by the St. Lawrence. It was, however, characteristic of the new period, when the parties fought more for political power than for social and political principles, that the question never became quite so acrimonious as it had been in the past. The reform party, educated out of its naïve agrarian idealism by the fact of the rebellions and by the leadership of such realistic economists as Francis Hincks, was prepared to come to terms with the business of the country. The tories, who had to win elections in the grain-producing counties of Canada West, were ready to make concessions to the farmers.[59] Canada East, and in particular the city of Montreal, was still unalterably opposed to duties on American produce which would interrupt the carrying-trade of the St. Lawrence. But even Montreal was prepared for a few losses which might be recompensed by greater gains; and it was apparently the Montreal merchants who first suggested the plan by which Great Britain, in return for a duty on American wheat entering Canada, would grant free entry for colonial wheat and flour into the British market.[60]

Everybody, merchants and farmers alike, looked expectantly to England; and in England the old land-owning tory party had just been returned to power. In theory, the Canadian conservatives preferred British tories to British whigs; but they suffered, and were to suffer, as much from men like Huskisson and Peel as they had benefited from men like Durham, Sydenham and Russell. The struggle between the theory of the old British Empire and the demands of the new British system of world trade, was approaching its climax in the old country. The year 1838, which in Canada had witnessed the first steps towards reorganization and recovery, was marked in Great Britain by the beginnings of the Chartist movement and the foundation of the Anti-Corn Law League. The bad harvests of the late thirties and early forties gave strength to the campaign against protection and the demand for cheap bread. The rise of the new industrialism and the failure of British agriculture, which were the obverse and reverse sides of the same phenomenon, were creating an almost chronic condition of unsettlement and agitation; and under the pressure, both material and moral, of the new conditions, the unpredictable tories began to remodel the ancient fiscal system with an irreverent thoroughness. Sir Robert Peel, who was first to rival and then to supersede, the record of Huskisson as a fiscal reformer, proposed a great series of tariff reductions in the famous budget of 1842. Despite all the clamours of the merchants of Quebec, Montreal and Bytown, the duties on foreign timber were reduced and the colonial preference suffered a net loss of 15s. The new corn law of 1842 scaled down the tariff on bread-stuffs, though at the same time, in recompense, it lowered the price level at which Canadian wheat was admitted at the nominal duty of 6d. per quarter. Moreover, Great Britain reduced the tariff on foreign produce entering its overseas possessions and practically abandoned the attempt to force the provision trade of the West Indies through the British North American provinces. Within a few years the Canadian trade with the islands, which had been dwindling steadily ever since the "reciprocity" of 1830, came virtually to an end.

All this was serious; and the gravity of the situation lay not only in the actual tariff reductions, but also in the approaching triumph of free trade which they appeared ominously to foreshadow. There was, for the Canadian merchants, only one element of comfort in the disquieting British parliamentary session of 1842. In the debates on the new corn law and on the revised tariff for the British possessions overseas, the whig opposition had sought to defend the Canadian commercial system and had moved in amendment that colonial corn be admitted at all times into the British market at a flat rate of 1s. per quarter. Stanley and Gladstone, for the government, objected that such legislation would in fact promote the import of American wheat *via* the St. Lawrence under the guise of encouraging the Canadian producer; and they implied that one of their main objections to a reduced tariff on colonial wheat and flour lay in the fact that American corn was admitted free of duty into Canada. This hint, which the Canadian papers immediately began to interpret at more than its face value, was made slightly more definite and official in Stanley's dispatch to Bagot of March 2, 1842.[61] The Canadian government construed this missive to mean that Great Britain was prepared to reduce her tariff on Canadian bread-stuffs if Canada, in return, would impose a duty on the import of American wheat. That autumn the Canadian parliament hurriedly performed its part of the proffered bargain. The three-shilling duty on American wheat, though it did not pass without opposition, was expected to perform various wonders for the commercial state.[62] It would help to satisfy the demand for agricultural protection; it would fatten the Canadian treasury; and, best of all, it would remove what appeared to be the last impediment to the virtually free admission of Canadian bread-stuffs into the British market.

In 1843, though with some grudging reluctance, the tory government in England proposed and carried the Canada Corn Act, by which Canadian wheat was admitted at a fixed duty of 1s. a quarter and flour milled in Canada at a proportionate amount a barrel. The Canada Corn Act both revived the hopes of the Canadians and aroused the fears of the United States; and an unnamed firm in Oswego, whose analysis was passed on to the august house of Baring Brothers, expected that the act would encourage a supply of bread-stuffs *via* the St. Lawrence, which would be regular and ample enough to lower prices in Great Britain and thereby raise the tariff against importations from the American Atlantic ports.[63] In the eyes of Canadians, the Canada Corn Act was a great concession, which balanced, though it barely balanced, the commercial injuries inflicted in 1842. The merchants' fears were not entirely consumed in their gratification. By 1843 the period of reconstruction and recovery, which had begun with the advent of Lord Durham, had ended in unsettlement. The support of Great Britain was as necessary as the reorganization of the colony to the success of the Canadian commercial system; and the concord which had been laboriously established in the Canadas was interrupted by the mother country, whose actions had always been uncontrollable and whose policy was becoming disquietingly uncertain.

CHAPTER XIII
FINAL COLLAPSE

I

THE cracks which in 1842 and 1843 had become apparent in the newly repaired structure of the commercial state, were multiplied and widened in the years which immediately succeeded. The era of reconstruction was as brief in its duration as it was deceptive in its promise; and the forces of disruption, as if renewed by their interval of inactivity, began now to effect the final downfall of the old commercial system of the St. Lawrence. The rivalry of the United States, the defection of Great Britain and the antagonism within Canada itself had been, since 1821, the three great factors which had threatened the achievement of the second commercial empire. In the half dozen years which elapsed between the passage of the Canada Corn Act and the publication of the annexation manifesto in Montreal, these antagonistic forces, united in irresistible combination, finally achieved their objective. The frustration of the old St. Lawrence system was finished and complete. It had not merely been defeated in a single battle; it had lost the second campaign and with it the entire war. And the material success of its enemies was accompanied by the loss of its own traditional support, the discredit of its ancient strategy, and the bankruptcy of its morale.

The St. Lawrence was a British imperial trade route in North America; and in these years its imperial connections were dissolving at the very moment when it was losing its American sources of supply. The renewal of American aggression was coincident with the decline of the second British Empire. On the one hand, the old colonial system was breaking up between the British declaration of economic independence and the Canadian demand for political autonomy; on the other, the expulsion of Canada from the trade of the United States was followed by the American commercial invasion of Canada. The Erie canal, which had diverted the trade of the American north-west away from the St. Lawrence, had been the work of New York state; but the drawback acts of 1845–

1846, which permitted Canada to export and import freely through the United States, were part of a deliberate scheme of the American federal government to tap the monopoly of Montreal in Canada West. The instinctive urge of the new agricultural Canada for the management of its own affairs was at last satisfied by the grant of responsible government; and the new British imperialism, based on capitalist manufacture and world trade, finally triumphed in the repeal of the corn laws. The collapse of its economic and political foundations brought about the wreck of the old colonial system. The St. Lawrence had almost ceased to be an international commercial system; it was ceasing to be a British imperial trade-route; and thus the material defeat of the northern trading organization was accompanied by the repudiation of basic purpose. The last rapid stage of this revolution reached its climax in 1849; but it began in 1842, with the commencement of fiscal reform in Great Britain and the renewal of party strife in Canada.

It was claimed at the time, and it has been asserted by historians of the present, that Lord Sydenham's political system was inherently temporary and only possible at all because of its author's instinct for domination and capacity for political management. Coming at the very end of the old empire, Sydenham had roughly achieved that balance of interests which had always been its ideal. He had pacified the party rivalries within the province: he had reconciled the demands of provincial self-government with the claims of imperial suzerainty. But Lord Sydenham was the last of the proconsuls which the imperial system demanded for its proper working; and under his successors, who were either more accommodating or less adroit, his political system began rapidly to disintegrate. Sir Charles Bagot, who succeeded to the governor-generalship at the beginning of 1842, was a man very different from his predecessor. He was old and mellowed, where Sydenham had been young and energetic. He came, not, like Sydenham, from the commercial middle class, but from the English land-owning society; and he had gained his political experience in diplomacy, whereas Sydenham had acquired his training in business and in the administration of the board of trade.

Bagot, therefore, was not unfitted for the role of political manœuvring and racial reconciliation which circumstances indicated he should play. His ministers, the ministers whom Sydenham had called to office, were convinced that the executive could not command a majority in the next session of the legislature, unless its strength were recruited by new members carrying more parliamentary votes. Francis Hincks was added to the ministry in the hope of gaining the Upper Canadian reformers; Henry Sherwood was included with the intention of winning the Upper Canadian tories. But the French, the largest and most compact group in the legislature, remained aloof; and it was Harrison's and Draper's conviction that in some way or another they must be brought in to the support of the ministry. It was advice which coincided with Bagot's own inclinations. The aged and affable statesman was attracted by the simple values of French-Canadian life; and the exclusion of the French from office and their opposition to the union constituted both a reproach to his sensibilities and a challenge to his diplomatic skill. To conciliate the two nations on the St. Lawrence, to complete his projected diplomatic revolution in Canadian politics, Bagot was even prepared to admit the French Canadians, as a party, to power. But this would mean admitting Robert Baldwin also, who all this time had been clinging to the French like a peculiarly adhesive barnacle. Bagot was not prepared to yield so far until the meeting of the legislature had convinced him and his ministers that they faced a hostile majority in the house. Then, by an adroit political manœuvre, he persuaded Baldwin, Lafontaine and three other reformers to enter his cabinet.[1]

Bagot's "great measure" was not, of course, the grant of the political principle of responsible government, but the conciliation of the French racial group. Bagot had kept the governor's initiative; and the new ministry was not a united reform cabinet, but a coalition, into which had been introduced a few new members who were acceptable to the French Canadians. The ministerial changes had actually been advised by tories like Draper; and, in carrying them out, Bagot had saved much of the old tory theory of colonial government. But, in spite of this, Canadian conservatives in general were unsparingly critical of the new arrangement. In their indignation they did not know whether to put the responsibility upon Bagot himself or, more charitably, upon the designing and unscrupulous men who had misled him. In one breath they denounced the governor as a Frankenstein, gazing with happy feelings on "the misshapen abortion which his audacious act has summoned into hideous existence";[2] and, in another, they laid the blame upon the circumstances which had victimized the unsuspecting Bagot and upon "the political *mesmerism* by which he was deliberately blinded and foully betrayed".[3] In part, they spoke as party men, indignant that the offices which they had always considered as their private property should be distributed to their opponents. But the tories were more concerned for fundamental than for immediate interests. They held a consistent and fully developed view of the economic and political future of Canada as a dependent unit within the second British Empire; and to them this whole conception was endangered by the political changes of 1842.

In particular, the tories objected to two things: to the inclusion of French Canadians in the ministry and to the doctrine of responsible government as they and Robert Baldwin interpreted it. It was to swamp the French and to make Canada a British province that Lord Durham had advocated the union of the provinces. It was for these salutary purposes, in the opinion of the tories, that union had been carried through. They apparently expected that the French Canadians would be left severely alone in the ignominy of social ostracism and political isolation, until they had learnt to abandon their absurd national pretensions and to accept in full the superior culture of the British. The fact that this process would probably require the time of generations seemed entirely equitable to the tories and left them cheerful and undismayed. "Every man . . .", declared one editor, "—outside the walls of a Lunatic Asylum or an Executive Council Chamber—was aware that it must be a futile attempt to expect the British population to forget, however willing they might be to forgive, the strife and bloodshed of 1837–8."[4] They looked upon the elevation of the French to office—at the invitation of a British governor-general—as something unnatural and revolting. "It was as great a shock to the loyal Canadians as the elevation of a Golden Calf or a Chinese Idol-Deformity would be in the eyes of a Christian People, with the addition of the spectacle of their High Priest and Monarch calling loudly on them to fall down and worship."[5]

There was more in all this than a natural revulsion to the rule of men who at least in sympathy had been rebels. The resurrection of the French Canadians, within two years of their official interment in the union, was a profoundly shocking event. The tories saw before them the frightful spectre of French domination, which they thought had been exorcized for ever. They envisaged the old sullen obstruction to commercial improvement and the obscurantist defence of antiquated law and custom. These Canadians were not modern Frenchmen; they were the almost unaltered survivors of the "priest-ridden and Lord-ridden" France of the past; and they "would neither reform themselves, nor permit those around them to exercise this privilege".[6] In the days before the rebellion they had used their obstructive power to the "embroilment of the whole country, the strangulation of public prosperity, and the paralysis of enterprise and improvement". Their return to office endangered the whole programme of anglification and reform which the Durham report and the union had promised. Already the judicature ordinance, which had been passed by the special council in Quebec for the reform of the Lower-Canadian legal system, had been suspended. "Every post from Kingston", declared the *Montreal Gazette*, "confirms the fact that the British party has been deliberately handed over to the vindictive disposition of a French mob, whose first efforts are directed to the abrogation of those laws which protect property and promote improvement, and render existence in this Colony desirable."[7]

The tories, however, objected not only to the admission of the French Canadians to office, but also to the political doctrine which they and Robert Baldwin professed. The term "responsible government", as it was defined and legitimized by Lord John Russell and Lord Sydenham, was gradually accepted by the reluctant tories; but they maintained as fiercely as ever that the new doctrine according to the reformers was objectionable in any country and completely inadmissible in a colony like Canada. In their view, the governor must be the controlling force of an administration whose members should be distinguished for their moderation and efficiency rather than for their party zeal. Responsible government, as the reformers defined it, would limit the superintendence of the governor and the imperial authorities, which had always been the wise practice of the British Empire. It would upset the equilibrium between the three branches of the legislature, which had been the boast of the English constitution. It would encourage, as a virtue, that party warfare which had distracted the Canadas and impeded their development. Stable government, under the operation of such a system, would be subjected to all the influences of widespread corruption and all the senseless shifts and changes of public opinion. Political authority would be "bandied and kicked about like a shuttle-cock, the prize to the stoutest parliamentary bully, or the most successful political swindler";[8] and an almost despotic power would fall into the hands of "any demagogue who may possess the vulgar art to head the House of Assembly, and the vigour to drive the cattle now harnessed, in the ricketty Omnibus of Responsible Government". The system which the reformers demanded would encourage the low ambition of upstarts for place, profit and patronage. It would take from public servants their security and drive them into an unending, corrupt campaign for the retention of their jobs. "We write without reference to party", declared one editor. "We care not what political sect may work this rotary machine. We reprobate and denounce the machine itself."[9]

Despite all the rant of the tories, the reforming ministers remained in office. But Sir Charles Bagot, who had effected the reconciliation of the French, died shortly after, a victim to that strange fatality which carried off three governors in succession during the 1840's. His successor was Sir Charles Metcalfe, a man who differed from both Sydenham and Bagot as much as they had differed from each other. Metcalfe was that typical production of the English governing class, the civil servant of the empire, the capable and authoritarian administrator of remote lands and strange races. He had spent a lifetime of service in India; he had handled capably a difficult situation in Jamaica. The instinct for authority, the stiff code of honour, the dogmatic simplicity of views which were characteristic of Metcalfe's class and profession were exaggerated by the governor's more personal qualities, his reserve, his uncompromising bluntness, his obvious incapacity for accommodation and compromise. He was a solitary figure in Canadian politics, grim, sombre, stoically unyielding; but for all the disaster

of his governorship and the turmoil which he helped to cause in
Canada, there was nothing sinister or unusual in the doctrine which
he held. He came to Canada, not to break responsible government,
but to work it in the only way in which it could be worked within
the limitations of the old empire. His views were the typical, the
normal, tory views, expressed on both sides of the Atlantic, by
British statesmen and Canadian publicists, in dispatches, speeches
and editorials. He interpreted the imperial connection as the
relationship of parent and child. He saw in the governorship an
institution through which the regulating control of the empire
could be used to improve the administration and moderate the
party passions of the province.

This had been the tory conception of how the union should be
worked. It had been put in practice by Lord Sydenham; it had
been maintained with difficulty by Sir Charles Bagot. But, under
Metcalfe, the old system of colonial administration was brought
once more into violent conflict with the doctrine of party government. In the autumn of 1843, the governor and his reforming
ministers quarrelled over a question which was almost entirely
unconnected with any of the serious social or political problems of
the colony.[10] In the various explanations and glosses which were
put upon the dispute after the event, Baldwin and Lafontaine
insisted that responsible government was in danger, while Metcalfe
maintained that the imperial authority was in jeopardy. In fact,
the quarrel was concerned with the distribution of the patronage
of the crown. The ministers demanded that no appointments to
office should be made without their consent and without due
attention to the needs of their party. The governor insisted that
appointments could only be made on his own responsibility, with a
view to efficient administration and with some effort at impartiality. The reformers had taken their stand upon what might well
appear to be one of the most odious corollaries of responsible
government. The governor had defended what many men would
regard as one of the most unassumingly legitimate exercises of the
gubernatorial authority.

The councillors, with the exception of Dominick Daly, resigned
in a body; and Metcalfe was left alone, tortured by the cancer which
was eating away his eyesight and his life, and oppressed by the

solemn duty of defending the British connection in Canada. He gathered about him a nondescript group of new councillors, trying, even in his extremity, to keep to his doctrine of non-partisan administration; and, since the governor had taken a stand, the tories and reformers returned to battle, using all their resources of vituperation, corruption and violence, to compass each other's defeat. The by-election in Montreal, which was contested by the tory Molson and the reformer Drummond in the spring of 1844, struck the strident and angry note which pervaded the subsequent general election. The reformers persuaded the Irish labourers on the Lachine canal to make common cause with the French. The canallers downed tools on April 16, marched to Montreal in hundreds, occupied the polling places in huge detachments, and intimidated and attacked all Molson supporters.[11] Molson resigned under protest. The military was called out; a French Canadian died of bayonet wounds; and this unfair and brutal contest was the prelude to a furious political campaign which culminated in the general election of that autumn. It was a repetition of the pre-rebellion electoral contests. It had all their violence. It pointed ominously to a re-enactment of their conclusion; and the tories urged every loyalist to defend the queen's government and the British connection. "*Indeed it would be difficult to imagine any occasion, short of invasion by an armed enemy,*" declared the *Montreal Gazette*, "*in which the services of all true patriots could be more peremptorily required.*"[12]

The issue upon which the reformers had taken their stand and the violence with which they tried to sustain it, drove many moderate, practical, peace-loving men into the company of the tories for the defence of the governor. Egerton Ryerson, the Methodist leader, who had broken with the extreme radicals in 1833 and who had done so much to quiet the Methodist farming community during the rebellions, was now impelled to re-enter political controversy; and his pamphlet, *Sir Charles Metcalfe Defended against the Attacks of his Late Counsellors*, was the most weighty and influential statement of the moderate point of view. The reformers themselves had written down responsible government in terms as low as any tory had ever imagined. For the benefit of the entire province, they had publicly defined their sacred doctrine as a

Canadian variant of the spoils system of the United States. They
had, in the biblical language of Ryerson, enshrined the new idol of
party patronage and party policy as the presiding deity of responsible government. "And this apple of discord—this premium for
partizanship . . . this system of political and moral corruption,
. . . is dignified as *the essence of responsible government;* and all
who do not fall down and worship this golden image of party
idolatry, are to be cast into the furnace of party proscription
and execration, heated seven times hotter than it was wont in
former days!"[13] It was in order to safeguard their party interests
as selfishly as the family compact had ever done, that the reformers
were prepared to resist the governor and to defy in his person the
prerogative of the crown and the moderating control of the colonial
office. The wise superintendence of the empire was to be flouted,
in order that some needy reformer might become clerk of the
peace in the Dalhousie district.

This was the reformers' interpretation of responsible government,
according to excited tories and indignant moderates. Against it
they placed their own version, based, so they claimed, on the
resolutions of 1841, the dispatches of the colonial secretaries and
the practice of Sydenham. Responsible government, they argued,
was desirable within the limits prescribed by the old colonial
system; and these limitations were wise and necessary, not merely
for the preservation of the imperial tie, but also for the moderation
of factional hatreds in Canada. In their view, the governor was an
umpire, an arbiter, a "generous rewarder of MERIT, no matter
what may be the fashion of its political motley. . . ".[14] The
imperial authority was a court to which right might appeal against
might; and this, far from being a disadvantage of the colonial
position, was actually its greatest merit. It enabled Canadians to
have what the constitution purported to give them, "a Government
so balanced that no party can be oppressed".[15] It encouraged
colonial politicians to lay their heads together, to reconcile clashing
interests, to give and to take. To the tories Canada was virtually
meaningless apart from the imperial connection; and they still
looked to Great Britain for protection, assistance and advice. They
refused to reduce the governor—the representative of imperial
authority—to a mere "machine for signing papers", to "the

degrading position of President of a partizan Council". They declined to accept without qualification a political principle which by the interpretation of its most earnest advocates appeared to revive those party hatreds which had distracted the province and plunged it into civil war.

The election of 1844, which the tories won under the leadership of Sir Charles Metcalfe, was the last victory in Canada for the old system of colonial government. It had been put once more upon the defensive, as it had been before the rebellions; and although the grimly serious Metcalfe had won, for somewhat the same reasons as the operatic Head, it was a difficult victory, achieved only after considerable strain. The forces which had made Canada a North American community instead of an imperial trading system were driving home, by new and more effective methods, the doctrine of local autonomy at the expense of imperial integration. The second British Empire could have been saved only by steady and determined resistance. And resistance was not to be expected from imperial statesmen who were now oppressed by the financial and commercial burdens of empire and irresistibly attracted by the promises of British industrialism and world trade.

II

In fact, the two years which followed the general election of 1844 witnessed the final downfall of a commercial system which for decades now had continued in a state of chronic insecurity. The doctrine of colonial autonomy had been defeated, though with difficulty, in Canada; but nothing the Canadians could do could forestall the British declaration of economic independence. That declaration was precipitated by a crisis in the imperial food supply and it was followed by a profound commercial depression. It was coincident, moreover, with the American drawback acts, by which the United States laid a claim to the trade of Canada West which Montreal had always regarded as its monopoly. And thus, in the years 1845–1846, the St. Lawrence commercial system was losing both its protected markets and its last uncontested sources of supply.

In 1845, the United States passed a drawback law, which

remitted the duties on its own imports from foreign countries when they were re-exported to Canada. In 1846, by an extension of the same principle, a second statute removed the duties on produce imported from Canada which was destined for exportation outside of the United States.[16] Back in 1835 and 1836 Mackenzie and others who were hostile to the northern trading system had agitated for the free importation and exportation of Upper Canadian goods *via* the New York route; and now the Americans, apprehensive of the imminent completion of the St. Lawrence canals, had spontaneously granted the boon for which the radicals had petitioned Great Britain to negotiate. Under the existing conditions of trade on the Great Lakes, the drawback laws were indeed a formidable attack on the St. Lawrence trading system. The British navigation laws had been inoperative on the inland waters of Canada; and by the interpretation which had been given by the authorities to clause 31 of the imperial statute 3 & 4 William IV, cap. 59, it was permissible for the Americans to import foreign as well as their own produce into Canada by their own vessels and carriages. Thus, by practice which had already become established, the Americans were competing for the carrying-trade to and from Canada on the Great Lakes. Now, by virtue of their own drawback acts, they were enabled to contend with Montreal for the carrying-trade between western Canada and the ocean. The drawback acts, together with the existing shipping regulations, provided an all-American trade route from the Canadian settlements to the sea.

In Canada, opinion on the new American drawback acts was divided, as Metcalfe found when he tried to discover the attitude of the Canadians.[17] The Montreal merchants and the forwarders predicted the most disastrous consequences to the carrying-trade of the St. Lawrence;[18] but the Toronto board of trade rejoiced that it now had a longer season for import and export and a chance to beat down high freight rates on the St. Lawrence.[19] Imports of refined sugar at Montreal dropped from 1,610,659 pounds in 1844 to 895,046 pounds in 1846; and imports of tea, in the same period, declined from 937,105 pounds to 603,038 pounds.[20] In the meantime, these and other commodities were coming in from the United States in rapidly increasing quantities; and whereas, in the past, the American tariff had discouraged the inland export of Canadian bread-stuffs, the drawback laws, by the year 1848, permitted Canada to export 277,031 barrels of flour and 297,011 bushels of wheat by the Erie route. It was perhaps impossible to check this; it was difficult even to devise expedients in the divided state of public opinion; and since the assembly and council had already petitioned for the repeal of clause 31 of 3 & 4 William IV, cap. 59 in an effort to protect the Canadian shipping interest, the government fell back upon the idea that some of the northern carrying-trade might be saved by a belated application of the navigation laws to the Great Lakes trade.[21] It was a curious example—on the very eve of the destruction of the old colonial system—of how tenaciously commercial Canada clung to the old expedients of empire, to the preferences and shipping regulations of the past.

At that very moment the most important of those preferences was exposed to the vagaries of the English weather and the changing convictions of a statesman's mind. Sir Robert Peel, the son of a cotton-spinner, the alien whom the great land-owning tory party had entrusted with its leadership, had realized with increasing clarity the changes which the industrial revolution had wrought in England. He had begun the wholesale reduction of the tariff in the great reform budget of 1842. He had been reluctantly converted by Cobden and the Anti-Corn Law Leaguers, those middle-class enthusiasts who saw the iniquities of agricultural protection in a revelation so blinding that it obscured the manifold abuses of their own cotton factories. By 1846 Peel was searching the barometer for the sign from heaven which would save or doom the corn laws; and the persistent, the implacable rains of that summer beat down the half-ripened wheat in England and completed the destruction of the rotted Irish potato crop. Peel was converted to the idea of immediate suspension and ultimate repeal. But the cabinet was divided and uncertain. Peel resigned; and it was only when Lord John Russell had refused to form a ministry that he returned to office, tense, nervously excited, fired with unalterable resolution. He would save the nation, even if it meant the ruin of his party. He would be the minister of the people if he could not be the leader of the tories.[22]

While this news arrived, in tantalizing, fragmentary instalments across the Atlantic, the Canadian commercial class waited in an agony of apprehension. The very names of the packet boats which carried this portentous information became known from one end of Canada to the other. "We do not believe", declared the *Patriot*, "that since Canada became a Province of the British Empire the arrival of any vessel from Europe was ever looked for with half the anxiety as that of the *Hibernia*."[23] The *Hibernia* brought the news that Peel was back again in office; and in January, 1846, when the imperial parliament met for its tumultuous session, the prime minister announced that he proposed to reduce the corn duties immediately and sharply and that he intended to abolish them, almost in their entirety, within three years. It was the black year of the Canadian commercial system, the year in which the American congress opened the republic to the free transit of Canadian produce destined for exportation abroad. The most ambitious advance of the United States and the final withdrawal of Great Britain had come together in a disastrous coincidence. The British had robbed the St. Lawrence of what was supposedly its greatest attraction at the very moment when the Americans had opened wide the Erie route to the produce of the Canadian commercial state.

These fiscal and commercial changes were followed by a profound depression; and through its gloom they assumed the aspect of fearful and abominable shapes. Canada, a staple-producing economy, tied to Great Britain and the United States, was subjected to the economic ills of both the old world and the new. On the one hand was the cycle of scarcity and over-production in Canada; and on the other were the calamitous ups and downs of prices in the United Kingdom and the United States. In the years 1845–1848 these circumstances combined to bring on a commercial depression which outweighed in gravity the shorter, sharper panic of 1836–1837. During 1842–1844, while the bounteous harvests in England had lowered prices in the home market, the exports from Canada of wheat and flour continued nevertheless to increase; and the timber trade, encouraged by rising British prices, expanded enormously during 1843–1845 to meet the needs of building and railway construction in Great Britain. In 1846, however, the glut in timber forced down prices. And in 1847 they were driven still lower by the dead weight of the unsaleable stocks in Canada and the declining demand in England.

In the meantime, while the timber trade was already in the throes of a collapse, the merchants in wheat and flour were responding all too eagerly to the speculative chances of the crisis in England. Peel's drastic modification of the corn laws could not lessen the attractions of a market where famine alternated with scarcity. Prices for bread-stuffs rose sharply and freights out of Quebec and Montreal were at a premium. The exports of wheat increased from 396,252 bushels in 1845 to 534,747 bushels in 1846; and during the same two years flour exports rose from 442,228 to 555,602 barrels.[24] For the first few months of 1847 prices were maintained. Then they fell suddenly in England, with the dead weight of a stone; and before the end of the year both the wheat trade and the timber trade of Canada were involved in a general depression which came to lie over the whole British and North American world.[25]

The slump, which continued until 1850, was just as severe and almost as complicated by concurrent misfortunes as the depression of 1836-1837 had been. Exports of wheat declined from 628,001 bushels in 1847 to 238,051 bushels in 1848; exports of flour fell off from 651,030 to 383,593 barrels; and imports for 1848 were valued at £2,107,264, which was a decrease of nearly a million from the estimated total of 1846.[26] By 1849, according to Governor Elgin's exaggerated statement, three-fourths of the commercial men were bankrupt; property in the principal Canadian towns had fallen nearly fifty per cent. in value. And, just as in 1836–1837, the commercial depression was accompanied by a crisis in provincial finance. By the end of 1846 the canals were uncompleted and the estimates had once more been shoved upwards; but the province was drawing the last of the £1,500,000 loan, and Grey, the new whig colonial secretary, refused to extend the imperial guarantee to fresh Canadian financing.[27] During 1847–1848, while the depression embarrassed the banks and reduced the provincial revenue, Canada found it difficult to negotiate its debentures at home; and although Cayley, the tory inspector-general, had gone to England in the summer of 1846 in the hope of obtaining further funds, he had found that the disfavour of Baring Brothers and the general discredit of the province made the floating of a new loan virtually impossible.[28] Canada did manage to secure some advances from the Bank of England; but it was certain that it would have to depend more upon its own resources for a time at least. Finally, in the midst of the depression and the financial stringency, came the notorious migration of the diseased and starving peasants from Ireland.

The famine in Ireland, which had precipitated the repeal of the corn laws, brought another calamity to Canada in the immigration of 1847. In that year the migrants flung themselves from Ireland as if from a burning house or a sinking vessel. They entered Canadian ports, to the number of nearly 100,000, a poverty-stricken, diseased and demoralized army. Over 30,000 were supposed to have been kept in the quarantine stations at Grosse Isle and at the various hospitals in the country. About 10,000 of them died there.[29] And while the diseased turned the hospitals into lazarettos, their children and orphans swelled the mass of the helpless and indigent for whom food, shelter and transportation had to be provided. The migration of 1847 produced a panic in Canada. It cost the provincial administration over £150,000, and it brought disease and death to the Canadian inhabitants.[30] It seemed as if Great Britain were willing to save herself from disaster, at any price to the empire. To parry the effects of famine and starvation she was willing to dump her diseased and destitute children upon the very colony which she had just robbed of its chief imperial advantage. Everything conspired, in these years of commercial depression and financial stringency, to exaggerate the iniquity of Great Britain; and it was only natural that the Canadians, with the concentration of fury, should fix upon the repeal of the corn laws as the grand cause of their misfortunes.

III

Though the economic effects of the repeal of the corn laws are still debated, there can be no doubt about its moral and political results. It began a series of changes which may be regarded as the second American revolution or as the long-delayed last chapter of the first. It contaminated the Canadians with that spiritual death of empire which had become chronic in England; and it unsettled a system which was too closely integrated for partial survival. The second British Empire was a great, complex, historical creation. It was an integration of law and custom which was supported by interests which were roughly complementary and sentiments which had much in common. It was made up of controls and devices, economic as well as political, which were designed to advance the prosperity and the power of the colonies and the mother country. Its purpose and, indeed, its partial accomplishment, was the reconciliation of interests, the just apportionment of burdens and the equalization of returns. But the faith which was necessary to give this system its vitality had long been declining, in England, into indifference, scepticism and an irked feeling of responsibility;[31] and in Canada, it ended, with the repeal of the corn laws, in a burst of resentful disillusionment. The second British Empire was left a brittle and ramshackle structure; and the very complexity of its ramifications involved the ruin of the whole in the destruction of one of its parts.

When Great Britain had renounced imperial preferences for the sake of world trade and when Canada had protested against imperial control in the interest of provincial autonomy, that delicate, critical balance, which had survived even the ruin of the first empire, was ended for ever. To contemporaries, who could best appreciate the interlocking mechanism of the old system, the action of Great Britain implied the almost inevitable break-up of the empire; and they felt the old ties loosen around them with both regret and a kind of bitter impatience to be free. In the opinion of the Montreal board of trade, the change effected by Great Britain was equivalent to the subversion "of an entire system of Government. . . ".[32] It was impossible, wrote one correspondent, to regard "the present condition of this Province, without serious apprehensions of changes, which may not only affect our commercial, but our political relations also. . . ".[33] With an almost indecent haste, both parties hastened to exchange old connections for new and to get rid of burdens which were now uncompensated by advantages. Great Britain looked beyond the restricted commerce of her colonies to the commercial dominion of the world; and Canada turned first to reciprocity and then to annexation, which were the two expressions, economic and political, of her instinctive recoil upon the United States.

To meet the crisis which seemed about to fall upon it, the province tried in desperation to realize its best advantages and to jettison its heaviest burdens. The government turned feverishly to complete the canals in the hope that while the diminished protective system still lasted in England, Canada could establish the superiority of the St. Lawrence route. There was no abandonment of the St. Lawrence; but, at the same time, the Canadians engaged as readily as the English in the reorganization of the structure which had been built up to support the northern commercial system. It was apparent in matters of finance, as well as in affairs of trade and politics, that the "parent state" and the "faithful colony" were gradually assuming that distant, calculating attitude appropriate to foreign powers. Though in 1850 the inspector-general Hincks managed, through Baring Brothers, to float a loan of £500,000 in England, it was not supported by an imperial guarantee; and during the depression, when Canadian finances were in great disorder, the financial relations between the mother country and the colony were seriously strained. On the one hand, the officials of the Bank of England alleged that Canada was occasionally negligent in paying the interest on its loans; and, on the other, Canadians grew angry over the ignorant depreciation of colonial debentures in England. The province repudiated the charges for the famine migration of 1847; and, at the same time, the imperial authorities were anxious to be rid of the burden of protecting the colonies.[34] "I confess", wrote the colonial secretary Grey to Elgin, "I think that now the Canadians have self Govnt so completely granted to them they ought also to pay all its expenses including military protection. . . ."[35] It was in February, 1848, within a month of the date of Grey's letter, that the inspector-general of Canada declared that the immigration expenditure "as a legitimate charge upon the revenues of the Province incidental to its position as a colony . . . has been distinctly repudiated by the Colonial Legislature".[36]

There were, however, other and more direct Canadian replies to Great Britain's proclamation of her new economic policy. The repeal of the duties on corn encouraged the colonists to tariff

changes, if not to tariff reprisals; and the new British Possessions
Act of 1846, which granted the colonies a considerable degree of
fiscal autonomy, enabled Canadians to proceed with their plans.
The Montreal board of trade, prompted as much by its bitter sense
of injury as by its appreciation of commercial realities, proposed
that in face of the new state of empire trade, Canada should repeal
the duty on American wheat and abolish the preferences on
British goods entering Canada.[37] The duty on American wheat,
which was part of the compact by which Canadian bread-stuffs
gained virtually free entry into the British market, was meaningless
without the corn laws; and the retention of the imperial preference
in Canada seemed clearly inequitable when it had been withdrawn
in England. Under the old balanced system, the advantages which
Canada gave to England were compensated by the advantages
which England accorded to Canada; but, argued the board of
trade, the Canadian differential duties were "at variance, under
present circumstances, not only with sound commercial principles,
but also with justice and abstract right".

Both parties and both sections of the province could agree
upon a low tariff for revenue purposes only. It was true that the
commercial class explored all possible fiscal avenues of escape
with the baffled, restless persistence of a caged beast. There were
free-traders and rabid protectionists in Montreal—symptoms, as
Elgin said, of the "generally uneasy and diseased condition of the
public mind which commercial depression has engendered".[38]
But in the matter of the tariff, as in so many other questions, the
two parties were in virtual agreement; and even the old conflict
between the claims of the transit trade and the demand for agricultural protection did not become a real issue in this period. In
1846, in anticipation of the final passing of Peel's corn law bill,
the Canadian legislature repealed the three-shilling duty on all
imported American wheat which was to be re-exported in its
natural state or milled in Canada for shipment abroad. In the
very next year, the tory administration, through its spokesman
the tory inspector-general Cayley, proposed and carried through
"a modified and uniform tariff for the purposes of revenue" which
reduced the duties on American manufactures and increased those
on British to a uniform level of about 7½ per cent. *ad valorem*[39].

The tories in Canada, instructed by the tories in Great Britain, had acted out of consideration for their own country, without reference to the empire as a whole. The repeal of the Canadian preferential tariff was, in its own way, just as decisive and significant as the repeal of the corn laws; and under these blows the old imperial fiscal system ceased to exist. "There was", wrote Elgin, with one of his few backward glances, "something captivating in the project of forming all the parts of this vast British Empire into one huge Zollverein with free interchange of commodities between its members, and uniform duties against the World without."[40] But the "zollverein" had vanished now; and all that remained were the vague regrets and longings of the commercial class for a system which, in a spasm of resentment and irritation, it had itself helped to destroy.

Amid the general wreck, both political and economic, of the second empire, one of the most venerable and fundamental parts of the structure still remained. The navigation laws dated from the Commonwealth and the Restoration, from the heroic period of the Dutch Wars; and the purpose which lay behind them had developed long ago, far back in the days when the first Tudors had begun to build the British navy and Englishmen had commenced to fight for the carrying-trade against the Venetians and the Hanseatic League. These ancient statutes had kept the allegiance of commercial Canada and continued to govern much of its activity. The liberal modifications of Robinson, Huskisson and their followers had, in the main, merely legitimized the breakdown of the navigation laws on the Great Lakes. The great bulk of the Canadian trade passed down the St. Lawrence and across the ocean to Great Britain; but the through journey down the St. Lawrence was closed to American vessels by decision of authority and the navigation laws still enjoined that the trade between Canada and England had to be carried on in British ships.

This monopoly, which was shared by both British and colonial shipping, had been accepted by Canadians, not merely for its intrinsic benefits, but also for the greater commercial advantages with which it was traditionally associated. But the repeal of imperial preference left the navigation laws exposed in a kind of meaningless isolation. And the rough adjustment of one part of a colonial system so complex and delicate in its organization, brought about, with a kind of fatal inevitability, the ruin of the whole. In one of the first reports which it prepared as a result of the "new commercial policy of England", the Montreal board of trade proposed that the navigation laws should be repealed and that the St. Lawrence should be thrown open to American shipping. There were cities like Quebec and Hamilton, which opposed repeal for a time, and there were always tories who remained dubious of its results. But, in the main, reformers agreed with conservatives, and Canada East was at one with Canada West, in an almost unanimous and an increasingly imperative demand for the abolition of the British shipping regulations.[41]

The Canadian case for repeal, like most of Canadian argumentation during this period of distress and imperial disintegration, was a mixture of commercial reasoning and emotional appeals to logic and justice. Transport from the west was cheaper to Montreal than to New York; but on the ocean all the old disabilities of the Canadian route increased its heavy charges. The Montreal board of trade and the Baldwin-Lafontaine government agreed that the yearly average freight on a barrel of flour between Montreal and Liverpool had varied between 4s. 6d. in 1844 and 5s. 1½d. in 1846, and that this rate was from 2 to 3 shillings more expensive than that from New York to Liverpool.[42] If the St. Lawrence was to be left a mere competitive route by the removal of imperial preferences, its attraction would depend entirely upon its cheapness; and the main argument for the repeal of the navigation laws and for the opening of the St. Lawrence to American shipping, was that it would reduce costs on the northern carrying route. The Canadian commercial system, the Canadian canals and the Canadian debt were so closely connected that they were almost indistinguishable, and the prosperity of the St. Lawrence system was simply another way of writing the solvency of the provincial government. The Canadians had now the best of reasons, commercial, political and financial, for making their route as cheap as possible. But, in addition, they emphasized their moral right to escape from burdens which were no longer balanced by privileges, and to extricate themselves from an entangling system, whose harmonious working had been stopped by Great Britain itself.

The repeal of the navigation laws in 1849, while it did not have the commercial results which the Canadians had hoped for, completed the destruction of the old mercantile system of the empire. Canada had helped Great Britain in the work of demolition; and it was almost as if she recoiled in disgust and contempt from the system she had once cherished. Inevitably her flight from the mother country was in the direction of the United States. In 1848, the Montreal board of trade had predicted that Canada and the United States would discover that their interests "under the changed policy of the Imperial Government are germane to each other, and under that system must sooner or later be politically interwoven".[43] But at first this instinctive gravitation towards the American republic, this immediate search of a weak dependency for a new empire, was expressed rather in the request for free trade relations than in the demand for political union. In the years which followed 1846 there arose an agitation of increasing intensity for reciprocal free trade between the British North American provinces and the United States in the natural products of both.[44] In Canada, which took the lead in the campaign, the scheme was first proposed in an address passed by the tory legislature in 1846. But, in general, reciprocity was more popular in Canada West than in Canada East; and it was not until the Baldwin-Lafontaine administration was returned to power in 1848, that the provincial government took the matter up seriously. Francis Hincks, the new inspector-general in whom Elgin placed such confidence, was in favour of reciprocity; and its greatest advocate was W. H. Merritt, who became president of the council from 1848 to 1850.

Merritt, who had voted with the tories in the days before the union, had been the promoter of the Welland canal and one of the great enthusiasts for the St. Lawrence trading system. In his mind, and doubtless in the minds of many others, reciprocity was intended to divert the wheat and flour of the western states into the St. Lawrence during the summer months. But though in this respect it could be reconciled with the historic commercial policy of the St. Lawrence, reciprocity was expected by its advocates to do other things besides increasing the exports of Montreal. It was expected to raise the price of the produce of the farmers and millers of Canada West by giving them another market within the

United States;[45] and Francis Hincks asserted that, as a result of England's free-trade policy, the Atlantic states would "frequently be the best market for the Agricultural products of Canada".[46] It was hoped, moreover, that reciprocity would give a more legitimate expression to that unworthy passion for annexation to the American republic; and it was this last argument which Lord Elgin pressed upon the imperial authorities in a series of letters and dispatches of great force, persuasiveness and eloquence. But the bills which were introduced into the American congress for the free admission of Canadian natural produce failed to pass; and despite the efforts of British and Canadian authorities, there was no immediate prospect of a reciprocity treaty. Canada had been disowned commercially by Great Britain and repulsed commercially by the United States. But there was one last, desperate remedy left; and Canadians were led on into a campaign for annexation, into the very agitation which reciprocity was designed to forestall.

IV

The movement for annexation to the United States was the appropriate conclusion of all the distresses, disappointments and resentments of these years. It was the last gesture of revulsion from a system which had been broken in pieces and a plan which had failed. Up to the very end the conservative merchants of Canada had accepted the economic limitations of the empire. Up to the very end they had defended the empire's regulating control. But when Great Britain had destroyed its old commercial system and had renounced its old political supervision, the tories recoiled from the unnatural mother country with a violence which simply revealed the extent of their dependence and the depth of their loyalty. To them the empire had been emptied of its value and their allegiance of its meaning. They capped the movement for commercial reciprocity with an agitation for political union. And the annexation manifesto proclaimed the spiritual death of the second empire in Canada.

The grant of responsible government, which ended the old practice of imperial governance, came, appropriately enough, in the midst of those releases, disavowals and renunciations by which the mercantile system was ended. The downfall of mercantilism and the grant of responsible government do not, of course, stand in the simple relation of cause and effect; but their coincidence in time reveals a deep relationship which the very organization of the old empire had established. The empire was a system, an integration of interdependent parts which had been welded together by generations of use and acceptance; and, just as the declaration of free trade in Great Britain was followed by the collapse of the entire mercantile system, so the break in the commercial connection was accompanied by the loosening of the political tie. Born in an atmosphere of indifference and discouragement, preceded and accompanied by other equally revolutionary changes, the grant of responsible government loses significance as a separate political achievement, while it gains in importance as an element in a more general upheaval. In 1775, when Great Britain was ready to fight for her colonies, responsible government would have been constructive statesmanship; but in 1848, when the mother country was prepared to anticipate the dissolution of her empire with equanimity if not with enthusiasm, the grant had a little too much the appearance of a benevolent formality.

The change came in the winter of 1848. The collapse of the tory party under Sir Robert Peel had brought the whigs back to power in England and the liberal Earl Grey to the colonial office. The new policy for the colonies had already been communicated to the lieutenant-governor of Nova Scotia; and when Lord Elgin arrived in Canada in 1847 he was determined and expected to accept without fear or favour whatever administration possessed the confidence of the assembly and the people. The new governor was a Scot who, like Sir Charles Metcalfe, had had experience in Jamaica. His was a vigorous and sanguine temperament; and he combined lively convictions with shrewd practicality and hard common sense. No Canadian governor, with the possible exception of Lord Durham, has received from posterity such unqualified approval; but—at the same time—no governor has ever been the object of more contemporary hatred and abuse. In fact, Lord Elgin, in a fashion somewhat like that of Lord Durham, occupies a dual position in Canadian history. He helped by his energy and enthusiasm to build up the new British Empire; but he also assisted by his well-meaning inertia in the destruction of the old. The uncertain tory majority and the ricketty tory administration which he found on his arrival in Canada were defeated in the general election of December, 1847. The tory ministers resigned in the first days of the new parliament; and Elgin automatically called on Lafontaine and Baldwin to form a government.

Thus was responsible government formally conceded. Whatever its ultimate benefits, its immediate effect was to precipitate a fresh outbreak of that violence which had disturbed the province for so long; and the explanation of this must be sought in the way in which contemporaries interpreted the events of the next two years. It was not their defeat in the winter election of 1847–1848 which drove the tories into action; and, once their downfall at the polls was incontestable, they looked forward with a kind of grumbling aversion to the inevitable formation of a reform ministry. There was nothing in their doctrine of colonial government which called, at this moment, for any really violent action. They admitted responsible government up to the limits of the colonial relation. They accepted the authority of provincial ministers in so far as it did not conflict with the power of the governor, who was at once a sovereign and a local minister, with high and peculiar functions for the preservation of British interests and the moderation of colonial partisanship. It was only when Lord Elgin had apparently abandoned these functions and had identified himself as much as Head or Metcalfe had ever done with the party in power, that the tories broke from him in indignation. Given the measures and the composition of the Baldwin-Lafontaine ministry, it was inevitable that they should have done so.

It was not the reforms of the new "reform" ministry which outraged the tories. According to radical contemporaries and to the legend of Canadian history, the coalition of 1848 was a real party of reform. But Lord Elgin agreed with the tories and the clear grits in refusing to take this highly complimentary label at its face value. "What", asked the *Montreal Gazette* of Robert Baldwin, "were the great questions upon which he quarrelled with the successive Governors of Canada? . . . It was all patronage. It was a quarrel about some petty office. Where was the great principle at stake?"[47] In this unpleasant caricature of Baldwin's political career, there was at least a modicum of truth; and it would be difficult to discover any number of great reforming measures with which the reform party was associated at this time in the public consciousness of Canada. The radicals were, of course, united in support in the extreme interpretation of the doctrine of responsible government; but responsible government was a method, not a measure; and the method was, so Elgin believed, the main bond of union between the eastern and western radicals. The French Canadians were not "reformers" as the word was understood then or since; they were bureaucrats in character and ministerialists in intention. The efforts, which Draper and Sherwood had made to induce them to enter the tory ministry, failed, not because they had an unalterable objection to holding office with conservatives, but because they were not permitted to enter on those terms of equality which their sense of a distinct culture and nationality required. "You will observe", wrote Elgin, "that no question of principle or of public policy has been mooted by either party during this negotiation. . . . The whole discussion has turned upon personal considerations. . . . It is not even pretended that the divisions of Party represent corresponding divisions of sentiment on questions which occupy the public mind. . . ."[48]

It was not positive reforms which the tories dreaded, but the old alien obstruction of the past. They pierced beneath the reformism of the reform party and discovered—or thought they discovered —the domination of the French. It was the genius of the reformers that they first accepted the duality of Canadian life. But the tories, though their leaders had been occasionally driven by expediency to approach the French Canadians, still held to the old view, which had been written into Lord Durham's report and put into practice by Lord Sydenham, that Canada was a British province, governed by British institutions and open to British capital and enterprise. The defeat of the rebellions had meant, in the opinion of the tories, the triumph of these ideas; and the union had been designed to convert them into actuality. But in fact, of course, one whole part of the tory programme of anglification, reform and material progress had completely miscarried. The union had never been really organic—perhaps not even Lord

Sydenham could have made it so; and though the French Canadians had given way to many national projects, their institutions and customs had been jealously guarded from profane reforms. The consciousness of this failure, of this defeat of the whole idea of the unitary commercial state, was growing slowly in the 1840's, eating its way into the minds of men already embittered by repeated frustrations and disillusionments. It was an almost unbearable realization. And if the French Canadians flaunted their successful immunity, if, by some significant action, they proclaimed their silent victory over the conquerors of 1837, then the tories might very easily be provoked to a sudden outburst of violence.

This was what happened in 1849. The bulk of the legislation introduced by the Baldwin-Lafontaine administration was sober and unprovocative. In its tariff policy, in its commercial measures, in its plans for the extension of local government, the reform ministry proceeded on lines which the tories had already laid down or with which they were unlikely to disagree; and the one seriously contentious measure in this almost unexceptionable programme was the Rebellion Losses Bill. The whole question of the indemnity awarded in Canada for losses sustained during the rebellions and invasions of 1837–1838 has never been subjected to a detailed and critical investigation; and it is dangerous to hazard generalizations on the wisdom or the equity of the act of 1849, which was passed to compensate the sufferers in the old province of Lower Canada. The view of radical contemporaries, which has become the accepted theory of Canadian history, was that the tory opposition to the bill was unreasoning and completely unjustified. There is a good deal of evidence in favour of this contention. Compensation had already been awarded for losses sustained in Upper Canada during the rebellion. The just claims of Lower Canada for similar indemnity had been accepted in principle by the tory legislature in 1845 and investigated in detail by a tory commission in 1846. Moreover, it had already been established, by the legislation for losses in Upper Canada, that the powers and duties of the commissioners were to extend to the investigation of all claims "in respect of any loss, destruction or damage of property occasioned by violence on the part of persons in Her Majesty's service, or by violence on the part

of persons acting or assuming to act on behalf of Her Majesty, in
the suppression of the said Rebellion. . . ".[49]

Nevertheless, there were problems connected with the payment
of losses in Lower Canada which gave pause to politicians and
aroused the suspicions of outsiders. Three commissions were
appointed before the matter was finally settled; and the evidence
presented by the second commission, in 1846, contains an illuminating revelation of the difficulties.[50] Dr. Wolfred Nelson, one of the
principal leaders of the rebellion in the lower province, put in a
modest bill for £12,000 against the government he had defied by
force of arms. Mr. B. Viger claimed damages of £2,000 for his
banishment to Bermuda. There were *patriotes*, burning, no doubt,
with unappreciated loyalty to Great Britain, who demanded compensation—with interest—for their arrest and imprisonment.
There were other and more wary *patriotes*, who had fled the
country at the time of the rebellion and who now claimed indemnity
—with interest—for their transportation charges out of the country
and back, and for all their expenses in exile. It was quite evident
that there were a good many people in Canada East who fully
intended to put an entirely novel construction upon the term
"Rebellion Losses"; and it is perhaps not altogether surprising
that the tory government gave up the attempt to satisfy an
insatiable generation which put forward such barefaced claims with
such complacent effrontery.

It was Lafontaine—another fugitive of 1837—who revived the
subject and made the matter of rebellion losses peculiarly his own,
while Baldwin, his chief colleague in office, remained significantly
silent during the earliest stages of debate. The original resolutions,
by which Lafontaine introduced the measure, did not even exclude
from the benefits of compensation those persons who had actually
been convicted of high treason or had been banished to Bermuda;
and the amendment, covering this omission, was proposed by
H. J. Boulton, who was not a member of the government.[51] It was a
questionable beginning for an act which awarded £100,000 to
Canada East in place of the £40,000 which had sufficed for Canada
West.[52] Perhaps Lafontaine had actually intended to pay convicted
rebels. It was a not unnatural conclusion that, blocked in this

endeavour, he would surreptitiously reward as many arrested, imprisoned and indicted rebels as he could.

The colony which had been commercially disowned by Great Britain and rejected by the United States had fallen under the domination of the Canadian French; and to the tories the final degradation of their slavery lay in the demand for tribute to reward the disloyalty of their masters. All the distresses of the depression, the resentment at Great Britain, the jealousy of American prosperity, and the deep despair at the frustration of the St. Lawrence, broke, in their minds, in a white blaze of anger. They opposed the measure in protracted and violent debates in parliament; they denounced it in tumultuous popular meetings; they derided it in editorials and reports and letters which filled the tory press for months. It was, they said, an act "unparalleled in the whole history of the world", an act which struck at the root of all government.

Loyalty was to be subjected to taxation in order that rebellion might be put on a firm commercial basis. This was the reward of the loyalists of 1837. "They shall now pay the losses of ruffians, who exist but by their mercy. . . . They shall submit to be taxed for the purpose of enriching a parcel of rebels, whose carcasses would have fattened the land, had they but met with their deserts."[53] The very men who had failed to deprive the British of their political rights by rebellion were now intent upon robbing them of their property by act of parliament. "If you do not resist that", appealed one editor to the volunteers of 1837, "you will submit to anything."[54] Sir Allan MacNab warned the legislature that "such acts of injustice would drive men to desperation"; and the *Montreal Gazette* declared that "the vote of the House will be the signal for a resistance, which will end in the complete prostration of the French Canadian race. . . ". The tories prophesied the renewal of civil war: they hinted darkly at the dismemberment of the empire. After all they could keep themselves English, if they were not permitted to be British. "They would not choose to be governed by foreigners, or they would rather choose the people of the United States."[55]

Defeated in the house, where the bill passed in spite of all their obstruction, the tories pinned their hopes upon the governor and the imperial authorities. They hoped that the governor would veto the bill and dissolve the house, or that he would reserve the bill and the imperial government would disallow it. They expected others to do for them what they were not politically strong enough to do for themselves. Largely their demand was made on grounds of political expediency; but at the same time it was in strict accordance with the views of colonial government which they had always professed. For them, the governor was at once a local sovereign and a local minister responsible to the British government. As the first he was one of the three branches of the legislature, equipped with a veto; and as the second he was charged with the duty of maintaining British interests and of moderating the rancorous prejudices of Canadian factions. In contempt of the assembly and the council, which to them were corrupted by their enemies, the tories appealed directly to the governor, to the final authority which they had so often influenced in the past. If the governor yielded, his surrender would confirm the domination of the French and the victory of the radical interpretation of responsible government. It would mean the end of the tory political theory of the commercial state.

On Wednesday, April 25, Lord Elgin drove into Montreal from Monklands. The unquiet city was waiting to receive him. The great river, which had made it the centre of the northern commercial system, had focused in it, as a natural consequence, all the ambitions and hatreds of the Canadian people; and it lay waiting, restless and ugly in its sense of injured vanity and disappointed hope. In the late afternoon, when the title of the Rebellion Losses Bill was read aloud for the signification of the governor's approval, there were hundreds of breathless citizens in the galleries. A moment of dead silence followed the words of formal consent. And then there arose a low but rapidly swelling murmur, a sound of groans and hisses and stamping feet. The crowd made for the gallery doors; the noise rose to yells and hootings as it clattered down the stairs; and when Elgin emerged from the house the furious citizens pelted him and his carriage with volleys of refuse.

As the April twilight descended the news spread and quickened the entire city. Broadsheets were struck off, proclaiming a meeting of the citizens at eight o'clock; the bells were rung; and men passed through the streets on foot and in carriages warning the people of the meeting. There were thousands assembled in the Champ de Mars when George Moffatt took the chair; and a few torches waved redly in the obscurity. The disallowance of the Rebellion Losses Bill and the recall of the governor were demanded. But the gathering of the respectable and the rowdy had now been transformed into a mob with a collective and passionate will; and, whether by impulse or by management, it moved off abruptly towards the parliament buildings.[56]

The house was in evening session, worriedly discussing a judicature bill. In the corridors the frightened clerks were whispering "Are they coming, are they coming?" And then the clamour could be heard outside and a rain of stones broke suddenly through the windows. Panic-stricken, the members and officials fled the building or cowered for safety in the lobbies and passages. The hall door burst open, breaking in atoms before the assault of the rioters. They swarmed into the room of the assembly; and in the confusion of smashing furniture and breaking lights, somebody marched off with the mace, while from the speaker's chair was heard a voice dissolving parliament in the Queen's name. Outside, in the darkness, a group of men were breaking other windows; and a knot of rioters collected at the west end of the building, by McGill Street, where there was a gallery or portico for the storage of stationery. They fired the papers; and in a minute the wooden gallery was ablaze.

It was a clear, cool, starry night. A high wind blew; and the flames were whipped like banners across the sky. Above the red blaze which broke from a hundred apertures in the building, the burning papers were borne upward in great bursts of white flame. The whole sky was bright with illumination; and the wide circle of watching faces was captured by a sudden magic from the obscurity. In the crowd of thousands which stood rooted as though in admiration before the spectacle, the commercial leadership of Montreal was collected; and the regrets for the loss of property were drowned in execrations for the governor and jeers for the sudden dissolution of parliament. All around rose the clamour of the aroused and turbulent city. And beyond that was the darkness and movement of the St. Lawrence.

In the next few days there was no cessation of violence and no regrets for what had been done. "The Chronicler of the past", prophesied the *Montreal Gazette*, "hereafter will say, that it was not unfitting, that an act which in principle and for atrocity is unparalleled in history, should be followed by the entire destruction of the Sodom and Gomorrah in which it was conceived and executed."[57] In this mood of vindictive elation, the mob jammed the streets on the morrow of the burning of the parliament buildings. It was angered, instead of sobered, when some of its members were arrested and when a guard was stationed before the gaol and the government house; and all day long, while the beleaguered executive council sat in permanence in its offices, the screaming crowd outside swayed uncertainly before the soldiery. When night fell on Thursday, the baffled rioters roamed in huge detachments through the city. They wrecked Hincks's house, smashed the windows in Baldwin's lodgings, fired Lafontaine's stables and destroyed his furniture, china, paintings and books.

The ministry, sleepless, fearful and tense with excitement, planned and debated all day and far into the night. The "Blockheads of ministers", as one of Elgin's own staff expressed it, "got in such a funk about themselves" that they enlisted hundreds of French Canadians as special constables;[58] and the tories raged at a government which armed "one portion of the population, so that they might murder the other". On Friday and Saturday, the crowds roamed the streets, apt for any violence and almost uncontrollable; and on Monday, April 30, when the governor came once more to the city to receive the loyal address of the assembly, he was pelted again with stones and rotten eggs. Volleys of missiles were fired over the heads of the soldiers at the members of parliament as they went to government house. Great beams were got in readiness to block Lord Elgin's exit from the city. And when the news came that the coachman had unexpectedly driven off by another route, the maddened British leaped into cabs, raced to intercept the governor, and fired a last shower of stones at the dragoons, the aides and the retreating carriage.

The abuse and execration of the governor continued. He was denounced as a renegade Bruce of whom every decent Scotsman ought to be ashamed; he was derided as a "disgraced weakling" who "came to the conclusion that he had nothing to do in Canada but obey Lafontaine and *draw his salary*". The Thistle Curling Club of Montreal expelled him as a patron; and the St. Andrews Society removed him from its honorary membership and returned "the paltry £10 he had given them for charity".[59] In tory experience, the governor, with a few regrettable exceptions, had been the leader of their party; in tory theory, he was the representative of British interests, which they identified as their own, and the pacificator of colonial partisanship, which they interpreted as the policy of their enemies. It was, as Elgin shrewdly suggested, "not the passage of the Bill by an overwhelming majority of the Representatives of the People . . . but the consent of the Governor which furnishes the pretext for an Exhibition of popular violence".[60] It was the abandonment, by a British official, of British interests and the old policy of making Canada a British province, which outraged the tories. The acceptance of the Rebellion Losses Bill was the political corollary of the repeal of the corn laws; and together they were "converting a dependent Colony into a foreign Nation".

There was one last court of appeal left—the British government and the imperial parliament; and as spring wore on into summer their incredible, adverse verdict was first suspected and then known. The London *Times* compared the "desperadoes" of 1849 with the "rebels" of 1837 to the evident disparagement of the former. The whig administration defended Lord Elgin's action and refused to advise the queen to disallow the bill. To the tories, it seemed as if Great Britain now regarded "*that fervor of loyalty, in which a portion of the Canadian people gloried, as a blind mistaken zeal,* or worse, *an officious impertinence* . . .".[61] Great Britain, who now considered the ownership of a few paltry provinces beneath her dignity, was now trying to turn the colonies adrift, as an animal turns off its cubs; and "a growl and a scratch in the one case, are only equivalent to an insult and an injury in the other". In the overheated imagination of the tories it even seemed as if Lord Elgin and the colonial office were twin conspirators in an evil plot to cast off an innocent and loyal people. "It is said", wrote one correspondent in an open letter to Lord Elgin, "that the policy of the present Cabinet is to get quit of Canada, and that your instructions were to endeavour to bring that about, now as you have done, by disgusting the British population of the Province. It was a dishonourable policy and your friends knew where to find a man for the dirty duty. Again I say, go home thou good and faithful servant, you have well performed the work assigned to you—go and receive your reward—"[62]

"Elginism", in the opinion of the tories, had thus completed the unnatural business which "Cobdenism" had begun. The acceptance of the Rebellion Losses Bill was Great Britain's official intimation that the empire was at an end and the despicable loyalty of the Canadians unwanted. The loyalists "not only against their will, but against their strongest and most affectionate remonstrances", had been driven to reconsider their status and to form new connections; and inevitably, in politics as in trade, the recoil of commercial Canada was in the direction of the United States. The new tory association, the British League, which was in session at Kingston during the summer, proposed the alternative policy of protection and a federal union of the British North American provinces—thus anticipating confederation and Sir John A. Macdonald's national policy. But Canada had become habituated to dependence upon an imperial metropolis; and it was natural, in the circumstances, that annexation should dominate men's minds. The answer to British free trade had been reciprocity, and the rejoinder to the new colonial policy was the annexation movement. On June 29, the *Montreal Herald* discussed annexation favourably; and, on the same day, Sydney Bellingham, one of the chief annexationists in the city, published the prospectus of a newspaper which was to advocate the peaceful separation of Canada from the imperial connection. Early in July, Lord John Russell's decision to uphold the Rebellion Losses Bill was known in Canada; and by the end of the summer, four of the principal English newspapers in Montreal, the *Herald*, the *Courier*, the *Gazette* and the *Witness* had declared themselves in favour of annexation.[63]

The annexation movement was a brilliant revelation of the composition of the now rapidly decaying commercial state. From its beginning, in the summer of 1849, the movement drew its main support from Canada East; and, wherever it showed itself in both sections of the province, it was urban, not rural, commercial, not agrarian, in character. The Eastern Townships, the old ally of Montreal, was the chief agricultural region to show a definite interest in annexation; and the convention of the British League at Kingston, which was well attended by delegates from Canada West, revealed how general and how strong the opposition in the old province of Upper Canada was likely to be. In Toronto, the reformers and the tories joined in a protestation of loyalty to the queen. The *Patriot*, which had scarcely ceased its abuse of Lord Elgin, united with the reformist *Globe* in denouncing annexation. Far back, in the days of the fur trade, when the transportation system of the St. Lawrence transcended the insignificant activities of its settlers, Montreal might almost have been said to be Canada; but that time had gone for ever, and the impending defeat of annexation was a victory of settlement over commerce, of self-government over the habit of political dependence, of incipient nationalism over the international commercial state. The northern trading system was incapable of carrying the country with it; but it plunged ahead blindly towards the logical conclusion of its long career. Montreal, which had always been its mouthpiece, pronounced its artistically appropriate valedictory; and early in October, 1849, in the annexation manifesto, it issued its vain appeal to the people of Canada.

V

With this repudiation of its past and this denial of its ancient principles, the history of the Canadian commercial state comes to a close. The years 1783 and 1821 had each brought down the curtain on an act; but 1849 meant the conclusion of an entire drama. The annexation manifesto was an epilogue which drove home the moral with an unendurable severity; but the course of events, like a play which has been played out, had already left behind it an empty feeling of finality, of conclusive defeat. The commercial empire of the St. Lawrence was bankrupt. Its material failure had been consummated at the very moment when its philosophical assumptions had been swept away. The failure to win the international commercial empire of the west and the forfeiture of part of the trading monopoly of western Canada had come home to a commercial generation whose historic weapons were broken in their hands and whose traditional support had vanished.

History does not readily accept finalities. It goes prosaically onwards, while its conclusions trail away in interminable addenda and its finales merge into transitional movements. The design of the St. Lawrence, as the Canadian merchants had always conceived it in the past, had been shattered beyond redemption; but there were component elements of the old and broken synthesis which survived to enter later into the composition of new and different patterns of thought and action. It is obvious that Canada remained bound to the imperial connection, from which, it is sometimes suggested, merely the "grosser elements" had been removed in 1848–1849; and it can be argued that though there were commercial changes in these years, there was no real commercial revolution. Canada, in fact, continued to do the bulk of its export trade in wheat and timber with the United Kingdom. The pull of the United States was incapable of breaking its historic dependence on the European market and its traditional reliance on the British imperial system. Montreal remained the focus of a great eastern and western trade route which continued to dominate the activities of Canadians and which led them, in the end, to a renewal of the continental strategy of the past. Above all, the river remained, the river which cared not whether it was valued or neglected, the river which would outlast all the ships that sailed upon it and survive all the schemes which it could possibly inspire.

But, though the theme of the St. Lawrence continued, it was no longer stated with the old solemn simplicity. It was heard now through novel variations and through the loud beginnings of new movements. Canadians no longer struggled to extend their commercial empire and to protect its political expression, the commercial state, with the old concentration, the old instruments and the old mental prepossessions. The coming of the railway introduced a profound change in technique. The opening of the New York route diverted an increasingly large part of the trade of the St. Lawrence and the Reciprocity Treaty partly deflected Canadian interests away from Great Britain and towards the United States. The national policy, which after an interval succeeded reciprocity, expressed the purpose of the northern economy to turn in upon itself rather than to rely once more upon the old transatlantic associations. Canada's designs in North America were destined to be more Canadian and less international in scope; and Canada's status in the western world had already become less imperial and more North American in character. It was true that the imperial connection revealed a toughness and an elasticity which commercial Montreal was incapable of foreseeing in 1849. But, with the removal of its grosser elements, it showed a tendency to dissipate into vaporous ethereality; and the tie which had once been the homely concern of practical, hard-headed men, threatened to become the object of the refined speculations of political theorists and the emotional outbursts of after-dinner speakers. Canada had ceased to be an imperial trade route which sought its sources of supply in the international American west, which built its political structure in the interests of commerce and which found its markets and its final court of appeal in the ample resources of the British Empire. It passed on to new endeavours, leaving behind it a cause which had been lost.

There was, in fact, some primitive defect, some fundamental weakness, in the society of the St. Lawrence, in the resources which it could bring to bear upon its problems, and in the very river itself which had inspired its entire effort. The St. Lawrence was a stream which dashed itself against the rocks and broke the hopes of its supporters; and all the long struggle, which had begun when the first ships of the French sailed up the River of Canada, had served, in the end, to establish a tradition of defeat. From the great northern bay and from the river which ran down to the ice-free port of New York, the invaders had pressed into the commercial empire of the St. Lawrence; and Henry Hudson, the Englishman who had given his name to both the river and the bay, had now at last been awarded his long-delayed, his double triumph over the Frenchman Champlain. The defeat of the French, the surrender of the western posts, the collapse of the North West Company and the failure of the St. Lawrence ship canal had followed each other slowly, with a kind of remorseless deliberation, in one long, unbroken record of disaster. It was to reach this appointed conclusion that La Salle had built the *Griffon*, that Pond had toiled northward to the Athabaska, that McTavish had founded the North West Company and that Richardson had planned the first Lachine canal. All these deeds and struggles took on, in retrospect, the appearance of episodes which had been intended merely to postpone the *dénouement* of a drama upon the last page of which there would inevitably be written the word defeat. In 1849, the accumulated sense of failure was so oppressive that it drove men to repudiate their unavailing loyalties and to destroy the cherished system which had failed them. The fire which broke out on that April evening of 1849, was symbolic of the blind urge towards disavowal and destruction; and the hopes of successive generations of Canadians, consumed in a last blaze of anger, were reflected in the red sky over Montreal.

BIBLIOGRAPHICAL NOTE

The manuscript materials, upon which this study is based to a considerable extent, are to be found chiefly in the Public Archives of Canada, at Ottawa. The two most important collections of state papers are the *G* series and the *Q* series which contain the originals or the transcripts of the correspondence between the provincial governments and the imperial authorities in England. Together these two series cover the entire period which is dealt with in this volume; and, up to about the end of the eighteenth century, they are supplemented by the *C.O. 42* series, which contains transcripts of the papers of the imperial board of trade. The official correspondence within the different Canadian provinces during the period is to be found in several collections which are variously designated. The *Upper Canada Sundries*, the *Secretary of State's Papers, Internal Correspondence* and the *Correspondence of the Governor-General's Secretary* are the series which have been principally used. The minutes of the executive councils of the different provinces—as well as the minutes of the council of the old province of Quebec in its legislative capacity—are preserved in manuscript volumes. These collections of state papers, and particularly the *Q* and *G* series, have long constituted the staple sources for the political and constitutional history of Canada; but, in addition, they contain a wealth of material on economic matters, which has been heavily drawn upon in the preparation of this volume.

In addition to these series of state papers, a number of other collections of manuscripts have been used. Among the most important of these collections are the following: the *Shelburne Manuscripts*, the *Richardson Letters*, the *Dalhousie Papers*, the *Merritt Papers*, the *Durham Papers* and the *Grey-Elgin Correspondence*. These sources yield a certain amount of information on the general financial and commercial problems of the colonies. They supply, in some cases, more intimate details concerning the relations between commerce and politics. Collections, such as that of the *Merritt Papers*, which illustrate the activities of people who were at once business men and politicians, have, of course, been particularly useful; and if more of these collections had been available, the task of writing the history of the commercial state would have been correspondingly more simple.

A portion of this contemporary manuscript material has been printed and published in recent times. The Public Archives of Canada has issued three invaluable collections of documents: A. Shortt and A. G. Doughty (eds.), *Documents Relating to the Constitutional History of Canada, 1759–1791* (Ottawa, 1918); A. G. Doughty and D. A. McArthur (eds.), *Docu-*

ments Relating to the Constitutional History of Canada, 1791–1818 (Ottawa, 1914); and A. G. Doughty and Norah Story (eds.), *Documents Relating to the Constitutional History of Canada, 1819–1828* (Ottawa, 1935). These collections, as their titles all imply, are intended to illustrate the constitutional problems of their respective periods; but, in addition, they contain material on land tenure, taxation and commercial regulations, and they provide some information on the political activities of the commercial group. The Ontario Historical Society has published *The Correspondence of Lieut.-Governor John Graves Simcoe* (Toronto, 1923–1931) and is now proceeding with the publication of *The Correspondence of the Honourable Peter Russell* (Toronto, 1932–36). These collections, which have been prepared under the editorship of Brigadier-General E. A. Cruikshank, are extremely useful in the study of the early development of Upper Canada. The publications of the Champlain Society have been of considerable service; and, in particular, W. S. Wallace (ed.), *Documents Relating to the North West Company* (Toronto, 1934) is of great value in understanding commercial organization during the period of the fur trade. Finally, the general economic history of Canada can be studied with the aid of two valuable collections of documents: H. A. Innis (ed.), *Select Documents in Canadian Economic History, 1497–1783* (Toronto, 1929); and H. A. Innis and A. R. M. Lower (eds.), *Select Documents in Canadian Economic History, 1783–1885* (Toronto, 1933).

Of the numerous collections of contemporary documents published in the United States, a few, which bear more particularly on Canadian problems, have been very useful. Occasional reference has been made to the *Documents Relating to the Colonial History of the State of New York*, an old series of volumes, edited by E. B. O'Callaghan and published in Albany during the 1850's. The fourth and fifth series of *American Archives*, edited by Peter Force and published in Washington 1837–1853, throw a great deal of light on the American invasion of Canada and the attitude of the commercial group during this crisis. From 1877 until 1912, the Michigan Pioneer and Historical Society issued a lengthy series of volumes intended to illustrate the early history of Michigan and the old west. These collections of documents, published most frequently under the general title, *Michigan Pioneer and Historical Collections*, deal in many cases with the period when the old west was part of the dominion of the St. Lawrence; and, indeed, the contents of a good many of the volumes were printed from the transcripts and the originals at the Public Archives of Canada.

Contemporary printed material is among the richest of all sources for the study of the commercial system of the St. Lawrence. The newspapers and pamphlets of the period give expression to the views of typical Canadian groups and interests. They supply detailed information on the character and course of political and commercial controversies. The newspapers are the only source for the debates of the Canadian legislatures during the period; and they provide a detailed record of Canadian commercial activities. Many newspapers of the period were ephemeral, and the files of the more enduring publications are in many cases broken and incomplete; but, within these necessary limitations, an attempt has been made to secure newspaper material which would at once reflect the interests of different sections of the provinces and the points of view of different political and commercial groups. The *Quebec Mercury*, the *Quebec Gazette*, *Le Canadien*, the *Montreal Gazette*, the *Montreal Herald*, the *Montreal Transcript*, the *Colonial Advocate*, the *Constitution* and the *Patriot* have all been used extensively in the preparation of this study.

Among other contemporary printed materials, the *Journals* of the legislative assemblies and councils are of first importance. The minutes of proceedings are of distinct though limited value; but the appendices, which, as time went on, were usually published as supplementary volumes to the Assembly's *Journal*, contain a mass of useful reports and statistical information. The accounts written by travellers and immigrants and the pamphlet literature of the period provide, like the newspapers, a very direct approach to the conditions and opinions of the time. There are two excellent guides to this material. *A Bibliography of Canadiana* (Toronto, 1935) has been prepared by Miss F. M. Staton and Miss Marie Tremaine and published by the Public Library of Toronto; and the *Catalogue of Pamphlets in the Public Archives of Canada* (Ottawa, 1931–1932) was edited by Miss M. Casey and issued as no. 13 of the publications of the Dominion Archives.

References to the secondary literature on the subject will be found in the notes.

NOTES

CHAPTER I

THE ECONOMY OF THE NORTH

1. M. I. Newbigin, *Canada, the Great River, the Lands and the Men* (London, 1926) pp. 157–161; H. A. Innis, "Interrelations between the Fur Trade of Canada and the United States" (*Mississippi Valley Historical Review*, vol. 20, December, 1933, pp. 321–332).

2. H. A. Innis, "An Introduction to the Economic History of the Maritimes" (*Canadian Historical Association Report*, 1931, pp. 89–90).

3. F. W. Pitman, *The Development of the British West Indies, 1700-1763* (New Haven, 1917).

4. J. B. Brebner, *New England's Outpost; Acadia before the Conquest of Canada* (New York, 1927); *The Neutral Yankees of Nova Scotia, a Marginal Colony during the Revolutionary Years* (New York, 1937).

5. H. Broshar, "The First Push Westward of the Albany Traders" (*Mississippi Valley Historical Review*, vol. 7, December, 1920, pp. 228–241); A. H. Buffinton, "The Policy of Albany and English Westward Expansion" (*Ibid.*, vol. 8, March, 1922, pp. 327–366).

6. G. P. de T. Glazebrook, "Roads in New France and the Policy of Expansion" (*Canadian Historical Association Report*, 1934, pp. 48–56).

7. H. A. Innis (ed.), *Select Documents in Canadian Economic History, 1497–1783* (Toronto, 1929), p. 367.

8. *Ibid.*, pp. 106, 113, 140.

9. H. A. Innis, *The Fur Trade in Canada, an Introduction to Canadian Economic History* (New Haven, 1930), pp. 122–123.

10. *Ibid.*, p. 393.

11. Innis, *Select Documents*, p. 429.

12. Innis, *The Fur Trade in Canada*, p. 117.

CHAPTER II

THE MERCHANTS' POLITICAL PROGRAMME

1. M. G. Jackson, "The Beginnings of British Trade at Michilimackinac" (*Minnesota History*, vol. 11, September, 1930, pp. 231–270).

2. A. L. Burt, *The Old Province of Quebec* (Toronto, 1933), p. 104.

3. J. Bain (ed.), *Travels and Adventures in Canada and the Indian Territories, between the Years 1760 and 1776, by Alexander Henry, Fur Trader* (Toronto, 1901), p. 3.

4. Public Archives of Canada, *Series Q.*, vol. 2, pp. 332–336, A list of Protestant house-keepers in Quebec and Montreal.

5. Public Archives of Canada, *Series C. O. 42*, Vol. 5, pp. 28–33, List of Protestants in the district of Montreal, November 7, 1765.

6. For details of the family relationships see the biographical dictionary in W. S. Wallace (ed.), *Documents relating to the North West Company* (Toronto, Champlain Society, 1934), pp. 425–505.

7. R. Campbell, *History of the Scotch Presbyterian Church, St. Gabriel Street, Montreal* (Montreal, 1887), pp. 81–82.

8. Peter Kalm, *Travels into North America* . . . (London, 1772), vol. 2, p. 236.

9. Isaac Weld, *Travels through the States of North America, and the Provinces of Upper and Lower Canada, during the Years 1795, 1796, and 1797* (London, 1799), p. 178.

10. E. Z. Massicotte, "Hôtelleries, Clubs et Cafés à Montréal de 1760 à 1850" (*Proceedings and Transactions of the Royal Society of Canada*, series 3, vol. 22, sec. 1, pp. 37–62).

11. D. S. Robertson (ed.), *An Englishman in America, Being the Diary of Joseph Hadfield* (Toronto, 1933), pp. 42, 147, 164–165.

12. Public Archives of Canada, *Dartmouth Papers*, vol. 2, part 1, List of British proprietors of lands in the Province of Quebec, 1773.

13. For merchants interested in the seal fishery see *Q.*, vol. 2, pp. 49–53, Memorial of the merchants of Quebec to Murray, February 16, 1764.

14. C. E. Lart, "Fur-Trade Returns, 1767" (*Canadian Historical Review*, vol. 3, December, 1922, pp. 351–358).

15. Bain, *Travels and Adventures in Canada* . . . *by Alexander Henry*, p. 10.

16. G. L. Nute, *The Voyageur* (New York, 1931), chaps. 3–5.

17. *See* the diary of John Macdonell in *Five Fur Traders of the Northwest*, C. M. Gates, ed. (University of Minnesota, 1933), pp. 67–119.

18. Innis, *The Fur Trade in Canada*, p. 245.

19. L. J. Burpee, "The Beaver Club" (*Canadian Historical Association Report*, 1924, pp. 73–92).

20. *Canadian Archives Report*, 1885, note A, pp. lxxx–lxxxvi, Copy of the register of the parish of Montreal, 1766–1787.

21. W. S. Wallace (ed.), *The Maseres Letters, 1766–1768* (University of Toronto Studies, History and Economics, Toronto, 1919), p. 44.

22. A. Shortt and A. G. Doughty, *Documents relating to the Constitutional History of Canada, 1759–1791* (Ottawa, 1918), vol. 1, pp. 150–153, Lords of trade to Egremont, August 5, 1763.

23. *Ibid*, vol. 1, p. 140, Lords of trade to Egremont, June 8, 1763.

24. For details concerning the characters and careers of Murray, Carleton and Haldimand, see: A. L. Burt, *The Old Province of Quebec;* R. H. Mahon, *The Life of General the Honourable James Murray* (London, 1921); A. L. Burt, "Guy Carleton, Lord Dorchester: An Estimate" (*Canadian Historical Association Report*, 1935, pp. 76–87); J. N. McIlwraith, *Sir Frederick Haldimand* (The Makers of Canada, Toronto, 1904).

25. Shortt and Doughty, *Constitutional Documents*, vol. 2, p. 721, Haldimand to Germain, October 25, 1780.

26. *Ibid.*, vol. 1, pp. 232–234, Petition of the Quebec traders.

27. D. M. Clark, *British Opinion and the American Revolution* (New Haven, 1930), p. 99.

28. *C. O. 42*, vol. 2, part 1, pp. 109–113, Memorial of the London merchants trading to Canada, April 18, 1765.

29. Shortt and Doughty, *Constitutional Documents*, vol. 1, pp. 235–236, Petition of the London merchants.

30. Wallace, *The Maseres Letters*, appendix A, p. 123.

31. *Ibid.*, p. 90.

32. *Canadian Archives Report*, 1918, appendix C., pp. 2–3.

33. C. W. Alvord, *The Mississippi Valley in British Politics, A Study of the Trade, Land Speculation, and Experiments in Imperialism culminating in the American Revolution* (Cleveland, 1917), vol. 1, pp. 290–291.

34. *Q*, vol. 4, pp. 200–207, Memorial upon the Indian trade, September 20, 1766; Public Archives of Canada, *Shelburne MSS.*, vol. 50, pp. 160–165, Observations on the Indian trade by B. Frobisher, November 10, 1766.

35. *C. O. 42*, vol. 5, pp. 158–160, Memorial of Fowler Walker to the lords of trade, June 26, 1766.

36. Jackson, *The Beginnings of British Trade at Michilimackinac*, p. 254.

37. M. G. Reid, "The Quebec Fur-Traders and Western Policy, 1763–1774" (*Canadian Historical Review*, vol. 6, March, 1925, pp. 25–26).

38. R. H. Fleming, *Phyn, Ellice and Company of Schenectady* (University of Toronto Studies, History and Economics, vol. 4, Toronto, 1932), pp. 18–19.

39. H. A. Innis, *Peter Pond, Fur Trader and Adventurer* (Toronto, 1930), pp. 24, 67.

40. Fleming, *Phyn, Ellice and Company*, pp. 29–30.

41. Public Archives of Canada, *Quebec Legislative Council Minutes*, vol. C, part 1, pp. 87–95.

42. E. B. O'Callaghan (ed.) *Documents relative to the Colonial History of the State of New York* (Albany, 1857), vol. 8, p. 216, Colden to Hillsborough, July 7, 1770.

43. *Legislative Council Minutes*, vol. C, part 2, pp. 201–205.

44. *Q*, vol. 8, pp. 47–48, Hillsborough to Carleton, July 19, 1771.

45. G. O. Rothney, "The Case of Bayne and Brymer" (*Canadian Historical Review*, vol. 15, September, 1934, pp. 264–275).

46. Shortt and Doughty, *Constitutional Documents*, vol. 1, pp. 422–423, Additional instruction to Carleton, July 2, 1771.

47. *Ibid.*, vol. 1, p. 295, Carleton to Shelburne, January 20, 1768.

48. *C. O. 42*, vol. 7, p. 3, H. Guinand *et al.* to Hillsborough, April 13, 1768; *ibid.*, vol. 7, p. 4, R. Hunter *et al.* to Hillsborough, September 20, 1768.

49. *C. O. 42*, vol. 7, pp. 58–61, Merchants of London trading to Canada to board of trade, July 11, 1770.

50. *Q*, vol. 7, p. 96, Memorial of merchants and other inhabitants of the city of Quebec to Carleton, April 10, 1770.

51. Shortt and Doughty, *Constitutional Documents*, vol. 1, pp. 533–534 (note).

52. *Ibid.*, vol. 1, pp. 486–502, for activities of the merchants in this crisis.

53. Francis Maseres, *An Account of the Proceedings of the British and other Protestant Inhabitants of the Province of Quebeck* . . . (London, 1775), pp. 30–31.

CHAPTER III

CANADA AND THE AMERICAN REVOLUTION

1. *Shelburne MSS.*, vol. 66, p. 32, Caldwell to Shelburne, January 9, 1775.

2. Wallace, *North West Company Documents*, p. 47, McTavish to Edgar, December, 24, 1774.

3. W. B. Kerr, "The Stamp Act in Quebec" (*English Historical Review*, vol. 47, October, 1932, pp. 648–651).

4. *C. O. 42*, vol. 5, pp. 252–255, Address of the merchants of Quebec to Carleton, September 26, 1766.

5. *Shelburne MSS.*, vol. 64, pp. 106–113, Copy of a letter from Quebec, September 30, 1766.

6. J. H. Smith, *Our Struggle for the Fourteenth Colony, Canada and the American Revolution* (New York, 1907), vol. 1, p. 90.

7. *Legislative Council Minutes*, vol. D, part 1, pp. 98–99.

8. Peter Force (ed.), *American Archives* (Washington, 1843), series 4, vol. 2, pp. 305–306, Committee of Montreal to committee of safety of Massachusetts, April 8, 1775.

9. *Ibid.*, series 4, vol. 2, p. 244, Brown to committee of correspondence in Boston, March 29, 1775.

10. Francis Maseres, *Additional Papers concerning the Province of Quebeck* (London, 1776), p. 86.

11. *Ibid.*, p. 101.

12. *Ibid.*, p. 92.

13. Smith, *Our Struggle for the Fourteenth Colony*, vol. 1, pp. 158–159.

14. H. A. Verreau, *Invasion du Canada: Collection de Mémoires* (Montreal, 1873), p. 50.

15. *Canadian Archives Report*, 1888, p. xiv.

16. Wallace, *North West Company Documents*, p. 49, McTavish to Edgar, May 12, 1776.

17. Force, *American Archives*, series 4, vol. 3, p. 1597, Articles of capitulation, November 12, 1775.

18. Smith, *Our Struggle for the Fourteenth Colony*, vol. 2, p. 227.

19. Force, *American Archives*, series 4, vol. 4, pp. 1001–1002, Wooster to president of congress, February 11, 1776; *ibid.*, series 4, vol. 4, p. 1215, Schuyler to president of congress, February 20, 1776.

20. Verreau, *Invasion du Canada*, p. 97.

21. Force, *American Archives*, series 4, vol. 4, p. 464, Montgomery to Schuyler, December 26, 1775.

22. *Ibid.*, series 4, vol. 5, p. 416, Wooster to Schuyler, March 5, 1776.

23. *Ibid.*, series 4, vol. 5, p. 752, Hazen to Schuyler, April 1, 1776.

24. *Ibid.*, series 4, vol. 4, p. 669, Wooster to Schuyler, January 5, 1776.

25. *Ibid.*, series 4, vol. 4, p. 668, Price to Schuyler, January 5, 1776.

26. *Ibid.*, series 4, vol. 5, p. 1166, Commissioners in Canada to president of congress, May 1, 1776.

27. G. C. Davidson, *The North West Company* (Berkeley, 1918). appendix H, pp. 277–279.

28. J. B. Tyrrell, *Journals of Samuel Hearne and Philip Turnor* (Toronto, Champlain Society, 1934), pp. 7–8.

29. Wallace, *North West Company Documents*, pp. 39–44, Graham to the governor and committee of the Hudson's Bay Company, August 26, 1772.

30. W. S. Wallace, "The Pedlars from Quebec" (*Canadian Historical Review*, vol. 13, December, 1932, p. 398).

31. Tyrrell, *Journals of Hearne and Turnor*, p. 37.

32. *Ibid.*, pp. 42–47.

33. G. A. Cuthbertson, *Freshwater* (Toronto, 1931), p. 283; R. H. Fleming, *Phyn, Ellice and Company*, p. 15.

34. *Canadian Archives Report*, 1888, pp. 61–62, Petition of the north-west traders to Haldimand, May 11, 1780; *Michigan Pioneer and Historical Collections* (Lansing, 1892), vol. 19, pp. 492–493, Petition of the merchants of Detroit to Haldimand, January 5, 1780.

35. *Canadian Archives Report*, 1886, pp. xxi-xxiv.

36. Wallace, *North West Company Documents*, pp. 40–41, Graham to the governor and committee of the Hudson's Bay Company, August 26, 1772.

37. *Tyrrell*, Journals of Hearne and Turnor, pp. 38–39, 53–55, 221.

38. Wallace, *North West Company Documents*, pp. 62–66, Grant to Haldimand, April 24, 1780.

39. H. A. Innis, "The North West Company" (*Canadian Historical Review*, vol. 8, December, 1927, p. 310).

40. Shortt and Doughty, *Constitutional Documents*, vol. 2, pp. 599–600, Instructions to Governor Carleton, 1775.

41. *Legislative Council Minutes*, vol. D, part 1, p. 96.

42. Burt, *The Old Province of Quebec*, pp. 254–256.

43. *Q*, vol. 17–1, pp. 140–147, Haldimand to Germain, October 25, 1780.

44. *Michigan Pioneer and Historical Collections*, vol. 19, pp. 492–493, Petition of the merchants of Detroit to Haldimand, January 5, 1780.

45. *C. O. 42*, vol. 10, p. 18, Report of R. Jackson, April 3, 1783.

46. *Legislative Council Minutes*, vol. D, part 1, pp. 94–100.

47. *Q*, vol. 17–2, pp. 666–671, Haldimand to Germain, October 25, 1780.

48. G. W. Brown, "The St. Lawrence in the Boundary Settlement of 1783" (*Canadian Historical Review*, vol. 9, September, 1928, p. 233).

49. Lord Fitzmaurice, *Life of William Earl of Shelburne, afterward first Marquess of Lansdowne* (London, 1912), vol. 2, p. 122.

50. Samuel Flagg Bemis, "Canada and the Peace Settlement of 1782–1783" (*Canadian Historical Review*, vol. 14, September, 1933, p. 281).

51. *Shelburne MSS.*, vol. 72, pp. 288–293, Canada merchants to Lord Shelburne, February 6, 1783 (with enclosures).

52. *Chatham MSS.*, vol. 343, pp. 7–10, Questions and answers on the American Treaty, February 6, 1783.

53. Fitzmaurice, *Life of Shelburne*, vol. 2, p. 220.

54. G. S. Graham, *British Policy and Canada, 1774–1791, A Study in 18th Century Trade Policy* (London, Royal Empire Society, 1930), chap. 4.

55. *Chatham MSS.*, vol. 343, pp. 7–8, Questions and answers on the American treaty, February 6, 1783.

56. *Ibid.*, p. 9.

57. *Shelburne MSS.*, vol. 72, p. 288, Canada merchants to Lord Shelburne, February 6, 1783.

CHAPTER IV

FIRST CONSEQUENCES OF 1783

1. W. E. Stevens, *The Northwest Fur Trade, 1763–1800* (University of Illinois, 1928), pp. 80–84.

2. *Canadian Archives Report*, 1890, pp. 48–49, North West Company to Haldimand, October 4, 1784.

3. *Canadian Archives Report*, 1888, pp. 63–64, Frobisher to Mabane, April 19, 1784.

4. *Canadian Archives Report*, 1890, p. 56, McGill to Hamilton, August 1, 1785.

5. Stevens, *Northwest Fur Trade*, pp. 92–93.

6. *Canadian Archives Report*, 1888, pp. 71–72, Matthew to Robertson, August 12, 1784.

7. *C. O. 42*, vol. 16, pp. 122–124, Memorandum on the Indian Trade, December 28, 1784; *Canadian Archives Report*, 1890, pp. 56–58, McGill to Hamilton, August 1, 1785.

8. *Michigan Pioneer and Historical Collections*, vol. 20, pp. 117–121, MacLean to Haldimand, May 18, 1783.

9. S. F. Bemis, *Jay's Treaty, A Study in Commerce and Diplomacy* (New York, 1923); A. L. Burt, "A New Approach to the Problem of the Western Posts" (*Canadian Historical Association Report*, 1931, pp. 61–75).

10. *Shelburne MSS.*, vol. 72, pp. 292–293, Regulations proposed by the merchants interested in the trade to the Province of Quebec, January 31, 1783.

11. A. R. M. Lower, "Credit and the Constitutional Act" (*Canadian Historical Review*, vol. 6, June, 1925, pp. 123–141).

12. H. Neatby, "The Political Career of Adam Mabane" (*Canadian Historical Review*, vol. 16, June, 1935, pp. 137–150).

13. A. L. Burt, *The Old Province of Quebec* (Toronto, 1933), pp. 401–402.

14. A. Shortt and A. G. Doughty, *Documents relating to the Constitutional History of Canada, 1759–1791* (Ottawa, 1918), vol. 2, p. 744, Petition for a house of assembly, November 24, 1784.

15. *C. O. 42*, vol. 17, p. 179, Finlay to Nepean, January 10, 1785.

16. *Ibid.*, p. 251, Finlay to Grant, August 9, 1785.

17. *Legislative Council Minutes*, D, part 2, pp. 223–224.

18. *C. O. 42*, vol. 17, p. 269, Finlay to Nepean, September 26, 1785.

19. *Canadian Archives Report*, 1890, pp. 61–62, Petition to the governor and council of Quebec, July 10, 1785.

20. *Ibid.*, pp. 59–60, Frobisher to Finlay, August 8, 1785.

21. *Q*, vol. 26–1, pp. 299–302, Memorial of the merchants and traders of Montreal, April 10, 1786.

22. *C. O. 42*, vol. 15, p. 29, Petition of the king's ancient subjects, September 30, 1783.

23. Shortt and Doughty, *Constitutional Documents*, vol. 2, pp. 742–746, Petition for a house of assembly, November 24, 1784.

24. *Legislative Council Minutes*, D, part 2, pp. 202–204.

25. *Q*, vol. 42–2, pp. 798–799, Fraser to Nepean, October 31, 1789.

26. Shortt and Doughty, *Constitutional Documents*, vol. 2, pp. 796–801, Memorial of the British merchants trading to Quebec, February 8, 1786.

27. *Legislative Council Minutes*, D, part 2, p. 311.

28. *Q*, vol. 24–1, pp. 247–249, Hamilton to Sydney, April 7, 1785.

29. G. S. Graham, *British Policy and Canada, 1774–1791, A Study in 18th Century Trade Policy* (London, Royal Empire Society, 1930), pp. 116-132.

30. *Legislative Council Minutes*, E, part 2, pp. 174, 214.

31. *C. O. 42*, vol. 16, p. 214, Finlay to Nepean, November 6, 1784.

32. *Legislative Council Minutes*, E, part 1, p. 163.

33. *Ibid.*

34. *Q*, vol. 28, pp. 4–6, Dorchester to Sydney, June 13, 1787.

35. *Ibid.*, pp. 28–43, Sydney to Dorchester (with enclosures), September 14, 1787; *Canadian Archives Report*, 1914–1915, pp. 203–205.

36. *Q*, vol. 45–2, pp. 532–534, Dorchester to Grenville, July 21, 1790.

37. "English Policy toward America in 1790–1791" (*American Historical Review*, vol. 8, October 1902, pp. 78–86).

38. *Statutes at Large*, United Kingdom, 30 George III, c. 29.

39. Graham, *British Policy and Canada*, chap. 5.

40. *Q*, vol. 40, pp. 14–16, Memorial of the merchants and manufacturers concerned in the flour and biscuit trade, November 29, 1788.

41. R. H. Fleming, "McTavish, Frobisher and Company of Montreal" (*Canadian Historical Review*, vol. 10, June, 1929, pp. 136–152).

42. W. S. Wallace (ed.), *Documents relating to the North West Company* (Toronto, the Champlain Society, 1934), pp. 84–89; H. A. Innis, "The North West Company" (*Canadian Historical Review*, vol. 8, December, 1927, pp. 308–321).

43. *Michigan Pioneer and Historical Collections*, vol. 24, p. 338, Memorial of the Montreal merchants respecting trade, December 9, 1791.

44. *Q*, vol. 49, pp. 287–294, Inglis to Grenville, May 31, 1790.

45. *Ibid.*, vol. 52, pp. 272–278, Detroit traders to Sir J. Johnson, August 10, 1791; *Michigan Pioneer and Historical Collections*, vol. 24, pp. 338–342, Merchants of Montreal to Simcoe, December 9, 1791.

46. *Canadian Archives Report*, 1890, pp. 172–174, Dundas to Dorchester, September 16, 1791.

47. *Legislative Council Minutes*, E, part 1, pp. 56–60.

48. *Q*, vol. 28, pp. 158–159, Dorchester to Nepean, October 24, 1787.

49. *The Parliamentary History of England*, vol. 27 (London, 1816), p. 511.

50. *Q*, vol. 43–2, pp. 757–770, Powers of attorney from the inhabitants of Quebec and Montreal to Adam Lymburner, October 23, 1788.

51. *Ibid.*, vol. 40, pp. 18–24, Memorial and petition of the subscribers, December 1–5, 1788.

52. Public Archives of Canada, *Richardson Letters*, p. 31, Richardson to Porteous, April 10, 1787.

53. *Privy Council Minutes*, H, part 4, pp. 601–603, Memorial of the Montreal merchants, October 26, 1790.

54. *Q*, vol. 57–1, pp. 48–49, Note from Lymburner.

55. *Privy Council Minutes*, H, part 1, p. 160.

56. *Q*, vol. 57–1, p. 115, Extract of a letter from the committee to Lymburner, June 22, 1791.

57. *The Paper read at the Bar of the House of Commons by Mr. Lymburner* . . . (Quebec, 1791), pp. 9–13.

CHAPTER V

THE RISE OF THE NEW STAPLE TRADES

1. A. C. Flick (ed.), *History of the State of New York* (New York, 1933–), vol. 5, pp. 143–175.

2. B. W. Bond, *The Civilization of the Old Northwest, A Study of Political, Social and Economic Development*, 1788–1812 (New York, 1934), chaps. 1–2.

3. C. M. Day, *History of the Eastern Townships* (Montreal, 1869).

4. La Rochefoucauld-Liancourt, *Travels Through the United States of North America, the Country of the Iroquois, and Upper Canada, during the Years 1795, 1796, and 1797* . . . (London, 1799), vol. 1, p. 225.

5. H. A. Innis, "An Introduction to the Economic History of Ontario" (*Ontario Historical Society, Papers and Records*, vol. 30, pp. 111–123).

6. C. E. Cartwright (ed.), *Life and Letters of the late Hon. Richard Cartwright* (Toronto, 1876), p. 82.

7. Isaac Weld, *Travels Through the States of North America, and the Provinces of Upper and Lower Canada, during the Years 1795, 1796 and 1797* (London, 1800), p. 284.

8. Cartwright, *Letters of Richard Cartwright*, pp. 76–77.

9. E. A. Cruikshank (ed.), *The Correspondence of Lieut-Governor John Graves Simcoe* (Toronto, 1923–31), vol. 1, pp. 97–100, Hamilton to Simcoe, January 4, 1792.

10. Weld, *Travels*, p. 284.

11. *Q*, vol. 281–1, pp. 184–185, Simcoe to lords of trade, December 20, 1794.

12. *Canadian Archives Report*, 1921, appendix B, pp. 30–31.

13. P. Campbell, *Travels in the Interior Inhabited Parts of North America in the Years 1791 and 1792* (Edinburgh, 1793), p. 160.

14. *Q*, vol, 74–1, pp. 176–179.

15. *Ibid.*, vol. 71–1, pp. 37–38, Portland to Dorchester, February 24, 1795.

16. *Ibid.*, vol. 74–1, pp. 176–179.

17. Cruikshank, *Simcoe Papers*, vol. 3, p. 223, Cartwright to Simcoe, December 15, 1794.

18. Cartwright, *Letters of Richard Cartwright*, p. 82.

19. Cruikshank, *Simcoe Papers*, vol. 1, p. 300, Gray to Simcoe, March 17, 1793.

20. *Ibid.*, vol. 3, p. 223.

21. E. A. Cruikshank (ed.), *The Correspondence of the Honourable Peter Russell* (Toronto, 1932–), vol. 1, p. 172.

22. Cartwright, *Letters of Richard Cartwright*, p. 74.

23. K. W. Porter, *John Jacob Astor, Business Man* (Cambridge, 1931), vol. 1, chap. 4.

24. I. Caron, *La Colonisation de la Province de Québec. Les Cantons de l'Est, 1791–1815* (Quebec, 1927), pp. 168–169.

25. Cruikshank, *Simcoe Papers*, vol. 1, pp. 182–183, Smith to Askin, July 26, 1792.

26. T. Chapais, *Cours d'Histoire du Canada* (Quebec, 1919–1934), vol. 2, pp. 42–43.

27. *Q*, vol. 66, p. 263, Monk to Nepean, January 3, 1793.

28. F. H. Soward, "The First Assembly in Lower Canada" (*Canadian Historical Review*, vol. 4, September, 1923, pp. 258–263).

29. A. G. Doughty and D. A. McArthur, *Documents relating to the Constitutional History of Canada, 1791–1818* (Ottawa, 1914), pp. 125–145.

30. H. A. Innis, *The Fur Trade in Canada* (New Haven, 1930), appendix G, pp. 423–424.

31. *Journal of the House of Assembly of Lower-Canada*, 1795–1796, vol. 4, pp. 249, 257.

32. *Q*, vol. 279–1, pp. 79–85, Simcoe to Dundas, November 4, 1792; *ibid.*, vol. 279–2, pp. 335–355, Simcoe to Dundas, September 16, 1793.

33. Doughty and McArthur, *Constitutional Documents*, pp. 91–100.

34. *Q*, vol. 281–2, pp. 462–475, Articles of provisional agreement and report of the commissioners of Upper Canada.

35. *Journal of the House of Assembly of Lower-Canada*, 1797, vol. 5, pp. 23–37.

36. *Ibid.*, 1799, vol. 7, pp. 32–38.

37. *Ibid.*, 1801, vol. 9, pp. 213–220.

38. Stevens, *Northwest Fur Trade*, pp. 162–185; Bemis, *Jay's Treaty*, chap. 6.

39. *Q*, vol. 52, pp. 272–278, Detroit traders to Sir J. Johnson, August 10, 1791.

40. Cruikshank, *Simcoe Papers*, vol. 1, pp. 91–94, Merchants of Montreal to Simcoe, December 9, 1791; *ibid.*, vol. 1, pp. 133–137, Merchants of Montreal to Simcoe, April 23, 1792.

41. M. M. Quaife (ed.), *The John Askin Papers* (Detroit, 1928–1931), vol. 1, pp. 407–410, Robertson to Askin, March 26, 1792.

42. *Q*, vol. 278, p. 111, Simcoe to Dundas, April 28, 1792.

43. *Ibid.*, vol. 58–1, pp. 86–92, Dorchester to Dundas, March 23, 1792.

44. Bemis, *Jay's Treaty*, chap. 8.

45. Cruikshank, *Simcoe Papers*, vol. 2, pp. 405–408.

46. The treaty is given in full in Bemis, *Jay's Treaty*, appendix 6, pp. 321–345.

47. *Canadian Archives Report*, 1921, appendix B, pp. 34–41.

48. *Journal of the House of Assembly of Lower-Canada*, 1797, vol. 5, pp. 23–37.

49. Cartwright, *Letters of Richard Cartwright*, p. 112.

50. *Statutes of Upper Canada*, 42 George III, c. 4.

51. Porter, John Jacob Astor, vol. 1, p. 52.

52. Cruikshank, *Russell Papers*, vol. 2, pp. 266–267, Memorandum on trade and commerce by R. Hamilton, September 24, 1798.

53. Cartwright, *Letters of Richard Cartwright*, p. 114.

54. *Q*, vol. 280–2, pp. 330–331, Simcoe to lords of trade, September 1, 1794.

55. Quaife, *John Askin Papers*, vol. 2, p. 343, Nichol to Askin, June 15, 1801.

56. *Q*, vol. 290–1, pp. 27–36, Report of the state of the several locks on the Cataraqui or St. Lawrence river, December 24, 1800.

57. *Ibid.*, vol. 57–2, pp. 375–381, Brickwood to King, June 12, 1795.

58. *Ibid.*, vol. 293, pp. 120–123, Memorandum concerning a canal projected by the American states from Albany to Lake Ontario . . . , December, 1801.

CHAPTER VI

THE CLASH WITH THE FRENCH CANADIANS

1. G. Heriot, *Travels through the Canadas* (London, 1807), p. 254; J. Lambert, *Travels through Canada and the United States of North America in the Years 1806, 1807, & 1808* . . . (London, 1816), vol. 1, pp. 145–146.

2. Heriot, *Travels*, p. 139.

3. H. A. Innis and A. R. M. Lower, *Select Documents in Canadian Economic History, 1783–1885* (Toronto, 1933), p. 138.

4. B. K. Sandwell, *The Molson Family* (Montreal, 1933), chap. 4.

5. *Montreal Gazette*, November 1, 1831.

6. Lambert, *Travels*, vol. 1, p. 524.

7. Quaife, *John Askin Papers*, vol. 2, pp. 624–625.

8. Simon McTavish's will is given in Wallace, *North West Company Documents*, pp. 134–143.

9. Adam Shortt, "Founders of Canadian Banking" (*Journal of the Canadian Bankers' Association*, vol. 30, January, 1923, pp. 154–166).

10. M. Q. Innis, *An Economic History of Canada* (Toronto, 1935), p. 91.

11. Shortt, "Founders of Canadian Banking" (*Journal of the Canadian Bankers' Association*, vol. 32, January, 1925, pp. 177–190).

12. *Ibid.*, vol. 30, pp. 34–47.

13. For the paragraphs which follow see: A. R. M. Lower, "The Trade in Square Timber" (*University of Toronto Studies, History and Economics*, vol. VI, Toronto,

1933), pp. 40–61; A. R. M. Lower, *History of the Canadian Timber and Lumber Trade prior to Confederation* (University of Toronto, unpublished M.A. thesis, 1923).

14. *Journals of the House of Assembly of Lower-Canada*, vol. 33, 1823–1824, appendix W, General table of exports, 1807–1822.

15. W. R. Riddell, "Joseph Willcocks" (*Ontario Historical Society, Papers and Records*, vol. 24, pp. 475–499).

16. W. R. Riddell, "Mr. Justice Thorpe" (*Canadian Law Times*, vol. 40, November, 1920, pp. 907–924).

17. *Canadian Archives Report*, 1892, note D, p. 40.

18. *Q*, vol. 106–1, pp. 51–52, Memorial of the undersigned merchants trading to Canada, February 11, 1807.

19. *Canadian Archives Report*, 1892, note D, p. 110.

20. *Ibid.*, note D, p. 90.

21. *Ibid.*, note D, p. 106.

22. *Journals of the House of Assembly of Lower-Canada*, 1805, p. 236.

23. *Ibid.*, p. 156.

24. *Q*, vol. 97, pp. 99–101, Petitions of the merchants of Montreal and Quebec, 1805.

25. *Quebec Mercury*, February 2, 1805.

26. *Q*, vol. 101–2, pp. 377–378, lords of trade to Shee, April 17, 1806.

27. *Montreal Gazette*, April 1, 1805.

28. *Journals of the House of Assembly of Lower-Canada*, 1806, pp. 64, 118.

29. *Ibid.*, pp. 80–94.

30. *Q*, vol. 98, pp. 109–112, Milnes to Camden, August 1, 1805.

31. Doughty and McArthur, *Constitutional Documents*, p. 310.

32. *Le Canadien*, January 17, 1807.

33. *Ibid.*, December 5, 1807, January 23, 1808.

34. Ibid., January 23, 1808.

35. Ibid., November 22, 1806.

36. *Ibid.*, January 17, 1807.

37. *Ibid.*, December 12, 1807.

38. *Ibid.*, November 28, 1807.

39. *An Apology for Great Britain* . . . (Quebec, 1809), pp. 13, 9.

40. *Quebec Mercury*, April 3, 1809.

41. *An Apology for Great Britain*, pp. 22–23.

42. *Quebec Mercury*, April 3, 1809.

43. *Journals of the House of Assembly of Lower-Canada*, 1808, p. 472.

44. *Q*, vol. 112, p. 39, Craig to Banbury, February 21, 1810.

45. *Ibid.*, vol. 107, pp. 318–321, Craig to Castlereagh, August 15, 1808.

46. *Some Considerations on this Question: Whether the British Government Acted Wisely in Granting to Canada her Present Constitution?* By a British Settler (Montreal, 1810).

47. *Quebec Mercury*, April 16, 1810.

48. Porter, *John Jacob Astor*, vol. 1, chap. 7.

49. *Q*, vol. 113, pp. 228–230, Agents of North West Company to correspondents in London, January 23, 1810.

50. *Ibid.*, pp. 221–227, McGillivray to Liverpool, November 10, 1810.

51. A. S. Morton, "The North West Company's Columbian Enterprise and David Thompson" (*Canadian Historical Review*, vol. 17, September, 1936, pp. 266–288).

52. *On the Origin and Progress of the North West Company of Canada, with a History of the Fur Trade as connected with that Concern* . . . (London, 1811).

53. C. G. Davidson, *The North West Company* (University of California Publications in History, Berkeley, 1918), pp. 284–285.

54. Public Archives of Canada, *Secretary of State's Papers*, S. 64, Memorial of the undersigned merchants of Montreal, November 8, 1805; *Q*, vol. 99, Dunn to Castlereagh (with enclosures), November 16, 1805.

55. L. P. Kellogg, *The British Régime in Wisconsin and the Northwest* (Madison, Publications of the State Historical Society of Wisconsin, 1935), pp. 261–262.

56. *Secretary of State's Papers*, S. 73, James McGill to Ryland, May 30, 1808; *ibid.*, S. 75, Memorial of merchants of Montreal, October 20, 1808.

57. *Ibid.*

58. *Michigan Pioneer and Historical Collections*, vol. 25, p. 268, Richardson to Forsyth, February 17, 1810.

59. Articles of agreement for the South West Fur Company, January 28, 1811, printed in Porter, *John Jacob Astor*, vol. 1, pp. 461–469.

60. *Journals of the House of Assembly of Lower-Canada*, 1823–1824, vol. 33, appendix W, General table of imports, St. Johns, 1807–1822.

61. *Ibid.*, appendix W, General table of exports, St. Johns, 1807–1822.

62. Davidson, *North West Company*, pp. 126–127.

63. *Q*, vol. 109, pp. 239–248, Memorial of the merchants of Lower Canada, May 29, 1809; *Michigan Pioneer and Historical Collections*, vol. 25, pp. 260–267, Memoranda of the committee of trade at Montreal, September 30, 1809.

64. F. L. Benns, *The American Struggle for the British West India Carrying-Trade, 1815–1830* (Indiana University Studies, vol. 10, Bloomington, 1923), chap. 1.

65. *Q*, vol. 109, p. 240, Memorial of the merchants of Lower Canada, May 29, 1809.

66. Public Archives of Canada, *Upper Canada Sundries*, July 25, 1823.

67. *Q*, vol. 115, pp. 38–47, Fawkener to Peel (with enclosures), February 7, 1811.

68. Nathaniel Atcheson, *American Encroachments on British Rights; or Observations on the Importance of the British North American Colonies* (London, 1808).

69. 52 George III, c. 55.

70. Public Archives of Canada, *G*, vol. 5, pp. 52–54, Liverpool to Prevost, April 13, 1812.

CHAPTER VII

THE END OF THE FUR TRADE

1. J. W. Pratt, *Expansionists of 1812* (New York, 1925) chap. 1.
2. F. A. Updyke, *The Diplomacy of the War of 1812* (Baltimore, 1915), chaps. 1–2.
3. *Q*, vol. 130–1, pp. 117–118, Memorial of merchants of Lower and Upper Canada, October 24, 1812.
4. *Michigan Pioneer and Historical Collections*, vol. 15, pp. 70–72, Gray to Prevost, January 13, 1812.
5. *Q*, vol. 119, pp. 185–188, To the British American committee, March 18, 1812; *Q*, vol. 120, pp. 35–39, Memorial of merchants interested in trade of British North American colonies, August 12, 1812.
6. *Q*, vol. 120, pp. 88–96, Atcheson to Bathurst (with enclosures), October 9, 1812; *ibid.*, pp. 154–162, same to same (with enclosures), November 19, 1812.
7. *Ibid.*, pp. 221–222, S. McGillivray to Goulburn, December 29, 1812; *ibid.*, vol. 123, pp. 143–146, same to same, January 2, 1815.
8. Porter, *John Jacob Astor*, vol. 1, pp. 259–260.
9. J. W. Pratt, "Fur Trade Strategy and the American Left Flank in the War of 1812" (*American Historical Review*, vol. 40, January, 1935, pp. 246–273).
10. *Q*, vol. 118, pp. 203–206, Hull to Eustis, August 4, 1812.
11. *Ibid.*, vol. 130–1, pp. 75–81, Merchants to Bathurst, January 31, 1814.
12. Kellogg, *British Régime in Wisconsin*, chap. 20.
13. *Q*, vol. 130–1, p. 129, Memorial of merchants of Lower and Upper Canada, October 24, 1812.
14. *Ibid.*; see also pp. 110–116, Inglis and Bainbridge to Liverpool, February 7, 1814.
15. *Ibid.*, vol. 126, p. 183, Extract of letters from committee of trade at Montreal to Atcheson, October 16–23, 1813.
16. Updyke, *Diplomacy of the War of 1812*, chap. 7.
17. *Q*, vol. 132, pp. 25–30, Richardson and McGillivray to Drummond, April 20, 1815.
18. *Ibid.*, vol. 134–2, pp. 385–392, Inglis, Ellice & Co., to Goulburn, July 25, August 2, 1815.
19. *Ibid.*, vol. 150–2, pp. 401–404, S. McGillivray to Bagot, November 15, 1817.
20. Porter, *John Jacob Astor*, vol. 2, p. 691.
21. *Q*, vol. 137, pp. 70–76, McDouall to Sherbrooke, August 7, 1816.
22. Innis, *Fur Trade in Canada*, pp. 265–284.
23. Chester Martin, *Lord Selkirk's Work in Canada* (Oxford and Toronto, 1916).
24. *Journals of the House of Assembly of Lower-Canada*, 1823–1824, vol. 33, appendix W.
25. *Montreal Gazette*, November 1, 1831.
26. D. G. Barnes, *A History of the English Corn Laws, from 1660–1846* (London, 1930), chap. 7.

27. *Q*, vol. 157–1, pp. 111–120, Memorial of committee of trade of Quebec to Bathurst, February 24, 1821; *ibid.*, vol. 158, pp. 4–13, Memorial of merchants of Montreal to Bathurst, September 9, 1821.

28. *Ibid.*, vol. 156–1, pp. 172–180, Petition of the merchants engaged in trade with the British colonies in North America, to the house of commons, June 19, 1820.

29. *Journals of the House of Assembly of Lower-Canada*, 1818, vol. 27, pp. 216–217.

30. *Montreal Gazette*, July 12, 1820; *Quebec Gazette*, May 24–June 4, 1821.

31. Lower, *Canadian Timber and Lumber Trade*, chap. 2.

32. *Q*, vol. 134–2, pp. 394–396, Inglis and Bainbridge to Bathurst, June 5, 1815.

33. *Ibid.*, vol. 324–1, pp. 180–185, Maitland to Bathurst, December 8, 1818.

34. *Ibid.*, vol. 136, pp. 127–129, Drummond to Bathurst, March 29, 1816; *Executive Council Minutes, State Book H., Lower Canada*, pp. 200–207, Report of March 26, 1816.

35. *Journals of the Legislative Assembly of Upper Canada* (Ontario Archives Report, 1912), pp. 546–547, 550–552.

36. *Q*, vol. 144, pp. 30–34, Petition of the undersigned inhabitants of Montreal; *ibid.*, vol. 149–1, pp. 142–153, Memorial of the merchants of Quebec and Montreal, October 26, 1818.

37. *G*, vol. 8, pp. 113–118, Bathurst to Sherbrooke, July 4, 1816; *Q*, vol. 144, pp. 21–24, Sherbrooke to Bathurst, May 20, 1817.

38. *Ibid.*, vol. 329, p. 195, Maitland to Bathurst, May 14, 1821.

39. *Montreal Gazette*, March 11, 1816.

40. *Quebec Gazette*, August 7, 1817.

41. *Ibid.*, June 12, 1817.

42. *Secretary of State's Papers*, S. 131, Petition of the inhabitants of Montreal, December 10, 1817.

43. Charles Stewart, *A Short View of the Present State of the Eastern Townships in the Province of Lower Canada. . . .* (London, 1817).

44. *Quebec Gazette*, January 14, 28, 1819.

45. *Ibid.*, January 16, 1817.

46. *Journals of the House of Assembly of Lower-Canada*, 1819, p. 95; *ibid.*, 1820–1821, vol. 30, p. 226.

47. *Journals of the House of Assembly of Lower-Canada*, 1820–1821, vol. 30, p. 177.

48. D. G. Creighton, "The Struggle for Financial Control in Lower Canada, 1818–1831" (*Canadian Historical Review*, vol. 12, June, 1931, pp. 120–144).

49. *Quebec Gazette*, January 16, 1817.

50. Robert Gourlay, *Statistical Account of Upper Canada, Compiled with a View to a Grand System of Emigration* (London, 1822).

51. *Journals of the House of Assembly of Lower-Canada*, 1815, vol. 24, pp. 104, 114.

52. *Quebec Gazette*, March 29, 1819; *Journals of the House of Assembly of Lower-Canada*, 1820–1821, vol. 30, pp. 90–91, 162, 264.

53. *Secretary of State's Papers*, S. 155, Report of commissioners for the Lachine canal, December 31, 1821.

54. *Journals of the House of Assembly of Lower-Canada*, 1819, vol. 28, appendix G.

55. *Journals of the Legislative Assembly of Upper Canada*, 1818 (Ontario Archives Report, 1912) pp. 446–450.

56. *Journals of the House of Assembly of Lower-Canada*, 1821–1822, vol. 31, appendix H.

57. *Q*, vol. 329, pp. 296–298, Maitland to Bathurst, August 20, 1821.

CHAPTER VIII
THE FAILURE OF UNION

1. R. G. Albion, "New York Port and its Disappointed Rivals, 1815–1860" (*Journal of Economic and Business History*, vol. 3, pp. 603–629); A. C. Flick (ed.), *History of the State of New York* (New York, 1933–), vol. 5, chap. 9.

2. *Census of Canada*, 1870–1871, vol. 4, pp. 83–171.

3. *Montreal Gazette*, February 1, 1826, November 1, 1831.

4. *The Colonial Advocate*, No. 6, *Containing an Essay on Canals and Inland Navigation* . . . (Queenston, U.C., 1824) p. 4.

5. *Montreal Gazette & Commercial Advertiser*, March 6, March 17, 1824; *Montreal Gazette*, May 21, 1825.

6. *Ibid.*, July 2, July 9, 1825; *Dalhousie Papers*, vol. 10, McGregor to Dalhousie, June 23, 1825.

7. *Q*, vol. 173–2, pp. 343–357.

8. T. Doige, *An Alphabetical List of the Merchants, Traders, and Housekeepers, residing in Montreal* (Montreal, 1819); J. Sansom, *Travels in Lower Canada* . . . (London, 1820).

9. *Montreal Gazette*, November 10, 1828.

10. *Ibid.*, December 1, 1824.

11. B. K. Sandwell, *The Molson Family* (Montreal, 1933), chap. 4; *Montreal Gazette & Commercial Advertiser*, July 21, July 24, 1824.

12. *Secretary of State's Papers*, S. 174, Report of the Montreal Harbour Commissioners, February 21, 1825.

13. W. H. Atherton, *Montreal, 1535–1914* (Montreal, 1914), vol. 2, pp. 585–587.

14. *Q*, vol. 153–2, pp. 480–488, Young to Wortley, May 15, 1819.

15. A. G. Doughty and Norah Story (eds.), *Documents relating to the Constitutional History of Canada, 1819–1828* (Ottawa, 1935), pp. 123–131.

16. *Letter from L. J. Papineau and J. Neilson, Esqs., addressed to His Majesty's Under Secretary of State on the Subject of The Proposed Union of the Provinces of Upper and Lower Canada* (London, 1824), p. 55.

17. *Q*, vol. 332–1, pp. 142–149, Robinson to ——, November 19, 1822.

18. *Q*, vol. 337–2, p. 433, Robinson to Horton, December 20, 1824.

19. *Quebec Gazette*, December 2, 1822.

20. *Montreal Herald*, September 2, 1822.

21. *Journals of the Legislative Council of the Province of Lower-Canada*, 1823, p. 27.

22. *Montreal Herald*, December 31, 1822.

23. *Ibid.*, December 14, 1822.

24. *Ibid.*, November 13, 1822.

25. [J. Stuart], *Observations on the Proposed Union of the Provinces of Upper and Lower Canada, under one Legislature* . . . (London, 1824), p. 16.

26. *Upper Canada Gazette & Weekly Register*, November 21, 1822.

27. *Montreal Herald*, November 9, 1822.

28. *Quebec Gazette*, October 24, 1822.

29. *Montreal Gazette*, October 26, 1822.

30. *Montreal Herald*, November 9, 1822.

31. *Montreal Gazette*, November 2, 1822.

32. *Ibid.*, March 14, 1823.

33. [J. Stuart], *Remarks on a Plan Intituled "A Plan for a General Legislative Union of the British Provinces, in North America"* (London, 1824).

34. R. W. Horton, *Exposition and Defence of Earl Bathurst's Administration of the Affairs of Canada* . . . (London, 1838), pp. 8–9.

35. *Montreal Gazette*, February 4, 1826.

36. *Quebec Gazette*, January 20, February 3, 1825.

37. *Secretary of State's Papers*, S. 156, Maitland to Dalhousie, January 24, 1822; *Journals of the House of Assembly of Lower-Canada*, 1825, vol. 34, pp. 187–188; *ibid.*, vol. 35, pp. 62–64, 331.

38. *Quebec Gazette*, January 15, 1824.

39. *Ibid.*, February 27, 1823.

40. J. L. McDougall, *The Welland Canal to 1841* (unpublished M.A. thesis, University of Toronto, 1923); L. B. Duff *et al.*, *The Welland Ship Canal* (St. Catharines, 1930), pp. 15–41.

41. *Q*, vol. 344–2, pp. 572–588, Maitland to Huskisson, December 31, 1827.

42. *Journals of the House of Assembly of Lower-Canada*, 1826, vol. 35, pp. 245–250.

43. *Quebec Gazette*, January 12, 1824.

44. *Ibid.*, April 19, 1827.

45. *Montreal Gazette*, January 11, 1827.

46. *Quebec Mercury* (quoted in *Montreal Gazette*, June 8, 1826).

47. *Quebec Gazette*, August 20, August 23, 1827.

48. *Q*, vol. 179–3, pp. 464–476, Dalhousie to Huskisson, December 10, 1827.

CHAPTER IX

THE REFORM OF THE OLD COLONIAL SYSTEM

1. Doughty and Story, *Constitutional Documents*, pp. 106–120.

2. *Ibid.*, pp. 98–104.

3. *Statutes at Large, United Kingdom*, 6 George V., cap. 114.

4. A. Brady, *William Huskisson and Liberal Reform; An Essay on the Changes in Economic Policy in the Twenties of the Nineteenth Century* (London, 1928), chaps. 4–6.

5. *Executive Council Minutes, Lower Canada, State Book J*, pp. 438–443, May 30, 1823; *Upper Canada Sundries*, Robinson to Hillier, July 25, 1823; *Q*, vol. 168–1,

pp. 37–39, Dalhousie to Bathurst, February 27, 1824; *ibid.*, vol. 335–2, pp. 324–335, Maitland to Bathurst, April 14, 1824.

6. G. W. Brown, "The Opening of the St. Lawrence to American Shipping" (*Canadian Historical Review*, vol. 7, March, 1926, pp. 4–12).

7. *Upper Canada Gazette & Weekly Register*, December 5, 1822.

8. *Q*, vol. 176–2, pp. 569–577.

9. *Montreal Gazette*, February 4, 1826.

10. *Quebec Gazette*, January 30, 1826.

11. *Q*, vol. 174–1, pp. 235–240; *ibid.*, vol. 176–1, pp. 22–32, Memorial of the under-signed merchants of Montreal, February 20, 1826; *Montreal Gazette*, August 14, 1826.

12. *Journals of the Legislative Council of the Province of Lower-Canada*, 1824, pp. 122–123.

13. *Statutes at Large, United Kingdom*, 7 George IV, cap. 48.

14. *Q*, vol. 180, p. 183, Lack to Herries, March 16, 1827.

15. *Statutes at Large, United Kingdom*, 7 and 8 George IV, cap. 56.

16. *Q*, vol. 170–3, pp. 710–715, Memorandum of the undersigned merchants interested in the trade of the provinces of Upper and Lower Canada, February 12, 1824.

17. F. L. Benns, *The American Struggle for the British West India Carrying-Trade, 1815–1830* (Indiana University Studies, Bloomington, 1923), chaps. 4–5.

18. *Q*, vol. 169, pp. 15–18, Memorial of certain merchants of Glasgow concerned with the trade of His Majesty's North American colonies, May 10, 1824.

19. *Statutes at Large, United Kingdom*, 6 George IV, cap. 64.

20. *Q*, vol. 339–1, pp. 234–239, Markland to Horton, April 27, 1825.

21. *Ibid.*, vol. 172–2, pp. 321–325, Memorandum on the admission of Canadian wheat into the British market, November 12, 1825; *ibid.*, vol. 172–2, pp. 436–441, Memorial of the subscribers of the city of Montreal, merchants, November 19, 1825.

22. *Journals of the House of Assembly of Lower-Canada*, vol. 35, p. 357; *Q*, vol. 179–1, pp. 12–14, Dalhousie to Horton, January 8, 1827.

23. *Statutes at Large, United Kingdom*, 7 & 8 George IV, cap. 57.

24. D. G. Barnes, *A History of the English Corn Laws, from 1660–1846* (London, 1930), pp. 200–202.

25. Benns, *The American Struggle for the British West India Carrying-Trade*, chap. 6.

26. *New York Morning Courier*, quoted in *Montreal Gazette*, January 25, 1830.

27. *Montreal Gazette*, December 21, December 28, 1829.

28. *Secretary of State's Papers*, S. 227, Memorial of the committee of trade of Quebec, January 12, 1830; *ibid.*, Petition of the undersigned members of the committee of trade of Montreal, February 10, 1830; *Montreal Gazette*, January 21, February 1, February 8, 1830.

29. A. R. M. Lower, *History of the Canadian Timber and Lumber Trade prior to Confederation* (unpublished M.A. thesis, University of Toronto, 1923), pp. 89–99.

30. *Montreal Gazette*, February 12, April 14, December 8, 1831.

31. *Q*, vol, 196–2, pp. 285–288, Memorandum of the undersigned merchants, members of the committee of trade, representing the mercantile body of Quebec, March 11, 1830; *ibid.*, vol. 354, pp. 101–104, Memorial of the president and directors of the Welland Canal Co., March 6, 1830.

32. *Statutes at Large, United Kingdom*, 1 William IV, cap. 24.

33. For example see details of imports at St. Johns, L.C., in 1830, *Journals of the House of Assembly of Lower-Canada*, 1831, appendix GG.

34. *Montreal Gazette*, March 15, 1832.

35. McDougall, *Welland Canal to 1841*, p. 77.

36. *Ibid.*, appendix E.

37. *Journals of the House of Assembly of Upper Canada*, 1833–1834, appendix, p. 95.

38. N. E. Whitford, *History of the Canal System of the State of New York* . . . (Supplement to the Annual Report of the State Engineer and Surveyor, Albany, 1906), vol. 1, pp. 950–954. The figures are given here in tons; I have altered them to barrels and bushels.

39. A. R. M. Lower, *The North American Assault on the Canadian Forest* (in press, Toronto, 1938.)

40. *Journals of the House of Assembly of Lower-Canada*, 1831, appendix GG; *Quebec Gazette*, February 13, 1836.

41. *Journals of the House of Assembly of Lower-Canada*, 1828–1829, vol. 38, appendix C; *Quebec Gazette*, February 13, 1836.

42. Benns, *The American Struggle for the British West India Carrying-Trade*, p. 157.

43. F. W. Burton, "Wheat in Canadian History" (*Canadian Journal of Economics and Political Science*, vol. 3, May, 1937, pp. 210–217).

44. *Montreal Gazette*, March 5, 1836.

45. Flick, *History of the State of New York*, vol. 6, chap. 10.

46. Albion, "New York Port," pp. 603–629.

CHAPTER X

COMMERCE *VERSUS* AGRICULTURE

1. *Quebec Gazette*, December 10, December 27, 1827.

2. *Montreal Gazette*, April 16, 1827.

3. *Q*, vol. 181, p. 120, Logan to Huskisson, October 8, 1827.

4. *Ibid.*, vol. 186–1, pp. 207–209, Gould to ——, March 7, 1828.

5. *Report from the Select Committee on the Civil Government of Canada* (London, 1828).

6. H. I. Cowan, *British Emigration to British North America, 1783–1837* (Toronto, 1928).

7. A. Shortt and A. G. Doughty (eds.), *Canada and its Provinces* (Toronto, 1914), vol. 4, p. 577.

8. H. A. Innis, "Unused Capacity as a Factor in Canadian Economic History"

(*Canadian Journal of Economics and Political Science*, vol. 2, February, 1936, pp. 1-15).

9. *Census of Canada*, 1870–1871, vol. 4, pp. 83–171.

10. C. B. Sissons, *Egerton Ryerson, His Life and Letters* (Toronto, 1937), vol. 1.

11. R. A. MacKay, "The Political Ideas of William Lyon Mackenzie" (*Canadian Journal of Economics and Political Science*, vol. 3, February, 1937, pp. 1–22).

12. *Montreal Gazette*, September 24, 1827.

13. A. Shortt, "Founders of Canadian Banking, The Hon. Wm. Allan, Merchant and Banker" (*Journal of the Canadian Bankers' Association*, vol. 30, January, 1923, pp. 154–166).

14. A. Shortt, *The Early History of Canadian Banking*, part 5, *The First Banks in Upper Canada* (Toronto, 1897), p. 21.

15. *Colonial Advocate*, September 16, 1830.

16. *Montreal Gazette*, June 9, 1831.

17. *Upper Canada Sundries*, Vankoughnet to Rowan, March 27, 1834.

18. *Montreal Gazette*, October 23, 1834.

19. *Q*, vol. 355, pp. 256–263, Yates to Murray, May 31, 1830.

20. *Ibid.*, vol. 378–2, pp. 322–325, Memorial of the stockholders of the Welland canal.

21. *Colonial Advocate*, February 17, 1831.

22. *The Patriot*, February 4, 1834.

23. *Secretary of State's Papers*, Lower Canada, Auldjo to Yorke, January 30, 1830; *Journals of the House of Assembly of Lower-Canada*, vol. 39, pp. 315, 332.

24. *Journal of the House of Assembly of Upper Canada*, 1833-1834, appendix, pp. 67–79; *Journals of the House of Assembly of Lower-Canada*, 1834, vol. 43, appendix Aa.

25. *The Patriot*, February 14, February 18, 1834.

26. *Quebec Gazette*, February 14, 1834.

27. *Montreal Gazette*, March 6, 1834.

28. *Quebec Gazette*, March 1, 1833.

29. *Report from the Select Committee on the Civil Government of Canada* (1828), p. 153, evidence of Viger.

30. *Montreal Gazette*, February 1, 1834.

31. *Journals of the House of Assembly of Lower-Canada*, 1831, vol. 40, p. 477.

32. *Montreal Gazette*, June 21, October 27, 1831.

33. R. Christie, *A History of the Late Province of Lower Canada, Parliamentary and Political, from the Commencement to the Close of its Existence as a Separate Province* (Montreal, 1866), vol. 3, pp. 382–383.

34. *Q*, vol. 201-2, p. 347, Memorial of the Quebec merchants, March 21, 1832.

35. *Journal of the House of Assembly of Upper Canada*, 1832–1833, pp. 89–91; *Q*, vol. 374–3, pp. 513–529, Memorial of the Society for the Relief of the Sick and Destitute of York, April 4, 1832.

36. *Montreal Gazette*, October 27, 1832.

37. Christie, *History of Lower Canada*, vol. 3, p. 409.

38. *Montreal Gazette*, September 11, 1832.

39. *Hamilton Mercury*, quoted in *Montreal Gazette*, September 25, 1832.

40. *Kingston Patriot*, quoted in *Montreal Gazette*, September 25, 1832.

41. *Quebec Gazette*, April 4, 1832.

42. *Q*, vol. 230–2, p. 282.

43. Christie, *History of Lower Canada*, vol. 3, p. 413.

44. *Q*, vol. 207–1, pp. 91–94, Aylmer to Goderich, March 18, 1833.

45. *Quebec Gazette*, March 25, 1833.

46. *Q*, vol. 207–2, p. 389, Address of the legislative council.

47. *Quebec Gazette*, May 8, 1833.

48. *Montreal Gazette*, April 1, 1830.

49. *Quebec Gazette*, March 7, 1831.

50. *Colonial Advocate*, May 6, 1830.

51. A. Shortt, *The History of Canadian Currency, Banking and Exchange*, part 5, *Prosperity and Expansion in Upper Canada* (Toronto, 1901), p. 14.

52. *Colonial Advocate*, January 14, 1830.

53. *Ibid.*, October 14, 1830.

54. *Q*, vol. 380–2, pp. 371–414, Mackenzie to Goderich, March 14, 1833.

55. *G*, vol. 70, pp. 214–233, Stanley to Colborne (with enclosures), May 30, 1833.

56. *Q*, vol. 378–1, pp. 6–39, Allan to Colborne, July 29, 1833; *ibid.*, pp. 105–109, Petition of the merchants and traders of the town of York, August 27, 1833; *ibid.*, vol. 379–1, pp. 103–104, Gould to Stanley, October 5, 1833.

57. *The Patriot*, January 10, 1834.

58. *Q*, vol. 381–1, pp. 233–235, Colborne to Hay, March 7, 1834.

59. *Journal of the House of Assembly of Upper Canada*, 1833–1834, appendix, pp. 122–129.

60. *Q*, vol. 378–1, pp. 49–52, Dunn to Rowan, August 1, 1833.

61. *Ibid.*, vol. 211–1, pp. 134 ff., Chipman to Stanley (with enclosures), July 25, 1833.

62. Christie, *History of Lower Canada*, vol. 3, pp. 423–427.

63. *Quebec Gazette*, January 7, 1833; *Q*, vol. 207–1, pp. 18–56, Hagerman on the annexation of Montreal, February 9, 1833.

64. *Quebec Gazette*, January 23, 1833.

65. *Q*, vol. 380–1, pp. 50–62, Mackenzie to Goderich, January 18, 1833.

66. *Montreal Gazette*, October 25, 1832.

67. *Ibid.*, December 8, 1832.

68. *Ibid.*, March 23, 1833.

CHAPTER XI

BREAKDOWN

1. R. C. McGrane, *The Panic of 1837* (Chicago, 1924), pp. 3–4.

2. *Montreal Gazette*, September 19, 1833, February 8, 1834.

3. *Q*, vol. 219–2, pp. 216–231, extract of a letter from Montreal, February 27, 1834.

4. *Ibid.*, pp. 236–238, Gillespie to Stanley, April 3, 1834.

5. *The Patriot*, May 23, 1834.

6. *Ibid.*, July 29, 1834.

7. *Upper Canada Sundries*, Vankoughnet to Rowan, February 27, 1834.

8. *The Patriot*, September 19, 1834.

9. *Colonial Advocate*, October 2, 1834.

10. *The Patriot*, December 9, 1834.

11. *Q*, vol. 383–2, pp. 232–238, Colborne to Spring Rice, November 20, 1834.

12. *Ibid.*, vol. 224–2, p. 336, Gould to Aberdeen, January 16, 1835.

13. *Montreal Gazette*, December 11, 1834.

14. *Ibid.*, November 6, November 8, 1834.

15. *Secretary of State's Papers*, Lower Canada, Auldjo *et al.*, to Craig, November 17, 1834.

16. *Montreal Gazette*, November 22, 1834.

17. *Secretary of State's Papers*, Lower Canada, Molson *et al.*, to Craig, November 22, 1834.

18. *The Patriot*, December 30, 1834.

19. *Ibid.*, January 16, 1835.

20. *Q*, vol. 224–2, p. 382, Gillespie to Aberdeen, January 25, 1835.

21. *Representation on the Legislative Union of the Provinces of Upper and Lower Canada* . . . (Montreal, 1837).

22. *Q*, vol. 221–2, p. 301, Aylmer to Hay, March 14, 1835.

23. *Mr. Walker's Report of His Proceedings in England, to the Executive Committee of the Montreal Constitutional Association* (Montreal, 1837).

24. *Q*, vol. 225–3, p. 540, Walker to Glenelg, June 17, 1835.

25. *Ibid.*, vol. 230–3, p. 399, ——? to Gillespie, December 31, 1835.

26. *Anti-Gallic Letters; addressed to His Excellency, The Earl of Gosford, Governor in Chief of the Canadas*. By Camillus. (Montreal, 1836).

27. *Q*, vol. 223–2, pp. 314–319, Gosford to Glenelg, December 28, 1835.

28. *Ibid.*, pp. 314–319, Gosford to Glenelg, December 28, 1835.

29. *Ibid.*, vol. 226–1, pp. 66–82, Gosford to Glenelg, January 15, 1836.

30. *Montreal Gazette*, January 21, 1836.

31. *Quebec Gazette*, January 25, 1836.

32. *The Patriot*, April 3, 1835.

33. McDougall, *The Welland Canal*, p. 55.

34. *Q*, vol. 388–3, pp. 577 ff.

35. *Merritt Papers*, vol. 3, Dalton to Merritt, December 12, 1835.

36. H. A. Innis and A. R. M. Lower (eds.), *Select Documents in Canadian Economic History, 1783-1885* (Toronto, 1933), pp. 178-179.

37. *The Patriot*, January 19, 1836.

38. *Ibid.*, April 3, 1835.

39. *Q*, vol. 388–3, p. 574, Mackenzie to Glenelg, December 17, 1835.

40. *The Patriot*, March 18, 1836; *Montreal Gazette*, May 19, 1836.

41. *The Patriot*, June 24, 1836.

42. *Montreal Gazette*, July 28, 1836.

43. Christie, *History of Lower Canada*, vol. 4, pp. 290.

44. *Montreal Gazette*, June 9, 1836.

45. *Ibid.*, June 30, July 2, 1836.

46. *Ibid.*, November 17, 1836.

47. *Ibid.*, March 12, 1836.

48. W. B. Smith and A. H. Cole, *Fluctuations in American Business, 1790–1860* (Cambridge, 1935), section 2.

49. McGrane, *Panic of 1837*, pp. 1-42.

50. *Quebec Gazette*, February 13, 1836, January 25, 1837.

51. *The Constitution*, January 18, 1837.

52. *Q*, vol. 237–1, pp. 28–31, Gosford to Glenelg, May 6, 1837.

53. *Merritt Papers*, vol. 3, W. B. Robinson to Merritt, July 21, 1836; *ibid.*, J. B. Robinson to Merritt, September 13, 1836.

54. *Q*, vol. 396–4, pp. 516–528, Head to Glenelg, April 4, 1837; *ibid.*, pp. 542–547, Head to Glenelg, April 5, 1837.

55. Quoted in Christie, *History of Lower Canada*, vol. 4, p. 354 (note).

56. *Montreal Gazette*, June 13, 1837.

57. *Q*, vol. 238-1, pp. 71-3, Gosford to Glenelg, September 2, 1837.

58. *Montreal Transcript*, May 18, 1837; *Q*, vol. 237-1, pp. 119-124, Gosford to Glenelg, June 2, 1837.

59. *Ibid.*, vol. 397–1, pp. 154–179, Head to Glenelg, May 23, 1837.

60. *Ibid.*, vol. 396–1, pp. 567–571, Head to Glenelg (with enclosure), April 23, 1837.

61. *Upper Canada Sundries*, J. H. Dunn to Civil Secretary, May 5, 1837.

62. *Ibid.*, Macaulay to Hagerman, n.d. (enclosed in Hagerman to Joseph, May 18, 1837).

63. *G*, vol. 81, p. 291, Glenelg to Head, July 22, 1837.

64. *Journal of the House of Assembly of Upper Canada, 1837–1838*, appendix, pp. 154–156.

65. *The Patriot*, June 27, June 30, 1837.

66. *Q*, vol. 397–2, pp. 475–479, Head to Glenelg, July 12, 1837.

67. A. Shortt, *The History of Canadian Currency, Banking and Exchange, Part 8, Crisis and Resumption* (Toronto, 1902), pp. 5–8.

68. *Merritt Papers*, vol. 4, McGill to Merritt, August 16, 1837.

69. *Montreal Courier*, quoted in *Quebec Gazette*, May 26, 1837.

70. *Montreal Transcript*, August 12, 1837.

71. *Upper Canada Sundries*, Carey to Head, May 8, 1837.

72. *The Constitution*, August 9, August 16, 1837.

73. *Ibid.*, August 16, 1837.

74. *Ibid.*

75. *The Patriot*, September, 29, November 24, 1837.

76. *Ibid.*, November 24, 1837.

77. *Ibid.*, October 20, 1837.

78. *Quebec Gazette*, October 25, 1837; *Montreal Herald*, quoted in *The Patriot*, November 14, 1837.

79. *Montreal Herald*, November 2, 1837.

80. *Q*, vol. 239–2, p. 372, Wetherall to Gosford, n.d.; *Montreal Herald*, quoted in *The Patriot*, November 14, 1837.

81. MacKay, "The Political Ideas of William Lyon Mackenzie," pp. 18–20.

CHAPTER XII
THE LAST RECOVERY

1. *Q*, vol. 243–2, p. 206, Gosford to Glenelg, January 30, 1838.

2. *Montreal Gazette*, February 17, 1838.

3. *Journal of the House of Assembly of Upper Canada*, 1837–1838, appendix, p. 104.

4. *Q*, vol. 409–2, pp. 456–467, Arthur to Glenelg (with enclosures), November 20, 1838.

5. *Journal of the House of Assembly of Upper Canada*, 1839, appendix, vol. 2, pp. 43–84.

6. Sissons, *Egerton Ryerson*, vol. 1, p. 460.

7. R. S. Longley, "Emigration and the Crisis of 1837 in Upper Canada" (*Canadian Historical Review*, vol. 17, March 1936, pp. 29–40).

8. *Journal of the House of Assembly of Upper Canada*, 1837–1838, pp. 351–353; *Montreal Gazette*, March 8, 1838.

9. *Ibid.*, February 13, 1838.

10. *Journal of the House of Assembly of Upper Canada*, 1837–1838, appendix, pp. 87–88.

11. C. W. New, *Lord Durham; a Biography of John George Lambton, first Earl of Durham* (Oxford, 1929), pp. 5–7, 12–13.

12. Public Archives of Canada, *Durham Papers*, sec. 6, vol. 1, pp. 414–435, Moffatt and Badgley to Durham, April 5, 1838.

13. *Ibid.*, pp. 631–658, Buller to Durham, June 21, June 25, 1838.

14. New, *Durham*, p. 419.

15. *Durham Papers*, sec. 2, vol. 1, pp. 169–177, Durham to Glenelg, July 16, 1838.

16. *Ibid.*, sec. 6, vol. 2, pp. 220–221, Thom to Durham, September 27, 1838.

17. *Montreal Gazette*, November 27, 1838.

18. Sir C. P. Lucas (ed.), *Lord Durham's Report on the Affairs of British North America* (Oxford, 1912), vol. 3, p. 363.

19. *Durham Papers*, sec. 6, vol. 3, pp. 194–198, Unsigned memorandum in Buller's hand, February, 1839.

20. New, *Durham*, p. 490.

21. *Montreal Gazette*, April 2, 1839.

22. William Smith, *Political Leaders of Upper Canada* (Toronto, 1931), chap. 10.

23. W. P. M. Kennedy (ed.), *Statutes, Treaties and Documents of the Canadian Constitution 1713–1929* (London and Toronto, 1930), pp. 374–382.

24. *Q*, vol. 266–2, pp. 190–207, Ninth report of the North American Colonial Association, April 17, 1839.

25. *Montreal Gazette*, September 3, 1839.

26. Adam Shortt, *Lord Sydenham* (The Makers of Canada, London and Toronto, 1926).

27. *Montreal Gazette*, December 19, December 24, 1839.

28. Chester Martin, *Empire and Commonwealth, Studies in Governance and Self-Government in Canada* (Oxford, 1929), pp. 242–243.

29. *Colonial Gazette*, quoted in *Montreal Gazette*, June 18, 1840.

30. *The Patriot*, October 8, 1841.

31. *Ibid.*, April 16, 1841.

32. Kennedy, *Documents*, p. 444.

33. Martin, *Empire and Commonwealth*, pp. 256–258.

34. *The Patriot*, September 15, 1843.

35. *Ibid.*

36. *Montreal Gazette*, July 16, 1841.

37. *The Patriot*, June 25, 1841.

38. G. E. Wilson, *The Life of Robert Baldwin, a Study in the Struggle for Responsible Government* (Toronto, 1933), pp. 133–138.

39. *Montreal Gazette*, May 5, 1847.

40. *Merritt Papers*, vol. 4, Keefer to Merritt, February 28, 1839.

41. *Montreal Gazette*, October 29, November 12, 1839.

42. *Journals of the Legislative Assembly of the Province of Canada*, 1841, appendix QQ.

43. *Montreal Gazette*, June 16, 1840.

44. New York *Journal of Commerce*, quoted in *Montreal Gazette*, May 11, 1841.

45. *Journals of the Legislative Assembly of the Province of Canada*, 1849, vol. 8, appendix Z.

46. *Journal of the House of Assembly of Upper Canada*, 1839, appendix, vol. 2, pp. 27–36.

47. *Q*, vol. 272-2, pp. 376–389, Thomson to Russell, June 27, 1840.

48. *G*, vol. 390, Sydenham to Russell, February 22, 1841.

49. *Q*, vol. 409-2, pp. 456–457, Arthur to Glenelg, November 20, 1838; *ibid.*, vol. 417-1, pp. 59–85, Arthur to Normanby, June 8, 1839.

50. P. Knaplund (ed.) *Letters from Lord Sydenham, Governor-General of Canada, 1839–1841, to Lord John Russell* (London, 1931), pp. 30–31.

51. *Montreal Gazette*, July 19, 1841.

52. R. S. Longley, "Francis Hincks and Canadian Public Finance" (*Canadian Historical Association Report*, 1935, pp. 30–39).

53. Public Archives of Canada, *Correspondence of the Governor-General's Secretary*, No. 3455, Killaly to Higginson, April 23, 1844.

54. *Montreal Gazette*, June 23, July 7, 1840, April 6, 1841.

55. *Journals of the Legislative Assembly of the Province of Canada*, 1841, appendix EE.

56. *Montreal Gazette*, September 6, 1841.

57. *Ibid.*, September 13, 1842.

58. *G*, vol. 389, pp. 206–209, Thomson to Russell, May 26, 1840; *ibid.*, vol 50, Russell to Sydenham, December 1, 1840; *Montreal Gazette*, December 9, 1841.

59. *The Patriot*, July 23, July 30, 1841.

60. *Montreal Gazette*, May 17, 1841.

61. *G*, vol. 112, Stanley to Bagot, March 2, 1842.

62. *Montreal Gazette*, September 30, October 1, 1842.

63. Public Archives of Canada, *Baring Papers, Official Correspondence*, Grinnell, Mintern & Co., to Baring Bros., January 10, 1844.

CHAPTER XIII

FINAL COLLAPSE

1. G. P. de T. Glazebrook, *Sir Charles Bagot in Canada, A Study in British Colonial Government* (London, 1929), chaps. 5–6.

2. *The Patriot*, September 27, 1842.

3. *Montreal Gazette*, December 13, 1842.

4. *The Patriot*, September 30, 1842.

5. *Ibid.*

6. *Montreal Gazette*, September 29, 1842.

7. *Ibid.*, October 6, 1842.

8. *The Patriot*, September 20, 1842.

9. *Montreal Gazette*, December 15, 1842.

10. Wilson, *Robert Baldwin*, chap. 8.

11. *Correspondence of the Governor-General's Secretary*, no. 3486, A, Wetherall to Daly, April 21, 1844; *Quebec Gazette*, April 22, April 24, 1844.

12. *Montreal Gazette*, quoted in *The Patriot*, October 1, 1844.

13. Egerton Ryerson, *Sir Charles Metcalfe Defended against the Attacks of His Late Counsellors* (Toronto, 1844), p. 143.

14. *The Patriot*, January 12, 1844.

15. *Quebec Gazette*, March 13, 1844.

16. G. N. Tucker, *The Canadian Commercial Revolution, 1845–1851* (New Haven, 1936), pp. 118–119, 210–212.

17. *G*, vol. 460, p. 440, Metcalfe to Stanley, May 8, 1845.

18. *Quebec Gazette*, March 19, 1845.

19. *Ibid.*, January 14, 1846.

20. *Journals of the Legislative Assembly of the Province of Canada*, 1849, vol. 8, appendix Z.

21. *Correspondence of the Governor-General's Secretary*, no. 4062, Smith to Higginson, April 26, 1845.

22. Bernard Holland, *The Fall of Protection, 1840–1850* (London, 1913), chaps. 7–8.

23. *The Patriot*, January 27, 1846.

24. *Journals of the Legislative Assembly of the Province of Canada*, 1849, vol. 8, appendix Z.

25. D. L. Burn, "Canada and the Repeal of the Corn Laws" (*Cambridge Historical Journal*, 1928, vol. 2, pp. 252–272.)

26. *Journals of the Legislative Assembly of the Province of Canada*, 1849, vol. 8, appendix Z.

27. *G*, vol. 125, Grey to Cathcart, August 18, 1846; *ibid.*, vol. 461, Cathcart to Grey, October 28, 1846.

28. *Ibid.*, pp. 106–107, Cathcart to Grey, December 28, 1846; R. S. Longley, "Francis Hincks and Canadian Public Finance" (*Canadian Historical Association Report*, 1935, pp. 30–39).

29. *Executive Council Minutes*, 1847–1848, State Book H, pp. 32–44.

30. Tucker, *Canadian Commercial Revolution*, pp. 155–177..

31. Edward Porritt, *The Fiscal and Diplomatic Freedom of the British Overseas Dominions* (Oxford, 1922), pp. 283–358.

32. *Montreal Gazette*, July 22, 1847.

33. *Ibid.*, March 5, 1847.

34. C. P. Stacey, *Canada and the British Army, 1846–1871, A Study in the Practice of Responsible Government* (London, 1936), chap. 4.

35. Public Archives of Canada, *Grey-Elgin Correspondence*, Grey to Elgin, March 22, 1848.

36. *Executive Council Minutes*, 1848, State Book H, pp. 249–254.

37. *Grey-Elgin Correspondence*, Papers on the navigation laws.

38. *Ibid.*, Elgin to Grey, January 4, 1849.

39. *Montreal Gazette*, June 24, 1847; Tucker, *Canadian Commercial Revolution*, pp. 104–106.

40. *Grey-Elgin Correspondence*, Elgin to Grey, June 6, 1848.

41. *Montreal Gazette*, January 15, March 5, July 21, July 22, 1847; Tucker, *Canadian Commercial Revolution*, pp. 121–126.

42. *Grey-Elgin Correspondence*, Papers on the navigation laws; *G*, vol. 461, pp. 208–220, Memorandum of the executive council, May 12, 1848.

43. Quoted in C. D. Allin and G. M. Jones, *Annexation, Preferential Trade and Reciprocity* (Toronto and London), p. 27.

44. D. C. Masters, *The Reciprocity Treaty of 1854, Its History, Its Relation to British Colonial and Foreign Policy and to the Development of Canadian Fiscal Autonomy* (London, 1936), pp. 3–27.

45. *Correspondence of the Governor-General's Secretary*, no. 4995, Merritt to Crampton (with enclosures), May 6, 1848.

46. *Ibid.*, no. 4957, Memorandum by Hincks.

47. *Montreal Gazette*, June 10, 1847.

48. *Grey-Elgin Correspondence*, Elgin to Grey, April 26, 1847.

49. *Statutes of Canada*, 4 and 5 Vic. cap. 39.

50. *Journals of the Legislative Assembly of the Province of Canada*, 1846, appendix X.

51. Wilson, *Robert Baldwin*, pp. 266–269.

52. *Statutes of Canada*, 12 Vic. cap. 58.

53. *Hamilton Spectator*, quoted in *Montreal Gazette*. March 2, 1849.

54. *Montreal Gazette*, February 12, 1849.

55. *Ibid.*, February 16, 1849.

56. "The Riots of 1849 in Montreal" (*Canadian Historical Review*, vol. 15, September, 1934, pp. 283–288); *Montreal Gazette*, April 27, 1849.

57. *Ibid.*, May 2, 1849.

58. Public Archives of Canada, *Canada Miscellaneous Documents*, Grant to Grant, May 1, 1849.

59. *Montreal Gazette*, April 30, 1849.

60. *G*, vol. 461, pp. 323–331, Elgin to Grey, April 30, 1849.

61. *Montreal Gazette*, July 13, 1849.

62. *Ibid.*, June 27, 1849.

63. Allin and Jones, *Annexation, Preferential Trade and Reciprocity*, pp. 49–98.

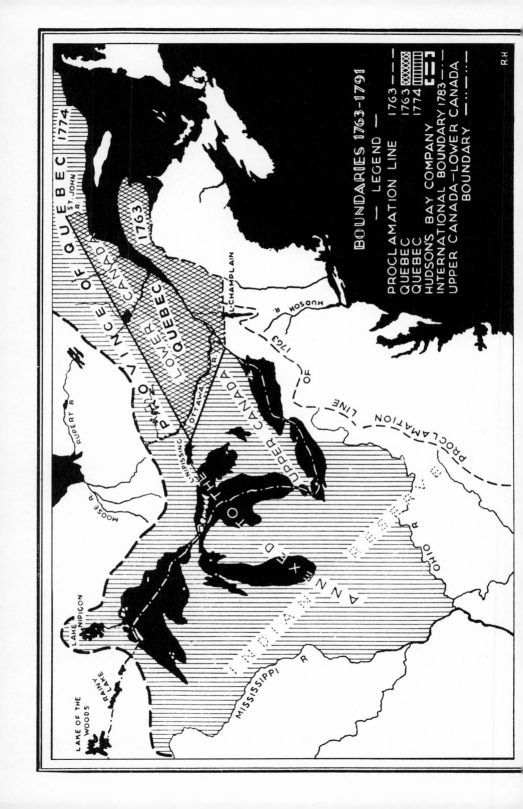

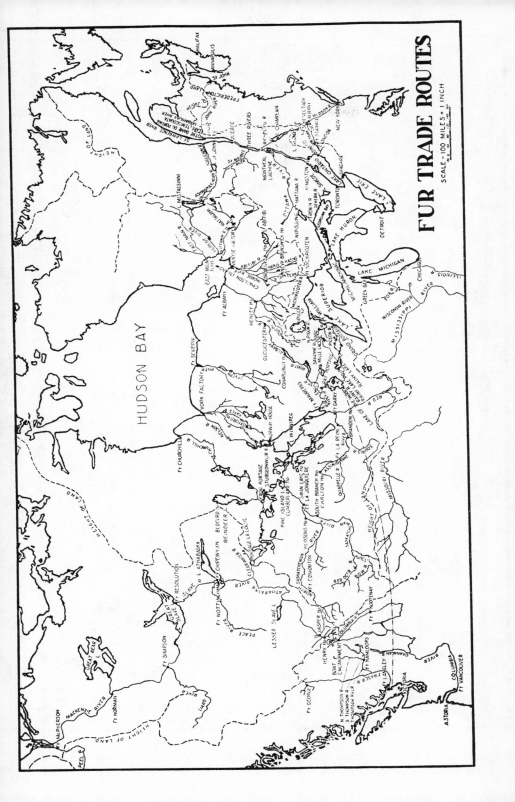

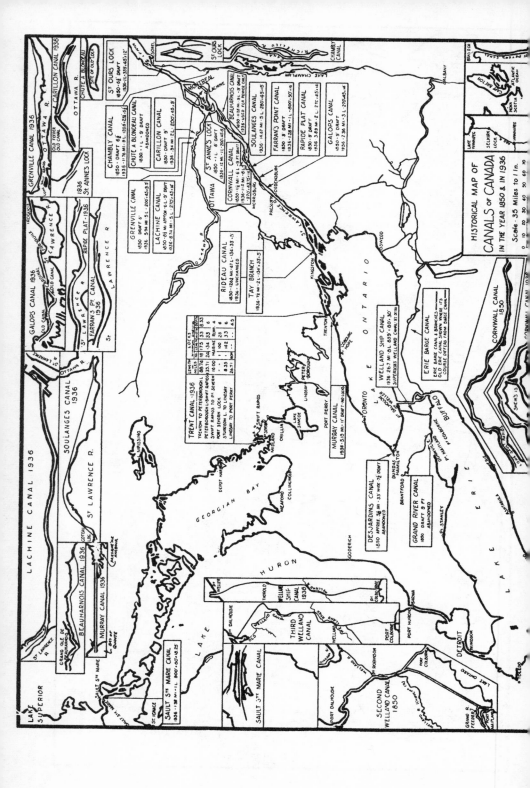

HISTORICAL MAP OF CANALS OF CANADA IN THE YEAR 1850 & IN 1936

Scale - 35 Miles to 1 in.

INDEX